Judicial Rhapsodies

Judicial Rhapsodies

Rhetoric and Fundamental Rights
in the Supreme Court

DOUG COULSON

Amherst
College
Press

Copyright © 2023 by Doug Coulson
Some rights reserved

This work is licensed under the Creative Commons Attribution- NonCommercial 4.0 International License. To view a copy of this license, visit http://creativecommons.org/licenses/by-nc/4.0/ or send a letter to Creative Commons, PO Box 1866, Mountain View, CA 94042, USA.

The complete manuscript of this work was subjected to a partly closed ("single-blind") review process. For more information, visit https://acpress.amherst.edu/peerreview/.

Published in the United States of America by
Amherst College Press
Manufactured in the United States of America

Library of Congress Control Number: 2022947603
DOI: https://doi.org/10.3998/mpub.12752816

ISBN 978-1-943208-46-3 (print)
ISBN 978-1-943208-47-0 (OA)

TABLE OF CONTENTS

Acknowledgments	vii
Introduction: Rhapsodic Jurisprudence	1
1. Judicial and Epideictic Rhetoric: A False Division	25
2. Freedom of Speech, Paramologia, and the Flag	71
3. Keeping Government Out of Religion and Vice Versa	101
4. Storms, Shadows, and Privacy	135
Conclusion: Truth Has No Bones	163
Notes	181
Glossary of Figures	237
Bibliography	239
Table of Cases	257
Index	261

ACKNOWLEDGMENTS

In many ways this project is the culmination of an odyssey that began with my earliest research into legal discourse after I left the practice of law for academia, and my gratitude extends to many who have offered support, encouragement, and conversation during that journey. I first formulated my interest in the role of epideictic in legal discourse during the years that I taught a course called Rhetoric and the Law at The University of Texas at Austin in graduate school. At the same time, I was cultivating an interest in classical rhetoric and its relationship to law as a student in Patricia Roberts-Miller's Classical Rhetoric course and Jeffrey Walker's Rhetoric and Poetics in Antiquity courses, among others. For this particular book, I would be remiss to not also recognize the impact of studying philosophy under Randall Auxier at Oklahoma City University—who first introduced me to Italian humanism—and to Donald Philip Verene, who once upon a time consented to serve as a commentator on a paper I delivered about Ernst Cassirer at a philosophy conference shortly after I concluded my undergraduate study.

During the development of this book, my ideas have benefited from discussions with students in my Law, Performance, and Identity, and History of Rhetoric: The Classical Age courses at Carnegie Mellon University, and from sharing a rich environment for the study of rhetoric alongside colleagues in the Rhetoric program and the Department of English at Carnegie Mellon. As research assistants, Colleen Storm and Benjamin Williams provided excellent support by coding cases for this book and copyediting a late draft, respectively. During the writing of the book, I benefited from a wide variety of conversations with more people than I can possibly tally, but chief among them are Marian Aguiar, Marilyn Altamira, Marilyn Coulson, Mary Coulson, Richard Coulson, Angela Daniels, Eugene Garver, Russell Holbert, Dave Kaufer, John O'Shea, Terry

Phelps, Jack Quirk, Andreea Ritivoi, Christian Shippee, Susan Tanner, and Pavithra Tantrigoda.

My thinking about this project has also been expanded or usefully mettled by panelists and audiences who attended panels or talks at which I presented portions of this book, including at the Association for the Study of Law, Culture, and the Humanities conferences in 2014 and 2017, the Rhetoric Society of America conference in 2016, the Law, Culture, and Ethics colloquium at Carnegie Mellon in 2019, the Classical Rhetoric as a Lens for Contemporary Legal Praxis Workshop at the William S. Boyd School of Law at the University of Nevada, Las Vegas in 2019, and Constitution Day 2022 at Carnegie Mellon in 2022. In addition, I am grateful for the institutional support provided by Carnegie Mellon both for travel to such conferences and for other research costs, as well as for reprieves from teaching which provided invaluable writing space.

Parts of this book were previously published in the form of articles and a chapter in a volume of conference proceedings, and I would like to thank the publishers for the permission to include the previously published material here. Specifically, Chapter 1 draws on "The Devil's Advocate and Legal Oratory in the *Processus Sathanae*," *Rhetorica: A Journal of the History of Rhetoric* 33, no. 4 (2015): 409–30; "Law as Epideictic: The Complex Publics of Legal Discourse," in *Rhetoric's Change*, ed. Jenny Rice, Chelsea Graham, and Eric Detweiler (Anderson: Parlor Press, 2018); and "More Than Verbs: An Introduction to Transitivity in Legal Argument," *The Scribes Journal of Legal Writing* 19 (2020): 81–125.

Finally, I would like to thank Amherst College Press, its editorial board, and Hannah Brooks-Motl and the rest of the editorial team for their support of this project and editorial assistance, as well as the Fulcrum production team at the University of Michigan. I would also like to thank Keith Bybee and my anonymous peer reviewers for their insightful comments on the manuscript.

Introduction: Rhapsodic Jurisprudence

> Legal discourse is a creative speech which brings into existence that which it utters. It is the limit aimed at by all performative utterances—blessings, curses, orders, wishes or insults....One should never forget that language, by virtue of the infinite generative but also *originative* capacity...which it derives from its power to produce existence by producing the collectively recognized, and thus realized, representation of existence, is no doubt the principal support of the dream of absolute power.
> —Pierre Bourdieu, *Language and Symbolic Power*[1]

> In epideictic oratory every device of literary art is appropriate, for it is a matter of combining all the factors that can promote this communion of the audience. It is the only kind of oratory which immediately evokes literature, the only one that might be compared to the libretto of a cantata.
> —Chaïm Perelman and Lucie Olbrechts-Tyteca, *The New Rhetoric*[2]

> The main opinion sounds like a bull elk trumpeting its virtues in the forest.
> —Justice Richard Maughan, dissenting in *Benevolent and Protective Order of Elks No. 85 v. Tax Commission* (1975)[3]

Legal decisions not only apply the law to particular cases but are often accompanied by discourse that magnifies the value of law and its applications. In his 2019 Year-End Report on the Federal Judiciary, United States

Supreme Court Chief Justice John Roberts recognized the importance of the promotional discourse that surrounds law in a democratic society. Roberts lamented the demise of democracy and civic education in the United States, writing that since constitutional ideals were first promoted in *The Federalist Papers* the country had "come to take democracy for granted," and "civic education has fallen by the wayside."[4] The federal judiciary plays an important role in civic education, he wrote, both through judicial outreach and the opinions judges write to justify their decisions.[5] Throughout his report, Roberts described the educational function of judicial activity as one of advancing public understanding of the legal system. Every generation has an obligation "to pass on to the next, not only a fully functioning government responsive to the needs of the people, but the tools to understand and improve it." In the penultimate paragraph of the report, however, Roberts shifted the focus from advancing understanding of the legal system to promoting and celebrating it, exhorting his colleagues in the federal judiciary to "promote public confidence in the judiciary" in their outreach and opinions and to "celebrate our strong and independent judiciary, a key source of national unity and stability."[6]

The relationship between advancing understanding of the legal system and promoting and celebrating it is the focus of this book, particularly a unique set of discursive practices that judges use to promote confidence in decisions regarding fundamental rights as applied to the states under the Due Process Clause of the Fourteenth Amendment. In the plurality opinion in *Planned Parenthood v. Casey* (1992), in which the Court reaffirmed the essential holding of *Roe v. Wade* (1973) regarding constitutional limits on abortion restrictions, United States Supreme Court Justices Sandra Day O'Connor, Anthony Kennedy, and David Souter recognized that the Court's legitimacy is largely a product of its opinion writing practices:

> As Americans of each succeeding generation are rightly told, the Court cannot buy support for its decisions by spending money and, except to a minor degree, it cannot independently coerce obedience to its decrees. The Court's power lies, rather, in its legitimacy, a product of substance and perception that shows itself in the people's acceptance of the Judiciary as fit to determine what the Nation's law means and to declare what it demands. The underlying substance of this legitimacy is...expressed in the Court's opinions.[7]

The legitimizing function of judicial opinions has also been recognized by scholars. As Lawrence Douglas writes, opinions often function as "dual performances, pronouncing judgment in the case at hand while simultaneously attempting to justify the authority of the Court to do so,"[8] and Chaïm Perelman notes that this leads judges to provide more than formal justifications for their decisions.[9] According to Eugene Garver, this legitimizing function is an even more difficult task for judges than addressing the parties or helping apply decisions to future cases.[10]

Although it often goes unrecognized, judges do not have to write or publish opinions, and in many cases they issue orders without explanation or they write cursory opinions of only a few sentences or less. Judges also write opinions that they choose not to publish in official reporter series, and some jurisdictions consider such unpublished opinions less precedential. A judge's decision both to write and to publish an opinion is, in other words, a rhetorical one, an effort either to shape public opinion on the issues in the case or to address doubts regarding the court's authority to make the decision. Despite the absence of any legal requirement that courts write opinions, however, the *Casey* plurality's comment that the Court's written opinions express the substance of its legitimacy echoes a long-standing recognition that the Court's power uniquely depends on its ability to persuasively justify its decisions. Indeed, judicial opinions form a core source of *stare decisis*, as judges typically pay attention both to the words and to the results of judicial decisions when identifying precedent.[11]

Previous studies have noted many rhetorical strategies judges use in their opinion writing to promote the legitimacy of judicial decisions, as well as how those strategies differ across jurisdictions and over time. These rhetorical strategies are significant in their own right, not only legitimizing the decisions but giving substance to the common law in the process, often revealing central gestures in the understanding and application of law. As Frank Upham writes, differences in judicial explanation both exemplify and create a "different understanding of the nature of society that may be fundamentally more important than any similarity in outcomes."[12] American courts often frame their decisions as the necessary outcome of first principles such as original intent, the plain or literal meaning of language, or precedent, all of which symbolize judicial restraint.[13] Regarding citations of precedent, Barbara Perry even notes that the broader the implications of a court's decision the more the majority may ground it in precedent and judicial restraint.[14]

At times judges self-dramatize their restraint, referring to the responsibility of deciding particular cases as "grave" or as taxing the "judicial conscience."[15] The United States Supreme Court has specifically orchestrated unanimous opinions in order to place its full institutional authority behind controversial decisions such as *Brown v. Board of Education* (1954), which held racial segregation in public schools to be unconstitutional,[16] and appellate courts often write majority opinions using the institutional third person ("the Court") or the first-person plural ("we") to invoke the court's institutional authority despite the fact that common law opinion writing characteristically permits multiple judgments and the first person ("I").[17] Some judicial opinions also adopt a "magisterial or omniscient tone" to convince "a skeptical audience of a dubious point,"[18] Barbara Perry writes, or opinions may be framed more ambiguously when opposition is anticipated in order to protect the institutional prestige of the court.[19]

In contrast to the use of precedent, judicial restraint, and institutional authority to legitimize judicial decisions, in certain situations judges also use remarkably unrestrained rhetorical practices to legitimize decisions. Opinion writing can be highly affective, laudatory, even operatic, on a wide array of subjects, particularly in cases that inaugurate legal changes with broad social consequences. Judicial writing in such cases often exhibits dense accumulations of discursive features that converge to performatively magnify the value of subjects ranging from individuals or entities, actions, activities, objects, and places, to concepts or principles such as liberty, equality, the jury system, the common law, and *stare decisis*, among others—features which reveal a unique earnestness and vulnerability in judicial discourse. The features that accumulate to perform this function include a vocabulary of praise describing subjects as superlative, unique, prior, or complete; figural amplification devices such as anaphora, paramologia, and chiasmus, among others, and patterns of amplification on the discourse level such as exergasia, accumulation, and enumeration (see Glossary of Figures). These lexical, syntactic, and discursive features are often accompanied by beautified or eloquent language and the gnomic aspect—a grammatical aspect that encompasses general truths found in proverbs, commonplaces, aphorisms, and maxims—in the unbounded present tense, or "eternal" present, about subjects such as liberty or equality which lack clear perceptual boundaries, as well as by a linguistic modality that abjures negation, qualifiers, or specific references to evidence.[20]

These features, I propose, constitute an epideictic register, a discursive form which from the classical rhetorical tradition of ancient Greece and Rome through at least the modern era has been associated with ritual and ceremonial occasions, literature and poetics, or as Chaïm Perelman and Lucie Olbrechts-Tyteca note in the epigraph above, the libretto of a cantata.[21] *Judicial Rhapsodies* examines the interdiscursive relationship between judicial discourse and ritual and ceremonial discourse through the lens of the relationship of the judicial and epideictic speech genres in rhetorical studies, contributing to the fields of law, literary and rhetorical studies, discourse analysis, and the history of rhetoric. The book offers a new register theory of epideictic and specifically examines epideictic features in the United States Supreme Court's fundamental rights jurisprudence, which has historically recognized that certain rights are so "implicit in the concept of ordered liberty" that restrictions on them must be regarded with heightened scrutiny,[22] extending previous studies both of epideictic and of its function in legal discourse. Although the doctrine of fundamental rights appears in many legal systems, in American jurisprudence it has particularly emerged in the extension of the Bill of Rights to the states through the "incorporation"[23] or "absorption"[24] of its most important guarantees into the Due Process Clause of the Fourteenth Amendment.

After the Fourteenth Amendment was ratified in the wake of the Civil War, the Supreme Court began to hold that many of the rights recognized in the Bill of Rights were merely enumerations of specific due process rights, and therefore, despite the fact that the Bill of Rights only expressly applied to the federal government, the Due Process Clause of the Fourteenth Amendment incorporated or absorbed them to limit state governments as well. According to Milton Konvitz, the process by which these rights have been given a "preferred dignity and majesty" is the "most significant and enduring development" in American constitutional history.[25] The extension of the Bill of Rights as a limitation on state governments impacts innumerable people and has often been attended by controversy. In this context, courts have written effusive paeans to rights such as freedom of expression, religious liberty, and privacy, among others, to promote confidence in their decisions. This jurisprudence not only forms an important part of American civic literature, but has inspired people across the globe.

I combine classical and contemporary rhetorical theory with linguistic analysis to argue that the use of epideictic registers in fundamental rights jurisprudence functions as an important legitimation strategy in controversial cases given the judiciary's unique dependence on public acceptance of its decisions, fulfilling what Eugene Garver describes as the judicial need to convince audiences that a judicial opinion "speaks *for* them" in order to legitimize decisions.[26] Functionally, epideictic responds to threats to social unity by converging in an honorific performance that produces a sublime cultural experience as a basis for cooperation, subsuming the individual agency of speaker and audience in a shared perspective through the power of language, described by Pierre Bourdieu in the epigraph above as the power to create the "collectively recognized, and thus realized, representation of existence."[27] The affective dimension of epideictic also reveals vulnerability and doubt as central impulses that have guided the Court's approach to fundamental rights, a conclusion which qualifies the observation of some commentators that judicial opinions seek to suppress doubt at all costs. I argue that the limitation of judicial authority implicit in the use of epideictic registers forms a perennial locus of conflict between law and rhetoric that can be found in the classical rhetorical tradition of ancient Greece and Rome as well as in contemporary legal discourse, suggesting more challenging questions about law and rhetoric than traditional narratives of their relationship reveal.

Judges themselves associate features of opinion writing with epideictic genres and forms, often referring to passages of judicial opinions containing such features with terms such as *paean, panegyric, encomium, rhapsody,* or—as reflected in the epigraph above from Justice Richard Maughan's dissenting opinion in *Benevolent and Protective Order of Elks No. 85 v. Tax Commission* (1975)—musical terms such as *trumpet*.[28] Opinion writing containing these features has at times been dismissed as political rather than legal rhetoric,[29] but it is prevalent in many of the most important opinions in the common law and possesses a rhetorical power evident in the fact that from the perspective of modern legal theory it is quoted in the popular press and later judicial opinions far out of proportion to its strictly legal significance. It possesses a "curious sublimity" more reminiscent of Christian sermons,[30] a sermonic quality that does not so much politicize subjects as sacralize them.[31]

Consider Justice William Douglas's eloquent mesodiplosis on the transcendent bond of marriage in the United States Supreme Court's majority opinion in *Griswold v. Connecticut* (1965), in which the Court held that a state contraceptive ban was unconstitutional:

> Marriage is a coming together for better or for worse, hopefully enduring, and intimate to the degree of being sacred. It is an association that promotes a way of life, not causes; a harmony in living, not political faiths; a bilateral loyalty, not commercial or social projects. Yet it is an association for as noble a purpose as any involved in our prior decisions.[32]

As a matter of propositional logic, Douglas's eloquent description of marriage in *Griswold* is not the sort of question one would expect to be debated by the parties to the case nor is it necessary or sufficient to explain the decision in the traditional sense expected to define a holding for purposes of *stare decisis*[33]—one would not expect to list among a court's factual findings that marriage is a "harmony in living," for example, or unrelated to "commercial or social projects," and it is difficult to imagine such propositions being subjected to legal argument in the customary mode. The passage is quoted eighty-four times in later judicial opinions in the United States, however, as well as in judicial opinions of the supreme courts of Canada, India, and Ireland.[34]

A half century after *Griswold*, Justice Anthony Kennedy quoted Justice Douglas's mesodiplosis on marriage in his majority opinion in *Obergefell v. Hodges* (2015), in which the Court held that same-sex couples had a constitutional right to marriage. In *Obergefell*, Kennedy offered his own paean to marriage before addressing the legal issue in the case:

> From their beginning to their most recent page, the annals of human history reveal the transcendent importance of marriage. The lifelong union of a man and a woman always has promised nobility and dignity to all persons, without regard to their station in life. Marriage is sacred to those who live by their religions and offers unique fulfillment to those who find meaning in the secular realm. Its dynamic allows two people to find a life that could not be found alone, for a marriage becomes greater than just the two persons. Rising from the most basic human needs, marriage is essential to our most profound hopes and aspirations.[35]

From start to finish, Kennedy's opinion in *Obergefell* is an extended paean to the institution of marriage. Later in the opinion, Kennedy wrote that "no union is more profound than marriage, for it embodies the highest ideals of love, fidelity, devotion, sacrifice, and family." He quoted other judicial praise of marriage as well, such as Justice Margaret Marshall's opinion on same-sex marriage for the Massachusetts Supreme Court in *Goodridge v. Department of Public Health* (2003), in which she wrote that because marriage "fulfils yearnings for security, safe haven, and connection that express our common humanity," it is "an esteemed institution, and the decision whether and whom to marry is among life's momentous acts of self-definition."[36]

Similar discursive features appear in the dueling Supreme Court opinions of Justices Felix Frankfurter and Robert Jackson addressing the constitutionality of compulsory flag salutes during the 1940s. In the first case, *Minersville School District v. Gobitis* (1940), the Court upheld the constitutionality of flag salutes before the Court reversed itself a mere three years later in the second case, *West Virginia State Board of Education v. Barnette* (1943).[37] Judge Richard Posner has argued that Justice Jackson's majority opinion in *Barnette* may be the "most eloquent majority opinion in the history of the Supreme Court."[38] In his opinion in *Barnette*, Jackson combines praise, enumeration, antithesis, asyndeton, eloquence, affirmative modality, and the gnomic aspect to elevate the significance of flag salutes as a form of speech:

> Causes and nations, political parties, lodges and ecclesiastical groups seek to knit the loyalty of their followings to a flag or banner, a color or design. The State announces rank, function, and authority through crowns and maces, uniforms and black robes; the church speaks through the Cross, the Crucifix, the altar and shrine, and clerical raiment....Associated with many of these symbols are appropriate gestures of acceptance or respect: a salute, a bowed or bared head, a bended knee. A person gets from a symbol the meaning he puts into it, and what is one man's comfort and inspiration is another's jest and scorn.[39]

Jackson uses similar features in *Barnette* to address the futility of coercing beliefs, writing that because those who attempt to coerce belief "soon find themselves exterminating dissenters," the effort to compel unity "achieves only the unanimity of the graveyard."[40] Such features pervade his opinion, culminating in a peroration in which Jackson introduces the now famous metaphor of a fixed star in our constitutional constellation to describe freedom of belief: "If there is any fixed star in our constitutional constellation, it is that no official, high or petty, can prescribe what shall be orthodox in politics, nationalism, religion, or other matters of opinion or force citizens to confess by word or act their faith therein."[41] Jackson's fixed star metaphor is quoted at least 256 times in later judicial opinions in the United States.[42]

Justice Jackson's opinion in *Barnette* was promptly quoted and heralded in the popular press. *The Christian Century* urged that the opinion form "part of the 'American Scriptures,' to be memorized and taken to heart by every patriot,"[43] and *Time* extolled the "ringing polysyllables" in which the Court "reaffirmed its faith in the Bill of Rights."[44] The opinion is significant not only for its form, however, but for its function. It was published during the early years of World War II, and the American framing of the war as a global struggle between freedom and tyranny was implicated in the question presented in the case. Jackson recognized early in the opinion that many complained the Bellamy salute which accompanied the Pledge of Allegiance was "too much like Hitler's."[45] His paean to freedom of belief in *Barnette* spoke to this global background while also specifically leveraging it in response to Justice Felix Frankfurter's majority opinion in *Gobitis*, the case *Barnette* overruled.

The exigency created by the Court's reversal of its precedent in such a short time had been exacerbated by Justice Frankfurter's own paean to national unity in *Gobitis*, which was quoted at length in the preamble of the West Virginia flag salute law at issue in *Barnette*.[46] No less eloquently than Justice Jackson extolled freedom of belief in *Barnette* did Frankfurter extol the importance of national unity in *Gobitis*:

> The preciousness of the family relation, the authority and independence which give dignity to parenthood, indeed the enjoyment of all freedom, presuppose the kind of ordered society which is summarized by our flag. A society which is dedicated to the preservation of these ultimate values of civilization may in self-protection utilize the educational process for inculcating those almost unconscious feelings which bind men together in a comprehending loyalty, whatever may be their lesser differences and difficulties.[47]

Frankfurter wrote in *Gobitis* that the ultimate foundation of a free society is the "binding tie of cohesive sentiment," fostered by "all those agencies of the mind and spirit which may serve to gather up the traditions of a people, transmit them from generation to generation, and thereby create that continuity of a treasured common life which constitutes a civilization."[48] In *Barnette*, Jackson's opinion may be read as a dueling refrain, or poetic *agôn*,[49] that not only responded to the logic of Frankfurter's opinion in *Gobitis* but responded to his paean to national unity as well.[50] Moreover, the form of the opinions was not determined by either justice's personal writing style. Both wrote important opinions during their tenure on the Court without such eloquent magnifications of their subjects.[51]

Judges have written paeans to a wide variety of subjects ranging from free speech to the rights of women, the common law, *stare decisis*, and Magna Carta. One court called Chief Justice Earl Warren's plurality opinion in *Sweezy v. New Hampshire* (1957), for example, in which the Court held that it was unconstitutional to arrest a professor for refusing to answer questions about a lecture he gave, a "paean to academic freedom,"[52] and in *Miller v. Board of Public Works* (1925) the California Supreme Court extolled the importance of the "civic and social value of American homes" to support its decision that a zoning ordinance prohibiting the construction of a four-family home in a particular area was lawful.[53] Judicial paeans also address more mundane subjects. In *Miller v. Clark County* (2003), for example, the United States Court of Appeals for the Ninth Circuit surveyed a lengthy history of "judicial literature" from the late nineteenth through the mid-twentieth century extolling the virtues of domestic dogs to support its decision that an arrest assisted by a police dog did not constitute an excessive use of force.[54] The *Miller* court began with *Maine v. Harriman* (1884), in which the court dismissed an indictment for killing a dog based on its conclusion that dogs were not domesticated animals but *ferae naturae*, or wild animals. In *Harriman*, Maine Supreme Court Justice John Appleton wrote a dissenting opinion that cited laudatory commentary on dogs by the Roman poet Virgil, French zoologist George Cuvier, and English lexicographer Samuel Johnson, among others, attributing civil society itself to the influence of dogs:

> From the time of the pyramids to the present day, from the frozen pole to the torrid zone, wherever man has been there has been his dog. Cuvier has asserted that the dog was perhaps necessary for the establishment of civil society and that a little reflection will convince us that barbarous nations owe much of their civilization above the brute to the possession

of the dog. He is the friend and companion of his master—accompanying him in his walks, his servant, aiding him in his hunting, the playmate of his children—an inmate of his house, protecting it against all assailants.[55]

Another court devoted 700 words to the praise of dogs despite denying a State Department employee's compensation claim for flying his dog from Egypt to the United States, writing among other things that "we have very little respect and no affection for anyone who has not at some time in his life loved a dog."[56] In *Miller v. Clark County*, the Ninth Circuit quoted these passages and many others from a long history of judicial opinions extolling the intelligence, friendliness, constancy, and loyalty of dogs in "song and story."[57]

What does all of this laudatory discourse have to do with justifying judicial decisions? I propose that it has more to do with it than is apparent at first glance. It reveals important truths about judicial authority and opinion writing practices, the relationship between law and rhetoric, and rhetoric itself. To better understand the rhetorical strategies that judges use in judicial opinion writing to justify their decisions it is worth studying epideictic rhetoric, and attention to the use of epideictic in judicial opinion writing can correspondingly improve our understanding of the form and function of epideictic more broadly. The epideictic features of judicial opinions sampled above are neither political nor aberrant, I propose, but necessary and endemic to judicial discourse and to legal discourse more broadly,[58] along with many other forms of practical discourse.[59]

A wide variety of speech forms have been categorized as epideictic, including ritual and ceremonial discourse, epic and lyric poetry, philosophy, and history, as well as sermons, occasional speeches, dedications, eulogies, memorials, and similar forms.[60] The conclusion that such forms are distinct from judicial discourse originated in the fourth-century BCE division of rhetoric into deliberative, judicial, and epideictic speech in Aristotle's *Rhetoric*. Aristotle concluded that deliberative speeches were delivered in legislative assemblies to persuade audiences of actions to be taken in the future, judicial speeches were delivered in courts to persuade audiences of the propriety or impropriety of past actions, and epideictic speeches were delivered on ritual or ceremonial occasions to audiences who merely judged the orator's skill in praising or critiquing a subject in the present.[61] Paradigmatic examples of epideictic include a variety of speeches that populate lists of great oratory, such as Athenian statesman Pericles's fifth-century BCE funeral oration, presidential inaugural addresses or accompanying forms such as Maya Angelou's inaugural poem "On the Pulse of Morning" or Amanda Gorman's inaugural poem "The Hill We Climb," the Nobel Prize acceptance speeches of William Faulkner or Martin Luther King, Jr., or Malala Yousafzai's speech on education to the United Nations.

Beyond describing epideictic as a skillful display of praise, Aristotle notes that amplification, or "heightening the effect" of praise to invest a subject with dignity or nobility, is the most appropriate topic of argument for epideictic speeches. "It is only natural that methods of 'heightening the effect' should be attached particularly to speeches of praise," Aristotle writes, and although amplification is common to all speeches it is most suitable to declamations, "where we take our hero's actions as admitted facts, and our business is simply to invest these with dignity and nobility."[62] More a function than a topic, however, amplification is accomplished by varied methods in many discursive situations. Kenneth Burke describes amplification as the most immutable of traditional rhetorical principles, aligned with poetic invention: "As extension, expatiation, the saying of something in various ways until it increases in persuasiveness by the sheer accumulation, amplification can come to name a purely poetic process of development, such systematic exploitation of a theme as we find in lyrics built about a refrain."[63] In contrast to the pragmatic reputation of deliberative and judicial rhetoric, epideictic is often associated with poetic or lyrical processes of development.

From the time that Aristotle conceived of epideictic as a separate rhetorical genre it has often been condemned as an inferior or degenerate form of speech that possesses an empty aesthetic appeal, branded as "ostentatious artistry"[64] or the playful display of an "oratorical virtuoso,"[65] characterized by "dazzling" techniques of "crowd-pleasing razzmatazz,"[66] producing only "ritualistic showpieces,"[67] "hollow bombast," "gaudy verbal baubles,"[68] or "vapid flattery,"[69] sometimes assuming the aspect of a "burlesque."[70] It is said to address only uncontroversial topics in a dogmatic mode, more closely associated with literature and propaganda than argument, or as Chaïm Perelman and Lucie Olbrechts-Tyteca note, the form of speech "most in danger of...becoming rhetoric in the usual and pejorative sense of the word."[71] Beginning with its association with Roman panegyrics—state-sponsored show speeches that lavished praise on Roman emperors[72]—epideictic has been specifically associated with the propaganda of illiberal regimes.⁷³ For example, the following excerpt from a Four Minute Man speech—public speeches given by volunteers during World War I on topics proposed by the United States Committee on Public Information—illustrates the form in American war propaganda:

> During all these years the Stars and Stripes have flung to the winds of the world the proud message that this was a free country—country of one people, one speech, and one social structure, into the fabrication of which has been woven the lives of generations of brave men and noble women."⁷⁴

Contemporary studies of propaganda recognize that poetic devices such as repetition and parallelism lend themselves to the power of propaganda to be detached from its original context and widely disseminated.⁷⁵

The relationship between epideictic and propaganda is also apparent in Antonio Gramsci's attribution of the rise of Italian fascism in part to what he called the "operatic conception of life," which he found to arise not only out of serial novels and other "mawkish, mellifluous, and whimpery" forms of popular literature but out of opera, its "most pestiferous" form, and the "collective expressions of oratory and theater." As representative examples of the forms of oratory that cultivated this "operatic taste" characterized by "'elevated' language," Gramsci particularly notes the influence of the funeral oratory marking important deaths which "always draw large crowds, often just to hear the speeches," as well as the oratory of "the local magistrate's court and law-courts," filled with people who memorized "the turns of phrase and the solemn words, feed[ing] on them and remember[ing] them."⁷⁶ Epideictic is evident in medieval morality plays, agitation trials in early Soviet Russia, and many other literary and rhetorical forms that promote specific versions of public morality.⁷⁷

The association of epideictic with the obfuscating quality of bureaucratic writing and propaganda substantially contributed to the Scientific Revolution and Enlightenment's perception of rhetoric as no more than a contamination of the preferred "plain style" of writing which continues to dominate prose today.⁷⁸ The association is a chief inspiration for modern language policies such as those of the Royal Society of London, founded in the seventeenth century to promote the advancement of science, which sought to eliminate all "amplification, digressions and swellings of style" in favor of a "primitive purity, and shortness," a "close, naked, natural way of speaking; positive expressions; clear senses; a native easiness; bringing all things as near…Mathematical plainness as they can."[79] Although in the sixteenth century figural discourse was viewed as necessary to give discourse "the persuasive aura of aristocracy in an aristocratic society,"[80] by the seventeenth century John Locke wrote that "all the artificial and figurative application of words eloquence has invented" merely "insinuate wrong ideas" and are "perfect cheats,"[81] and by the end of the eighteenth century Immanuel Kant wrote that rhetoric borrows from poetry only what is needed to "win over men's minds…before they have weighed the matter, and to rob their verdict of its freedom," meriting "no *respect* whatsoever."[82] In the nineteenth century, John Genung noted that amplification was regarded with suspicion, "as if it were merely spreading the thought out thin, or putting what is called 'padding,'" and that "no advice about writing is more popular than the advice to 'boil it down.'"[83] In contrast to the austere impulse of such modernist exhortations, epideictic expounds on its topics with psychagogic intensity.[84]

Consistent with this history, the amplification practices that have historically been associated with epideictic conflict with the concise and plain quality often called for in judicial opinions. A common complaint about opinions is their length and extraneous content, giving rise to advice such as to avoid lengthy discussions of established principles and to prefer "plain words and sentences that communicate rather than befuddle,"[85] or that "deliberate brevity insures lucidity."[86] As Nevin Laib writes, as a result of its association with bureaucratic writing and propaganda amplification has come to represent an "evil, sophistic, and impersonal system bent on suppression of personal freedom and manipulative deception of an innocent public."[87]

I began my study of epideictic in judicial discourse after finding the more limited framework of argumentation inadequate to present a complete picture of legal discourse, even when an argumentation focus is expanded to encompass informal logic and epistemic modality. In particular, such an exclusive focus on argumentation neglects more performative and symbolic dimensions of legal discourse which are particularly apparent in its epideictic registers. Although judicial opinions are not the only legal discourse containing such registers, they serve as useful artifacts to examine the role of epideictic in legal discourse given the important role they play in classrooms, law offices, courtrooms, and media representations of law, representing records of legal judgments, precedent for future cases, and exemplars of legal reasoning.[88]

While standard histories of rhetoric have defined epideictic as a secondary, derivative, or inferior form of speech that portends a "decline" of rhetoric compared with the practical civic oratory of legislative assemblies and courts, Jeffrey Walker argues that rhetoric itself is "centrally and fundamentally an art of epideictic argumentation/persuasion" that extends to practical discourse and constitutes a major source of the emergence of rhetorical knowledge.[89] According to Walker, Aristotle turned his conception of deliberative, judicial, and epideictic rhetoric into "abstract universal types," an "all too tidy" classification scheme that obscured the specificity of the genres encompassed by the terms and improperly sought to turn them into "a set of timeless paradigms with only an approximate correspondence to actual speaking practices."[90] Other commentators have observed that epideictic originally referred to a quality of discourse or an entire approach to rhetoric characteristic of the ancient Greek sophists rather than to a genre and that it performed important social, cultural, and political functions that Aristotle neglected.[91] The fact that epideictic was ubiquitous in ancient Greece is even evident in Aristotle's own preference for illustrating the points in his *Rhetoric* using epideictic rather than deliberative and judicial sources.[92]

As Walker notes, before Aristotle the Greeks distinguished epideictic not as a genre but by its function of "suasive 'demonstration,' display, or showing-forth (*epideixis*) of things, leading its audience…to contemplation (*theôria*) and insight and ultimately to the formation of opinions and desires on matters of philosophical, social, ethical, and cultural concern." In Greek antiquity, epideictic established and mnemonically sustained the "culturally authoritative codes of value and the paradigms of eloquence" from which deliberative and judicial rhetoric derived their "'precedents,'… language, and…power," a sort of substratum of all speech. What distinguished epideictic and pragmatic speech, Walker writes, had little to do with subject matter, a fact he notes is obscured by the conventional translation of the pragmatic genres as "'deliberative' and 'forensic' or (worse) as 'political' and 'legal' discourse," and that the distinction is not strictly formal.

Instead, Walker concludes, the division of pragmatic and epideictic discourse in ancient Greece represented different registers that existed along a spectrum rather than as a dichotomy. Practical speech existed as a "continuation and further evolution of the poetic tradition (and its methods of argument) into new stylistic registers" often "punctuated and pervaded by sententious flights of wisdom-invoking eloquence," which reflected differing purposes or functions overlapping or blending in various discourse situations.[93] Other commentators have described isolated praise registers as "miniature panegyric,"[94] or as "mixed or hybrid" structures reflecting a "mixed purpose,"[95] sometimes including only epideictic "elements,"[96] "dimensions,"[97] or "parts or moments,"[98] or as a "persuasive gesture or mode we might locate in any number of discourses," including judicial discourse.[99] The recognition that epideictic functions as a register in a wide range of rhetorical situations, often appearing only in parts or moments of discourse or as a gesture or mode rather than as genre, accounts for a wealth of commentary by both ancient and contemporary sources that suggests epideictic features have always extended beyond forms such as funeral and festival speeches to more pragmatic forms of discourse.

The related concepts of genre and register refer to the perspective that discursive features perform sociocultural functions in response to situational variables. To the extent that similar situations recur, in other words, so do similar ideas and discursive forms. Along with the concept of style, the concepts of genre and register have been used in conflicting ways,[100] but a genre approach to discourse generally considers features common to an entire type of text such as a eulogy while a register approach considers features that regularly occur across many types of texts.[101] Some commentators have also described hybrid or fused genres. Kathleen Jamieson and Jennifer Stromer-Galley, for example, note that a genre may exist as a "fusion of elements that may be energized or actualized as a strategic response" to unique situations.[102] As Mikhail Bakhtin writes, because the possibilities of human activity are inexhaustible, linguistic diversity is ultimately limitless, each sphere of activity containing "an entire repertoire of speech genres that differentiate and grow as the particular sphere develops and becomes more complex."[103] Because all situations contain incommensurable elements, inviting or demanding a variation of responses, genres are dynamic rather than static.[104] This relationship of form and function results in what Norman Fairclough calls interdiscursivity, or the "heterogeneity of texts in being constituted by combinations of diverse genres and discourses" that constantly transform past discursive practices into the present.[105]

Approaching epideictic as a register rather than a genre emphasizes the range of epideictic features manifest across genres and the fact that even in genres traditionally classified as epideictic its features may only exist in parts or moments of particular texts. Such an approach also explains the wealth of sources that have noted the incoherence of the epideictic genre from its inception.[106] As John O'Malley writes, epideictic "often transgressed the limits set for it" in the ancient world. The deliberative, judicial, and epideictic genres were considerably blurred in both theory and practice in ancient Greece and Rome, as praise and blame constituted expected and proper elements of both deliberative and judicial discourse.[107] The fourth-century BCE Greek rhetorical handbook *Rhetorica ad Alexandrum* teaches that deliberative, judicial, and epideictic oratory should be employed "both separately, when suitable, and jointly, with a combination of their qualities—for though they have very considerable differences, yet in their practical application they overlap."[108] Although Aristotle does not consider amplification the primary focus of deliberative and judicial oratory, he recognizes that it may play a "subsidiary" role in each,[109] and many ancient Greek sources exemplify the interdiscursivity of judicial and epideictic discourse, such as Gorgias of Leontini's *Encomium to Helen*, Isocrates's *Antidosis*, or Demosthenes's *On the Crown*, which exhibit epideictic features in judicial forms.

By the late Roman Republic, epideictic was inseparable from other rhetorical genres.[110] The author of the oldest surviving rhetorical handbook in Latin, for example, the first-century BCE *Rhetorica ad Herennium*, states that epideictic is "only seldom employed by itself independently," but instead deliberative and judicial rhetoric often devote "extensive sections... to praise or censure."[111] According to Roger Rees, praise was "as much a part of free-flowing generic traffic as any other discourse" in ancient Rome and "similarly open to innovation and growth."[112] In his *Institutio Oratoria*, Quintilian notes the importance of praise and blame in the practical life of Rome. Funeral orations were imposed as a duty on public officeholders or magistrates. The praise or blame of a witness in court could "carry weight," and it was a recognized practice to "produce persons to praise the character of the accused."[113] The practical forms of epideictic required proof, and a "semblance of proof" was at times required by speeches "composed entirely for display."[114] The Roman speech exercises known as declamations also used epideictic features to address judicial subjects, and their "grandiloquent phraseology" influenced courtroom oratory.[115]

The significance of epideictic in practical argument has also been recognized in contemporary rhetorical studies. Chaïm Perelman notes that epideictic tends to effect change no less than any of the forms of practical argument,[116] and Perelman and Lucie Olbrechts-Tyteca stress that epideictic is a "central part of the art of persuasion" from which all practical speech arises, functioning to intensify adherence to the values on which arguments rest.[117] Jeremy Engels notes that in the Early American Republic the lines between deliberative and epideictic rhetoric blurred as "tactics typically associated with more ceremonial rhetoric—for instance, the passionate denunciation of enemies—were characteristic of rhetoric in more deliberative settings."[118] At times the distinction between epideictic and practical argument has been limited only by the immediacy of its effects. Perelman and Olbrechts-Tyteca propose that epideictic is distinguishable from practical argument only by its temporality, because it creates a disposition to act at a future moment rather than immediately,[119] and Eugene Garver similarly writes that epideictic is "less urgent" than deliberative and judicial speech but "more lasting."[120] In the early pages of Perelman and Olbrechts-Tyteca's *New Rhetoric*, they emphasize that of his three rhetorical genres Aristotle's characterization of epideictic is "particularly unsatisfactory."[121]

Recently studies have also recognized epideictic features in certain forms of legal discourse, such as the design of legal trials, witness testimony, and the power of legal discourse to secure compliance with legal decisions or promote legal values. For example, Mark Osiel aligns the decisions of Allied prosecutors after World War II to narrow the scope of trials for wartime atrocities to the conduct of officials rather than broader power structures with the "pedagogic, 'epideictic' mode" of historical writing.[122] Lawrence Rosenfield suggests that the records of modern genocides may represent "the most authentic epideictic literature produced by our age," citing Aleksandr Solzhenitsyn's *Gulag Archipelago* as an example which commemorates "our capacity for life, truth, and human dignity even as it disparages the venality" of those responsible for the atrocities in Soviet concentration camps. Solzhenitsyn's work is not simply polemical, Rosenfield writes, but "bore witness" to Soviet atrocities.[123] Similarly, Bradford Vivian has noted the epideictic quality of witnessing, writing that witnesses to atrocity "ostensibly communicate, with optimum moral if not factual authenticity, indubitable lessons in justice applicable to entire communities," representing "exceptional and commonplace epideictic agent[s] in modern liberal-democratic institutions."[124]

With regard to the power of legal discourse to secure compliance with decisions and promote legal values, Perelman and Olbrechts-Tyteca illustrate their explanation of epideictic with the Greek statesman Demosthenes's effort to not only get Athenians to make legal decisions but to convince them, "by every means at his command, to carry out the decisions once they were made," recognizing that "a decree is worthless in itself, unless you add to it the willingness to carry out resolutely what you have decreed."[125] Perhaps in contrast to the irrelevance of decrees that are not carried out, Eugene Garver argues that although the Emancipation Proclamation "freed no slaves," it nonetheless "proclaimed a new orientation of the political community by definitively offering a new set of values."[126] In addition, Garver writes that the Court's opinion regarding racial desegregation of public schools in *Brown v. Board of Education* (1954) constituted an "epideictic declaration that equality and antidiscrimination are fundamental American constitutional values" which committed the Court and the nation to a new constitutional *ethos* connecting *Brown* to President Lincoln's Gettysburg Address and later to the Court's opinion in *Loving v. Virginia* (1967), in which the Court held miscegenation laws to be unconstitutional.[127] Although *Brown* was premised on the value of education to democracy, Garver writes, it created an "ethical surplus" in the antidiscrimination principle it embraced which committed the Court to desegregation beyond schools.[128]

Similarly, Robert Tsai argues that constitutional jurisprudence fosters "bonds of fellowship," legitimizes institutional relationships, and repairs "rifts in the political imagination" created by social and political change,[129] and Colin Starger concludes that Justice Antonin Scalia's dissenting opinions in a series of First Amendment cases involving the free speech rights of abortion protesters reflect epideictic discourse by promoting an antiabortion perspective in opposition to *Roe v. Wade* (1973), which transcended the First Amendment issues in the cases.[130] Perhaps most broadly, Francis Mootz argues that the natural law commonplaces that form our general conception of "the Law" serve "an epideictic role as much as a forensic or logical one."[131]

As noted earlier, not only have scholarly commentators recognized epideictic features in legal discourse but judges have as well, often using terms closely associated with epideictic such as *paean, panegyric, encomium,* or *rhapsody* to describe judicial opinion writing, brief writing, and legislation. In *Georgia v. Randolph* (2006), for example, Justice Scalia described the concurring opinion of Justice John Paul Stevens as a "panegyric." In *Randolph*, the Court held that a warrantless search by the Georgia police of a married couple's home was unconstitutional because it was based on the consent of only one spouse while the other refused consent. In a concurring opinion, Stevens wrote that the case illustrated the limits of an originalist interpretation of the Constitution because even the most ardent originalist must "recognize the relevance of changes in our society." Citing the common law castle doctrine which protects a person's home against intrusion, Stevens acknowledged that in the eighteenth century the consent of a husband alone would have been enough for the police to search a couple's home given the differences between the property rights of husband and wife at the time. He argued that the history of the doctrine was not dispositive in 2006, however, because "it is now clear, as a matter of constitutional law, that the male and the female are equal partners," neither one "a master possessing the power to override the other's constitutional right to deny entry to their castle."[132]

Justice Scalia responded to Justice Stevens's critique of originalism in a dissenting opinion, writing that Stevens's "panegyric to the *equal* rights of women" did not support the conclusion that "the spouse who *refuses* consent should be the winner of the contest."[133] Although the term *panegyric* is relatively archaic, other judges have used the term to refer to judicial panegyrics to free speech,[134] the marketplace of ideas,[135] freedom of the press,[136] liberty,[137] the right of privacy and personal security,[138] the common law and Magna Carta,[139] the jury trial,[140] *stare decisis*,[141] anonymous political discourse,[142] arbitrator impartiality,[143] the polygraph,[144] and religion,[145] among other subjects. In an opinion describing the "extravagant panegyric" to the jury system found in many judicial opinions, one court noted that some opinions have "even found evidence of its sacred character in Holy Writ, pointing with reverential awe to the twelve apostles, twelve tribes, twelve stones, etc."[146]

The term *panegyric* occurs in at least eighty-one judicial opinions issued by federal and state courts in the United States, both to refer to a judge's own opinion writing practices and to those of his or her colleagues, in positive, negative, and strictly descriptive senses.[147] Judges have also described judicial opinion writing with related terms such as *paean*,[148] *encomium*,[149] *rhapsody*,[150] *eulogy*,[151] or *trumpet*.[152] One court compared judicial panegyrics with eulogies and taps—the ceremonial bugle call played at military funerals—to describe judicial precedent, holding that it is better to sacrifice safety than freedom: "Panegyrics to 'essential liberty' from those who, in the comfort of their judicial chambers, do not face the dangers of the streets are of little comfort to those who all too often have to listen to eulogies and taps for those killed trying to protect society from the lawless."[153]

In addition to judicial opinions, epideictic registers are found in constitutions, legislation, pleadings, oral arguments and briefs, the examination of witnesses at trial, and other forms of legal discourse. Beyond the references cited above in which judges describe judicial opinions with terms such as *paean, panegyric, encomium,* or *rhapsody,* for example, judges have referred to legislation and appellate briefs in such terms. Judge Eugene Strassburger of the Superior Court of Pennsylvania, for example, called the Pennsylvania Right to Farm Act "a paean to agribusiness,"[154] and in Justice Samuel Alito's dissenting opinion in the United States Supreme Court's consideration of the Stolen Valor Act which criminalized lying about receiving military decorations, Alito wrote that "Respondent's brief features a veritable paean to lying."[155] Judicial opinions are the most generally read form of legal discourse, however, and the most significant form read by legal experts,[156] offering a voluminous and accessible corpus that illustrates the epideictic features of legal discourse not only in the arguments presented by lawmakers, parties, and witnesses, but in the development of the law itself.

This book's focus on judicial opinion writing in fundamental rights jurisprudence is intended to illustrate dimensions of legal discourse largely neglected in contemporary studies of judicial opinions rather than to be exhaustive. I first identified a set of prevalent registral features of epideictic by reviewing rhetorical artifacts that have been traditionally categorized as epideictic and classical and contemporary scholarly commentary on epideictic in rhetorical studies. After identifying such features, which encompass situation, form, and function, I reviewed state and federal judicial opinions considered important or influential to determine whether they possessed convergences of the epideictic features that I identified. I also searched case law databases for references to specific features of epideictic in judicial opinions, such as references to judicial praise, figures of speech and arrangement, eloquence, and maxims, and for descriptions of opinions using terms closely associated with epideictic such as *paean, panegyric, encomium, rhapsody,* and *eulogy,* looking not only for the isolated presence of such features but for their convergence with others. Although I discovered many examples of epideictic registers beyond those considered here, they appeared prominently in fundamental rights jurisprudence.

By focusing on a discrete doctrinal area of law, I am also able to demonstrate epideictic's intertextual power in opinion writing and the central gestures that often emerge out of it, such as the Court's repeated use of paramologia, or strategic concession, in its free speech jurisprudence, or the prevalence of chiasmus in the Court's early religion cases.

In Chapter 1, "Judicial and Epideictic Rhetoric: A False Division," I develop a register theory of epideictic through an analysis of discourse traditionally classified as epideictic and classical and contemporary commentary on epideictic. I argue that the situations of epideictic are prototypically those in which social relationships begin, end, or in which an exigency arises to threaten social unity, and among its more pervasive features are praise, amplification devices, eloquence, the gnomic aspect, affirmative modality, and nonverbal elements of the occasions on which epideictic discourse is delivered, such as the date, time, location, venue, the speaker and their attire, all of which respond to potential division by subsuming the individual agency of speaker and audience within a collective perspective so unifying that it often leads to descriptions of the experience in mystical terms. Drawing on speech act theory and Chaïm Perelman and Lucie Olbrechts-Tyteca's concept of the ways in which arguments interact by convergence to augment each other, I conclude that successful epideictic preserves and restores social unity through dense performative convergences of many of the registral features identified to magnify the value of subjects beyond the perceptual capacities of participants.[157]

In Chapters 2 through 4, I illustrate the convergence of these registral features in three bodies of the United States Supreme Court's fundamental rights jurisprudence. In Chapter 2, "Freedom of Speech, Paramologia, and the Flag," I examine the epideictic registers in the United States Supreme Court's jurisprudence regarding the First Amendment's Free Speech Clause, first in the Court's opinions regarding the constitutionality of compulsory flag salutes in *Minersville School District v. Gobitis* (1940) and *West Virginia State Board of Education v. Barnette* (1943), and then in the opinions of Justices William Brennan, Anthony Kennedy, and William Rehnquist regarding prosecutions for desecration of the American flag in *Texas v. Johnson* (1989). I argue that these cases reveal the central role that the figure of paramologia, or strategic concession, played in the Court's thought regarding freedom of speech, acknowledging and lamenting the dangers of free speech while amplifying its benefits by contrast. I also critique Justice Frankfurter's use of epideictic in the flag salute cases as a failure to accurately apprehend the nation's beliefs, desires, and ethical commitments on the issue and the efficacy of Justice Rehnquist's infamous opinion extolling the flag's place in American history.

In Chapter 3, "Keeping Government Out of Religion and Vice Versa," I examine the epideictic registers in the Court's early Religion Clause jurisprudence regarding the relationship between religion and public schools, focusing on *Everson v. Board of Education* (1947), *McCollum v. Board of Education* (1948), and *Lemon v. Kurtzman* (1971). I pay particular attention to the intertextual role played by Madison's *Remonstrance and Memorial* in the epideictic registers of *Everson* and *McCollum* as majority, concurring, and dissenting justices quote and interpret Madison's *Remonstrance* in their opinions. Attending to this dimension of the Court's epideictic registers in its early Religion Clause jurisprudence reveals the central role that the figure of chiasmus plays in the Court's thought regarding the Religion Clauses. A chiasmatic relationship is prevalently expressed both in Madison's thought and in the Court's early Religion Clause jurisprudence, and I argue that the prevalence of this figure serves to interpret the wall of separation between church and state as a more indeterminate, flexible, or unstable relationship than traditional interpretations reflect and one that ultimately ended in irresolution.

In Chapter 4, "Storms, Shadows, and Privacy," I examine the epideictic registers in the Court's privacy jurisprudence as the right of privacy was found to inhere in the penumbras of the Bill of Rights and in the liberty protected by the Due Process Clause of the Fourteenth Amendment, proceeding by means of an analysis of Justice Anthony Kennedy's majority opinion in *Obergefell* and a genealogy of the leading cases on which he relied, particularly *Lawrence v. Texas* (2003), *Griswold v. Connecticut* (1965), *Loving v. Virginia* (1967), and related cases. I argue that Chief Justice John Marshall's immortal constitution metaphor, which viewed the Constitution as a vessel designed to weather "storms and tempests," and Justice William Douglas's metaphor of "emanations" of the Bill of Rights which form "penumbras," serve as important foundations of the Court's privacy jurisprudence, functioning as central figurations in epideictic registers that amplify the basis of judicial authority to recognize rights such as privacy that are not explicitly enumerated in the Constitution. The often expansive intertextual power of epideictic registers is at its height in the Court's privacy cases, I argue, as the Court's affective commitments to the relationship between liberty and privacy accrue and take on new meanings across a wide range of subjects from searches and seizures to wiretapping, contraceptive use, sexual relations, and marriage. I argue that this jurisprudence and the metaphors on which it relied magnified the value of figurative reasoning itself to a sublime level as a premise of the Court's interpretive authority.

In the conclusion, "Truth Has No Bones," I compare Justice Antonin Scalia's criticism of epideictic when it appeared in the writing of other justices with his own uses of epideictic and those of the Roberts Court. I illustrate how the conflict of belief, desire, and ethical commitment between originalism and living constitutionalism which supported the opposing positions on abortion in *Dobbs v. Jackson Women's Health Organization* (2022) is particularly evident in the epideictic registers of its opinions, and I assess the implications of the register theory of epideictic considered in the book for identifying, predicting, critiquing, and producing epideictic, as well as the limits of the theory. I discuss the importance of recognizing that the divide between judicial and epideictic discourse existed in the classical rhetorical tradition and is not a modern development, and I argue for a "humanist jurisprudence" or "rhetorical jurisprudence" that recognizes the role of temporality in judicial discourse. Contrary to the perspective that the more "rhapsodical strains" of judicial opinion writing reflect only an inferior, degenerate, and empty form of speech, I propose that such writing often reflects moments when judges acknowledge the limits of their power and seek to exercise their authority ethically and rhetorically by addressing the consequences of their decisions and seeking public acceptance rather than relying on power alone, not as an anomaly or a corruption of disciplined legal reasoning but as necessary and endemic to it.

CHAPTER 1

Judicial and Epideictic Rhetoric: A False Division

Legal discourse is antirhetorical, or so we are told. It relies on reduction and certainty in order to resolve disputes with finality. It promotes, as Sanford Levinson writes, "the one right (or best) answer to questions and the one true (or best) meaning of texts."[1] It disciplines rather than cultivates speech. According to Levinson, lawyers and judges tend to adopt an overconfident tone, dismissing opposing views as "without merit," and they rarely characterize a question as "exceedingly close" with "much to be said on both...sides."[2] Peter Goodrich writes that the foundational texts of the English common law are motivated by the figure of antirrhesis, a denunciation of others as outsiders, heretics, or iconoclasts.[3] Legal discourse aims to obtain a judgment predicated on proof "beyond the course of doubt," he writes, a form that depends on dismissal and repression, "a refusal to listen, a void or absence of speech in which the other is characterized not simply as without jurisdiction but as mendacious, demanding, inconsistent and without credibility or right."[4] Those who challenge the law are viewed not merely as wrong, Goodrich writes, but as "sacrilegious, unnatural and irrational if not explicitly insane."[5]

According to Robert Ferguson, the driving impulses of judicial opinions include a controlling voice in which "the goal of judgment is to subsume difference in explanation and decision,"[6] an interrogative mode guided by questions only asked "with an answer already firmly in mind,"[7] and a declarative tone that "resists mystery, complexity, revelation, and even exploration" in favor of "hyperbole, certitude, assertion, simplification, and abstraction."[8] These impulses combine to form what Ferguson calls a "rhetoric of inevitability" which presents decisions as predetermined.[9] Similarly, Eugene Garver writes that although judges may struggle with doubts regarding more than one rational decision in a case, "when it comes time to write an opinion, each judge writes as though his or her decision is ineluctable, necessary, and inevitable."[10] It is evident from these and other commentators that, much like scientific discourse, legal discourse promotes an image of itself as a hermetic domain unaffected by rhetorical considerations.[11]

The antirhetorical quality that is believed to characterize legal discourse today has often been contrasted with the close relationship believed to have existed between rhetoric and law in the classical rhetorical tradition of ancient Greece and Rome, the influence of which extended through European history to the Middle Ages and the Renaissance.[12] The development of rhetorical knowledge in ancient Greece reputedly began in response to the rise of property litigation, the emergence of written judicial opinions and legal doctrines such as equity have been attributed to the proliferation of rhetorical training in ancient Rome, and modern rules of evidence and procedure are in part codifications of principles that first arose in the classical rhetorical tradition.[13] The rhetorical handbooks of the classical tradition included prescriptive instruction in legal advocacy, and the highest lesson of the series of prose composition exercises known as *progymnasmata* which emerged from the tradition and on which classical rhetorical theory often reflected was an exercise in which a student spoke for and against a proposed law.[14] As Chaïm Perelman notes, "in Greece, Rome, the Middle Ages and the Modern Era legal development went hand in hand with rhetorical development."[15] During the Renaissance the legal career was particularly instrumental in reviving rhetorical study, and a legal career has always been a destination for those who have pursued a rhetorical education.[16]

The perceived disparity between contemporary and classical perspectives on the relationship between law and rhetoric has prompted many to lament the divide between the fields today. Legal historian David Cairns writes that no history of modern legal advocacy has been written nor has anyone considered it in the depth that Aristotle or Quintilian did the legal oratory of ancient Greece and Rome,[17] and Michael Frost concludes that the classical rhetorical tradition is an "unequaled source" of wisdom on legal advocacy, "the most coherent and experience-based discussion of legal reasoning, analytical methods, and argumentative strategies ever devised."[18] According to Frost, contemporary approaches to legal discourse lack "the breadth, depth or tone of...classical sources," with their attention to philosophy, poetics, and politics.[19]

The contemporary divide between law and rhetoric has been variously attributed to the decline of the Roman Republic, the professionalization of law and legal apprenticeship that began with the rise of law schools in the late Middle Ages, the codification of rhetorical principles in modern rules of evidence and procedure which have rendered their separate study unnecessary, and the effect of the Scientific Revolution and Enlightenment's insistence that invention be exclusively governed by deductive logic and the scientific method rather than included in the study of rhetoric.[20] In the sixteenth century, the pedagogical reformer Peter Ramus directed that invention along with arrangement and memory be eliminated from rhetorical studies entirely and assigned exclusively to philosophy, leaving rhetorical studies only the study of style appended separately from the development of content, and even limiting rhetorical studies of style to consideration of tropes and figures—mostly tropes—while etymology and syntax were separately assigned to grammatical studies.[21] The Ramist approach to rhetoric reduced rhetoric, in other words, to an ornamental role more than, in Walter Ong's assessment, "any other rhetoric ever has."[22] The modern elimination of invention from rhetorical studies beginning with Ramus has diminished the study of the rhetorical dimensions of knowledge not only in law but in every discipline, a development further compounded by René Descartes's rationalism and the modern language policies of Francis Bacon and the Royal Society of London which rejected rhetoric along with all other humanistic knowledge in the pursuit of an exclusively scientific model of invention.[23]

The relationship between law and rhetoric today is often explained, in other words, as a drift away from an original unity. According to Ronald Matlon, despite an originally close relationship between law and rhetoric, "the road traveled has been a rocky one,"[24] and Michael Frost subtitled his book on classical legal rhetoric *A Lost Heritage*.[25] Although over the past half century many commentators have begun to question the antirhetorical portrait of contemporary legal discourse—including those who pursued the "jurisprudential turn" in argument theory led by philosophers Chaïm Perelman and Stephen Toulmin to prefer a juridical model of argument over a strictly logical one[26]—the story of the relationship between law and rhetoric has generally been one of growing alienation. As a result, rhetorical studies have borne the burden of proving their relevance to legal discourse.[27]

While the historical forces to which the contemporary divide between law and rhetoric have been attributed have undoubtedly shaped the divide in the ways commentators have noted, representations of an original unity between law and rhetoric in the classical tradition are also overstated and appear to suffer from a certain nostalgia that fails to recognize divisions between the fields of law and rhetoric in the classical tradition as well as in contemporary thought. It is unclear whether Aristotle, Quintilian, or any other classical rhetorician considered legal discourse all that deeply either. They seldom wrote about particular legal cases or historical contingencies in great depth, and they largely limited their study of legal discourse to its eristic dimension, the pragmatic consideration of how lawyers succeed or fail to secure the outcomes they desire in legal cases. Sources of division between law and rhetoric are evident in many classical sources on law and rhetoric, suggesting a more perennial and fraught relationship than historical drift alone explains.

One of the most important classical sources of the division between law and rhetoric is Aristotle's effort to separate judicial and epideictic speech in his *Rhetoric*, an example of a broader perspective in the ancient world that at times viewed judicial discourse as beyond the scope of rhetoric at all. The first-century Epicurean philosopher Philodemus, for example, concluded that Epicureanism not only rejected the view that epideictic—which he equated with sophistic amplification practices—belonged to a single genre of rhetoric, but he concluded that it constituted the entire realm of rhetoric to the exclusion of deliberative and judicial discourse.[28] The distinction continues to appear in contemporary sources. Walter Berns, for example, writes that "it is not clear that there is a proper place for rhetoric in the judiciary, even at the highest level," although it is necessary for judicial rhetoric "to strengthen, or 'fortify,' the popular attachment to the Constitution, or, to cause it to be venerated by the people."[29]

Previous commentators have noted that Aristotle's division of rhetoric into deliberative, judicial, and epideictic genres sought to discipline the epideictic rhetorical practices of the ancient Greek sophists,[30] but it is important to understand that the division concomitantly sought to discipline judicial rhetoric as well and what that disciplinary effort suggests about attitudes toward legal discourse in ancient Greece. In the opening pages of his *Rhetoric*, after arguing that rhetoric is an art that can be treated systematically, Aristotle complains that the authors of rhetorical treatises preferred the "accessory" and "non-essential" topics of emotional rather than logical modes of persuasion. According to Aristotle, the logical modes of persuasion are the "only true constituents of the art" of rhetoric, particularly the enthymeme, which he calls "the substance of rhetorical persuasion." Although enthymemes existed as a category of rhetorical activity before his *Rhetoric*, Aristotle conceives of enthymemes as "rhetorical syllogisms" because they adhere to logic in the same manner as logical syllogisms, distinguished only by the fact that enthymemes address contingent issues or rely on tacit premises, as "conclusions that state what is merely usual or possible must be drawn from premises that do the same."[31]

For Aristotle, the enthymeme, then, is a counterpart (*antistrophos*) of strictly logical reasoning because "the true and the approximately true are apprehended by the same faculty," and "the man who makes a good guess at truth is likely to make a good guess at probabilities."[32] Enthymemes are particularly suitable to judicial discourse, he writes, because "it is our doubts about past events that most admit of arguments showing why a thing must have happened or proving that it did happen."[33] Much as Stephen Toulmin introduced epistemic modality into argument theory in the twentieth century by recognizing the role that backing, warrants, and qualifiers play in argument, Aristotle introduced modality into rhetorical theory in the ancient world by recognizing the value of contingent reasoning.

Despite Aristotle's recognition of contingent reasoning, however, he distinguishes emotional and logical modes of persuasion in the opening pages of his *Rhetoric* by critiquing the advice provided for legal advocates in the rhetorical handbooks of the era. Specifically, Aristotle positions his *Rhetoric* as a response to the focus of such handbooks on methods of arousing prejudice, pity, anger, and other emotions, which he concludes are improper because they have "nothing to do with the essential facts" of a case but are purely personal appeals to a judge. It is wrong for a litigant to "pervert" the judge by "moving him to anger or envy or pity," Aristotle argues. Instead, a litigant has "nothing to do but to show that the alleged fact is or is not so, that it has or has not happened." A judge should ignore pleas from a litigant regarding whether a thing is important or just, Aristotle writes, deciding such matters for himself to the extent that their value is not already defined by the legislature. In addition, legislatures should allow judges "to decide as few things as possible."[34] Because legislators consider "wider issues" and vote in their own self-interest rather than as bystanders, Aristotle concludes that deliberative rhetoric is less susceptible than judicial rhetoric to exploitation by unscrupulous rhetorical practices.[35] For Aristotle, as Eugene Garver explains, "we all have a stake in getting the answers right" in deliberative rhetoric,[36] but in judicial rhetoric the speaker must "create the motivation" by making people take arguments "personally and morally."[37] For Aristotle, appealing to a judge in this way should be strictly limited.[38]

In contrast to his recognition of contingent reasoning or at least qualifying that recognition, Aristotle also announces early in his *Rhetoric* a general preference for the prospective and general decision-making of legislatures to the retrospective and casuistical reasoning of judges, citing the particularism of judicial reasoning as the "weightiest reason of all" for preferring legislative authority.[39] This preference also subordinates Aristotle's development of the concept of equity, or situational principles of justice that serve to correct the generality of legislation, to legislative decision-making,[40] and he commends strict procedures to regulate the narrow scope of authority that legislatures give judges. He even writes that if the rigorous rules for trials in "well-governed" states such as those in the Council of Areopagus were applied everywhere, the writers of rhetorical treatises would "have nothing to say."[41] The Council of Areopagus consisted of former consuls with jurisdiction over intentional homicide and sacrilege cases, observed severe procedures that included ritual oaths performed over animal sacrifices and exclusionary practices directed at emotional or irrelevant pleading, and conducted its own inquiries into cases as a basis for independently challenging pleadings and evidence presented by the parties.[42] By contrast, popular jury courts had larger audiences and permitted the sort of emotional appeals excluded by the Areopagus.[43]

Considering Aristotle's admonitions against legal advocacy in the introductory pages of his *Rhetoric* in their entirety, it may not be surprising that in Cicero's first-century BCE dialogue *De Oratore* the interlocutor Antonius remarks that Aristotle "disdained" (*despiciebat*) rhetoric.[44] For Aristotle, the epideictic function of shaping beliefs, desires, and ethical commitments on matters of philosophical, social, ethical, or cultural concern is entirely improper in legal advocacy. Instead, he promotes a narrow and mechanical function of factfinding for judges with the consequences of such findings strictly determined by the legislature. The introductory paragraphs of Aristotle's *Rhetoric*, in other words, all but prefigure Shakespeare's famous line, "The first thing we do, let's kill all the lawyers."[45]

A closer examination of Aristotle's approach to the enthymeme and of the enthymeme's pre-Aristotelian history, however, reveals a more affective, epideictic dimension to Aristotle's logical modes of persuasion than is suggested by his tripartite division of genres and his condemnation of moving judges "to anger or envy or pity."[46] Despite Aristotle's early contrast between emotional appeals and the enthymeme as a logical mode of persuasion, for example, he writes later in his *Rhetoric* that speeches relying on enthymemes "excite the louder applause" than those that rely on examples, suggesting that enthymemes possessed emotional potency.[47] More importantly, he betrays recognition of a close connection between enthymemes and epideictic by recognizing that maxims (*gnomoi*)—defined as general statements about practical courses of conduct—constitute the premises and conclusions of enthymemes.[48] An enthymeme is "a syllogism dealing with...practical subjects," Aristotle writes, and he provides the following enthymeme from Euripides's tragedy *Medea* as an example:

Never should any man whose wits are sound
Have his sons taught more wisdom than their fellows
It makes them idle; and therewith they earn
Ill-will and jealousy throughout the city.

Aristotle similarly notes, again citing Euripides, that the maxim *there is no man among us all is free* forms an enthymeme when combined with the maxim *for all are slaves of money or chance*. He also includes among his examples the maxims *chiefest of blessings is health for a man, no love is true save that which loves forever*, and *mortal creatures ought to cherish mortal, not immortal thoughts*.[49]

Although Aristotle concludes that such declarations of general principles are only appropriate for speakers with experience in their subjects, he notes that they invest speech with moral character and can arouse strong emotion. "Even hackneyed and commonplace maxims" are effective if they suit a speaker's purpose, because everyone loves to hear the opinions they hold about particular cases expressed as general truths. On the other hand, Aristotle recognizes that maxims can be used agonistically to advance a dispute. "When working up feelings of horror and indignation" in an audience it is useful to declare something to be universal when it is not, he writes, and speakers should not avoid maxims that contradict commonly accepted knowledge, such as the maxims *know thyself* or *nothing in excess*. The use of maxims to contradict such commonly accepted knowledge can raise an audience's opinion of the speaker's character "or convey an effect of strong emotion." As an example, Aristotle writes it will raise an audience's estimation of a speaker for the speaker to say "we ought not to follow the saying that bids us treat our friends as future enemies: much better to treat our enemies as future friends," an enthymeme combining the gnomic aspect with the figure of chiasmus, or specifically antimetabole. If accepted by an audience, such declarations of moral principle reveal the speaker as a person of good moral character.[50] As Lawrence Rosenfield and Thomas Mader note, enthymemes also give pleasure because "their maxim-like injunctions come to the audience as dramatic revelations."[51]

The relationship between enthymemes and the gnomic aspect reveals a close connection between Aristotle's conception of the enthymeme, the sophistic background of his *Rhetoric*, and epideictic rhetoric, contradicting any clean separation of judicial and epideictic discourse into separate genres. According to Jeffrey Walker, the civic speeches in Homer's works of the seventh or eighth centuries BCE are "punctuated with sententious, gnomic sayings that invoke general truths or premises," which probably constitute "poetic formulae derived from traditional epideictic registers." Skillful speakers seamlessly wove such material together with "'original,' pragmatic utterance" that applied to the case at hand.[52] In the eighth century BCE, the Greek poet Hesiod described the eloquence of the wise prince (*basileus*) in civic forums using the term *epea* (words, tales, songs, or sayings) rather than *logos* (word, speech, discourse) or *onoma* (name, utterance).[53] Several commentators have suggested that Hesiod's use of the word *epea* may signify the oral-formulaic phrases of *epos*, the "winged words" of gods and bards or verses or rhythmic formulae which, Walker writes, constitute "the entire range of cultural lore an oral society cultivates, disseminates, and preserves in rhythmic discourse," including "discursive and/or catalogic representations of knowledge and belief—genealogies, hymns, prayers, curses, proverbs, instructions, 'scientific' or technical information, ethical exhortation, praise and blame, and so on."[54]

According to Walker, the cultural lore encoded in *epea* generally included "the customary laws or 'precedents,' the *themistas*, on which the civic rhetoric of the basileus is grounded." For the wise prince to be persuasive in civic forums he had to be able to "recall, interpret, and apply to the question at issue the memorious lore" encoded in *epos* and to "compose his own speech in rhythmic phrases and formulae, sententious language resembling traditional *epea*, as he carries off the mind of the fractious crowd on the stream of his 'honeyed' discourse."[55] Epideictic not only rehearses such conventional codes of value and meaning, Walker notes, but can "work to challenge or transform conventional beliefs" by shaping "the fundamental grounds, the 'deep' commitments and presuppositions, that will underlie and ultimately determine decision and debate in particular pragmatic forums."[56]

Although Aristotle emphasized the logical function of enthymemes when he appropriated the term from Isocrates and other sophists, the numerous enthymematic topics he lists in his *Rhetoric* almost exclusively reflect various antitheses which serve to amplify subjects.[57] Before Aristotle's reconceptualization of the enthymeme, Walker writes, the term generally referred to "heartfelt reasoning," the related adjective *enthymios* meant "taken to heart," and enthymemes were often used in epideictic speeches.[58] The term *enthymeme* was not used as a term of art before the fourth century BCE,[59] and pre-Aristotelean conceptions were as important as the Aristotelean conception of the enthymeme to later writers.[60] The enthymeme was a commonly occurring discursive practice, in other words, like the amplifying figures it often employed.[61] Walker explains that Aristotle's conception of the enthymeme presupposes a long sophistic tradition in which it was approached either as a general quasi-syllogistic discursive figure or procedure combining intuitive inference with affective force and passionate response,[62] or more technically a "turn or 'cap' " in argumentation that exploited "a cluster of emotively resonant, value-laden representations and systems of oppositions" made present through amplification devices such as figures and rhythm to produce a "passional identification" with a stance.[63]

In both pre-Aristotelian and Aristotelian rhetoric, the enthymeme possessed a powerfully affective dimension closely intertwined with the performative amplification of subjects characteristic of epideictic, and, accordingly, Aristotle's emphasis on the enthymeme as "the substance of rhetorical persuasion"[64] substantially qualifies his contrast between those who used enthymemes and those who sought to move judges to "anger or envy or pity"[65] as less of a contrast between logic and emotion than a particular approach to their relationship.[66] Moreover, Aristotle's emphasis on the enthymeme as most suitable to judicial discourse specifically casts doubt on his division of judicial and epideictic discourse into separate genres.[67] In sum, Aristotle's effort to discipline epideictic and separate it from judicial discourse conflicts with his own emphasis on the enthymeme, and may be read as a sort of whistling in the dark which arose from a fear of sophistic amplification practices.

The separation of judicial and epideictic discourse into separate genres arose concomitantly with the belief in the classical world that the province of rhetoric should be limited to case-specific questions, or *hypotheses*, while *theses*, or general questions, should be the domain of philosophy. In the classical world no less than today, legal and rhetorical reasoning have both been associated if not equated with the case-specific reasoning of equity and casuistry. Like Aristotle's definition of the equitable person as "no stickler for his rights in a bad sense but [one who] tends to take less than his share though he has the law on his side,"[68] the legal concept of equity refers to the power granted to a judge to apply broad principles of fairness in order to "mitigate the harshness of strict application of a statute, or to allocate property or responsibility according to the facts of the individual case."[69] For this reason, Chaïm Perelman refers to equity as "the crutch of justice."[70] Principles of equity empower a court to consider the particularity of cases in order to mitigate the unforeseeable effects of general rules. The practice of appealing to equity against the rigid application of laws was commonly taught in the schools of the Roman Republic and rewarded by Roman judges,[71] and George Kennedy has suggested that Roman rhetoric may have supported the "relaxation of rigid interpretation of word in favor of intent" which epitomized Roman equity.[72] Since its development in Roman law, the legal concept of equity has been so closely associated with rhetoric that the two are sometimes synonymous.[73]

The connection between equity and the facts of particular cases closely parallels casuistry, a case-based method of resolving moral conflicts by analogical reasoning from precedents arranged according to their proximity to paradigmatic cases. In *The Abuse of Casuistry*, Albert Jonsen and Stephen Toulmin compare casuists to "Supreme Court justices who eschew *obiter dicta* and refuse to present opinions going beyond the facts of the immediate case."[74] Separately, Toulmin proposes that we understand the historical development of philosophical concepts in the same manner as "common-law historians have characterized the historical development of legal concepts," citing Justice Oliver Wendell Holmes's *The Common Law* and Edward Levi's *An Introduction to Legal Reasoning*.[75] Jonsen and

Toulmin link casuistry to the Aristotelian tradition of practical reasoning, contrasting deductive reasoning with a rhetorical perspective that reasons not from "single chains of unbreakable deductions" but by "accumulating many parallel, complementary considerations."[76] Due to this contrast, casuistry like equity is often simply equated with rhetorical reasoning.[77] In an 1839 essay, Thomas De Quincey defends casuistry's particularism as a practical necessity despite its frequent ill-treatment by rule-bound moralists, and he specifically aligns it with legal advocacy by defining a casuist as

> a kind of lawyer or special pleader in morals, such as those who, in London, are known as Old Bailey practitioners, called in to manage desperate cases—to suggest all available advantages—to raise doubts or distinctions where simple morality saw no room for either—and generally to teach the art, in nautical phrase, of sailing as near the wind as possible, without fear of absolutely foundering.[78]

"The name, the word casuistry, may be evaded," De Quincey writes, "but the thing cannot; nor *is* it evaded in our daily conversations."[79]

As intuitive as the connection of lawyers and cases may be, the casuistical dimension of legal reasoning provides only one side of a common topic of legal discourse regarding the relationship between particular facts and broader truths. In Cicero's early rhetorical treatise *De Inventione*, he ridicules the Stoic philosopher Hermagoras for including within the purview of rhetoricians not only those "special questions" that pertain to specific people, places, or things, but such "general questions" as "Is there any good except honor?" Another favorite example of such general questions in the classical world was "Is marriage good?"[80] According to the young Cicero, it was "the height of folly to assign to an orator as if they were trifles these subjects in which we know that the sublime genius of the philosophers have spent so much labor."[81]

In his more mature writing on rhetoric, however, Cicero famously reversed his view that special questions belonged to rhetoric and general questions to philosophy, as reflected in the following comment of the interlocutor Crassus in Cicero's *De Oratore*, written in the form of a dialogue between accomplished Roman trial lawyers:

> The most ornate speeches are those which take the widest range and which turn aside from the particular matter in dispute to engage in an

explanation of the meaning of the general issue, so as to enable the audience to base their verdict in regard to the particular parties and charges and actions in question on a knowledge of the nature and character of the matter as a whole."[82]

Cicero rejected the entire approach to rhetoric in his earlier treatise *De Inventione* as nothing more than a "long string of precepts…which slipped out of the notebooks of my boyhood," unworthy of his later age and experience "gained from the numerous and grave causes in which I have been engaged."[83] While *De Inventione* elaborated the technical precepts of Roman scholastic rhetoric,[84] after a lifetime of experience as a legal and political orator—including his election to the offices of quaestor, aedile, praetor, and consul—Cicero expressed contempt for such scholastic rhetoric and instead claimed that the ideal orator must pursue a broad education not only in philosophy but in "all the liberal arts."[85]

The broad education that Cicero recommended in his later work would enable the orator to "argue every question on both sides, and bring out on every topic whatever points can be deemed plausible," much as the interlocutors of *De Oratore* themselves agree to argue every question on both sides.[86] In this way, Cicero sought to join rhetoric and philosophy, *hypotheses* and *theses*, in a single approach to rhetoric characterized by a "discrimination of perspectives and the differentiation of frames of reference."[87] In *De Oratore*, the participants in the dialogue virtually lampoon the formulaic approach of *De Inventione* and similar handbooks prevalent in Rome at the time, but for reasons that differ markedly from Aristotle's critique of rhetorical handbooks.[88] Antonius complains that the precept-taught youth were "redolent rather of the training-school and its suppling-oil than of our political hurly-burly and of the Bar,"[89] and he warns that the "requirements of a pitched battle are not those of a sham fight or our own training-ground,"[90] and Crassus remarks that if his audience is content with the rules drawn up by the writers of rhetorical handbooks, "you are making the orator abandon a vast, immeasurable plain and confine himself to quite a narrow circle."[91] Unlike Aristotle's rejection of rhetorical handbooks on legal advocacy for their focus on methods of arousing prejudice, pity, anger, and other emotions—which have "nothing to do with the essential facts" of a case but are merely personal appeals to a judge"[92]—the interlocutors of Cicero's *De Oratore* reject handbooks only for being narrowly formulaic.

Cicero's critique of the formulaic precepts found in such handbooks is closely related to his inclusion of *theses*, or general questions, within the purview of orators and his belief in the unity of rhetoric and philosophy. Early in the prologue to the first book of *De Oratore*, Cicero contrasts his own view that eloquence depends on "the trained skill of highly educated men" to his brother Quintus's view that eloquence must be "separated from the refinements of learning and made to depend on a sort of natural talent and on practice,"[93] views occupied by Crassus and Antonius, respectively, in the dialogue of *De Oratore*.[94] Crassus argues that the ideal orator requires "profound insight into the characters of men, and the whole range of human nature, and those motives whereby our souls are spurred on or turned back," knowledge previously considered to be the exclusive province of philosophers.[95] Accordingly, an orator may be expected to know "of the immortal gods, of dutifulness, harmony, or friendship, of the rights shared by citizens, by men in general, and by nations, of fair-dealing, moderation or greatness of soul, or virtue of any and every kind."[96]

It is obvious whether a speaker in the courts and assemblies has "merely floundered about in this declamatory business," Crassus argues, "or whether, before approaching his task of oratory, he has been trained in all the liberal arts,"[97] and he criticizes orators who "flit around the Courts, to loiter about the Bench and judgment-seats of the praetors" without even knowing the common law, when rights are debated concerning "long user, guardianship, clanship, relationship through males, alluvial accessions, the formation of islands, obligations, sales, party-walls, ancient lights, rain-drop from the eaves, the revocation or establishment of wills."[98] He describes the statesmen of old as men consulted not only on points of law but about "marrying off a daughter, buying a farm, tilling their estates, and in short every sort of liability or business," both religious and secular.[99] The overarching argument of *De Oratore* seeks to emphasize the value for an orator of a broad education compared to the "rigid formulism of contemporary handbooks."[100]

According to Antonius, the division of general and special questions is even "ludicrous," because all specific cases turn on general questions:

> Indeed, even where the question is one of pure fact, such as 'Did Publius Decius take moneys unlawfully?' the evidence for prosecution and defense alike must have reference to general terms and essential qualities: to convict of extravagance you must refer to profusion; of covetousness, to greed;

of sedition, to turbulent and wicked members of the community; to prove that the defendant's accusers are many, you must deal with witnesses in the mass: and conversely all the evidence for the defense will have to turn away from the particular occasion and individual to general conceptions of circumstances and kinds.[101]

In his *Orator*, Cicero clarifies the relationship between *theses* and *hypotheses* by noting that "no one can discuss great and varied subjects in a copious and elegant style without philosophy,"[102] and he clarifies the relationship between *theses* and arguing both sides of a case:

> To be able to use these the orator—not an ordinary one, but this outstanding orator—always removes the discussion, if he can, from particular times and persons, because the discussion can be made broader about a class than about an individual, so that whatever is proved about the class must necessarily be true of the individual. Such an inquiry, removed from particular times and persons to a discussion of a general topic, is called [*thesis*]. Aristotle trained young men in this, not for the philosophical manner of subtle discussion, but for the fluent style of the rhetorician, so that they might be able to uphold either side of the question [*in utramque partem*] in copious and elegant language.[103]

As Thomas Sloane notes, Cicero's philosophical point always rested in part on the premise that "it's folly to argue an *hypothesis*,…without giving some thought to the *thesis*, to argue a specific matter without considering the general belief or value or even fact which encompasses it."[104]

This premise was also evident in Cicero's practice of recording and circulating his oral arguments in writing for posterity. According to Richard Enos, Cicero used the publication of his oral arguments, which he edited before and after their delivery, as an opportunity to "make a larger social statement, one that transcended the particulars of the case."[105] Cicero's legal debates would thereby "elevate the argument to higher levels than the fine points of jurisprudence," and "tend to transcend petty debates and stress more captivating social issues."[106] Jeffrey Walker explains that the *thesis* introduced "strategies of argument (and additional topics) by which one might, for example, argue about what 'tyranny' is, what the definition includes and implies, whether it is bad, or whether it should be opposed," and thereby amplifies and intensifies general premises grounded in the "deep communal beliefs and emotions of the audience."[107] The ideal orator imagined in Cicero's *De Oratore*, Walker writes, "looks remarkably like a sophist...whose major sources of emotive eloquence and power derive from epideictic registers: from poetry, from philosophic dialogue and dialectic, from history, from panegyric."[108] Theodor Burgess also notes that the classical rhetorical practice of arguing both sides of a case "has naturally a strong epideictic tendency."[109] Both Aristotle's exclusion of epideictic from judicial discourse and the classical belief that *theses*, or general questions—often the subject of maxims—were not the province of legal orators reveal a long-standing effort to discipline legal discourse in the classical rhetorical tradition which persists in contemporary attitudes to the relationship between law and rhetoric.

For purposes of considering the epideictic features of judicial opinions in the following chapters, the remainder of this chapter develops a register theory of epideictic through an analysis of discourse traditionally classified as epideictic and classical and contemporary commentary on epideictic, illustrated with examples from legal discourse. I argue that the situations of epideictic are prototypically those in which social relationships begin, end, or in which an exigency arises to threaten social unity, and among its more pervasive features are praise, amplification devices, eloquence, the gnomic aspect, affirmative modality, and nonverbal elements of the occasions on which epideictic discourse is delivered, such as the date, time, location, venue, and the speaker and their attire, all of which respond to potential division by subsuming the individual agency of speaker and audience within a collective perspective so unifying that it often leads to descriptions of the experience in mystical terms. Drawing on speech act theory and Chaïm Perelman and Lucie Olbrechts-Tyteca's concept of the ways in which arguments interact by convergence to augment each other, I conclude that epideictic preserves and restores social unity through dense performative convergences of the registral features identified to magnify the value of subjects beyond the perceptual capacities of participants.[110]

Epideictic Situations

A register of communication is a functional variety of symbolic activity organized as a model of communicative conduct to suit a particular situation and purpose, such as the formal register often used in legal proceedings, which is typically impersonal, tends to use more complete sentences and complex lexical, morphological, and syntactic features absent in everyday conversation, refers to people and places by their official titles and full or last names, and is largely devoid of slang, sarcasm, and humor.[111] Although registral analyses often focus on the lexical, morphological, or syntactic features of speech and are often predominantly linguistic, communication registers also include nonlinguistic signs such as gestures and situational features such as the relationship between the participants, the channels and modes of communications, the circumstances in which they take place, and their purpose.[112]

The social practices encompassed by registers are more complex than can be explained by lexical, morphological, or syntactic features alone.[113] Registers are also continuously undergoing development—dynamic and portable routines or repertoires that presuppose situations, identities, and values.[114] Registers emerge through the interrelationship of situational features, formal features, and functions, the situational features being the most basic. Rather than merely identifying unique formal features of language, a register analysis considers the distribution of particularly pervasive communicative features of specific situations,[115] and registers are identified by different levels of generality or specificity. As Douglas Biber and Susan Conrad note, "there is no one correct level on which to identify a register," but registral features can be identified for general registers such as public speaking or academic prose or for specific registers such as Presbyterian sermons, botany textbooks, or sociological research articles. The course of a registral inquiry may also begin by identifying a general register before proceeding to more specific registers over time.[116] This chapter identifies general registral features of epideictic, recognizing that additional features or subregisters may be identified with further study.

The situations in which epideictic discourse arises represent the beginnings or ends of social relationships, particularly occasions when such beginnings or endings are memorialized or moments when they are called into question. Chaïm Perelman and Lucie Olbrechts-Tyteca write that epideictic seeks to "increase the intensity of adherence" to specific values when they conflict with other values.[117] Similarly, Celeste Condit writes that epideictic helps to define a community in terms of its core values and beliefs "when some event, person, group, or object is confusing or troubling,"[118] and Gray Matthews notes that if epideictic has traditionally been viewed as a form of inspirational discourse it is important to examine what creates the need for inspiration.[119] As Lloyd Bitzer conceives rhetorical situations, discourse responds to exigencies created by people, events, objects, and relations "which can be completely or partially removed if discourse, introduced into the situation, can so constrain human decision or action as to bring about the significant modification" of the exigency.[120] An exigency, according to Bitzer, is an "imperfection marked by urgency," a "defect, an obstacle, something waiting to be done, a thing which is other than it should be," and exigencies are rhetorical when they can be modified or assisted by discourse.[121]

Based on Bitzer's premise that rhetorical situations arise from exigencies provoking discursive responses and Condit's claim that epideictic fosters community in response to confusing or troubling events, James Jasinski proposes that epideictic addresses "communal exigencies" that threaten social unity, particularly problems that cannot be resolved by policy changes. Even a holiday or wedding toast, the profession of thanks at a Thanksgiving dinner, or a child thanking a parent for support in difficult times, Jasinski writes, are "variations on traditional epideictic themes that help to maintain a community," and this function is equally served by many leaders in public and private life. "A corporation, a university community, a congregation, or a nation," Jasinski writes, "are sustained or held together by this...discursive practice."[122] In speeches that mark social or institutional change, for example, such as those of weddings, commencements, inaugurals, or coronations, Condit concludes that an audience "seeks an understanding of the value of what has been completed and a hint at how they might judge what is to come."[123] The same may be said of speeches that mark the end of relationships, such as eulogies or consolation speeches, farewell speeches, or the sendoff hymns to the gods on their departure listed among epideictic speeches by the third-century CE Greek rhetorician Menander of Laodicea.[124]

Like many other epideictic occasions, legal decisions inaugurate changes that threaten social unity, often with broad social consequences. Gerald Wetlaufer writes that in judicial opinions on "politically sensitive" topics such as racial discrimination, the scope of the First Amendment, the American flag, the death penalty, and rights regarding privacy, abortion, and sexuality, judges are at times "attentive to a range of persuasive possibilities" broader than the traditionally antirhetorical features of judicial opinions, abandoning syllogisms and writing with "a passion that sounds more like the rhetoric of politics."¹²⁵ He dismisses such rhetoric as that of politics rather than law, merely an additional means by which majority opinions seek "popular assent to a potentially unpopular decision" and by which dissents seek popular support for legal change.¹²⁶ Courts make unpopular decisions on a much wider array of topics than Wetlaufer identifies, however, and opinions such as Justice Robert Jackson's opinion in *West Virginia State Board of Education v. Barnette* (1943) address decisions that are largely popular.¹²⁷

What distinguishes opinion writing in which judges abandon their typical syllogistic mode of writing to attend to a broader range of persuasive possibilities and write more passionately on topics such as the American flag, racial discrimination, and privacy is that decisions in such cases often inaugurate social or institutional change in much the same way as arrivals, commencements, coronations, and other situations inaugurate change, calling for similar inaugural discourse. It is not unpopularity, but change, that prompts such writing. In such situations, judicial opinion writing often responds not only to those who disapprove of the decisions but also to those who approve of them, addressing the inauguration of change itself.

Praise

The feature most closely associated with epideictic from its earliest emergence as a rhetorical genre is praise, particularly lexical content overtly praising a subject. In Laurent Pernot's *Epideictic Rhetoric: Questioning the Stakes of Ancient Praise*, he largely approaches epideictic as a discourse of praise,¹²⁸ and J. Richard Chase criticizes modern commentary that classifies discourse as epideictic without the presence of overt praise or blame. According to Chase, to indiscriminately describe either performative discourse or all discourse that is not deliberative or judicial as epideictic without praise or blame lacks any foundation in the rhetorical tradition.¹²⁹ In Aristotle's *Rhetoric*, he identifies the function of praising or critiquing a subject as the distinguishing feature of epideictic, subordinating all other considerations to that of establishing a subject's nobility.¹³⁰ He describes the varieties of nobility as the common topics of epideictic along with methods of "heightening the effect" of praise by, for example, describing a subject as superlative, unique, or prior. Such heightening methods are most appropriate to epideictic, he concludes, because in epideictic facts are not contested but only invested with nobility.[131]

Praise and blame are also identified as the distinguishing features of epideictic by Anaximenes in his fourth-century BCE rhetorical handbook *Rhetorica ad Alexandrum*,[132] by both the author of the first-century CE rhetorical handbook *Rhetorica ad Herennium* and Cicero in his first-century CE *De Inventione*,[133] and by Menander of Laodicea in his third-century CE analysis of epideictic speeches.[134] The prose composition exercises known as *progymnasmata*, which were mentioned as early as the *Rhetorica ad Alexandrum* and flourished between the first and eleventh centuries CE, included an exercise in encomium which taught students to write about good qualities belonging to the gods, people, animals, plants, cities, mountains, and rivers, as well as about the good qualities of concepts such as justice. It also included an exercise in invective which taught students to write about their bad qualities.[135]

The most common lexical or morphological dimensions of praise are terms of comparative superiority such as *more, better, higher, preferable,* or *transcendent,* or related terms such as *essential, critical,* or *fundamental,* indicating a subject's centrality in contrast to ancillary subjects. The same effect can be created with intensifiers such as *very* or *exceedingly*. In *Lawrence v. Texas* (2003), for example, Justice Anthony Kennedy wrote that "when sexuality finds overt expression in intimate conduct with another person, the conduct can be but one element in a personal bond that is more enduring."[136] Praise is indicated by describing subjects with superlatives such as *best, first, last, ultimate,* or *paramount,* or with adjectives and adverbs modified by *most,* as in Justice Felix Frankfurter's comment in *Minersville School District v. Gobitis* (1940) that "the ultimate foundation of a free society is the binding tie of cohesive sentiment."[137] Subjects can be praised as unique with terms such as *unique, original, distinctive, singular, alone,* or *only,* or as anterior with terms such as *prior, old, time-honored, ancient,* or as having stood the "test of time." Among the more conspicuous commonplaces of ancient Greek funeral orations was the praise of Athenians as autochthonous,[138] and in encomium, Laurent Pernot notes, "the prestige of seniority is mentioned often."[139] In *Obergefell v. Hodges* (2015), Kennedy described marriage as "one of civilization's oldest institutions."[140] Subjects can also be praised using terms such as *total, complete, perfect, consummate, exhaustive,* or *thorough*.

These and similar lexical and morphological items are pervasive features of epideictic,[141] but the same function is served by terms that merely attribute to a subject qualities an audience considers positive. Among praiseworthy qualities, for example, the author of the fourth-century BCE *Rhetorica ad Alexandrum* includes the just, lawful, expedient, noble, pleasant, and ease of accomplishment, citing the "unwritten custom" of humanity for basic principles of justice such as honoring one's parents, benefiting friends, and repaying favors, because "these and similar rules are not enjoined on men by written laws but are observed by unwritten custom and universal practice." The author also lists strength, beauty, health, wealth, peace, and friendship among desirable qualities.[142] Similarly, Aristotle lists justice, courage, temperance, magnificence, magnanimity, liberality, gentleness, prudence, and wisdom among the common topics of epideictic.[143] John O'Malley notes of the sermons delivered in the papal court of the Renaissance that if a sermon announced that it was dealing with "God's *facta, opera, gesta, magnalia,* or *beneficia,*" it was "inevitably leading into epideictic."[144] Not only can generally approbative or laudatory terms such as *great, excellent,* or *wonderful* be used to magnify value, but metaphorical uses of terms such as *saint* can as well.

Praise can also be conferred metonymically by praising the positive qualities of a subject's origins, education, or associations, or by praising a subject for qualities near to the ones they actually possess.[145] In Menander's third-century CE analysis of epideictic speeches, for example, he treats as separate speech topics how to praise cities, how to praise a city for its origin, and how to praise cities for their activities.[146] Aristotle refers to topics of indirect praise such as good birth or education as "accessories," subordinate to the subject's own accomplishments, but notes that when we praise or blame something we must assume qualities closely aligned with those actually possessed to be identical with them, so that "the cautious man is cold-blooded and treacherous, and...the stupid man is an honest fellow or the thick-skinned man a good-tempered one." In addition, Aristotle writes, we can always idealize a subject by "drawing on the virtues akin to his actual qualities," so that "we may say that the passionate and excited man is 'outspoken'; or that the arrogant man is 'superb' or 'impressive,'" and extreme cases will possess corresponding qualities so that "rashness will be called courage, and extravagance generosity."[147]

Despite the pervasiveness of praise in epideictic, Celeste Condit notes that using its presence as a criterion for classifying discourse as epideictic is unsatisfying because all discourse contains praise, and given the variety of forms that praise takes, its pervasiveness in a particular type of speech is not a useful measure.[148] Perhaps most importantly, because praise is as much a function as a form of discourse, to insist on it being lexically apparent is artificial. Laurent Pernot notes that praise was only one possible content of ancient Greek *epideixis*,[149] and despite J. Richard Chase's insistence on the presence of praise or blame to classify epideictic he recognizes that before Aristotle's *Rhetoric* praise and blame were "called just that" rather than distinguishing a genre.[150] Lawrence Rosenfield argues that instead of praise and blame, epideictic's fundamental function is acknowledgment and disparagement, "the recognition of what *is* (goodness, grace, intrinsic excellence) or the refusal to so recognize in a moment of social inspiration."[151] He contrasts acknowledgment with extravagant praise, but nonetheless describes the experience of epideictic as a celebratory one of witnessing reality with "appreciative" or "loving" attention.[152] When value inheres in a subject, he writes, "it 'cries out' for recognition and remains recognition-demanding regardless of any praise heaped on it."[153]

It is also important that Aristotle identifies epideictic with ceremonial "display" and an orator's "skill" in praising or blaming a subject, which has led many commentators to associate epideictic with theatrical display.[154] Chase concludes that after Aristotle the display element of epideictic held a secondary function in rhetorical treatises and had largely disappeared as a distinguishing feature of epideictic by the time of the Roman Empire.[155] In Quintilian's first-century CE *Institutio Oratoria*, however, Quintilian questions the classification of epideictic by gesturing to a variety of speech acts that are not neatly encompassed by Aristotle's separation of genres:

> Indeed if we place the task of praise and denunciation in the third division, on what kind of oratory are we to consider ourselves to be employed when we complain, console, pacify, excite, terrify, encourage, instruct, explain obscurities, narrate, plead for mercy, thank, congratulate, reproach, abuse, describe, command, retract, express our desires and opinions, to mention no other of the many possibilities?[156]

John Austin's speech act theory developed the idea that language contains a performative as well as representational function, because the sole purpose of linguistic utterances is not only "to 'describe' some state of affairs, or to 'state some fact'…either truly or falsely," but to perform actions such as questioning, commanding, wishing, or conceding.[157] Some have found Austin's term *performative* to be essentially synonymous with rhetoric because it captures a common focus of rhetoric on language as gesture.[158]

In Walter Beale's discussion of epideictic, he synthesizes praise and display along with modern perspectives on epideictic by drawing on Austin's speech act theory to define epideictic as a "unified act of rhetorical discourse which does not merely say, argue, or allege something about the world of social action," but "constitutes…a significant social action in itself."[159] While recognizing that language's performative and representational functions exist simultaneously, Beale claims that in situations conventionally associated with epideictic the audience's attention is "typically drawn" to the performative function of speech, "the communal or historical significance of the speech itself."[160] To console or thank is also, in a sense, to confer praise. Epideictic features an honorific performance that magnifies the value of its subject, and the presence of lexical and morphological praise is a pervasive but neither necessary nor sufficient feature of the register, only sharing an honorific function in common with other features.

Amplification Devices

As previously noted, Aristotle finds amplification, or "heightening the effect" of praise to invest a subject with dignity or nobility, to be the topic of argumentation most appropriate to epideictic.[161] It is possible to magnify the value of a subject indirectly by using patterns of arrangement known as figures of thought such as repetition or antithesis, which develop or amplify a theme, and through syntactic amplification devices known as figures of speech. These devices are a pervasive feature of epideictic, often converging with other features to serve a common function. In Longinus's first-century CE rhetorical treatise *On the Sublime*, although Longinus subordinates amplification to the sublime, he defines amplification as "the accumulation of all the small points and incidental topics bearing on the subject matter; it adds substance and strength to the argument by dwelling on it."[162] He explains the effect as that which follows "when the matters under discussion or the points of an argument allow of many pauses and many fresh starts from section to section, and the grand phrases come rolling out one after another with increasing effect,"[163] prefiguring

Kenneth Burke's description of amplification as a poetic or lyrical process of development by "extension, expatiation, the saying of something in various ways until it increases in persuasiveness by the sheer accumulation."[164]

Epideictic has often been associated with a prevalence of figures, as it is described by Theodor Burgess as "expansive and exuberant in style, full of antithesis, rhetorical question, asyndeton, extravagant statement."[165] In the classical rhetorical tradition, epideictic was sometimes called "Asianic," a term derived from ethnic stereotypes of Asian luxury, effeminacy, and extravagance. The term was used to characterize any highly figured or artificial style of prose featuring balanced clauses, conspicuous rhythms, repetition, poetic diction, and figurality as a vulgar, bombastic, theatrical, and luxurious form of rhetoric.[166] Longinus states that although amplification can take many forms, it is usually accomplished "either by the rhetorical development of a commonplace, or by exaggeration, whether facts or arguments are to be stressed, or by the building up of actions or emotions."[167]

As Chaïm Perelman and Lucie Olbrechts-Tyteca note, the simplest methods of amplification depend on repetition, such as the figure of anaphora, in which the same word or phrase is repeated at the beginning of successive clauses or sentences.[168] The opposite figure, epistrophe, which repeats the same word or phrase at the end of successive passages, has similar effects, along with mesodiplosis, which repeats the same word or phrase in the middle of successive passages, and mesarchia, which repeats the same word or words at the beginning and in the middle of successive passages. Other common figures of repetition include anadiplosis, which repeats the end of a clause or sentence at the beginning of the next; chiasmus or antimetabole, in which items are repeated in transposed order in successive passages; polysyndeton, in which unnecessary conjunctions are added, or hyperbole. From the classical tradition through the Renaissance, rhetorical treatises were at times obsessed with cataloging such figures, culminating in Erasmus's sixteenth-century *Copia: Foundations of the Abundant Style*.[169] A list of figures referenced in this book can be found in the Glossary of Figures.

The use of figures is not limited to style, but they can also be found in patterns of arrangement on the discourse level in what are often called figures of thought to distinguish them from figures of speech. Perelman and Olbrechts-Tyteca note, for example, that exergasia, by which a single idea is repeated in different forms, "conveys presence by using a form that suggests progressive correction," and is similar to correctio or epexegesis, a form in which one expression is explained or interpreted by another "not so much for purposes of clarification as to increase the feeling of presence."[170] Stylistically, President Lincoln exemplified exergasia or epexegesis in the Gettysburg Address when he stated that "we cannot dedicate, we cannot consecrate, we cannot hallow this ground," combining anaphora with a substantive repetition of meaning in alternative forms.[171]

In the following passages of Chief Justice Warren Burger's majority opinion in *United States v. Nixon* (1974), Burger combines praise and exergasia on the discourse level:

> The need to develop all relevant facts in the adversary system is both fundamental and comprehensive. The ends of criminal justice would be defeated if judgments were to be founded on a partial or speculative presentation of the facts. The very integrity of the judicial system and public confidence in the system depend on full disclosure of all the facts, within the framework of the rules of evidence. To ensure that justice is done, it is imperative to the function of courts that compulsory process be available for the production of evidence needed either by the prosecution or by the defense.[172]

Similar patterns of arrangement include accumulation, which Longinus associates most closely with amplification, and enumeration, which Perelman and Olbrechts-Tyteca note is often nearly indistinguishable from accumulation.[173] As John Genung notes, because figures can be used both stylistically and on the discourse level, "invention and style are equally concerned" in amplification.[174]

According to Perelman and Olbrechts-Tyteca, when a figure of thought or speech changes an audience's perspective it is considered argumentative and its use normal, but if it fails to secure the "adherence" of the audience it will be considered mere ornamentation. "It can excite admiration, but this will be on the aesthetic plane, or in recognition of the speaker's originality."[175] This commentary addresses a centuries-old dismissal of figurality as a merely ornamental feature of language divorced from content which Perelman and Olbrechts-Tyteca attribute to the "tendency of rhetoricians to restrict their study to problems of style and expression."[176] As previously discussed, this tendency emerged with the rise of critical approaches to rhetoric in the early modern era developed by reformers such as Peter

Ramus and René Descartes who sought to separate style from invention, culminating in language policies such as those of the Royal Society of London which sought to eliminate all "amplification, digressions and swellings of style" in favor of a plain style of writing.[177] According to Perelman and Olbrechts-Tyteca, this modern bias against figures is revealed in the fact that when a figure is "detached from its context and pigeonholed," or when form is attended to more than substance, "it is almost necessarily perceived under its least argumentative aspect." In less conspicuous uses, however, this bias can be avoided: "party dresses are in order in certain surroundings, and do not attract attention."[178]

This observation neglects the fact that in epideictic discourse figures are often displayed conspicuously as part of an honorific performance but remain inseparable from the content or function of the discursive act. In Jeanne Fahnestock's study of rhetorical figures in science, she notes that the "tight focus on metaphor in science studies, like the fixation on metaphor and allied tropes in textual studies," has removed attention from figures of speech despite the fact that the figures come from the same tradition that produced metaphor.[179] Although modern thought has often condemned tropes and figures as misleading because they appeal to the senses rather than reason and metaphor transfers and transforms meaning in a manner that frustrates logical precision,[180] Fahnestock notes that contemporary commentary on metaphor typically indicates confidence that it provides "a window on a fundamental, generative cognitive process."[181] Like Perelman and Olbrechts-Tyteca's conclusion that figures are not merely stylistic but argumentative, Fahnestock concludes that figures of thought "belong in the pragmatic or situational and functional dimension of language."[182] The functional significance of figures reveals them as "vehicles of impressiveness or vividness or force," conveying both "the speaker's point and the degree of intensity or conviction behind it," rather than embellishments or as the mere expression of emotion.[183]

Figures are not merely expressive, Fahnestock notes, but are found as often in philosophy and science as in poetry.[184] In contrast to mere ornamentation or artistic expression, she writes, figures are more or less "constitutive or iconic,"[185] forming a "verbal summary that epitomizes a line of reasoning," a "condensed or even diagram-like rendering of the relationship among a set of terms, a relationship that constitutes the argument and that could be expressed at greater length."[186] Although figures may be either expanded or condensed, a figured or plain style cannot be translated into verbosity or concision but reflects only a method of amplifying or muting material.[187] In contrast to Perelman and Olbrechts-Tyteca, Fahnestock's recognition of the fact that figures combine the cognitive and affective dimensions of language, through which the intensity or conviction of a claim is communicated, explains how even the most conspicuous figures function in argumentation. This function of figures is particularly important in epideictic, in which the proclamation of belief, desire, or ethical commitment forms a central purpose. In epideictic, even the most conspicuous forms fuse with content in honorific performances.

Eloquence

The third-century CE rhetorician Pseudo-Dionysius of Halicarnassus writes that in panegyric speeches it is proper for a speaker to grace the festival with oratory much like "athletes grace the festival with their physical strength, as do those who are servants of the Muses and Apollo with their musical performances," composing an artful speech "so that it may avoid being merely ordinary."[188] He advises against using a uniform style instead of a "varied and mixed" style, "treating some subjects with simplicity, some with Isocratean antithesis and balancing of clauses, and others in an elevated style."[189] As Elaine Fantham notes, eloquence is "something more than mere style, and should not be limited to the embellishments of figures of speech or thought; instead, it may entail sophisticated thinking in simple language."[190] Similarly, classical authors approved a variety of styles appropriate to epideictic, from an elegant style characterized by parallelism, a politically charged and contentious style, a majestic style, a simple or gentle style, and a display of virtuosity.[191] The second-century CE rhetorician Hermogenes, for example, writes that "Solemnity can be used alone" to constitute panegyric, or "Simplicity or Sweetness or Purity or a carefully wrought style" can be used, among other styles.[192] Eloquence is also a pervasive feature of epideictic, the aesthetic quality of which serves an honorific function independent of figurality, although they are often combined.[193]

Perelman and Olbrechts-Tyteca attribute the fact that epideictic has often been more closely connected with literature and poetics than argument—or with the "libretto of a cantata"[194]—to the fact that from the time of Aristotle rhetoricians "confused the concept of the beautiful, as the object of the speech (which was, besides, equivalent to the concept of 'good') with the aesthetic value of the speech itself." Accordingly, Perelman and Olbrechts-Tyteca emphasize epideictic's capacity to intensify adherence to the premises on which arguments rest in contrast to the beauty of speech itself, which they relegate to a peripheral role in epideictic.[195] Similar to their conclusion that figures are perceived as mere embellishment when divorced from content, they note that a speaker with a reputation for eloquence may be vulnerable to the charge of "pretence, artifice, a contrived means to an end."[196] As a result, they appear to accept the idea that rhetoric is a deftly conceived artifice.

In contrast to the mistrust of eloquence that Perelman and Olbrechts-Tyteca apply to epideictic, Elaine Fantham writes that eloquence is "undoubtedly most necessary and least suspect" in epideictic.[197] The mistrust of eloquence that Perelman and Olbrechts-Tyteca betray in their approach to epideictic neglects its situational efficacy as well as how even conspicuously beautified speech converges with other features of epideictic to performatively honor a subject and is inconsistent with modern commentary that finds eloquence to exclude artificiality by definition. Elsewhere Perelman and Olbrechts-Tyteca recognize that in epideictic more than in any other type of oratory a speaker must not only possess a unique stature in the community but "be skillful in…presentation" if they are not "to appear ridiculous."[198] In epideictic situations, eloquence is not perceived as contrived but is expected, much like "athletes grace the festival with their physical strength," to return to Pseudo-Dionysius of Halicarnassus's analogy.[199]

In modern commentary, eloquence has been defined not only as beautiful but also as copious and fitting thought, providing new perspectives that enlarge an audience's understanding both on the world and itself. In other words, for speech to be eloquent its form must be suited to its function and situation which in epideictic includes an honorific performance. In Celeste Condit's approach to epideictic, she includes eloquence among its functions, defining it as a "combination of truth, beauty and power in human speech" which allows us to "stretch our capacities and identities in the human quest for improvement." Through eloquence, Condit claims, epideictic speakers are able to display "broad humane capacities" and audiences are allowed to "stretch their daily experiences into meanings more grand, sweet, noble, or delightful."[200] Ralph Waldo Emerson describes the eloquent speaker as "fluent, various and effective," able to "command the whole scale of the language, from the most elegant to the most low and vile," in order to "translate a truth into language perfectly intelligible" to an audience,[201] and Dale Sullivan concludes that in epideictic an audience finds that "the speaker is saying exactly what needs to be said."[202]

Eloquent speakers do not merely rehearse conventional values in order to flatter an audience, but place matters in a perspective that lends "new solidity and worth" to them, introducing a "new principle of order."[203] Similar to Emerson and Sullivan, Thomas Farrell describes eloquence as "a recognizable honorific quality" in language use with a power that derives from "its ability to subsume particulars within themes and frames of larger generality,"[204] much like Cicero approved using *theses*, or general topics such as dutifulness, harmony, friendship, fairness, or moderation "not for the philosophical manner of subtle discussion, but for the fluent style of the rhetorician, so that they might be able to uphold either side of the question in copious and elegant language."[205] In this respect, contemporary commentary follows classical commentary which defined eloquence as the combination of wisdom with beautiful and fitting expression, summarized in Giambattista Vico's definition of eloquence as "wisdom, ornately and copiously delivered in words appropriate to the common opinion of mankind."[206] In ordinary language use, epideictic is often described simply as eloquent—whether it occurs in judicial or other types of discourse—and in both its ordinary and technical sense eloquence is a pervasive feature of epideictic.

The Gnomic Aspect

While prior commentary on epideictic has noted that it features praise, figurality, and eloquence, though not their functional convergence, less attention has been paid to the grammatical aspect of epideictic which tends to be imperfective and often specifically gnomic. As previously mentioned, the gnomic aspect expresses general truths or aphorisms in the unbounded present tense, or "eternal" present, about subjects lacking clear perceptual boundaries. It is the aspect exemplified in the maxims that Aristotle observes to serve as premises or conclusions of enthymemes, such as *no love is true save that which loves forever* and *mortal creatures ought to cherish mortal, not immortal thoughts*,[207] and legal maxims such as *no one is bound to do what is impossible, when opinions are equal a defendant is acquitted*, or, with regard to property rights, *water runs and ought to run*.[208] Legal maxims remain in use in legal canons of interpretation, both in statutory form and in common law jurisprudence,[209] and like figures, they have at times been criticized as "ostentatious," holding little strictly legal significance. They are sometimes held to serve only as "a way to show off in court or in writing," but they also function as condensed forms of argumentation.

Despite their condensed form, the term *maxim* derives from the Latin *maxima propositio*, or "largest proposition," signifying a wider scope, deeper normative basis, or greater weight or importance than ordinary legal rules.[210] Maxims serve to amplify both legal principles and general principles of belief, desire, or ethical commitment. In *Sweezy v. New Hampshire* (1957), for example, the majority opinion stated that "scholarship cannot flourish in an atmosphere of suspicion and distrust,"[211] and in Justice Robert Jackson's concurring opinion in *Douglas v. Jeanette* (1943) he used the gnomic aspect to promote the importance of judicial clarity: "Forthright observance of rights presupposes their forthright definition."[212] In *Cabell v. Markham* (1945), Judge Learned Hand wrote that "it is one of the surest indexes of a mature and developed jurisprudence not to make a fortress out of the dictionary."[213] and Justices Stephen Breyer, Sonia Sotomayor, and Elena Kagan wrote in their dissenting opinion in *Dobbs v. Jackson Women's Health Organization* (2022) that "human bodies care little for hopes and plans."[214] The gnomic aspect is a pervasive feature of epideictic which often converges with praise, figurality, and eloquence to produce a characteristic register.

Without specifically discussing aspect, some commentators have noted that epideictic speakers tend to express general or universal truths, sometimes in the form of maxims. For example, Richard Weaver writes that epideictic is characterized by "spaciousness," a quality of speech in which concepts have literary and historical "resonances" but are "general, and as it were, mobile," lacking concrete referents yet "with full expectation that they will be received as legal tender" by an audience. Weaver compares this quality to the lawyer's right to assume that precedents are valid, that what has been "sanctified with usage has a presumption in its favor," and he concludes that spaciousness has "a certain judicial flavor about it."[215] He offers President Lincoln's Gettysburg Address as an example, in which Lincoln "spoke in terms so 'generic' that it is almost impossible to show that the speech is not a eulogy of the men in gray as well as the men in blue, inasmuch as both made up 'those who struggled here.' "[216]

Citing Weaver, Dale Sullivan notes that epideictic creates an image of orthodoxy through an orator's "use of generalities that reflect the culture's definition of reality, wisdom, and prudence." While epideictic speakers may allude to history, Sullivan writes, they are less likely to "ground their assertions with meticulous detail" than to make broad claims without citing proof. "One of the major ways to create the sense of prudence or wisdom required of epideictic," he claims, is to cite maxims.[217] Similarly, Celeste Condit writes that in the Boston Massacre orations delivered from 1771 to 1783, speakers expended more effort "belaboring" the maxim "standing armies bring evil" than discussing self-government or the evils of taxation without representation, and the orations featured no "direct descriptions" of the massacre.[218] Rather than dwelling on concrete details of the events, the orators "depicted events on a larger canvas," emphasizing what had happened in the days and months before the massacre and the emotions it engendered. Condit argues that the massacre had to be contextualized in a manner that invested the event with motive and meaning, subsumed within the community's history and values, which could not be accomplished by recounting the events in a "newspaper-like reportorial" manner.[219]

According to Perelman and Olbrechts-Tyteca, epideictic speakers not only draw on the general principles found in maxims, but *convert* what has standing through social unanimity into "universal values, if not eternal truths." Epideictic, they write, is "most prone to appeal to a universal order, to a nature, or a god that would vouch for the unquestioned, and supposedly unquestionable, values."[220] Similarly, Eugene Garver argues that epideictic does not merely rehearse or recirculate established values but converts knowledge from "something that each person knows to something that everybody knows and which therefore can figure in deliberations"—including through "ritual trials"—and that the function of epideictic is "making common knowledge truly common," giving the community possession of the truth. As Garver describes this conversion of individual knowledge to collective knowledge, "I can know that the government uses torture, but my knowledge is transformed when I find that you know it as well."[221] According to Ernesto Grassi, the primacy of metaphorical thought and language in the humanistic tradition is not derived from rational logic but from the sense of the community, or *sensus communis*, through which we "continually transform reality in the human context by means of 'fantastic' concepts."²²² The panegyric or eulogy, he writes, presents "a measure or standard according to which the past and future can be evaluated," or "what is exemplary and to which every judgment about men, actions, or situations must be referred."²²³ The gnomic aspect is essential to this relationship between epideictic and common sense.

Epideictic is often associated with the present tense in a manner that is highly suggestive of the gnomic aspect. Aristotle writes that the epideictic speaker is concerned with the present, "since all men praise or blame in view of the state of things existing at the time."²²⁴ It is not the simple present that is most characteristic of epideictic, however, nor is it accurate to say it appeals to a universal order. Instead, it favors the unbounded present, often referred to as universal or "eternal" only because its boundaries are unmarked. As Cynthia Sheard notes, the themes and exigencies of epideictic "might *appear* to its audience as timeless and transcendent or 'universal.' "²²⁵ This is the present that Perelman and Olbrechts-Tyteca describe as expressing "the universal, the law, the normal," the tense of "maxims and proverbial sayings, of that which is always timely and never out of date." In a phrase such as *women like to talk*, Perelman and Olbrechts-Tyteca write, "one insists on the normal to the extent of making it a general characteristic." They note that the present also conveys most readily the feeling of presence, which they align with amplification.²²⁶ Not only do maxims condense common wisdom, but they reflect one of the most effective means of promoting and developing it, emphasizing the role played by accepted values and how they are circulated and transferred to new situations.²²⁷

The association of epideictic with the present is better understood as a matter of aspect than tense. Epideictic's present does not so much orient its subject to past or future events as depict a continuous or eternal state within a boundless or transcendent framework of meaning. The property of language known as aspect is generally divided into the perfective and imperfective aspects according to whether events are depicted as completed. The perfective aspect depicts events as completed and the imperfective aspect depicts events without reference to their completion. Aspect conveys different perspectives on the temporal constituency of a situation, or how an event is distributed through time and distinguished from other events.²²⁸

The perfective aspect depicts an event from an external perspective, as a complete, unanalyzable whole by referencing its beginning, middle, or end, without distinguishing the internal phases or elements of the event (for example, *she signed the contract*). As Paul Hopper notes, in the perfective aspect "the idea of speaker distance from the narrated events is paramount."[229] The imperfective aspect, by contrast, depicts a situation from an internal perspective, as a continuous state or an incomplete, unfolding, or endless process, viewing the situation from within. It includes depictions of situations as habitual (for example, *she has always signed contracts*), continuous (*she signs contracts*), or progressive (*she is signing the contract*).[230]

While aspect is conveyed through morphological and syntactic features of language, it is also semantic and contingent on interpretive practices.[231] A common test for perfectivity is whether a predicate may be used with adverbials of completion such as *in a minute*, *in an hour*, or *in a day*. Adverbials of completion are compatible with perfective forms (for example, *the house collapsed in less than a minute*), but not with imperfective forms (*he wrote in a week* is not grammatically coherent, in contrast to *he wrote for a week* or *he wrote the report in a week*). Because perfectivity depends not only on the verb but on its object, when the object of a verb is unbounded, such as a mass noun, an imperfective interpretation is indicated. The action in the sentence *they drank water*, for example, is imperfective even though the verb *drank* is in the perfect tense. The action cannot be viewed as completed because its object is unbounded.[232]

The dependence of perfectivity on bounded objects can be observed in the language of judicial opinions such as the frequently quoted passage from Justice Louis Brandeis's dissenting opinion in *Olmstead v. United States* (1928): "The greatest dangers to liberty lurk in insidious encroachment by men of zeal, well-meaning but without understanding."[233] Not only does Brandeis use the present tense of the intransitive verb *lurk* in this sentence, but even if the verb *encroach* were translated into an active verb, to encroach on liberty is imperfective because liberty is unbounded in contrast to *a* liberty. Although aspect is often confused with tense, a proposition can be presented in the perfect tense without being perfective in aspect. Tense refers to the function of language that relates events to the present time,[234] the simple present merely denoting the position of current events relative to past and future ones. The perfective aspect can occur in past or future tenses (for example, *they will open the store tomorrow*), but the present tense necessarily indicates an imperfective aspect because it lacks the boundaries required for an event to be depicted as completed.

The perfective aspect serves the function of foregrounding the central events of a narrative while the imperfective aspect provides the background of such events, contextualizing, amplifying, or commenting on the events in ways that shape our understanding of the motives or attitudes the speaker believes the events reflect.[235] As Paul Hopper explains, the events in any narrative sequence are each contingent on the completion of the preceding event, and "it is from this contingency that the notion of completeness which is characteristic of perfective aspect derives—the idea of the action viewed 'as a whole.'"[236] Ronald Langacker notes that the imperfective aspect is qualitatively different in that it is not sequenced but represents the perception of "constancy through time instead of change,"[237] and Hopper emphasizes the subject focus of the imperfective due to the capacity of the simultaneous or overlapping background to change subjects more than the events in a narrative sequence in the foreground, which typically focus on a smaller number of subjects that drive a narrative.[238] The two aspects combine to create what Hopper calls a "flow-control mechanism":

> The aspects pick out the main route through the text and allow the listener (reader) to store the actual events of the discourse as a linear group while simultaneously processing accumulations of commentary and supportive information which add texture but not substance to the discourse itself.[239]

The accumulation of commentary and supportive information provided in the imperfective aspect, Hopper notes, does not introduce new information so often as "old already-related events are retold and amplified."[240] The qualities of constancy through time and amplification reflected in the imperfective aspect serve the unifying function of epideictic.

This unifying function of the imperfective aspect is evident in studies of both aspect and epideictic. In Keith Tandy's aspectual study of Ælfric of Eynsham's eleventh-century hagiography *Lives of Saints*, for example, Tandy argues that Ælfric presented the moral divide between pagans and Christians through his use of aspect by depicting Christians from an internal perspective and pagans from an external one:

> In [Ælfric's] scheme pagans and Christians are distinguished, the former characterized as active, punctual, imperative, nondurative; the latter are virtually nontemporal, all their actions having moral goals and contexts. The distinctions drawn arise from a dichotomous view of acts and states,

from a complex range of aspectual features, and from careful variations of agentive features of verbs.[241]

Both Bradford Vivian and Jeremy Engels have noted the role praise and blame play in shaping unities and divisions through enmities.[242] Vivian notes that "despite roseate perceptions to the contrary," the appeal of epideictic is "often ardently nationalistic (if not xenophobic or militaristic)."[243] Hugh Lee notes that the victory odes of the fifth-century BCE Greek lyric poet Pindar not only featured praise but hymnal features, mythical narratives, and gnomic sayings, among other material, the "resulting complex whole" of which "aims to glorify the victor."[244] The boundless quality of epideictic speech serves a unifying function, investing events with motive, meaning, and normality subsumed within a community's history and values, framing events from an internal perspective as an undifferentiated whole.

According to Hopper, because backgrounded content includes states which are not part of the sequence of foregrounded events and does not move discourse forward, it has access to a wider spectrum of time and is less constrained by tense, making it a sort of temporal "distortion." Thus, such content can form part of the prehistory of foregrounded events (for example, *the Founders had fought*), provide a total perspective of the events (*the decision will ensure* or *freedom of speech will not be infringed*), or suggest contingent but unrealized events (*if privacy were limited*).[245] Both the form and function that linguists attribute to backgrounded content is characteristic of epideictic and may also explain the quality by which eloquence is observed to place matters in a perspective that lends "new solidity and worth" to them,[246] or place them in "themes and frames of larger generality."[247] As Barbara Czarniawska notes, "gnomic utterances are the opposite of narrative ones" because "they are situated neither in place nor in time," creating a discursive situation in which "there is no base on which to contest a statement in the gnomic present." Instead, gnomic utterances are "situated no-place in no-time" and feature "abstract protagonists."[248]

The less bounded the referential limits of lexical or morphological items the more restricted the viewing frame, allowing viewers to see only a portion of the referents and opening space for variable interpretations.[249] By addressing subjects without perceptual boundaries in a temporal "distortion," the gnomic aspect not only magnifies the value of its subjects but evades challenge by presenting itself as generally known truth rather than new information, a self-enclosed discourse of belief, desire, or ethical commitment discoverable only through the practical imagination or as common knowledge. This quality also aptly characterizes epideictic. As Eugene Garver writes, "as self-contained," epideictic "becomes a more organic body with its own internal standards for success."[250] In addition to the commonly recognized amplification devices previously discussed, the gnomic aspect is a powerful form of amplification and a pervasive feature of epideictic.

Affirmative Modality

Another pervasive feature of epideictic is a tendency toward affirmative polarity and a relatively sparse use of epistemic qualifiers. As William Frawley explains the linguistic category of modality, speakers often qualify their statements "with respect to believability, reliability, and general compatibility with accepted fact." This area of semantics is called modality, which indicates a speaker's attitude or opinion toward the factual status of propositions.[251] In contrast to tense and aspect, modality does not refer directly to events but only to the status of propositions related to them.[252] The most fundamental category of modality is whether a speaker expresses a proposition with affirmative or negative polarity, or whether a proposition is stated as a fact or negated.[253] Negation is most often indicated by the negative particle *not* or the article *no*, or by pronouns such as *none* or *nothing* and adverbs such as *never* or *nowhere* (for example, *he opened the package* reflects affirmative polarity while *he did not open the package* reflects negative polarity).

John O'Malley writes that "confrontation was hardly [the] first impulse" of epideictic sermons in the papal court of the Renaissance. Epideictic sermons, instead, evinced a "resoundingly affirmative," "world-affirming" rhetoric.[254] Their most arresting quality, he observes, was the "extraordinarily affirmative interpretation of man and the world" that they promoted.[255] Similarly, Perelman and Olbrechts-Tyteca note that there is "an optimistic, a lenient tendency in epideictic discourse which has not escaped certain discerning observers" because it intensifies the adherence to traditional and accepted values rather than those that "stir up controversy and polemics."[256] According to Celeste Condit, epideictic tends to be "relatively non-controversial and focus on universal (that is, broad and abstract) values," presenting "no overt conflict of ideas and values."[257] Instead, a focus on fractious interests is "anathema" to it, and audiences feel an occasion is "misused" when speakers make arguments to which the audience does not assent.[258] Condit distinguishes judicial and legislative discourse from epideictic by the fact that judicial and legislative discourse "pit[s] two sides against each other," focusing inevitably on refutation rather than unity and sharing.[259]

The preference for affirmation in epideictic has often led to labeling it dogmatic. An epideictic oration, O'Malley notes, is "a 'dogmatic' exercise and hence it does not dispute 'disputed questions.'"[260] Epideictic is more agonistic, however, than most commentators recognize.[261] Jeffrey Walker notes, for example, that the enthymematic topics Aristotle lists in his *Rhetoric* almost exclusively constitute antitheses,[262] and antithesis is a familiar figure in epideictic along with other forms of refutation. In the opening remarks of Pericles's funeral oration, he refuted the common belief that the oration was necessary to honor those who died in war, stating that "I could have wished that the reputations of many brave men were not to be imperiled in the mouth of a single individual, to stand or fall according as he spoke well or ill."[263] More broadly, Nicole Loraux has noted the persistently "agonistic motif" of ancient Greek funeral orations, which are pervaded by a "struggle for prestige" between Athens and its neighbors.[264] As previously mentioned, Aristotle recognizes that maxims can be used agonistically,[265] and Quintilian notes that proofs were required in both practical and display varieties of epideictic.[266] In Nicolaus the Sophist's fifth-century CE commentaries on the *progymnasmata*, he devotes an entire paragraph to the importance of refutation in the encomium exercise,[267] and as previously noted, Theodor Burgess writes that the ancient practice of arguing both sides of a case "has naturally a strong epideictic tendency."[268] For all of epideictic's affirmative qualities, any irenic qualities that it may have cannot be noted without qualification.

In some ways, conflict inheres in the logic of praise and blame itself. When a subject is praised it implies divisive grounds for blame,[269] and some commentators have recognized that epideictic is involved in both critique and reform. Perelman notes that epideictic tends to effect change no less than any other form of practical argument.[270] Frederick Ahl argues that even in the panegyrics addressed to Roman emperors, orators were trained to use "figured speech" that both flattered and indirectly criticized them—a practice he labels "safe criticism"[271]—to such an extent that panegyric was broadly recognized as insincere during the period.[272] Similarly, O'Malley notes that praise is sometimes "thinly disguised blame,"[273] and that to epideictic preachers in the papal court of the Renaissance, "reform talk fell to them almost as their proper métier."[274]

According to Bradford Vivian, not only do community members sometimes disagree with epideictic pronouncements of collective memory but "publicly praising certain ideals of communal conduct…doesn't necessarily provide sufficient or widely agreeable motivations for peaceful participation in political or legal institutions." Instead, epideictic speeches may either intentionally or unintentionally produce "collective responses that undermine peaceful political and legal decision-making."[275] Others have reached similar conclusions, finding that eulogies delivered during the same funeral presented competing claims,[276] for example, or that Abraham Lincoln's 1842 Temperance Address functioned as an act of cultural criticism in epideictic form.[277] Although epideictic tends toward affirmative polarity in what Condit describes as a "humane vision" of a community's motive and meaning,[278] it does so only by subordinating rather than entirely eliminating negative polarity which often appears in antitheses that amplify the positive qualities of a subject by contrast.

The dogmatic reputation of epideictic may also derive from its relatively low use of epistemic qualifiers despite its agonism and use of proofs. Closely related to polarity is epistemic modality, based on the distinction between the realis mode in which the actual world and the expressed world coincide and the irrealis mode in which some distance is marked between the actual and expressed worlds.[279] In contrast to the realis mode, which depicts situations as having actually occurred, the irrealis mode depicts situations as "purely within the realm of thought, knowable only through imagination."[280] Epistemic modality reflects the ways in which language expresses concepts such as possibility, necessity, inference, belief, report, hearsay, conclusion, deduction, opinion, commitment, speculation, quotation, doubt, and evidence.[281] In many instances, epideictic not only avoids negation but epistemic qualifiers as well. As Ernesto Grassi notes of sacred language, "it never arises out of a process of inference."[282] Rather than dogmatism, epideictic expresses a faith or resolve in the form of a community's beliefs, desires, and ethical commitments.

In contrast to the complete "mismatch" of the actual and expressed worlds reflected in negative polarity, William Frawley writes, epistemic modality reflects "the *convergence of the [actual and expressed worlds]*, particularly...the *likelihood* of that convergence and the *evidence* that a speaker marshals to assert this convergence."[283] Epistemic modality relativizes truth to speakers by "relating their current state of knowledge or belief to the content of their expressions."[284] It is indicated by qualifiers that can be categorized according to whether they express degrees of convergence between the actual and expressed worlds or refer to the grounds for finding such a convergence. Qualifiers that express degrees of convergence between actual and expressed worlds range from verbs such as *seem, tend, appear, believe, think,* or *assume,* and auxiliary verbs such as *can, may, might, could, would,* or *should,* to adverbs such as *probably, likely, possibly, perhaps,* or *conceivably,* or adjectives such as *probable, possible,* or *conceivable,* and adverbs of frequency such as *often, usually, sometimes, occasionally,* or *seldom.* Qualifiers that refer to the grounds for finding a convergence between actual and expressed worlds include verbs such as *indicate, suggest, see, hear, witness, testify, claim, argue, imply, infer,* or *guess*; adverbial forms such as *presumably, supposedly, allegedly, according to, if,* or *even if*; adjectives such as *presumed, supposed, alleged, claimed,* or *so-called,* and clauses such as *heard that, saw that, learned that, said that, testified that, assumed that, if that is true,* or *if you believe that.*

Much like its use of the gnomic aspect, epideictic does not present propositions as entirely beyond doubt but tends to leave their epistemic limits less marked than more logical registers. Given that it often addresses unbounded subjects in the unbounded present tense, perhaps the contingency of epideictic premises and conclusions are simply too apparent to induce reference. Attributing maxims and proverbs to specific authors or qualifying how likely they are to be true in the same manner as a logical demonstration, for example, may be unnecessary or inappropriate. In John O'Malley's comparison of thematic and epideictic sermons in the papal court of the Renaissance, he distinguishes epideictic sermons not only by their lyrical quality but by how they used sources. The fewer quotations a sermon contained, he observes, the more likely it was to have other epideictic qualities. "They utilize, but do not explicitly quote, their sources," he notes. "The allusions, paraphrases, and even the actual quotations are woven into their text in such a way that they fit the rhythm and do not attract attention to themselves."[285] This tendency toward an absence or subordination of attribution of sources can be found in many examples of epideictic discourse. As Dale Sullivan notes, epideictic speakers are vested with an authority that allows them to "make broad characterizing statements without providing evidence."[286] They are expected to speak on behalf of their audience, channeling the audience's beliefs, desires, and ethical commitments in a manner that neither requires nor permits the same level of qualification and attribution as logical demonstration.

In Eugene Garver's discussion of *Brown v. Board of Education* (1954), which he describes as an "epideictic declaration that equality and antidiscrimination are fundamental American constitutional values," he argues that "the brevity of the *Brown* opinion, which critics quickly characterized as 'containing almost no law,' is part of its persuasiveness because it is part of its legitimacy." The Court presents the opinion as "ethically necessary and inevitable," he writes, "precisely because it is not necessary and inevitable by narrow logical and legal criteria." Although the Court could have written a detailed deductive argument containing lengthy citations to constitutional precedent, Garver writes, "for a case as monumental as *Brown* such a deduction would have been perceived as the Court hiding behind legal precedent and not taking responsibility for the decision." The Court instead committed itself and the nation to an ethical principle which Garver argues extended beyond *Brown*.[287] The relative absence and subordination of negation and epistemic qualifiers in epideictic may be due not to any assertion that propositions are incontrovertibly true, as many commentators have concluded, but to the performance of a faith or resolve in which the speaker and audience unite.

Structured Occasions

Although it is beyond the scope of the chapters that follow to consider the nonverbal epideictic features of the occasions on which particular judicial opinions regarding fundamental rights were delivered, it is noteworthy that judicial discourse is delivered on occasions designed to elevate its importance through various nonverbal ritual and ceremonial elements such as a court's location, architecture, and decor, judicial reputation and attire, and the ritual actions that attend judicial discourse, such as the custom of standing while a judge or jury enters or leaves a courtroom, the swearing of testimonial oaths, the formal reading and proclamation of judgments, and general rules of decorum. Pierre Bourdieu writes that ritual is "designed to intensify the authority of the act of interpretation" in which courts engage, such as the formal reading of the texts and proclamation of judgment, which "adds to the collective work of sublimation designed to attest that the decision expresses not the will or the world-view of the judge but the will of the law or the legislature."[288] Such nonverbal ritual elements are designed to respond to epideictic situations in the same manner as discursive features.

In ancient Greece, epideictic emerged directly from ritual, particularly from funeral orations (*epitaphios logos*) and festival speeches (*panegyric*) which were attended by nonverbal ritual elements.[289] Based in part on epideictic's long connection to ritual, Michael Carter even argues that epideictic is only successful when it "achieves the qualities of ritual."[290] In Menander of Laodicea's third-century CE handbook on epideictic speeches, in addition to funeral orations and related forms expressing consolation and grief, he discusses a variety of arrival and farewell speeches, coronation speeches, the speeches of ambassadors addressed to distressed cities, birthday and wedding speeches, and bedtime speeches exhorting a newly married couple to consummate their marriage,[291] occasions which typically included nonverbal ritual elements. Today similar elements attend epideictic occasions such as inaugurals, commencements, commemorations, and memorials. The time and place of epideictic is often significant and specifically designed to infuse an event with impressiveness and solemnity, supporting the extemporaneous exploitation of possibilities immanent in a situation with a careful design of the space of performance to enhance the effect of the speech.[292]

As Bradford Vivian notes, "memorials are often staged on the sites of historic events and thereby provide a sense of material connection with the past,"[293] and Edmund Thomas explains that the epideictic speakers of the Second Sophistic during the first and third century CE of the Roman Empire were "not just aware of their architectural surroundings" but "positively fed off them," their speech and tone dependent on their experience of the setting and the acoustics of the venue. Epideictic speakers considered appropriate posture and gesture, he writes, and they "wore clothes, which, like the architectural decoration, were beautiful without being distracting." The "ostentatious style" of epideictic performance and its "glamorous and impressive settings" in the early Roman Empire created an expectation comparable to opera, Thomas concludes, their effect derived both from the form of the speeches and from their "theatrical use of the spatial settings in which they took place."[294]

Numerous commentators have recognized that law is pervaded by ritual and ceremony.[295] Following the rise of law schools in the twelfth century and the rise of a civil legal profession by the end of the thirteenth century, authorities spanning many times, places, and jurisdictions "sought to bond individuals to them and to legitimate their powers" through "the display of judicial authority."[296] This included the construction of courts housed in governmentally sponsored venues, often located near churches or city centers and architecturally designed to dominate their surroundings. Judith Resnik and Dennis Curtis note that early European courthouses often included "depictions of the Virtues and allegorical scenes of religious stories and classical myths to link their regimes to prosperity, peace, and history."[297] The public display of legal authority in early modern Europe included public readings of law such as those in mid-sixteenth-century Germany, where "rulers staged public readings of basic rights as a *quid pro quo* for obtaining the loyalty oath from their subjects."[298]

Court architecture in early America followed familiar formulas which served to legitimize the legal profession by defining law as separate from and untainted by the market,[299] a monumental architecture that invested jurists with professional values.[300] Contemporary judicial architecture reflects a similar purpose. The 1991 version of the *U.S. Courts Design Guide* directed that the architectural design of federal courts should "symbolize the Judiciary as a co-equal branch of Government," for example, through a monumental scale and durable materials, exuding an "impressive and inspiring" spirit that reflected the judiciary's "seriousness." In 1997, the *Guide* directed federal courthouses to "promote respect for the tradition and purpose of the American judicial process," expressing "solemnity, stability, integrity, rigor, and fairness." The same principles guided selection of the artwork and decor of federal courthouses.[301]

The United States Supreme Court building designed by Cass Gilbert exemplifies these principles. Gilbert designed the Court in the style of a classical Roman temple, inspired by Pierre Vignon's Église de la Madeleine in Paris, and he surrounded the building with symbols suitable to its monumental image. These symbols include lampposts with ram heads and lion paws symbolizing strength, resting on bronze tortoises symbolizing the deliberate pace of justice. Relief panels on the front doors of the building depict the growth of the law beginning in ancient Greece and Rome, and allegorical figures representing the "Contemplation of Justice" and the "Authority of Law" flank the entrance, above which the front pediment displays allegorical figures representing Liberty, Justice, Order, Authority, Council, and Research Past and Present. As Barbara Perry describes the Court's entrance, "after climbing up the broad, white steps, stepping under the Corinthian columns, and passing through the foyer, visitors...enter the 'Great Hall,'" designed to "dramatize the approach to the courtroom of the highest tribunal in the land." The Court's building also affected the manner in which the Court published its opinions, as the Court established a Public Information Office in conjunction with its new building and began providing journalists with copies of its opinions the day they were announced.[302]

Another nonverbal element of epideictic that serves to magnify the value of its subjects is the reputation of epideictic speakers, often selected to speak on epideictic occasions based on their stature in the community. Many classical commentators associated epideictic with established speakers selected for their wisdom or authority. As previously mentioned, Aristotle concludes that the maxims which form the premises and conclusions of enthymemes are only appropriate for speakers with experience in their subjects,[303] and Walter Beale notes that ceremonial speakers are "generally expected to hold credentials appropriate to the event."[304] According to Dale Sullivan, epideictic audiences bring to the speech a "willingness to accept the speaker's assertions because of the speaker's generally perceived *ethos*," allowing the speaker to draw on their own authority rather than that "derived through citing others or evidence."[305] Although epideictic speakers are not always established leaders,[306] they are often at least drawn from locally recognized spokespersons. Bradford Vivian notes that the collective knowledge and motivations epideictic engenders circulates and becomes recognized as common wisdom "through the public speech of a community's most widely accepted spokespersons (including elected leaders, public servants, intellectuals, religious authorities, military heroes, and communal advocates)."[307]

Judges obviously merit inclusion in this group of recognized community spokespersons. They are appointed or elected to their positions in part on that basis. The recognition that judges will hold important roles as community spokespersons is further enhanced by judicial attire, selected and regulated to magnify the value of their speech. As W. N. Hargreaves-Mawdsley writes, one of the best ways to promote the dignity of the law is to give legal officials a "dignified costume."[308] Judicial attire was designed for this purpose as soon as the civil legal profession arose in

Europe alongside the development of civil courtrooms. Today the judicial robe may be the most widely recognizable feature of this attire (and in some jurisdictions the coif), but historically judicial attire was also distinguished by special mantles, hoods, shoulder pieces, caps, collars or ruffs, gloves, and cuffs, often by specific decree and dependent on rank and ceremonial occasion.[309] The attire of civil judges imitated that of the ecclesiastical authorities and nobles they succeeded, as well as the fashion of upper class laypeople, to secure an image of power and authority,[310] and similar purposes continue to inform the regulation of judicial attire.

In 2015, the Florida Supreme Court adopted a new rule requiring that "during any judicial proceeding, robes worn by a judge must be solid black with no embellishment," a rule issued in response to complaints of judges wearing colored robes, including one judge who wore a camouflage robe and a judge in the Keys who wore a flowered robe that resembled a Hawaiian shirt.[311] The court wrote that the people of Florida "should not have to question whether equal justice is being dispensed based on the color of a judge's robe," and that the rule was intended to emphasize that "the attire worn by judges during judicial proceedings must promote public trust and confidence in the proceedings and the judicial system as a whole."[312] Jerome Frank notes that the judicial robe "announces in impressive terms that the judge is a member of a caste at once mysterious and aristocratic" and gives the public an impression of uniformity, that judicial wisdom derives from "a single, superhuman source," although Frank criticizes the intimidating effect of the robe and notes that many judges try to assuage the effect.[313] Through many nonverbal elements, the occasions on which judicial discourse is delivered are structured to magnify its value, converging with verbal features to intensify the effect of epideictic registers in judicial opinions and promote confidence in judicial decisions.

Transcendent Function

A register approach to epideictic comprehends its ubiquity across many discourses and texts and its function as a central element of persuasion in all practical speech genres,[314] as well as how it serves the immediate purposes of argument. Among its most pervasive features are praise, amplification, eloquence, the gnomic aspect, affirmative modality, and nonverbal elements of the occasions of its delivery, all of which performatively magnify the value of its subject in response to situations that threaten social unity. As previously noted, because these features exist on a general registral level does not preclude the identification of additional features or more specific epideictic registers.[315] As Cynthia Sheard writes, epideictic constitutes a "multivalent" and "composite but fluid whole which any particular definition can describe only in part."[316] According to Sheard, epideictic is less of a genre or fixed set of rhetorical elements than a "persuasive gesture or mode we might locate in any number of discourses, including those we might regard as deliberative or forensic."[317]

The presence of the registral features identified in this chapter will never be identical in particular examples of epideictic, but in prototypical examples the features appear in dense convergences in which they augment one another to magnify the value of subjects beyond the perceptual capacities of participants, fostering social unity by shifting the perspective of participants to a shared and unbounded object of contemplation. Even though the registral features identified may not all be found in a particular instance of epideictic, the accumulation of the features in varying combinations unifies participants by subsuming the individual agency of speakers and audience members within a common framework of value and meaning, what Kenneth Burke refers to as rhetorical transcendence—the adoption of a perspective in which oppositions are dissolved. Although Burke observes that transcendence is basic to all thought, he particularly associates it with didactic-moralistic literature, which is conventionally associated with epideictic.[318]

In epideictic, according to Perelman and Olbrechts-Tyteca, "every device of literary art is appropriate, for it is a matter of combining all the factors that can promote this communion of the audience,"[319] and they note that arguments interact and augment one another in a process they elsewhere call convergence.[320] "If several distinct arguments lead to a single conclusion," they write, "the value attributed to the conclusion and to each separate argument will be augmented, for the likelihood that several entirely erroneous arguments would reach the same result is very small." This convergence can either be explicit or arise from the mere enumeration or systematic exposition of elements.[321] What Perelman and Olbrechts-Tyteca suggest in the latter conclusion is that convergence has both a representational and performative dimension closely connected with their emphasis on presence in argumentation, by which the importance of the elements of any argument is increased by the simple act of paying attention to them.³²² Presence "acts directly on our sensibility," they write, making present what is absent "by verbal magic alone,"³²³ valorizing the elements of an argument.³²⁴ In epideictic, praise, amplification, eloquence, the gnomic aspect, affirmative modality, and nonverbal elements of the occasions of its delivery performatively augment one another to magnify the value of a subject in the same manner as accumulations of logic and evidence. The import of epideictic is not simply identified, rehearsed, or recirculated, but created and magnified through performance.

The effects of epideictic's convergence of features are often profound. Commentators describe the experience as "mystical,"³²⁵ "prophetic,"³²⁶ or an "encounter with Being,"³²⁷ occurring in the sacred time of ritual³²⁸ and possessing the "curious sublimity" of religious rhetoric.³²⁹ Michael Carter describes its "esoteric—even mysterious—nature," achieving "a meaning and function that is beyond the potential of ordinary, pragmatic language."³³⁰ These commentators reference an experience reflected not only in the social and political life of a community produced by the speech, but the immediate experience of the speaker and audience being subsumed within a common framework of value and meaning. Christine Oravec, for example, argues that epideictic involves the speaker and audience in "a reciprocal relationship in which the listener actively supplies materials for discourse and judges the speaker's abilities to construct illuminating and important statements from those materials."³³¹

As discussed above regarding the gnomic aspect and affirmative modality characteristic of epideictic, its speakers are expected to speak on behalf of their audience in a manner that simultaneously channels and shapes the audience's beliefs, desires, and ethical commitments. As Cristian Tileagă writes of the relationship of the speaker and audience in national commemorative addresses, for example, "the perspective espoused in commemorative contexts is not necessarily that of the 'member' with representative duties, but rather *the* representative point of view, acceptable to the nation and expressed *in the name* of the nation,"³³² similar to Eugene Garver's explanation of the judicial need to convince audiences that a judicial opinion "speaks *for* them" in order to legitimize decisions.³³³ Likewise, E. Johannes Hartelius and Jennifer Asenas note that epideictic "transcends identity even in the humanist condition insofar as [it] subordinates individualism to the rehearsal of values and signs that are not of the speaker's making,"³³⁴ much as the speaker in a funerary lament may perform the grief of a deceased's relatives.³³⁵ In ritual, writes Edmund

Leach, "there is no separate audience of listeners," but instead "the performers and the listeners are the same people" and "we engage in rituals in order to transmit collective messages to ourselves."[336]

The collective experience of epideictic is closely connected to the powerful transcendence that it can achieve and which is its chief function, a fitting response to situations in which social unity is threatened. In the classical rhetorical tradition, Isocrates and Plato both conclude that epideictic promotes social, cultural, and political cohesion,[337] and the subject of Gorgias of Leontini's Olympic oration was *homonmia*, or concord, arguing that Greeks should wage war with barbarians rather than each other. The Greek sophist Hippias of Elis also advocated Greek unity.[338] In contemporary commentary, Bradford Vivian writes that epideictic is used to establish solidarity by providing "common explanations of a people's historical past and the lessons (whether peaceful or violent) it betokens for the group's present and future."[339] In their study of southern speeches in the aftermath of the Civil War, Waldo Braden and Harold Mixon conclude that for southerners epideictic became an "amalgam or binding element, drawing together in a single oration shared aspirations, deep sentiments, memories, and fantasies of listeners and speaker, enshrined in communal values and myths."[340] These and other commentators have noted the power of epideictic to unify a community and legitimize decisions by grounding them in a common framework of value and meaning. The following chapters illustrate how the registral features of epideictic identified in this chapter have functioned in the United States Supreme Court's fundamental rights jurisprudence to legitimize judicial decisions that inaugurated constitutional change with broad social consequences.

CHAPTER 2

Freedom of Speech, Paramologia, and the Flag

Many of the epideictic features of judicial opinions may be classified as dicta—commentary that either gratuitously extends to questions beyond the facts of the immediate case or is unnecessary to support the logical propositions a case represents and therefore not considered binding precedent in later cases.[1] Justice Edward Fadeley objected in his concurring opinion for the Oregon Supreme Court in *Snow v. Oregon State Penitentiary* (1989), for example, that the praise in a "panegyric to the polygraph" which he perceived in the majority opinion was "neither presented as if it were dicta nor based on an analysis of appropriateness for admission which relies upon the facts and circumstances of this case."[2] As noted in the previous chapter, praise comes in many forms, including performative, nonpropositional ones. The incontestability of gnomic sayings which Barbara Czarniawska notes, because they are "situated no-place in no-time" and feature "abstract protagonists"[3]—much like the self-enclosed quality of epideictic itself[4]—also reflects an inherent contingency that limits their determinacy. Both legal maxims and maxims on general subjects have been criticized as "ostentatious," holding little legal significance but serving only as "a way to show off."[5] Amplification devices such as metaphors and other figures of thought and speech, particularly those involving repetition, may also be dismissed as superfluous rather than necessary elements of legal reasoning. Reducing legal reasoning to a set of logical propositions in the manner a traditional analysis of dicta recommends will necessarily neglect much of its epideictic content.

Because dicta is not binding in future cases, it is often considered not only peripheral but even damaging to the clarity of judicial opinions. For some commentators, gnomic sayings such as "liberty finds no reference in a jurisprudence of doubt,"[6] "the greatest dangers to liberty lurk in insidious encroachment by men of zeal, well-meaning but without understanding,"[7] "the secular state is not an examiner of consciences,"[8] or "one man's vulgarity is another's lyric,"[9] and densely figured descriptions such as Justice Louis Brandeis's account of the American colonists' belief that "fear breeds repression; that repression breeds hate; that hate menaces stable government; that the path of safety lies in the opportunity to discuss freely supposed grievances and proposed remedies; and that the fitting remedy for evil counsels is good ones,"[10] are mystifying distractions that only serve a stylistic function. To the extent they are taken seriously as legal propositions rather than stylistic flourishes, they may be considered dogmatic or illiberal because they do not constitute the fully elaborated reasons which "build the bridge between the authorities they cite and the results they decree" in order to legitimize judicial opinions in democratic societies.[11]

Other commentators have been more skeptical of the distinction that the concept of dicta signifies, however, and of dismissive attitudes toward it. In Robert Tsai's study of how the rhetorical strategies of activists, lawyers, and presidents created a "faith community based on rule of law values" which shaped the development of First Amendment culture, for example, he argues that the widespread dissemination of judicial metaphors regarding the First Amendment in public discourse suggests that "one should pay careful attention to dicta, for it is in the so-called nonessential portions of judicial rulings, legal memoranda, and policy statements that such direct appeals to the populace are to be found."[12] Tsai notes that the metaphorical content of opinions plays an important role "in the construction of the political imagination," with the potential to cultivate "political intimacy" or "a sense of affinity among citizens who disagree about the good life," a "regenerative power" with the capacity to "level and legitimate the law."[13] Like Tsai, Paul Kahn writes that dicta is as important as the content of a judgment to the rhetoric of a judicial opinion. With regard to the unifying work of the judiciary, Kahn writes, the logical content of opinions is the "least interesting aspect."[14] Similarly, Don Le Duc argues that the means of persuasion available to courts make dicta a "far more potent force for legal change than the rather abstract descriptions of legal references would suggest," noting that "the more vigorous or eloquent the judicial passage being quoted, the less likely it is to be an expression of existing law."[15]

Although many commentators have focused exclusively on the stylistic dimension of judicial metaphors rather than their function in legal reasoning, Haig Bosmajian claims that the tropological language of opinions helps us understand the logical basis of decisions. In response to a history of commentary that condemns judicial metaphors for many of the same reasons that modern language policies condemned all metaphor, Bosmajian writes that we should be "a bit wary of the tropology of the law" because it can narrow thinking and result in "outmoded and dangerous legal language and precedents," but for the most part Bosmajian defends the importance of tropological language to judicial thought against those who would dismiss it as mere stylistic ornamentation.[16] Similarly, Maksymilian Del Mar recognizes both metaphor and figures as important artifacts of legal inquiry, forms of language that "signal their own artifice" and "call upon us to participate" in legal thought, enabling and sustaining inquiry in important ways.[17]

Studies of legal discourse have also largely neglected figures of thought and speech in favor of an exclusive focus on metaphor in a manner that parallels the focus on metaphor that Jeanne Fahnestock notes of science and textual studies.[18] Bosmajian acknowledges this limitation of his own study, writing that his analysis is restricted to tropes and does not deal with that "other group of figures of speech, schemes," because he concludes that figures such as antithesis, asyndeton, anaphora, and antimetabole "do not have the impact on meaning or conceptualization that tropes do."[19] Similarly, Chaïm Perelman and Lucie Olbrechts-Tyteca acknowledge that they subordinate the study of figures to argumentation.[20] As explained in the previous chapter, however, not only do Chaïm Perelman and Lucie Olbrechts-Tyteca recognize the argumentative power of figures but other commentators such as Jeanne Fahnestock note that figures share a common origin with metaphor and belong equally to the "pragmatic or situational and functional dimension of language,"[21] forming a "verbal summary that epitomizes a line of reasoning"[22] with the capacity to change an audience's perspective.[23] Del Mar is the most notable exception to the neglect of figurality in legal thought, noting that his study of judicial figures such as antithesis, parataxis, antimetabole, and personification was inspired by Fahnestock's work on figures in science.[24]

Despite the fact that judicial metaphors and figures may be dismissed as dicta, they substantially contribute to the intertextual power of opinions as evidenced by the frequent quotation of the figurative language of opinions both in the popular press and later opinions. In Bosmajian's study of judicial metaphors, for example, he notes that they are often "cited as support in the reasoning of subsequent decisions," such as many of the opinions of Justice Robert Jackson, who "often developed his arguments in nonliteral, figurative terms, some of which were subsequently cited again and again by courts at all levels."[25] Del Mar notes that figures are "highly memorable," making them "more likely to be re-used," perhaps because they are "kinesically resonant" and invite our interaction with them.[26] According to Tsai, the power of judicial metaphors is furthered by the fact that their moving quality tends to find reception in a wider circulation in later opinions and secondary media, which "increases the chance that it will be appropriated by others."[27]

Many traditionally recognized examples of epideictic outside of the judicial context reflect this intertextual power. As James Jasinski notes, for example, Abraham Lincoln's three-part tricolon structure in the peroration of his Gettysburg Address, in which Lincoln resolved that "government of the people, by the people, for the people, shall not perish from the earth," is borrowed without attribution from Daniel Webster's 1830 speech in reply to Robert Hayne regarding a proposal to limit the sale of land in Western states: "The people's government, made for the people, made by the people, and answerable to the people."[28] Paul Baker and Sibonile Ellece similarly note that Martin Luther King, Jr.'s "I Have a Dream" speech refers to Abraham Lincoln's Gettysburg Address by using the phrase "five score years ago," as well as to the Bible, Shakespeare, and the Declaration of Independence,[29] often without attribution.

This chapter examines the epideictic registers in the Court's jurisprudence regarding the First Amendment's Free Speech Clause, first in the Court's opinions regarding the constitutionality of compulsory flag salutes in *Minersville School District v. Gobitis* (1940) and *West Virginia State Board of Education v. Barnette* (1943), and then in the opinions of Justices William Brennan, Anthony Kennedy, and William Rehnquist regarding prosecutions for desecration of the American flag in *Texas v. Johnson* (1989). I argue that the cases reveal the central role that the figure of paramologia, or strategic concession, played in the Court's thought regarding freedom of speech, acknowledging and lamenting the dangers of free speech while amplifying its benefits by contrast. I also critique Justice Frankfurter's use of epideictic in the flag salute cases as a failure to accurately apprehend the nation's beliefs, desires, and ethical commitments on the issue and the efficacy of Justice Rehnquist's infamous opinion extolling the flag's place in American history.

Fundamental Rights

The doctrine of fundamental rights did not originate with the United States Supreme Court nor is it unique to American law.[30] As developed in American law, however, historically the doctrine has recognized that certain rights are so "implicit in the concept of ordered liberty" that restrictions on them must be regarded with heightened scrutiny.[31] It has particularly emerged in the extension of the Bill of Rights to state governments through the "incorporation"[32] or "absorption"[33] of its most important guarantees into the Due Process Clause of the Fourteenth Amendment. As Milton Konvitz explains, the process of identifying some rights and liberties that enjoy more dignity or have a higher rank than others and therefore deserve more vigilance and protection can be traced to the early years of the American colonies.[34] The primary drafter of the Bill of Rights, James Madison, first identified certain rights as preeminently important "natural rights," speaking of "the great rights, the trial by jury, freedom of the press,…liberty of conscience," while more reluctantly recognizing other guarantees in the Bill of Rights.[35]

Madison initially opposed the idea of a Bill of Rights because he thought their enumeration was unnecessary and inconsistent with the idea of popular rights, but he eventually supported the enumeration of certain rights in response to public outcry for a Bill of Rights and the usefulness of the constitutional enumeration of certain rights in public debate.[36] Producing a discursive commitment to certain rights in a "solemn manner" so that they became "incorporated with the national sentiment," Madison concluded, could promote political acculturation and be a "good ground for an appeal to the sense of the community."[37] For Madison, in other words, the compelling purpose of the Bill of Rights was an epideictic one of shaping belief, desire, and ethical commitment in the American people through the inscription of certain rights in the Constitution, independent of its strictly legal significance.

In American law, the fundamental rights doctrine first emerged in early interpretations by the Court of the term "liberty" in the phrase "life, liberty and property" in the Fifth and Fourteenth Amendments to the United States Constitution.[38] It was not until after the Civil War and passage of the Fourteenth Amendment, however, that the Court developed the doctrine known as substantive due process by which the Court held that certain rights found in the Bill of Rights inhere in the meaning of due process and therefore serve to limit not only the federal government but state governments under the Due Process Clause of the Fourteenth Amendment. Justice John Harlan advocated this view in dissenting opinions in cases before the Court in 1884 and 1908, but it was only in *Gitlow v. New York* (1925) that the Court first recognized the doctrine, writing that "freedom of speech and of the press...are among the fundamental personal rights and liberties protected by the due process clause of the Fourteenth Amendment from impairment by the States."[39] Soon after *Gitlow*, in *Stromberg v. California* (1931), the Court declared California's Red Flag Law unconstitutional on First Amendment free speech grounds as a violation of the liberty protected by the Fourteenth Amendment, and in *Palko v. Connecticut* (1937) the Court first formulated the doctrine under which guarantees in the Bill of Rights could be accepted or rejected as fundamental based on whether they were "implicit in the concept of ordered liberty."[40] In *Palko*, Justice Benjamin Cardozo wrote for the Court that freedom of speech is "the matrix, the indispensable condition, of nearly every other form of freedom," while the right to trial by jury, immunity from prosecution in the absence of an indictment, and immunity from self-incrimination "may have value and importance" but "are not of the very essence of a scheme of ordered liberty."[41]

According to Milton Konvitz, the fundamental rights doctrine aligns with a general compulsion to bring hierarchical order "as soon as a reflective mind faces a large body of legal enactments, or religious precepts, or moral maxims, or the world of phenomena," identifying what is relevant and irrelevant or important and marginal.[42] The drive for fundamentals, he writes, is "not essentially different from the compulsion felt by theologians to formulate the essentials or primary, fundamental beliefs of a religious faith."[43] He notes that in law, however, the term *fundamental* is often imprecise, including honorific purposes and the expression of beliefs, desires, and ethical commitments:

> It is at times used in an honorific sense, to underscore the importance of the idea or value in question, and it may suffice for the purpose and in the context in which it is used. It may contribute some intelligibility to a classification, it may make some decisions more predictable; it may help bring decisions or principles into a larger order of consistency. It may be used, not to describe or explain, but to guide conduct. It may express a wish or hope.[44]

Decisions regarding whether guarantees in the Bill of Rights place limits on state governments often inaugurate changes that threaten social unity, as reflected in the controversy such decisions engender, which invites epideictic registers from the Court speaking to the importance of such rights to who we are or resolve to be as a polity.

Flag Salutes

Both *Minersville School District v. Gobitis* (1940) and *West Virginia State Board of Education v. Barnette* (1943) involved Jehovah's Witness children who refused to participate in compulsory flag salutes in public schools. Discriminatory incidents regarding Jehovah's Witnesses in the United States preceded the two cases by decades, including acts of violence and legal cases targeting Witnesses. They faced particularly harsh treatment during this period for opposing the American war effort during World War I through activities such as the dissemination of extensive anti-war propaganda, and some Witnesses were sentenced to imprisonment. Before World War II began, Witnesses had also opposed saluting the American flag on religious grounds, but the patriotic fervor of World War II after decades of nationalistic grievances toward Witnesses brought the conflict into particularly high relief. In one act of wartime hysteria, Witnesses were feared as a Fifth Column and physically attacked as suspected Nazi agents.[45]

This was the context in which two children, aged ten and twelve, were expelled from the public schools of Minersville, Pennsylvania, for refusing to participate in a Pledge of Allegiance ceremony required by the local board of education which required teachers and students to recite the Pledge of Allegiance every day while performing the Bellamy salute by extending their right hands in salute to the American flag. The Gobitis children were Witnesses who believed that such a gesture was prohibited by the Bible, particularly by the proscription in the Ten Commandments against worshipping other gods or graven images. Thus, the central conflict of *Gobitis* was about honorific performances. Because their attendance at the public school was compulsory, the children's expulsion required their parents to place them in private school.[46] When the school expelled them for refusing to participate in the ceremony, their family sued the school, seeking an injunction prohibiting the school from requiring the children to participate in the pledge ceremony based on the assertion that insisting the children participate in it violated without due process of law the religious liberty they were entitled to under the Fourteenth Amendment.

Before discussing Justice Felix Frankfurter's majority opinion for the United States Supreme Court in *Gobitis*, it is useful to recognize the rhetorical context in which he wrote. Both the district court and the court of appeals granted the injunctive relief sought and included epideictic registers prominently in their judicial opinions. Judge Albert Maris of the United States Court for the Eastern District of Pennsylvania wrote two opinions in the case, one responding to the request for a preliminary injunction and one following trial. In his first opinion, Maris recognized the right of conscience referred to in the Pennsylvania Constitution as

> one of the fundamental bases upon which our nation was founded, namely, that individuals have the right not only to entertain any religious belief but also to do or refrain from doing any act on conscientious grounds, which does not prejudice the safety, morals, property or personal rights of the people.[47]

In this passage and elsewhere in his opinion, Maris used praise, enumeration, *dirimens copulatio*, eloquence, the gnomic aspect, and affirmative modality to magnify the value of freedom of conscience. He wrote that freedom of conscience meant freedom for each individual to decide for themselves what is religious, and to permit the state to determine whether religious objections were sincere "would be to sound the death knell of religious liberty."[48]

Following the trial in *Gobitis*, Judge Maris also prefigured Justice Jackson's attack on compelled belief in *Barnette* by referencing the context of the war and incorporating praise, exergasia, and antithesis to amplify his conclusion that religious liberty was crucial to national security because it cultivated independent thought in contrast to totalitarian conformity:

> We need only glance at the current world scene to realize that the preservation of individual liberty is more important today than ever it was in the past. The safety of our nation largely depends upon the extent to which we foster in each individual citizen that sturdy independence of thought and action which is essential in a democracy. The loyalty of our people is to be judged not so much by their words as by the part they play in the body politic. Our country's safety surely does not depend upon the totalitarian

idea of forcing all citizens into one common mold of thinking and acting or requiring them to render a lip service of loyalty in a manner which conflicts with their sincere religious convictions. Such a doctrine seems to me utterly alien to the genius and spirit of our nation and destructive of that personal liberty of which our flag itself is the symbol.[49]

The transcendent purpose of Maris's epideictic register in this passage is augmented by his frequent use of the first-person plural (*we*, *our*) and references to democracy and the body politic.

The school appealed Judge Maris's decision to the United States Court of Appeals for the Third Circuit. Writing for the court of appeals, Judge William Clark wrote a lengthy opinion so saturated in epideictic features, particularly the gnomic aspect, that it is impossible to do all of the features justice here. The case raised questions "within the aura of conscience,"[50] Clark wrote, and he included a quotation from the Puritan minister Roger Williams, who Clark introduced as a "champion of religious liberty," discussing the Latin maxim *salus populi suprema lex* ("let the welfare of the people be the supreme law"). In addition, Clark elevated religious faith above respect for secular laws through a dense convergence of praise, eloquence, the gnomic aspect, and a relatively affirmative modality:

> Reverence is manifestly something deeper than law. The mere creation by fiat of a particular moral standard would not mean that its violation might reasonably be expected to arouse the passions productive of peace breaches. There are, however, certain "ethics" whether furnished with legal sanctions or not, that do plumb those reaches of our emotions.[51]

The opinion also included more specifically gnomic sayings, such as that "compulsion rather than protection should be sparingly exercised," for "harm usually comes from doing rather than leaving undone, and refraining is generally not sacrilege." Similarly, Clark wrote that "departure from a recently evolved ritualistic norm of patriotism is not clear and present assurance of future cowardice or treachery," for "we do not find the essential relationship between infant patriotism and the martial spirit."[52]

Judge Clark's opinion quoted George Washington's praise of freedom of conscience in his October 1789 letter to Quakers, which the opinion introduces with the remark that "the almost universal character" of

Washington's wisdom "always freshly surprises." In the passage of the letter quoted in the opinion, Washington says:

> I assure you very explicitly, that in my opinion the conscientious scruples of all men should be treated with great delicacy and tenderness; and it is my wish and desire, that the laws may always be as extensively accommodated to them, as a due regard to the protection and essential interests of the nation may justify and permit.

Weaving Washington's language from the letter into his opinion, Clark then wrote that the school that had expelled the Gobitis children had "failed to 'treat the conscientious scruples' of all children with that 'great delicacy and tenderness.'"[53] He quoted at length from Daniel Webster's 1820 Speech in Commemoration of the First Settlement of New England, in which Webster wrote eloquently of the love of religious liberty, calling it "a stronger sentiment than an attachment to civil or political freedom," prominently featuring praise, metaphor, antithesis, parallelism, the gnomic aspect, and affirmative modality:

> History instructs us that this love of religious liberty, a compound sentiment in the breast of men, made up of the dearest sense of right and the highest conviction of duty, is able to look the sternest despotism in the face.[54]

In separate places in his opinion, Judge Clark also prominently quoted without attribution portions of the gnomic saying of Jesus in Matthew 19:14 of the Christian scriptures: "Suffer little children, and forbid them not, to come unto me: for of such is the kingdom of heaven." Clark first quoted the verse in the opening sentence of his opinion: "Eighteen big states have seen fit to exert their power over a small number of little children ('and forbid them not')." He quoted the verse a second time some ten paragraphs later, writing, "These little children ('suffer them') are asking us to afford them the protection of the First Amendment (Bill of Rights) to the Constitution and to permit them the 'free exercise' of their 'religion.'"[55] By neglecting to attribute the saying to its biblical source, Clark creates a more affirmative modality characteristic of epideictic, and combined with the praise, figurality, eloquence, and gnomic aspect that pervade the opinion, it is clear that Clark responded to the situation of *Gobitis* with an insistent paean to religious liberty.

When the school appealed Judge Clark's decision to the United States Supreme Court, the Court agreed to hear the appeal. In an 8:1 decision that met with substantial criticism from the legal community and the popular press, the Court reversed the district court and the court of appeals and held that Pennsylvania's compulsory flag salute statute did not violate the rights of the Gobitis children. Justice Frankfurter began the Court's majority opinion in *Gobitis* with a somber tone of self-dramatization that elevated the Court's authority through praise, repetition, parallelism, eloquence, the gnomic aspect, and affirmative modality:

> A grave responsibility confronts this Court whenever in course of litigation it must reconcile the conflicting claims of liberty and authority. But when the liberty invoked is liberty of conscience, and the authority is authority to safeguard the nation's fellowship, judicial conscience is put to its severest test.[56]

This opening passage of *Gobitis* illustrates how appeals to judicial restraint and epideictic registers, while often alternative rhetorical strategies for legitimizing decisions, can also be combined to dramatic effect.

After reciting the facts and identifying the legal issue in the case, Justice Frankfurter praised the capacity of religious liberty to deal with the "ultimate mystery of the universe." He used praise, metaphor, antithesis, repetition, asyndeton, eloquence, the gnomic aspect, and a relative absence of epistemic qualifiers to magnify the value of religious liberty around this theme:

> Certainly the affirmative pursuit of one's convictions about the ultimate mystery of the universe and man's relation to it is placed beyond the reach of law. Government may not interfere with organized or individual expression of belief or disbelief. Propagation of belief—or even of disbelief—in the supernatural is protected, whether in church or chapel, mosque or synagogue, tabernacle or meeting-house.

Despite his praise of religious liberty, however, Frankfurter concluded that at times the "manifold character of man's relations may bring his conception of religious duty into conflict with the secular interests of his fellowmen."[57] Although Justice Frankfurter acknowledged that the Court dealt with "interests so subtle and so dear, every possible leeway should be given to the claims of religious faith," and "no single principle can answer all of life's complexities," he nonetheless argued that the right to religious liberty, "however dissident and however obnoxious to the cherished beliefs of others—even of a majority—is itself the denial of an absolute." To affirm freedom of conscience without limits, he wrote, "would deny that very plurality of principles which, as a matter of history, underlies protection of religious toleration."[58]

The basic gesture of these early passages of Frankfurter's opinion in *Gobitis*, in other words, was to magnify the value of religious liberty only as a form of paramologia, or strategic concession, serving to amplify by contrast his greater paean to national unity which animated the rest of the opinion. A paramologia nearly reversing these priorities—conceding the value of national unity to amplify freedom of expression and belief by contrast instead—would later find expression in *Barnette* as it did in First Amendment jurisprudence both before and after *Gobitis*. This central gesture of the epideictic registers of Frankfurter's opinion demonstrates the anachronistic quality of his opinion and may help explain why the case was reversed in such rapid fashion.

Justice Frankfurter began his paean to national unity in *Gobitis* by extolling the importance of an individual's corresponding duty to secular law. "In the course of the long struggle for religious toleration," he wrote, the right of conscience did not relieve the individual from obedience to "a general law not aimed at the promotion or restriction of religious beliefs." The mere possession of religious convictions which contradict secular law, he wrote, did not relieve anyone of their political responsibilities.[59] Then in a gnomic saying that forms one of the most famous lines of *Gobitis*, Frankfurter shifted attention from unity to security: "National unity is the basis of national security," an interest "inferior to none in the hierarchy of legal values."[60] With unity thus tied to security, Frankfurter finally framed the issue in dramatically existential terms by comparing it to the Civil War, describing it as a phase of the "profoundest problem confronting a democracy—the problem which Lincoln cast in memorable dilemma: 'Must a government of necessity be too *strong* for the liberties of its people, or too *weak* to maintain its own existence?'"[61] Lincoln's question derives from his Address to a Special Session of Congress on July 4, 1861, addressing whether to go to war with the seceding states.[62]

With the apparent conflict between religious liberty and national security established in these terms, Justice Frankfurter's paean to unity and the American flag began in earnest, incorporating praise, exergasia, enumeration, antithesis, parallelism, eloquence, the gnomic aspect, and affirmative modality:

> The ultimate foundation of a free society is the binding tie of cohesive sentiment[,]...fostered by all those agencies of the mind and spirit which may serve to gather up the traditions of a people, transmit them from generation to generation, and thereby create that continuity of a treasured common life which constitutes a civilization. "We live by symbols." The flag is the symbol of our national unity, transcending all internal differences, however large, within the framework of the Constitution. This Court has had occasion to say that "the flag is the symbol of the Nation's power, the emblem of freedom in its truest, best sense it signifies government resting on the consent of the governed; liberty regulated by law; the protection of the weak against the strong; security against the exercise of arbitrary power; and absolute safety for free institutions against foreign aggression."[63]

This passage and accompanying language in *Gobitis* caused some editorials in major newspapers to attribute the decision to war hysteria.[64]

In a commonplace of debates regarding the conflict between security and other values, Frankfurter concluded by arguing that without respect for the flag no other rights were possible: "The preciousness of the family relation, the authority and independence which give dignity to parenthood, indeed the enjoyment of all freedom, presuppose the kind of ordered society which is summarized by our flag." A society dedicated to preserving "these ultimate values of civilization," he wrote, may "in self-protection utilize the educational process for inculcating those almost unconscious feelings which bind men together in a comprehending loyalty, whatever may be their lesser differences and difficulties."[65]

The Court's decision in *Gobitis* was poorly received by the overwhelming majority of law and political science journals and by popular media outlets. The editorial comments in 171 of the larger newspapers throughout the country disapproved of the decision. Despite this public disapprobation, the refusal of Jehovah's Witness children to participate in compulsory flag salute ceremonies resulted in the expulsion of children in at least thirty-one states following the decision,[66] and on January 9, 1942, the West Virginia Board of Education ordered that the flag salute become "a regular part of the program of activities in the public schools."

The school board's resolution requiring the salute required that all teachers and students "participate in the salute honoring the Nation represented by the Flag" and that refusal to salute the flag be regarded as "an act of insubordination," and it was preceded by a preamble containing lengthy recitals from Justice Frankfurter's opinion as justification.[67] It was in this context that after only a few years the Court reversed *Gobitis* in *Barnette* when the parents of Witness children sought an injunction prohibiting enforcement of the West Virginia order that had been premised on the Court's own opinion.

In his opinion for the majority in *Barnette*, Justice Robert Jackson began in simpler terms than Justice Frankfurter had in *Gobitis*. Jackson first recited the facts and concerns that had brought the case before the Court, recognizing both that the West Virginia flag salute resolution contained recitals from the Court's opinion in *Gobitis* and that many had complained that the Bellamy salute required by the resolution was "too much like Hitler's."[68] Amplifying the harm that *Gobitis* had caused, Jackson noted that Jehovah's Witness children had been expelled and threatened with expulsion for refusing to participate in the salute, that officials had threatened to send them to reformatories maintained for criminally inclined juveniles, and that their parents had been prosecuted and threatened with prosecution for causing delinquency.[69]

Rather than frame the case in terms of religious liberty as the courts had in *Gobitis*, Justice Jackson approached compulsory flag salutes as compelled speech that violated the First Amendment's free speech protections. He began by establishing the flag salute as a form of utterance using a characteristically epideictic register:

> Symbolism is a primitive but effective way of communicating ideas. The use of an emblem or flag to symbolize some system, idea, institution, or personality, is a short cut from mind to mind. Causes and nations, political parties, lodges and ecclesiastical groups seek to knit the loyalty of their followings to a flag or banner, a color or design. The State announces rank, function, and authority through crowns and maces, uniforms and black robes; the church speaks through the Cross, the Crucifix, the altar and shrine, and clerical raiment. Symbols of State often convey political ideas just as religious symbols come to convey theological ones. Associated with many of these symbols are appropriate gestures of acceptance or respect: a salute, a bowed or bared head, a bended knee. A person gets from a symbol

the meaning he puts into it, and what is one man's comfort and inspiration is another's jest and scorn."⁷⁰

The dense convergence of praise, exergasia, enumeration, antithesis, asyndeton, parallelism, eloquence, the gnomic aspect, and affirmative modality in this passage is augmented by its historical scope and by Jackson's alignment of political with religious symbols.

Justice Jackson then discussed First Amendment precedent before shifting to an epideictic register again in the last several pages of the opinion, a lengthy peroration that began with a gnomic saying that incorporated epanalepsis or perhaps a form of chiasmus: "Government of limited power need not be anemic government."⁷¹ Jackson then specifically responded to Justice Frankfurter's provocative quotation of Lincoln in *Gobitis*, writing that "without promise of a limiting Bill of Rights it is doubtful if our Constitution could have mustered enough strength to enable its ratification," and "to enforce those rights today is not to choose weak government over strong government." Instead, Jackson wrote, "it is only to adhere as a means of strength to individual freedom of mind in preference to officially disciplined uniformity for which history indicates a disappointing and disastrous end."⁷²

Justice Jackson characterized Justice Frankfurter's paean to unity in *Gobitis* as the "very heart of the *Gobitis* opinion," then derided it in a lengthy invective that culminated in an enthymematic cap in the gnomic aspect:

> Struggles to coerce uniformity of sentiment in support of some end thought essential to their time and country have been waged by many good as well as by evil men. Nationalism is a relatively recent phenomenon but at other times and places the ends have been racial or territorial security, support of a dynasty or regime, and particular plans for saving souls. As first and moderate methods to attain unity have failed, those bent on its accomplishment must resort to an ever-increasing severity. As governmental pressure toward unity becomes greater, so strife becomes more bitter as to whose unity it shall be. Probably no deeper division of our people could proceed from any provocation than from finding it necessary to choose what doctrine and whose program public educational officials shall compel youth to unite in embracing. Ultimate futility of such attempts to compel coherence is the lesson of every such effort from the Roman drive to

stamp out Christianity as a disturber of its pagan unity, the Inquisition, as a means to religious and dynastic unity, the Siberian exiles as a means to Russian unity, down to the fast failing efforts of our present totalitarian enemies. Those who begin coercive elimination of dissent soon find themselves exterminating dissenters. Compulsory unification of opinion achieves only the unanimity of the graveyard.[73]

Jackson quickly followed this invective with a rapid succession of highly conspicuous figures including antithesis, conduplicatio, and chiasmus, writing that the First Amendment was "designed to avoid these ends by avoiding these beginnings" and that "authority here is to be controlled by public opinion, not public opinion by authority."[74]

Justice Jackson wrote that the case was only difficult because "the flag involved is our own," and he argued that "we apply the limitations of the Constitution with no fear that freedom to be intellectually and spiritually diverse or even contrary will disintegrate the social organization." A fear that free and voluntary patriotism will fail to appear, he wrote, is "to make an unflattering estimate of the appeal of our institutions to free minds." In the form of a paramologia which contests Justice Frankfurter's paramologia in *Gobitis*, Jackson wrote that individualism and the cultural diversity of "exceptional minds" come "at the price of occasional eccentricity and abnormal attitudes," but "when they are so harmless to others or to the State as those we deal with here, the price is not too great." In the final lines of his peroration, Jackson repeated this argument by stating that if freedom to disagree were "limited to things that do not matter much," it would be "a mere shadow of freedom." Instead, "the test of its substance is the right to differ as to things that touch the heart of the existing order."[75]

Finally, Justice Jackson concluded the opinion with his famous metaphor of a fixed star in a constitutional constellation: "If there is any fixed star in our constitutional constellation, it is that no official, high or petty, can prescribe what shall be orthodox in politics, nationalism, religion, or other matters of opinion or force citizens to confess by word or act their faith therein."[76] Haig Bosmajian describes this metaphor from *Barnette* as "the most memorable and influential tropological passage" among many of Jackson's metaphors to be quoted in later opinions,[77] and Sanford Levinson describes it as "one of the most quoted sentences in all constitutional law."[78] Jackson's constellation metaphor magnifies the value of freedom from compelled speech not only beyond the reach of any other constitutional value but beyond the audience's perceptual capacities to the level of the sublime.

Justices Hugo Black and William Douglas wrote a brief concurring opinion in *Barnette* explaining their "change of view" on the flag salute issue since *Gobitis*, which they had joined. They began their opinion by acknowledging that although the principle *Gobitis* recognized of deferring to state legislation believed to be inimical to the public good was sound, "its application in the particular case was wrong,"[79] and they concluded their opinion with a peroration that featured a brief epideictic moment reflecting praise, repetition, parallelism, eloquence, the gnomic aspect, and affirmative modality:

> Words uttered under coercion are proof of loyalty to nothing but self-interest. Love of country must spring from willing hearts and free minds, inspired by a fair administration of wise laws enacted by the people's elected representatives within the bounds of express constitutional prohibitions."[80]

Although Justice Frankfurter unsurprisingly wrote a dissenting opinion in *Barnette*, it differed substantially from his opinion in *Gobitis*. In *Barnette*, Frankfurter distanced himself from his paean to national unity in *Gobitis* and instead limited his opinion to magnifying the value of judicial restraint.[81]

"Were my purely personal attitude relevant I should wholeheartedly associate myself with the general libertarian views in the Court's opinion," Justice Frankfurter wrote in *Barnette*, "representing as they do the thought and action of a lifetime." He wrote that as a justice on the Court, however, "I am not justified in writing my private notions of policy into the Constitution, no matter how deeply I may cherish them or how mischievous I may deem their disregard."[82] These words hardly form a rousing refrain in support of the transcendent unity symbolized by the flag which Frankfurter advanced in *Gobitis*, a refrain that led to his words populating the preamble of the flag salute resolution at issue in *Barnette*. In *Gobitis*, Frankfurter had used the passive subjunctive phrase *even were we convinced of the folly* to refer to the flag salute in order to distance himself from substantive disagreement with the salute,[83] while in *Barnette* he used the active form *we may deem it a foolish measure*, consistent with his new-found declaration that he did not agree with the salute.[84] By the end of his dissent in *Barnette*, Frankfurter even framed the conclusion as obvious: "Of course patriotism can not be enforced by the flag salute."[85] The point was not the wisdom or folly of the salute, he argued in *Barnette*, but that "this Court is not the organ of government to resolve doubts as to whether it will fulfill its purpose."[86]

Justice Frankfurter's dissenting opinion in *Barnette* spanned a lengthy twenty-five pages almost entirely devoted to the use of exergasia to magnify the value of judicial restraint, developing this central tenet in varied forms. "The admonition that judicial self-restraint alone limits arbitrary exercise of our authority is relevant every time we are asked to nullify legislation," he wrote, a deference to legislative authority that he called "the very essence of our constitutional system and the democratic conception of our society."[87] He emphasized that "this is no dry, technical matter," nor of "ephemeral significance," but an "august" one that "cuts deep into one's conception of the democratic process."[88] He warned the Court against succumbing to "the pressures of the day," writing that "our system is built on the faith that men set apart for this special function, freed from the influences of immediacy and from the deflections of worldly ambition, will become able to take a view of longer range."[89] Although Frankfurter devoted some attention to magnifying the value of judicial restraint in *Gobitis*, it held a secondary emphasis compared to his soaring paean to national unity which is entirely absent from his opinion in *Barnette*.

In Justice Frankfurter's peroration in *Barnette*, he quoted extensively from legal theorist James Thayer's autobiography of Chief Justice John Marshall, introducing Thayer's autobiography as a competing paramologia in response to Justice Jackson's concession of the dangers of free speech. Frankfurter's competing paramologia in *Barnette* also differed substantially from the paramologia that he had advanced in *Gobitis*. In contrast to *Gobitis*, in which Frankfurter had conceded the importance of religious liberty only to magnify the value of national unity by contrast, in *Barnette* he conceded that the invalidation of unconstitutional legislation could sometimes be justified only to magnify the value of legislative supremacy as a privileged forum for free speech which outweighed the value of all but the most conservative approaches to judicial review. As quoted by Frankfurter, Thayer wrote:

> I venture to think that the good which came to the country and its people from the vigorous thinking that had to be done in the political debates

that followed [the passage of unconstitutional laws], from the infiltration through every part of the population of sound ideas and sentiments, from the rousing into activity of opposite elements, the enlargement of ideas, the strengthening of moral fiber, and the growth of political experience that came out of it all—that all this far more than outweighed any evil which ever flowed from the refusal of the court to interfere with the work of the legislature.[90]

In *Barnette*, not only did Frankfurter abandon his paean to national unity but he also abandoned the paramologia at the heart of his *Gobitis* opinion in which he had argued that national unity, as the basis of national security, constituted an interest "inferior to none in the hierarchy of legal values."[91] In his dissenting opinion in *Barnette*, Frankfurter argued that judicial deference to the legislature outweighed judicial authority to invalidate legislation that violated the First Amendment's free speech protections. According to the Thayer excerpt which Frankfurter relied on in *Barnette*, the "tendency of a common and easy resort to this great function" of judicial review, "now lamentably too common, is to dwarf the political capacity of the people and to deaden its sense of moral responsibility."[92] The Court's majority was not protecting freedom of speech in its greatest forum, Frankfurter concluded, which was the legislature.

The Fitting Remedy for Bad Speech

Robert Tsai writes that *Barnette* "simultaneously affirmed the integrity of individuals' intensely held outlook and ethics and required that they subscribe to a particular set of democratic values."[93] Justice Jackson's opinion responded to the threat to social unity posed by the flag salute issue by incorporating extended epideictic registers proclaiming a set of beliefs, desires, and ethical commitments he believed would legitimize it, but in a manner substantially different from Justice Frankfurter's response to a similar situation, separated only by the distance of World War II, in which Frankfurter had promoted national unity. Jackson's paramologia in *Barnette* proclaiming that the First Amendment guarantee of freedom of speech came "at the price of occasional eccentricity and abnormal attitudes" revealed a common gesture in First Amendment jurisprudence expressed in its epideictic content. The figure is made all the more salient by its conflict with Frankfurter's paramologias in both *Gobitis* and *Barnette* as well as by the fact that the form of Jackson's paramologia, not Frankfurter's, is more closely aligned with the predominant gesture of American jurisprudence regarding the values that inform the interpretation of the First Amendment's protections of freedom of speech both before and since *Gobitis*.

In the following passage from Justice Louis Brandeis's concurring opinion in *Whitney v. California* (1927), for example, in which the Court upheld a conviction under the California Criminal Syndicalism Act for allegedly promoting the violent overthrow of government—later overruled by *Brandenburg v. Ohio* (1969)—Brandeis offered a powerful paramologia to the inherent risks of freedom of speech using a combination of praise, antithesis, anadiplosis, eloquence, the gnomic aspect, and a relatively affirmative modality aside from its grounding in the perspective of the American colonists:

> Those who won our independence believed...that public discussion is a political duty; and that this should be a fundamental principle of the American government. They recognized the risks to which all human institutions are subject. But they knew that order cannot be secured merely through fear of punishment for its infraction; that it is hazardous to discourage thought, hope and imagination; that fear breeds repression; that repression breeds hate; that hate menaces stable government; that the path of safety lies in the opportunity to discuss freely supposed grievances and proposed remedies; and that the fitting remedy for evil counsels is good ones. Believing in the power of reason as applied through public discussion, they eschewed silence coerced by law—the argument of force in its worst form. Recognizing the occasional tyrannies of governing majorities, they amended the Constitution so that free speech and assembly should be guaranteed.[94]

This passage of Brandeis's opinion in *Whitney* has been quoted in many later judicial opinions, including Brandeis's gnomic saying "the fitting remedy for evil counsels is good ones," which has itself been quoted fifty-five times.[95]

Writing for the majority in *Bridges v. California* (1941), in which the Court overturned contempt of court fines for threatening a strike if a judicial case resulted in an unfavored outcome and for publishing the threat,

Justice Hugo Black wrote that "it is a prized American privilege to speak one's mind, although not always with perfect good taste, on all public institutions."[96] Similarly, in *United States v. Associated Press* (1943), in which the United States District Court for the Southern District of New York held that the First Amendment did not protect newspapers from liability under the Sherman Antitrust Act, Judge Learned Hand wrote that the First Amendment's protection of freedom of speech "presupposes that right conclusions are more likely to be gathered out of a multitude of tongues, than through any kind of authoritative selection," and that while "to many this is, and always will be, folly[,] we have staked upon it our all."[97]

In *New York Times v. Sullivan* (1964), in which the Court held that the First Amendment's protection of freedom of speech requires that a public official must prove actual malice to establish a claim for defamation, Justice William Brennan acknowledged the risks that freedom of speech would yield uncivil speech:

> We consider this case against the background of a profound national commitment to the principle that debate on public issues should be uninhibited, robust, and wide-open, and that it may well include vehement, caustic, and sometimes unpleasantly sharp attacks on government and public officials.[98]

Finally, concession to the risks of free speech appears in Justice William Douglas's dissenting opinion in *United States v. White* (1971), in which the Court held that the admission of evidence from conversations between a defendant and an undercover informant collected through electronic surveillance did not violate the Fourth Amendment protection against unreasonable searches and seizures:

> Free discourse—a First Amendment value—may be frivolous or serious, humble or defiant, reactionary or revolutionary, profane or in good taste; but it is not free if there is surveillance. Free discourse liberates the spirit, though it may produce only froth. The individual must keep some facts concerning his thoughts within a small zone of people. At the same time he must be free to pour out his woes or inspirations or dreams to others. He remains the sole judge as to what must be said and what must remain unspoken. This is the essence of the idea of privacy implicit in the First and Fifth Amendments as well as in the Fourth.[99]

In these and many other examples, courts have used epideictic registers to magnify the value of free speech through strategic concessions to its risks, positioning the risks as a sacrifice worthy of the high value that the freedom affords. The Court could alternatively have minimized the risks of free speech or the scope of the risks rather than acknowledge them. As Chaïm Perelman and Lucie Olbrechts-Tyteca note, "concession is above all the antidote to lack of moderation" which strengthens an argument and makes it easier to defend by restricting the scope of a claim while expressing the fact that "one gives a favorable reception to some of the opponent's real or presumed arguments."[100] In addition to this quality, however, paramologia amplifies by creating a contrast between the elements of an argument conceded and those that are not.

Desecrating the Flag

Paramologia also formed a central gesture of epideictic registers in the Court's First Amendment jurisprudence in *Texas v. Johnson* (1989), in which the Court held that a criminal law prohibiting the desecration of the American flag violated the First Amendment.[101] *Johnson* emerged from an event in which Gregory Johnson burned an American flag during a protest of the Reagan administration at the 1984 Republican National Convention in Dallas, Texas, while protesters chanted "America, the red, white and blue, we spit on you." As a result of his act of burning the flag, Johnson was arrested and convicted of desecrating a flag in violation of Texas law.[102] Justice William Brennan wrote the majority opinion for the Court, and Justice Anthony Kennedy wrote a concurring opinion, both of which featured paramologias to free speech. Joined by Justices Byron White and Sandra Day O'Connor, Justice William Rehnquist published an infamously hyperbolic dissenting opinion which has been characterized by one commentator as a "flowery description of history and significance of the flag,"[103] to which both Brennan and Kennedy responded. Both Brennan and Kennedy lamented the Court's decision in dramatic paramologias despite their support of the decision, and all three of the opinions exhibited epideictic features that spoke to the threat to social unity the case posed.

In his majority opinion in *Johnson*, Justice Brennan wrote that "the flag's deservedly cherished place in our community will be strengthened, not weakened, by our holding today," and he expounded the principles represented by the flag in an eloquent statement exhibiting praise, metaphor, antithesis, repetition, eloquence, the gnomic aspect, and affirmative modality:

> Our decision is a reaffirmation of the principles of freedom and inclusiveness that the flag best reflects, and of the conviction that our toleration of criticism such as Johnson's is a sign and source of our strength. Indeed, one of the proudest images of our flag, the one immortalized in our own national anthem, is of the bombardment it survived at Fort McHenry. It is the Nation's resilience, not its rigidity, that Texas sees reflected in the flag—and it is that resilience that we reassert today.[104]

Brennan followed his antithesis that the community would be strengthened, not weakened, by tolerating criticism with another antithesis extending the point: "The way to preserve the flag's special role is not to punish those who feel differently about these matters. It is to persuade them that they are wrong."[105]

One's response to flag desecration may "exploit the uniquely persuasive power of the flag itself," Justice Brennan wrote, because

> we can imagine no more appropriate response to burning a flag than waving one's own, no better way to counter a flag burner's message than by saluting the flag that burns, no surer means of preserving the dignity even of the flag that burned than by—as one witness here did—according its remains a respectful burial. We do not consecrate the flag by punishing its desecration, for in doing so we dilute the freedom that this cherished emblem represents.[106]

Brennan's eloquent paean to the liberty represented by the flag in these passages used praise, antithesis, mesarchia, asyndeton, and affirmative modality that culminated in a gnomic saying that formed an enthymematic cap to the argument, exhibiting an epideictic register echoed in the other opinions in *Johnson* as the justices engaged in a dueling refrain, or poetic *agôn*,[107] like that between Justices Frankfurter and Jackson in *Gobitis* and *Barnette*. Each of the opinions in *Johnson* performatively responded to the other justices' paeans to patriotism and the flag, revealing the central gestures of belief, desire, and ethical commitment that supported their decisions.

In Justice Kennedy's concurring opinion in *Johnson*, he also lamented the circumstances of the case. "The hard fact is that sometimes we make decisions we do not like," he wrote, conceding the high costs of free speech in what almost constitutes a jeremiad to honoring the flag:

> I agree that the flag holds a lonely place of honor in an age when absolutes are distrusted and simple truths are burdened by unneeded apologetics. With all respect to those views, I do not believe the Constitution gives us the right to rule as the dissenting Members of the Court urge, however painful this judgment is to announce. Though symbols often are what we ourselves make of them, the flag is constant in expressing beliefs Americans share, beliefs in law and peace and that freedom which sustains the human spirit. The case here today forces recognition of the costs to which those beliefs commit us. It is poignant but fundamental that the flag protects those who hold it in contempt.[108]

He concluded his opinion by noting that Johnson "was not a philosopher and perhaps did not even possess the ability to comprehend how repellent his statements must be to the Republic itself," but whether or not Johnson could appreciate "the enormity of the offense he gave, the fact remains that his acts were speech, in both the technical and the fundamental meaning of the Constitution."[109]

In Justice Rehnquist's "flowery" dissenting opinion,[110] he devoted more than the first half of its fifteen pages to cataloging many ways in which the American flag had held an exalted place in American history, including lengthy quotations of poetry and the entire national anthem. These features may tempt the reader to consider his opinion an epideictic register magnifying the value of the flag, and in some measure it is, but Rehnquist's opinion is instructive for how poor an example it is of epideictic despite its reputation for ardent Americanism. It relied almost exclusively on praise and enumeration—and even its praise is less overtly laudatory but presented in the sort of "newspaper-like reportorial" style that Celeste Condit distinguishes from the epideictic accounts of history in the Boston Massacre orations[111]—primarily cataloging evidence of the flag's significance in American history. It offered no particular eloquence aside from brief examples in the poetry and song that Rehnquist quoted, and it incorporated little gnomic content aside from the opening sentence in which Rehnquist quoted Justice Oliver Wendell Holmes's aphorism that "a page of history is worth a volume of logic," which is itself carefully attributed to Holmes both on the text level and with a complete citation. The opinion relied heavily on the perfective aspect rather than offering a poetic refrain in honor of the flag and exhibited highly qualified modality. Perhaps as a result of these features, the opinion is widely criticized as a patriotic caricature rather than emotionally moving prose.

"For more than 200 years," Rehnquist began, "the American flag has occupied a unique position as the symbol of our Nation, a uniqueness that justifies a governmental prohibition against flag burning."[112] At the time of the American Revolution, Rehnquist wrote, "the flag served to unify the Thirteen Colonies at home, while obtaining recognition of national sovereignty abroad." He then quoted the following passage from Ralph Waldo Emerson's "Concord Hymn," which references the flag's presence in the first skirmishes of the Revolutionary War:

> By the rude bridge that arched the flood
> Their flag to April's breeze unfurled,
> Here once the embattled farmers stood
> And fired the shot heard round the world.

Following these introductory passages, Rehnquist cataloged numerous colonial and regimental flags, including their symbols such as pine trees, beavers, anchors, and rattlesnakes, bearing slogans such as "Liberty or Death," "Hope," "An Appeal to Heaven," and "Don't Tread on Me," as well as the flag's appearance on battleships, airplanes, military installations, and public buildings, often in excruciating detail ("the first distinctive flag of the Colonies was the 'Grand Union Flag'—with 13 stripes and a British flag in the left corner—which was flown for the first time on January 2, 1776, by troops of the Continental Army around Boston"). In addition, Rehnquist noted that countless flags are placed by the graves each year on Memorial Day ("the flag is traditionally placed on the casket of deceased members of the Armed Forces, and it is later given to the deceased's family"), and listed the many laws that regulate the care of flags.[113]

Alongside his catalog of historical events, Justice Rehnquist cited poetry and song at some length, including the entire text of the "Star-Spangled Banner" and John Greenleaf Whittier's poem "Barbara Fritchie," but he did not weave the content of the poetry or lyrics into the rhythm of his own writing and always provided careful attribution.

At times the opinion did not even rise to the level of history so much as mere chronicle:

> No other American symbol has been as universally honored as the flag. In 1931, Congress declared "The Star-Spangled Banner" to be our national anthem. 36 U. S. C. § 170. In 1949, Congress declared June 14th to be Flag Day. § 157. In 1987, John Philip Sousa's "The Stars and Stripes Forever" was designated as the national march. Pub. L. 101–186, 101 Stat. 1286. Congress has also established "The Pledge of Allegiance to the Flag" and the manner of its deliverance. 36 U. S. C. § 172. The flag has appeared as the principal symbol on approximately 33 United States postal stamps and in the design of at least 43 more, more times than any other symbol. United States Postal Service, Definitive Mint Set 15 (1988).[114]

Even in the peroration of his discussion of the flag, Rehnquist relied heavily on logical demonstration which gave the opinion a more refutational quality than is typically characteristic of epideictic. While claiming that the flag inspired a mystical reverence among millions of Americans (curiously qualified as "*almost* mystical"), Rehnquist's opinion failed to inspire such reverence:

> The American flag, then, throughout more than 200 years of our history, has come to be the visible symbol embodying our Nation. It does not represent the views of any particular political party, and it does not represent any particular political philosophy. The flag is not simply another "idea" or "point of view" competing for recognition in the marketplace of ideas. Millions and millions of Americans regard it with an almost mystical reverence regardless of what sort of social, political, or philosophical beliefs they may have.[115]

Beyond his sparse use of epideictic features in the opinion, Rehnquist's praise of the flag is also divorced from his legal argument in the latter half of the opinion and features little recognition of alternative epideictic refrains in the majority and concurring opinions or elsewhere, lending it an isolated quality that fails to transcend the threat to social unity posed by the case.

The failure of Justice Rehnquist's paean to the American flag as epideictic explains the criticism the opinion has received and why it has not been cited favorably in later opinions. It lacked the memorable and invitational quality that derives from the convergence of epideictic features which serve epideictic's transcendent function of subsuming the individual agency of speaker and audience within a common framework of value and meaning. Its highly qualified modality in particular failed to sacralize its subject in the manner of successful epideictic. It did not evince a "resoundingly affirmative," "world-affirming" rhetoric like that which John O'Malley attributes to the epideictic sermons of the papal court of the Renaissance,[116] an "extraordinarily affirmative interpretation of man and the world,"[117] nor the "optimistic,…lenient tendency" that Chaïm Perelman and Lucie Olbrechts-Tyteca note of epideictic.[118] There is little leniency in Rehnquist's opinion, and only with difficulty could it be characterized as "mystical,"[119] "prophetic,"[120] or an "encounter with Being."[121]

Dueling Refrains

The register theory of epideictic developed in the previous chapter provides a framework for predicting, identifying, and analyzing epideictic both in discursive genres traditionally classified as epideictic as well as in those perceived to be largely pragmatic such as the judicial opinions in the Court's First Amendment free speech jurisprudence, including the flag salute and desecration cases of *Gobitis*, *Barnette*, and *Johnson*. The epideictic registers in these cases illustrate the interdiscursive relationship between judicial discourse and the ritual and ceremonial discourse of epideictic, in which epideictic forms a central element of judicial persuasion that is neither separate nor secondary to logical demonstration but a primary form of judicial discourse on which logical demonstration depends. Attending to epideictic registers in judicial opinion writing often reveals central gestures that inform opinions, such as the pervasiveness of paramologia in the Court's free speech jurisprudence, figural gestures that link an audience's emotions, senses, and embodied knowledge and which, as Maksymilian Del Mar notes, "simply cannot be captured by explicit propositions."[122]

Far from being dicta, the epideictic registers of judicial opinions form primary and endemic elements of judicial thought grounded in the social dimension of practical reasoning. Such registers serve not only to shape attitudes for future action but form an immediate response to situations that inaugurate change with broad social consequences in order to legitimize decisions. In both *Gobitis* and *Barnette*, the justices accused each other of succumbing to wartime hysteria, and after *Johnson* the United States Congress passed an amendment to the Flag Protection Act to prohibit the desecration of the American flag in an effort to legislatively overrule *Johnson*, an act promptly declared unconstitutional by the Court in *United States v. Eichman* (1990).[123] In both the flag salute and desecration contexts, the controversial quality of the situations is readily apparent, a condition that invites epideictic registers such as those found in the cases. The question of honor implicated by the flag controversies may have particularly intensified the need for such registers.

The dueling refrains, or poetic *agôns*,[124] of the epideictic registers in *Gobitis*, *Barnette*, and *Johnson* not only illustrate the agonistic dimension of epideictic as justices responded to each other's paeans to national unity, freedom of conscience, legislative supremacy, freedom of speech, and the American flag, but reveal a specific conflict between the justices surrounding the central figure of paramologia that emerged in the registers. In both *Gobitis* and *Barnette*, Justice Frankfurter sought to advance alternatives to the predominant form that paramologia took in the Court's free speech jurisprudence before and after the cases, a predominant form which consistently acknowledged and lamented the dangers of free speech while amplifying its benefits by contrast. In *Gobitis*, Frankfurter acknowledged the importance of religious liberty only to amplify the benefits of national unity by contrast, and in *Barnette* he acknowledged judicial authority to invalidate compulsory flag salutes only to amplify a preference for legislative speech by contrast. The anachronistic quality of Frankfurter's paramologias in the cases serves to explain the Court's reversal of *Gobitis* in such a short span of time better than a logical analysis can, as the beliefs, values, and ethical commitments of Frankfurter's opinions were inconsistent with those of the Court's First Amendment free speech jurisprudence across the wider era. They reflect a failure to recognize the nation's character or what it had resolved to become.

A similar failure is evident in Justice Rehnquist's dissenting opinion in *Johnson*, which despite its catalog of the exalted place the American flag had held in history and its lengthy quotations of poetry and song, relied on the perfective aspect and a highly qualified modality in a manner that privileged inexorable logic over the impassioned promotion of beliefs, desires, and ethical commitments that would legitimize his decision. Rehnquist's opinion neither responded to the epideictic refrains in the majority and concurring opinions nor conceded any dangers to freedom of speech by prohibiting the burning of the flag in protest, even in the form of a paramologia that would amplify the benefits of protecting the flag. The opinion instead largely declined to respond to the epideictic situation of the case, rendering it isolated, peevish, and caricatured.

In Ernesto Grassi's discussion of rhetorical thought as the primary form of philosophy, he argues that the original assertions on which rational thought are based are figurative and metaphorical rather than argumentative, noting that "even logical language must resort to metaphor."[125] Such original assertions cannot have "an apodictic, demonstrable character and structure but are thoroughly *indicative*" or "allusive," he writes, providing "the framework within which…proof can come into existence" while being incomprehensible through rational language and thought alone. Their "primal clarity" stands in contrast to the clarifying function of logical demonstration because they do not arise from logic but from indicative language which possesses a "prophetic" and "'evangelic' character," a "showing" that is both figurative and imaginative.[126] The panegyric or eulogy, Grassi writes, presents "a measure or standard according to which the past and future can be evaluated," or "what is exemplary and to which every judgment about men, actions, or situations must be referred."[127] The development of such standards through epideictic discourse accordingly cultivates an ethical dimension of judgment.

Because indicative language is figurative, Grassi writes, it possesses an "original pathetic essence" and from a formal perspective belongs to the "sacred, religious word" outside of historical time. The fact that "every original, former, 'archaic' speech…cannot have a rational but only a rhetorical character" signifies the primacy of rhetorical thought as philosophy rather than a mere art or "technique of an external persuasion,"[128] an original unity of *pathos* and *logos* rather than a "posterior synthesis" of the two derived from rational thought.[129] True rhetorical speech, Grassi writes, is "nondeducible, moving, and indicative, due to its original images," that of "the wise man, or the *sophos*, who is not only *epistetai* [knowing], but who with insight leads, guides, and attracts,"[130] a description that closely parallels Cicero's description of the ideal statesmen who is consulted not only on points of law but about "marrying off a daughter, buying a farm, tilling their estates, and in short every sort of liability or business."[131]

Although Eugene Garver emphasizes the unity of *ethos* and *logos*, like Grassi he questions the separation of form and content represented by modern rationalism and sees in epideictic a paradigmatic form of practical reasoning. According to Garver, practical reasoning "flourishes when a community recognizes that impractical-looking forms of discourse such as philosophy, epideictic rhetoric, and the celebration of common symbols are indeed practical."[132] To hide one's commitments and act "as though practical reasoning was an inferential relation between propositions, not between the assertion of propositions," he writes, "may be not only an ethical error but a less rational argument,"[133] as "an ethical or an emotional argument can sometimes be more rational than an argument that tries to rely on reason alone."[134] The epideictic registers of judicial opinions which speak to the beliefs, desires, and ethical commitments that may legitimize judicial decisions, in other words, do not reflect improper or superfluous content but practical reasoning, and failing to respond appropriately to the threat to social unity posed by such situations is an ethical failure. "If jurisprudence is an ethical rather than a mathematical matter," writes Garver, "the exclusion of *ethos* is itself unethical and untrustworthy."[135] Behind the "ritualized dance of carefully balanced reasons" in judicial opinions, he writes, "lies something that both judges and their audience must believe in order to find the assertion of authority morally convincing" rather than a raw assertion of power.[136]

The epideictic registers in the Court's First Amendment free speech jurisprudence discussed in this chapter reveal the relationship between epideictic and practical reasoning along with the ethical dimensions of epideictic in judicial opinion writing as judges move beyond the certain knowledge on which mathematical models of legal reasoning are based and accept responsibility for the beliefs, desires, and ethical commitments on which their decisions are based, not concealing them but openly and passionately magnifying them. Such discourse reveals judges as the *sophos* who Grassi describes as not only knowing but who with insight "leads, guides, and attracts,"[137] or in Jeffrey Walker's words, leads their audience "to contemplation (*theôria*) and insight and ultimately to the formation of opinions and desires on matters of philosophical, social, ethical, and cultural concern."[138] The following chapter examines the epideictic registers in the Court's early Religion Clause jurisprudence regarding the proper relationship between religion and government in public schools. In this jurisprudence, much like the central role that paramologia played in free speech jurisprudence, the figure of chiasmus emerged as a central gesture in the epideictic registers of the Court's opinions regarding the relationship between religious and secular life.

CHAPTER 3

Keeping Government Out of Religion and Vice Versa

In *Goodson v. Northside Bible Church* (1966), Judge Daniel Thomas of the United States District Court for the Southern District of Alabama wrote that "no constitutional principle is more firmly imbedded in our heritage" than "what Jefferson termed 'the wall of separation between Church and State,'" a principle that Thomas wrote was "fundamental to our liberty."[1] To support this conclusion, Thomas cited both the wall metaphor drawn from Thomas Jefferson's 1802 letter to the Danbury Connecticut Baptist Association—in which Jefferson wrote that he revered the Religion Clauses of the First Amendment for "building a wall of separation between Church and State," a phrase perhaps inspired by early American sources such as Roger Williams's 1644 letter to John Cotton[2]—and the precursor of the Religion Clauses found in James Madison's 1785 *Remonstrance and Memorial against Religious Assessments*.[3] As Haig Bosmajian notes of the wall metaphor often attributed to Jefferson, "no other metaphor has been so directly defended and challenged" by Supreme Court justices or had its figurality highlighted as extensively and consciously.[4] "The words 'separation of church and state' are an accurate and convenient shorthand [for] the First Amendment itself,"[5] writes R. Freeman Butts, and the words have become, as Daniel Dreisbach describes, "more familiar to the American people than the actual text of the First Amendment."[6]

Although the wall metaphor was first cited by the Court in a nineteenth-century polygamy case, its power as a means of understanding the Religion Clauses and the controversy surrounding the metaphor began with Justice Hugo Black's majority opinion in *Everson v. Board of Education* (1947). In *Everson*, Black wrote that "the First Amendment has erected a wall between church and state" which "must be kept high and impregnable," preventing "the slightest breach"[7]—a formulation which Robert Tsai notes is "clean, if somewhat chilling"[8]—and for years after *Everson* the metaphor proliferated in Religion Clause opinions written by justices on all sides of the issue.

As early as *McCollum v. Board of Education* (1948), however, not only did Justice Stanley Reed object that "a rule of law should not be drawn from a figure of speech"—a statement that itself combines the gnomic aspect, metaphor, and parallelism[9]—but four of the concurring justices expressed doubts about the wall of separation metaphor, and over time the metaphor met with substantial critique and disfavor on the Court for its sweeping and rigid implications.[10] The Court explored alternative metaphors over the years by construing the Religion Clauses as representing an imperfect "line," a "scale" in which religion and government are balanced, a "boundary" designed to avoid excessive "entanglements," and a "tight rope" to be "traversed,"[11] but Chief Justice Warren Burger's majority opinion in *Lemon v. Kurtzman* (1971) perhaps epitomized opposition to the metaphor by stating that "the line of separation, far from being a 'wall,' is a blurred, indistinct, and variable barrier depending on all the circumstances of a particular relationship."[12] While the status of the wall of separation metaphor has deteriorated in the Court's opinion writing since *Lemon*, it still persists both in judicial opinion writing on the Religion Clauses and in the public imagination of the constitutionally defined relationship between religion and government.

Attending to the epideictic registers in the Court's early Religion Clause jurisprudence reveals the central role that another figure plays in the Court's thought regarding the Religion Clauses, however, specifically the figure of chiasmus exemplified in Justice Robert Jackson's expression of the relationship between the Religion Clauses in his dissenting opinion in *Everson*, as one "intended not only to keep the states' hands out of religion, but to keep religion's hands off the state."[13] As a figure of thought or arrangement, the term *chiasmus* derives from the Greek letter *chi* (X), referring to a transposition or crossing, and is used to refer to any inverted parallelism or repetition of ideas or grammatical structures in reverse order, whether on the discourse level across large portions of a text or entire text or distilled stylistically in the sort of inverted bicolon reflected in Jackson's dissent in *Everson*. When words are repeated in reverse order at the level of inverted clauses, particularly in a bicolon such as Jackson's, a specific variety of chiasmus known as antimetabole is formed, sometimes expressed in shorthand by the Latin phrase vice versa.[14] Justice Hugo Black, for example, wrote in his majority opinion in *Everson* that "neither a state nor the Federal Government can, openly or secretly, participate in the affairs of any religious organizations or groups and *vice versa*."[15] The relationship between religion and government is prevalently expressed through the figure of chiasmus both in Madison's *Remonstrance and Memorial* on which many of the Court's justices rely in their early writing on the Religion Clauses and in the Court's Religion Clause jurisprudence itself, serving as a central gesture in the Court's epideictic registers in religion cases.

The inverted parallelism reflected in the figure of chiasmus has an ancient lineage that predates its appearance in Greek rhetoric, appearing much earlier in Sumero-Akkadian and Ugaritic texts from the third millennium BCE as well as in the Hebrew and Christian scriptures,[16] and the figure is ubiquitous in ancient rhetoric, poetics, and wisdom literature, including eulogies.[17] It is sometimes noted for its "almost ritual enactment."[18] Far from representing a merely stylistic figure, chiasmus is "one of the earliest forms of thought," Rodolphe Gasché writes, an "originary form" that "allows the drawing apart and the bringing together of opposite functions or terms and entwines them within an identity of movements" while also infinitely deferring closure through the "substitutability implied by its asymmetry."[19] According to Robert Hariman, the chiasmus "moves one towards a center that proves to be empty, a space only for crossing," a movement that ultimately lends itself to "mystification."[20]

Among famous examples of chiasmus, Gorgias of Leontini famously advised advocates to "kill your opponents' earnestness with jesting and their jesting with earnestness."[21] Parallel chiasms bracket Jesus's Parable of the Workers in the Vineyard in the Christian scriptures, offered in response to the apostle Peter's question of what the apostles would receive for their sacrifice. The parable starts with the prophetic expression "many that are first shall be last; and the last shall be first" and ends with the explanatory chiasmus "so the last shall be first, and the first last."[22] The chiasmus has sometimes even simply been called *hysteron proteron* (that is, "the latter first").[23]

Chiasmus has also served as an important organizing principle for philosophical and legal thought. In the famed Taoist allegory of transformation, the ancient Chinese philosopher Zhuangzi writes that after waking from a dream in which he was a butterfly he questioned whether he was really a man dreaming of being a butterfly or a butterfly dreaming of being a man.[24] Maurice Merleau-Ponty imagines the body-world relationship through a chiasmus, writing that "what begins as a thing ends as consciousness of the thing, what begins as a 'state of consciousness' ends as a thing,"[25] and Ernesto Grassi writes that "the true philosophy is rhetoric, and the true rhetoric is philosophy."[26] In legal thought, Cicero writes that "a magistrate is a speaking law, and a law is a silent magistrate,"[27] and Justice Robert Jackson famously wrote that the Supreme Court is "not final because we are infallible, but we are infallible only because we are final."[28]

Chiasms appear prominently in both the language and structure of Madison's *Remonstrance and Memorial*, a document itself informed by the epideictic situation of the church-state battles of the 1780s and which forms an important precursor of the Religion Clauses.[29] The *Remonstrance* consists of fifteen paragraphs which structurally form a single chiasmus centered around the eighth paragraph, itself containing two chiasms on the sentence level, a figurality which echoed a broader tendency of Madison toward eloquent moderation and harmony.[30] In the first and last paragraphs of the *Remonstrance*, Madison appeals to a general theory of inalienable rights; in paragraphs 2 and 14, he addresses the limits of legislative power; in paragraphs 3 and 13, he addresses the imprudence or impracticability of using law to uphold religion; in paragraphs 4 and 12, he extols the necessity of freedom to religious belief; in paragraphs 5 and 11, he claims the bill will upset an existing harmony between religion and government; and in paragraphs 6–7 and 9–10, he enumerates the corrosive effect the bill will have on religion and government, respectively. In paragraph 8, Madison indicts religious establishment as in some cases erecting a "spiritual tyranny on the ruins of Civil authority" and in others "upholding the thrones of political tyranny"—a chiastic movement depicting religious establishment as either religion exploiting government or government exploiting religion—and concludes with the chiasmus that a just government protects its citizens in their religious freedom no less than in their property, "neither invading the equal rights of any Sect, nor suffering any Sect to invade those of another."[31]

The structure of Madison's *Remonstrance* moves, in other words, from inalienable rights to legislative power to prudence to freedom to harmony to the bill's consequences to the central chiastic paragraph and back again from the bill's consequences to harmony, freedom, prudence, and legislative power. The final paragraph then returns to inalienable rights, proclaiming that we must either say that the legislature may "sweep away all our fundamental rights; or, that they are bound to leave this particular right untouched and sacred."[32]

The claim of the *Remonstrance*'s central paragraph that a just government protects religious freedom no less than property is represented in more explicitly chiastic form in Madison's 1792 essay on property, in which he writes that "as a man is said to have a right to his property, he may be equally said to have a property in his rights." Madison explains the balance of liberty and government which immediately follows this chiasmus with a similar form. "Where an excess of power prevails, property of no sort is duly respected," he writes, because "no man is safe in his opinions, his person, his faculties, or his possessions," but correspondingly "where there is an excess of liberty, the effect is the same, though from an opposite cause." He then repeats the initial chiasmus in the final sentence of the essay: "If the United States mean to obtain or deserve the full praise due to wise and just governments, they will equally respect the rights of property, and the property in rights."[33] If Madison cannot be characterized as a "chiastic personality," in which the chiasmus was so central to his thought that it constituted a psychological condition,[34] the figure was at least central to his thinking about rights and religious freedom in particular, and it is an important precedent to the Religion Clauses of the First Amendment and their interpretation by the Court.

Chiasmus not only "entwines" opposing functions or terms in an "identity of movements,"[35] but as Robert Hariman notes it is fundamentally "a figure of social interaction."[36] Emmanuel Levinas describes "a pleasure of contact at the heart of the chiasm,"[37] and Hariman writes that this social dimension of the figure activates "the cognitive reciprocity of interpersonal exchange prior to all other social patterning."[38] It is "precisely analogous to the visual experience of looking at another person or at one's mirror image," Hariman writes, an experience of doubling which depends on both "proximity and distance, and on there being empty space between one and one's double."[39]

John Ruffin notes that chiasmus "emphasizes both sides of an antithesis,"[40] and Jeanne Fahnestock explains that a chiasmus can suggest "not identity but mutual constitution," as "one term so depends on the other, it does not matter which comes first, an indifference displayed iconically in the syntax of the figure."[41] This leads to a relationship more aligned with abeyance than obstruction,[42] one that according to Hariman "profoundly destabilizes the principles of similarity and difference" and "does not allow one to settle on either side of the equation,"[43] resulting in a "hermeneutical miasma"[44] used when "what needs to be said eludes representation."[45] It is available when "one needs to suggest that there remains more work to do."[46] The basis for resolution between the terms of a chiasmus, Hariman writes, is "always signified only by the crossing, which itself supplies no principle of resolution but rather perpetual oscillation," a "ping-ponging back and forth" like a "small prison house of language."[47] It is also a highly conspicuous figure particularly suited to epideictic. As Elie Assis notes, chiasmus constructs *ethos* because it "often directs the reader to the fact that the text is constructed."[48]

The chiasmatic relationship between religion and government reflected in Madison's *Remonstrance*, in the Religion Clauses of the First Amendment, and in the Court's early Religion Clause jurisprudence represents the "blurred, indistinct, and variable barrier" that Chief Justice Burger described in *Lemon*[49] more than the "high and impregnable wall" of *Everson*.[50] The Court's reliance on the chiasmus in its early cases also suggests, however, that *Lemon*'s interpretation of the Religion Clauses was incipient in the Court's earliest uses of the wall metaphor.

This chapter examines the epideictic registers in the Court's early Religion Clause jurisprudence regarding the relationship between religion and public schools, focusing on *Everson v. Board of Education* (1947), *McCollum v. Board of Education* (1948), and *Lemon v. Kurtzman* (1971). I pay particular attention to the intertextual role played by Madison's *Remonstrance and Memorial* in the epideictic registers of *Everson* and *McCollum* as majority, concurring, and dissenting justices quote and interpret Madison's *Remonstrance* in their opinions. Attending to this dimension of the Court's epideictic registers in its early Religion Clause jurisprudence reveals the central role that the figure of chiasmus plays in the Court's thought regarding the Religion Clauses. A chiasmatic relationship is prevalently expressed both in Madison's thought and in the Court's early Religion Clause jurisprudence, and I argue that the prevalence of this figure serves to interpret the wall of separation between church and state as a more indeterminate, flexible, or unstable relationship than traditional interpretations reflect and one that ultimately ended in irresolution.

The High and Impregnable Wall

The United States Supreme Court first held that the First Amendment's Establishment Clause applied to the states under the Fourteenth Amendment's Due Process Clause in *Everson v. Board of Education* (1947), a case that arose out of a New Jersey bus voucher program that reimbursed parents for money they spent on bus transportation to send their children to and from school, including Catholic schools that gave students both secular education and religious instruction conforming to the Catholic faith.[51] Although the Court concluded in a 5:4 decision that the Establishment Clause applied to the states under the Fourteenth Amendment—intended to create what Thomas Jefferson called a "wall of separation between Church and State" which the Court described as "high and impregnable," admitting not "the slightest breach"—the majority nonetheless found that New Jersey had not breached the high and impregnable wall of separation in the case.[52] The bus voucher program, the Court concluded, amounted only to "public welfare" legislation or "general government services" like police and fire protection, utilities, or public highways and sidewalks, and the Establishment Clause was not designed to deny such services to religious schools.[53]

Justice Hugo Black wrote the majority opinion, Justice Wiley Rutledge published a lengthy dissenting opinion in which Justices Felix Frankfurter, Robert Jackson, and Harold Burton joined, and Justice Jackson published a separate dissenting opinion. Because the case inaugurated a new line of constitutional interpretation with broad social consequences by applying the Establishment Clause to the states, it is not surprising that all of the opinions in the case featured epideictic registers. Both Black's majority opinion and Rutledge's dissent developed their epideictic registers in part through James Madison's *Remonstrance and Memorial* and other writings as well as the text of Thomas Jefferson's *Virginia Bill for Religious Liberty*, which Madison's *Remonstrance* supported, and the epideictic registers of all of the opinions centrally featured chiasms to describe the relationship between religion and government.

Justice Black began his discussion of the constitutional issue in *Everson* by dramatizing the experience of early Americans which led to the Religion Clauses, stating that the clauses "reflected in the minds of early Americans a vivid mental picture of conditions and practices which they fervently wished to stamp out in order to preserve liberty for themselves and for their posterity." Although Black lamented that their goal had "doubtless" not been reached, he wrote that "so far has the Nation moved toward it that the expression 'law respecting an establishment of religion,' probably does not so vividly remind present-day Americans of the evils, fears, and political problems that caused that expression to be written into our Bill of Rights."[54] Building on these features of praise, metaphor, eloquence, and affirmative modality, Black then adopted a sublime historiography, eloquently describing the early American history of the Establishment Clause with enumeration, repetition, and a variety of parallelisms, including chiasmus:

> With the power of government supporting them, at various times and places, Catholics had persecuted Protestants, Protestants had persecuted Catholics, Protestant sects had persecuted other Protestant sects, Catholics of one shade of belief had persecuted Catholics of another shade of belief, and all of these had from time to time persecuted Jews. In efforts to force loyalty to whatever religious group happened to be on top and in league with the government of a particular time and place, men and women had been fined, cast in jail, cruelly tortured, and killed.[55]

In another dramatic history containing all of the features of epideictic except the gnomic aspect and prominently featuring metaphor, enumeration, and asyndeton, Black wrote of the transplantation of these practices from the old world to the new:

> Catholics found themselves hounded and proscribed because of their faith; Quakers who followed their conscience went to jail; Baptists were peculiarly obnoxious to certain dominant Protestant sects; men and women of varied faiths who happened to be in a minority in a particular locality were persecuted because they steadfastly persisted in worshipping God only as their own consciences dictated.[56]

These practices became so commonplace, Black wrote, "as to shock the freedom-loving colonials into a feeling of abhorrence," which the Religion Clauses expressed.[57]

With this historical foundation laid, Justice Black then quoted extensively from the epideictic registers contained in a 1774 letter from Madison to a friend, Madison's *Remonstrance and Memorial*, and the preamble to Jefferson's *Virginia Bill for Religious Liberty*. Beginning with the letter, Black quoted Madison's invective against "that diabolical, hell-conceived principle of persecution [that] rages among some," which he wrote "vexes me the worst of anything whatever." As Madison writes in the letter quoted by Black in *Everson*, "I have squabbled and scolded, abused and ridiculed, so long about it to little purpose, that I am without common patience," and Madison begs his friend to pity him and "pray for liberty of conscience to all."[58] Black then effusively praised Madison's "great" *Remonstrance and Memorial*, paraphrasing Madison's "eloquent" argument as that

> a true religion did not need the support of law; that no person, either believer or non-believer, should be taxed to support a religious institution of any kind; that the best interest of a society required that the minds of men always be wholly free; and that cruel persecutions were the inevitable result of government-established religions.

Black wrote that Madison's arguments received "strong support throughout Virginia," eventually leading the religious assessments bill, against which it remonstrated, to die in committee and to the enactment of Jefferson's bill for religious liberty.[59]

Justice Black then quoted at length from the powerful paean to freedom of conscience in Jefferson's bill for religious liberty, which found among other things that

> Almighty God hath created the mind free; that all attempts to influence it by temporal punishments or burdens, or by civil incapacitations, tend only to beget habits of hypocrisy and meanness, and are a departure from the plan of the Holy author of our religion, who being Lord both of body and mind, yet chose not to propagate it by coercions on either…; that to compel a man to furnish contributions of money for the propagation of opinions which he disbelieves, is sinful and tyrannical; that even the forcing him to support this or that teacher of his own religious persuasion, is depriving him of the comfortable liberty of giving his contributions to the particular pastor, whose morals he would make his pattern.[60]

Toward the conclusion of Black's epideictic treatment of the Religion Clauses he surveyed prior First Amendment cases, concluding that "there is every reason to give the same application and broad interpretation" to the Establishment Clause, a conclusion which he supported with a chiasmus from *Watson v. Jones* (1871): "The structure of our government has, for the preservation of civil liberty, rescued the temporal institutions from religious interference. On the other hand, it has secured religious liberty from the invasion of the civil authority."[61]

Before turning to the Court's holding, Justice Black then wrote a lengthy and densely figured passage featuring various forms of repetition, particularly anaphora, along with asyndeton and the chiasmus referenced in the introduction to this chapter that is signified with the Latin phrase *vice versa*, culminating in Jefferson's wall of separation metaphor. The passage has been quoted at least 123 times in later judicial opinions in the United States[62]:

> The "establishment of religion" clause of the First Amendment means at least this: Neither a state nor the Federal Government can set up a church. Neither can pass laws which aid one religion, aid all religions, or prefer one religion over another. Neither can force nor influence a person to go to or to remain away from church against his will or force him to profess a belief or disbelief in any religion. No person can be punished for entertaining or professing religious beliefs or disbeliefs, for church attendance or non-attendance. No tax in any amount, large or small, can be levied to support any religious activities or institutions, whatever they may be called, or whatever form they may adopt to teach or practice religion. Neither a state nor the Federal Government can, openly or secretly, participate in the affairs of any religious organizations or groups and *vice versa*. In the words of Jefferson, the clause against establishment of religion by law was intended to erect "a wall of separation between Church and State."[63]

After the lengthy and rousing paean to separationism which formed the core of Justice Black's opinion—from the dramatic history of religious persecution in England and early America to the eloquent precursors of the Religion Clauses in the writings of the Founders, prior cases extolling the importance of separationism, and his peroration culminating in Jefferson's wall metaphor—he abruptly returned to a pragmatic register in the final two and a half pages of the opinion. In the final pages, Black argued that while the Religion Clauses had "erected a wall" between religion and government which "must be kept high and impregnable," preventing even the "slightest breach," New Jersey had not breached the wall because reimbursement for busing was similar to other governmentally provided services such as the police, fire department, or public roads.[64] As Justice Robert Jackson wrote in his dissenting opinion, the "undertones" of Black's opinion, advocating "complete and uncompromising separation of Church from State, seem utterly discordant with its conclusion yielding support to their commingling in educational matters." Jackson quoted a passage from Lord Byron's satirical epic *Don Juan* to support this observation: "The case which irresistibly comes to mind as the most fitting precedent is that of Julia who, according to Byron's reports, 'whispering "I will ne'er consent,"—consented.'"[65]

The First Experiment on Our Liberties

Justice Wiley Rutledge wrote a dissenting opinion in *Everson* twice the length of Justice Black's majority opinion not counting its appendices which included the entirety of Madison's *Remonstrance and Memorial* and the proposed bill for religious assessments to which the *Remonstrance* responded. Rutledge started his opinion with two epigraphs: the full text of the Religion Clauses of the First Amendment and the following passages from the preamble and text of Jefferson's 1786 *Virginia Bill for Religious Liberty*:

> Well aware that Almighty God hath created the mind free;...that to compel a man to furnish contributions of money for the propagation of opinions which he disbelieves, is sinful and tyrannical.

> *We, the General Assembly, do enact,* That no man shall be compelled to frequent or support any religious worship, place, or ministry whatsoever, nor shall be enforced, restrained, molested, or burdened in his body or goods, nor shall otherwise suffer, on account of his religious opinions or belief.[66]

The portions of Jefferson's bill for religious liberty in the latter epigraph were also among those quoted in Black's majority opinion.[67]

Justice Rutledge began the opinion with disbelief that the Founders would have joined the majority in *Everson* and lamented that "neither so high nor so impregnable today as yesterday is the wall raised between church and state by Virginia's great statute of religious freedom and the First Amendment."[68] In keeping with his epigraphs, Section I of Rutledge's opinion offered an effusive paean to the text of the Religion Clauses, which he described as "broadly but not loosely phrased," the "compact and exact summation of its author's views formed during his long struggle for religious freedom," and a "'Model of technical precision, and perspicuous brevity.'"[69] As a result, he concluded, Madison "could not have confused 'church' and 'religion,' or 'an established church' and 'and establishment of religion,'" but instead the Religion Clauses were intended to create a "complete and permanent separation of the spheres of religious activity and civil authority by comprehensively forbidding every form of public aid or support for religion."[70] Rutledge then tied the Religion Clauses to their history, writing that "no provision of the Constitution is more closely tied to or given content by its generating history" and that the clauses were at once "the refined product and the terse summation of that history."[71]

What followed in Section II of Justice Rutledge's opinion was a lengthy paean to the history of the Religion Clauses and Madison's struggle for religious liberty, including liberal paraphrases and quotations from Madison's *Remonstrance and Memorial*, a history Rutledge considered "irrefutable confirmation of the Amendment's sweeping content." For both Jefferson and Madison, Rutledge wrote, "religious freedom was the crux of the struggle for freedom in general."[72] As a member of Virginia's General Assembly, Madison threw his "full weight" behind Jefferson's bill for religious liberty, wrote Rutledge, a bill which formed "a prime phase of Jefferson's broad program of democratic reform."[73] According to Rutledge, Madison was "unyielding at all times" in his struggle for religious liberty, opposing the religious assessments bill "with all his vigor" before finally publishing his "historic" *Remonstrance and Memorial*. Rutledge described the *Remonstrance* as Madison's "complete...interpretation of religious liberty," a "broadside attack upon all forms of 'establishment' of religion," at once "the most concise and the most accurate statement" of Madison's views regarding establishment.[74] "Because it behooves us in the dimming distance of time not to lose sight of what he and his coworkers had in mind," Rutledge wrote, "when, by a single sweeping stroke of the pen, they forbade an establishment of religion and secured its free exercise, the text of the *Remonstrance* is appended at the end of this opinion for its wider current reference."⁷⁵

Justice Rutledge concluded Section II of his opinion with a powerful amplification of separationism, first by insisting that Madison's struggle for religious liberty in Virginia was essential to an understanding of the Religion Clauses:

> All the great instruments of the Virginia struggle for religious liberty thus became warp and woof of our constitutional tradition, not simply by the course of history, but by the common unifying force of Madison's life, thought and sponsorship. He epitomized the whole of that tradition in the Amendment's compact, but nonetheless comprehensive, phrasing.⁷⁶

For Madison, Rutledge wrote, "'establishment' and 'free exercise' were correlative and coextensive ideas, representing only different facets of the single great and fundamental freedom," a passage that gestured to the chiasmatic relationship between the Religion Clauses. Because Madison believed it was dangerous to tolerate "any fragment" of establishment, Rutledge concluded, Madison sought to "tear out the institution not partially but root and branch, and to bar its return forever."⁷⁷

Justice Rutledge asserted that Madison was "more unrelentingly absolute" in opposing state support or aid by taxation than in any other area of religious establishment, and Rutledge quoted the following passage of Madison's *Remonstrance and Memorial* in support of the unrelenting separatism that he attributed to Madison:

> Because it is proper to take alarm at the first experiment on our liberties.... the freemen of America did not wait till usurped power had strengthened itself by exercise, and entangled the question in precedents. They saw all the consequences in the principle, and they avoided the consequences by denying the principle. We revere this lesson too much, soon to forget it.⁷⁸

Rutledge concluded his paean to separationism with a chiasmus based on one found in paragraph 5 of Madison's *Remonstrance and Memorial*, writing that "the principle was as much to prevent 'the interference of law in religion' as to restrain religious intervention in political matters." To support this chiasmus, Rutledge quoted Madison's chiasm in paragraph 5 of the *Remonstrance*, in which Madison wrote that "the bill implies either that the Civil Magistrate is a competent Judge of Religious truth; or that he may employ Religion as an engine of Civil policy."[79]

It is only after Justice Rutledge's lengthy paean to separationism across the first three sections of his opinion that he turned to applying the Religion Clauses to New Jersey's bus voucher program in a more pragmatic register in Sections III and IV of the opinion, arguing that "commingling the religious with the secular teaching does not divest the whole of its religious permeation and emphasis or make them of minor part, if proportion were material."[80] He rejected the majority's comparison of New Jersey's voucher program with public welfare legislation or general government services, writing that "of course paying the cost of transportation promotes the general cause of education and the welfare of the individual," but so does paying all other items of educational expense." "By casting the issue in terms of promoting the general cause of education and the welfare of the individual," he wrote, the majority's argument "ignores the religious factor and its essential connection with the transportation, thereby leaving out the only vital element in the case."[81] Even in this pragmatic register Rutledge drew on a chiasmus, arguing that the majority opinion "concedes that the children are aided by being helped to get to the religious schooling," but "by converse necessary implication..., it must be taken to concede also that the school is helped to reach the child with its religious teaching."[82]

Almost as soon as Justice Rutledge's pragmatic register had begun, he returned toward the end of section IV of the opinion to an epideictic register which liberally paraphrased and cited Madison's *Remonstrance and Memorial*. By the time Rutledge wrote toward the end of section IV, with only a fifth of the body of the opinion to go, that "this is not...just a little case over bus fares," he had hardly even mentioned New Jersey's voucher program. Beginning with the chiasmus that "there cannot be freedom of religion, safeguarded by the state, and intervention by the church or its agencies in the state's domain or dependency on its largesse," he used praise, exergasia, polyptoton, mesodiplosis, eloquence, the gnomic aspect, and affirmative modality to magnify the value of separationism:

> The great condition of religious liberty is that it be maintained free from sustenance, as also from other interferences, by the state. For when it comes to rest upon that secular foundation it vanishes with the resting. Public money devoted to payment of religious costs, educational or other,

brings the quest for more. It brings too the struggle of sect against sect for the larger share or for any. Here one by numbers alone will benefit most, there another. That is precisely the history of societies which have had an established religion and dissident groups....The end of such strife cannot be other than to destroy the cherished liberty. The dominating group will achieve the dominant benefit; or all will embroil the state in their dissensions.[83]

To end Section IV of his opinion, Justice Rutledge paraphrased Madison to write that "either we must say, that the will of...the Legislature is the only measure of their authority; and that in the plenitude of this authority, they may sweep away all our fundamental rights; or, that they are bound to leave this particular right untouched and sacred,"[84] and he elevated religious liberty to a sacred right in the final lines of the section:

The realm of religious training and belief remains, as the Amendment made it, the kingdom of the individual man and his God. It should be kept inviolately private, not "entangled in precedents" or confounded with... what legislatures legitimately may take over into the public domain.[85]

In the final sections of his opinion, Justice Rutledge first addressed the feelings of religious observers, writing that "no one conscious of religious values can be unsympathetic toward the burden which our constitutional separation puts on" the religious instruction of children, but "if those feelings should prevail, there would be an end to our historic constitutional policy and command."[86] Although "hardship in fact there is which none can blink," he wrote, "we have staked the very existence of our country on the faith that complete separation between the state and religion is best for the state and best for religion."[87] Referencing the writings of the apostle Paul in the Christian scriptures, Rutledge framed the pursuit of religious instruction without governmental support as a noble sacrifice, writing that "like St. Paul's freedom, religious liberty with a great price must be bought." For those who insisted on mixing religious education for their children with secular education, Rutledge wrote, "by the terms of our Constitution the price is greater than for others."[88]

Justice Rutledge then renewed his challenge to the majority's comparison of New Jersey's bus voucher program to ordinary public safety measures before extolling separationism in the peroration of his opinion by again liberally paraphrasing Madison's *Remonstrance and Memorial* with attribution of the author only:

> Two great drives are constantly in motion to abridge, in the name of education, the complete division of religion and civil authority which our forefathers made. One is to introduce religious education and observances into the public schools. The other, to obtain public funds for the aid and support of various private religious schools. In my opinion both avenues were closed by the Constitution....Now as in Madison's day it is [a matter] of principle, to keep separate the separate spheres as the First Amendment drew them; to prevent the first experiment upon our liberties; and to keep the question from becoming entangled in corrosive precedents. We should not be less strict to keep strong and untarnished the one side of the shield of religious freedom than we have been of the other.[89]

Rutledge relied heavily on chiasmus in this passage, the chiastic movement of the dual threats to separationism crossing in the introduction of religion into public education and of public funds into religious education.

A Backward Turn

At only ten pages, Justice Jackson's separate dissenting opinion in *Everson* is considerably shorter than both the majority opinion and Justice Rutledge's dissent, but like the other opinions it contains substantial epideictic registers. Jackson began his opinion by expressing sympathy, "though it is not ideological," with Catholics who were "compelled by law to pay taxes for public schools, and also...constrained by conscience and discipline to support other schools for their own children."[90] He challenged the majority's finding that the New Jersey voucher program was equally available to everyone by noting that it limited reimbursement to those attending public schools and Catholic schools, excluding private schools operated in whole or in part for profit including those serving children with disabilities or special needs.[91] In other words, it privileged the students attending schools of one religious denomination.[92]

After beginning on a relatively pragmatic note, Justice Jackson shifted into an epideictic register in the third section of his opinion to magnify the value of religious liberty, beginning with a chiasmus:

Keeping Government Out of Religion and Vice Versa 117

It is of no importance in this situation whether the beneficiary of this expenditure of tax-raised funds is primarily the parochial school and incidentally the pupil, or whether the aid is directly bestowed on the pupil with indirect benefits to the school.

The Establishment Clause cannot be circumvented, Jackson wrote, by "a subsidy, bonus or reimbursement of expense to individuals for receiving religious instruction and indoctrination."[93]

Responding to the majority's claim that the New Jersey voucher program had a public rather than a private purpose, Justice Jackson wrote in a passage densely figured with antithesis, mesodiplosis, and consonance that

of course, the state may pay out tax-raised funds to relieve pauperism, but it may not under our Constitution do so to induce or reward piety. It may spend funds to secure old age against want, but it may not spend funds to secure religion against skepticism. It may compensate individuals for loss of employment, but it cannot compensate them for adherence to a creed.[94]

He then concluded his response to the majority's comparison of the voucher program to public welfare or general government services with a pair of parallel chiasms:

A policeman protects a Catholic, of course—but not because he is a Catholic; it is because he is a man and a member of our society. The fireman protects the Church school—but not because it is a Church school; it is because it is property, part of the assets of our society.[95]

The movement from policeman and Catholic to Catholic and society in the first sentence and from fireman and Church to Church and society in the second reflects a fundamentally chiastic movement further amplified by repetition.

In the peroration of his opinion, Justice Jackson extolled religious liberty as a preeminent right, featuring praise, chiasmus, anadiplosis, mesodiplosis, consonance, eloquence, the gnomic aspect, and affirmative modality:

This freedom was first in the Bill of Rights because it was first in the forefathers' minds; it was set forth in absolute terms, and its strength is its rigidity. It was intended not only to keep the states' hands out of religion, but to keep religion's hands off the state, and, above all, to keep bitter religious controversy out of public life by denying to every denomination any advantage from getting control of public policy or the public purse. Those great ends I cannot but think are immeasurably compromised by today's decision.

The Religion Clauses of the First Amendment had never pleased religious groups, Jackson wrote, but instead "they all are quick to invoke its protections; they are irked when they feel its restraints."[96] The same people who complained of its burdens enjoyed its protections, he wrote, and "we cannot have it both ways." He concluded with the metaphor of the Court turning back the clock on religious liberty:

> The great purposes of the Constitution do not depend on the approval or convenience of those they restrain. I cannot read the history of the struggle to separate political from ecclesiastical affairs..., without a conviction that the Court today is unconsciously giving the clock's hands a backward turn.[97]

Rules of Law and Figures of Speech

The judicial authors of all of the opinions published in *Everson* devoted substantial attention to the epideictic function of shaping beliefs, desires, and ethical commitments in response to the inauguration of a new line of jurisprudence that would apply the Establishment Clause to state governments under the Due Process Clause of the Fourteenth Amendment. As Robert Tsai notes, the Court "consistently paid homage to the wall of separation by using it as the undisputed starting point for legal inquiry" in the early years of the Court's Religion Clause jurisprudence, a metaphor Tsai describes as among "the precepts of eloquence governing the era," nearly all of the justices assuming that "the words of the First Amendment, 'properly interpreted,' had 'erected' a wall." Conservative opponents of a strict separationist interpretation of the Religion Clauses immediately challenged the rigidity of the wall metaphor, however, which they believed to symbolize the liberalism of the Warren Court more generally.[98]

According to Tsai, this reactionary movement emerged in the 1950s and 1960s, eventually leading to an "emerging counterdiscourse" on the Court itself reflected in Chief Justice Earl Warren's majority opinion in *McGowan v. Maryland* (1961), in which Warren defensively wrote that to hold Sunday closing laws to be unconstitutional based solely on their "undeniably religious…origin," despite their secular purpose of setting aside one day a week for "rest, repose, recreation, and tranquility," would "give a constitutional interpretation of hostility to the public welfare rather than one of mere separation of church and state."[99] An "adaptive period" followed in the 1970s, Tsai writes, which "tried to save the wall by softening its appearance,"[100] the paradigm of which is Chief Justice Warren Burger's majority opinion in *Lemon v. Kurzman* (1971), in which Burger openly acknowledged that "total separation" was not possible "in an absolute sense" and wrote that the language of the Religion Clauses was "not precisely stated" but "at best opaque," characterizing the separation of religion and government prescribed by the Religion Clauses as "a blurred, indistinct, and variable barrier" rather than a wall.[101]

Another part of the story, however, is that well beyond Justice Stanley Reed's remark in *McCollum v. Board of Education* (1948) that "a rule of law should not be drawn from a figure of speech,"[102] doubts about the wall of separation metaphor were expressed by many of the Court's justices almost immediately after *Everson*. Haig Bosmajian notes that in *Zorach v. Clauson* (1952), for example, Justice Jackson wrote in a "strongly worded" dissenting opinion that "the wall which the Court was professing to erect between Church and State [in *McCollum*] has become even more warped and twisted than I expected,"[103] a comment which reveals not only that Jackson had doubts about the efficacy of the wall of separation metaphor in *Zorach* but that his doubts had preceded the case.[104] Jackson's doubts about the metaphor, as discussed in the next section of this chapter, emerged in his concurring opinion in *McCollum* the year after *Everson*, along with similar doubts expressed in Justice Frankfurter's concurring opinion which Jackson joined along with Justices Wiley Rutledge and Harold Burton.

While the wall metaphor immediately met with doubt and eventually with qualification, if not dismay, the prevalence of chiasmus in the Court's early Religion Clause jurisprudence serves to interpret the wall metaphor as less stable than *Everson*'s "high and impregnable"[105] wall suggested, signifying instead a "perpetual oscillation" between religion and government that "eludes representation"[106] even as the First Amendment proscribes certain forms of contact between them,[107] an infinitely deferred closure[108] suggesting that "there remains more work to do,"[109] leading to a relationship that "does not allow one to settle on either side of the equation."[110] The "blurred, indistinct, and variable barrier" of *Lemon*[111] was already incipient in the chiasms of *Everson* and of Madison's *Remonstrance and Memorial* on which the justices in *Everson* drew, as well as in the continuing prevalence of chiasmus in *McCollum* and even in Chief Justice Burger's opinion in *Lemon*.

Madison's *Remonstrance and Memorial* was written in response to a bill authored by Patrick Henry to establish a provision for religious teachers, which Henry introduced into the Virginia legislature with what Eva Brann describes as a "fervent speech tracing the downfall of ancient and modern polities to the decay of religion," and the floor debate between Madison and Henry over the bill anticipated and shaped the *Remonstrance*.[112] Madison's notes from the floor debate indicate that he "intended to divert the argument from the preoccupation with the social need for religion to the 'true question': Are religious establishments necessary for religion?"[113] As discussed in the introduction to this chapter, the centrality of chiasmus to Madison's thinking about rights in general and religious freedom in particular is not only evident in the language and structure of the *Remonstrance* but in Madison's essay on property and the Religion Clauses themselves. It is also evident in this formative moment in Madison's floor debate with Patrick Henry over the religious assessments bill as he inverts the question from whether religion is necessary for the state to whether the state is necessary for religion.

Although Madison's inversion of Patrick Henry's preoccupation with the social need for religion was a refutative one, it was not a complete reversal of emphasis but reflected chiastic reasoning which proposed that religious establishment posed a threat to both church and state by upsetting a harmonious balance between them. Implicit in the inversion is at least a parity between church and state, or it could even suggest a privilege accorded to religion. The duty of religious conscience, Madison writes in the *Remonstrance*, is "precedent, both in order of time and in degree of obligation to the claims of Civil Society," for a person "must be considered a subject of the Governor of the Universe" before they "can be considered as a member of Civil Society." Every person who becomes a member of "any particular Civil Society," Madison writes, must do it with "a saving of [their] allegiance to the Universal Sovereign." Yet this precedence, for

Madison, entails that religion is "wholly exempt" from the "cognizance" of civil society.[114] It is not that the jurisdiction of religious conscience is inferior to law; it is simply outside of its cognizance and can neither aid nor be aided by the state, a close approximation of the statement of Jesus to the Pharisees in the Christian scriptures to "render…unto Caesar the things which are Caesar's; and unto God the things that are God's."[115]

In all the chiasms in *Everson*, what is important is the inversion, or crossing, and the parity of respect for both religion and government evinced by the crossing. In the context of the Court's Religion Clause jurisprudence, the chiastic relationship between the Establishment Clause and the Free Exercise Clause values religion and government equally even as it expresses the urgency of their respective sovereignties. Combined with the other amplifying features of the epideictic registers in which the chiasms appear, religious liberty is infused with a value beyond perceptible limits, ultimately eluding representation. The Religion Clauses reflect not a wall of separation between church and state, but a chiasm of church and state. This relationship becomes more apparent as the Court's Religion Clause jurisprudence expands, from *McCollum* to *Lemon*, and chiasms continue to appear while the wall of separation faces increasing critique.[116]

Good Fences Make Good Neighbors

Although the Court first held that the Establishment Clause applied to the states under the Fourteenth Amendment in *Everson*, the Court first found the Establishment Clause to be violated by a state the following year in *McCollum v. Board of Education* (1948). In *McCollum*, the Court held in an 8:1 decision that an Illinois school's released time program, in which students were released from their secular classes on a voluntary basis during regular school hours to attend religious instruction led by Protestant teachers, Catholic priests, or Jewish rabbis according to their faith, was an unconstitutional establishment of religion.[117] As in *Everson*, Justice Black wrote the majority opinion in *McCollum*, Justice Frankfurter wrote a concurring opinion joined by Justices Jackson, Rutledge, and Burton—the same four justices who joined Rutledge's dissenting opinion in *Everson*—and Jackson wrote a separate concurring opinion. As the sole dissenting justice, Justice Reed wrote a dissenting opinion.

In Justice Black's majority opinion in *McCollum*, he wrote a brief statement of the facts before concluding that they "show the use of tax-supported property for religious instruction and the close cooperation between the school authorities and the religious council in promoting religious education," which was "beyond all question a utilization of the tax-established and tax-supported public school system to aid religious groups to spread their faith" in violation of the Establishment Clause of the First Amendment.[118] Black wrote his majority opinion in an almost strictly pragmatic register, but the syllogistic logic of his opinion flowed from the epideictic register of his peroration in *Everson* which he quoted in its entirety in *McCollum*, including the chiasmus signified with the phrase vice versa:

> Neither [a state nor the Federal Government] can pass laws which aid one religion, aid all religions, or prefer one religion over another. Neither can force nor influence a person to go to or to remain away from church against his will or force him to profess a belief or disbelief in any religion....Neither a state nor the Federal Government can, openly or secretly, participate in the affairs of any religious organizations or groups and *vice versa*.[119]

The counsel defending Illinois's released time program in *McCollum* challenged this passage of *Everson* as having been dicta and urged the Court to reconsider and repudiate it. In *McCollum*, Black did not expressly reject the charge that the *Everson* passage was dicta,[120] but when the Court was again challenged to repudiate the passage as dicta in *Torcaso v. Watkins* (1961), Black wrote for the majority that "we declined to do this" in *McCollum*, but "instead strongly reaffirmed what had been said in *Everson*."[121]

Justice Frankfurter's concurring opinion in *McCollum*, which all of the justices who had dissented in *Everson* joined, is the longest opinion published in *McCollum*, although Justice Reed published a dissenting opinion of comparable length. It is useful to begin with Frankfurter's concluding paragraph in *McCollum*, in which he wrote that "we renew our conviction that 'we have staked the very existence of our country on the faith that complete separation between the state and religion is best for the state and best for religion,'" before quoting without attribution Robert Frost's poem "Mending Wall" on a more poignant note in the final sentence of his opinion: "If nowhere else, in the relation between Church and State, 'good fences make good neighbors.'"¹²² Frankfurter's qualifying phrase *if nowhere else* and the gnomic saying *good fences make good neighbors* from Frost's poem gesture to a discomfort with the wall metaphor even among the justices who had dissented in *Everson*. Justice Jackson's concurring opinion in *McCollum*, discussed below, reflected a similar discomfort with the sweeping scope of the wall metaphor and the prospect that the floodgates of litigation had been opened by the Court's opinion in *McCollum*, despite his concurrence in the decision.

The opening line of Frost's poem "Mending Wall," *something there is that doesn't love a wall*, which is repeated near the end of the poem, is as famous as the poem's final line *good fences make good neighbors*, quoted by Justice Frankfurter at the end of his *McCollum* opinion. The neighbor in Frost's poem who tells the narrator "good fences make good neighbors" is portrayed as a dark and enigmatic figure in the poem:

He moves in darkness as it seems to me,
Not of woods only and the shade of trees.
He will not go behind his father's saying.

The neighbor does not answer the narrator's argument that the wall is unnecessary since neither of the two own livestock, but only repeats unresponsively that "good fences make good neighbors" in the final line of the poem.¹²³

An allusion to Frost's poem also seems to have begun Justice Frankfurter's opinion in *McCollum*, forming a poetic frame through which the opinion considered separationism. In the third sentence of the opinion, Frankfurter wrote that "the mere formulation of a relevant Constitutional principle is the beginning of the solution of a problem, not its answer."¹²⁴ The meaning of a "spacious conception" like the separation of church and state, he wrote, is "unfolded as appeal is made to the principle from case to case," and the agreement in the abstract that the Religion Clauses were designed to erect a wall of separation between church and state "does not preclude a clash of views as to what the wall separates,"¹²⁵ a phrase that echoes Frost's line in "Mending Wall":

Before I build a wall I'd ask to know
*What I was walling in or walling out.*¹²⁶

Although Justice Reed's comment in *McCollum* that "a rule of law should not be drawn from a figure of speech"[127] has received more scholarly attention, Frankfurter explained his statement about the inevitable clash of views regarding what the wall separates by stating similarly that "accommodation of legislative freedom and Constitutional limitations upon that freedom cannot be achieved by a mere phrase." The wall metaphor, he wrote, could not be "illuminatingly" applied until the history of religious education in America was considered, along with the place of released time programs in that history.[128]

After these introductory remarks, Justice Frankfurter devoted roughly half of the remainder of the opinion to his account of the history of released time programs. Although he recognized that "traditionally, organized education in the Western world was Church education," he concluded that the evolution of colonial education into the modern public school system was "the story of changing conceptions regarding the American democratic society."[129] Noting that Madison's *Remonstrance and Memorial* arose out of a proposal to support religious education, Frankfurter wrote that the modern public school "derived from a philosophy of freedom reflected in the First Amendment."[130] This evolution of separationism was not imposed on the states, he wrote, but "merely reflected a principle then dominant in our national life" in which states were willing participants as Americans responded to "the particular needs of a young and growing nation" with "zealous watchfulness against fusion of secular and religious activities."[131]

Justice Frankfurter punctuated his history of separationism in American schools with his first shift into an epideictic register to support the assertion that "the secular public school did not imply indifference to the basic role of religion in the life of the people." The "deep religious feeling of James Madison is stamped upon the *Remonstrance*," Frankfurter wrote, and the secular public school was the "means of reconciling freedom in general with religious freedom."[132] Combining praise, exergasia, repetition, parallelism, asyndeton, ploce, the gnomic aspect, and affirmative modality, he magnified the value of modern secular education to cohesive sentiment in a democracy:

> The sharp confinement of the public schools to secular education was a recognition of the need of a democratic society to educate its children, insofar as the State undertook to do so, in an atmosphere free from pressures

in a realm in which pressures are most resisted and where conflicts are most easily and most bitterly engendered. Designed to serve as perhaps the most powerful agency for promoting cohesion among a heterogeneous democratic people, the public school must keep scrupulously free from entanglement in the strife of sects. The preservation of the community from divisive conflicts, of Government from irreconcilable pressures by religious groups, of religion from censorship and coercion however subtly exercised, requires strict confinement of the State to [nonreligious] instruction.[133]

He repeated this focus on cohesion later in his opinion when he stressed that public education "should be the training ground for habits of community" and that separation of religion and government was "one of the vital reliances of our Constitutional system for assuring unities."[134] This focus echoed Frankfurter's majority opinion in *Minersville School District v. Gobitis* (1940), discussed in Chapter 2, particularly his statement in *Gobitis* that "the ultimate foundation of a free society is the binding tie of cohesive sentiment" and his conclusion that as a result society may "utilize the educational process for inculcating those almost unconscious feelings which bind men together in a comprehending loyalty."[135]

Before turning to the rise of released time programs in the United States, Justice Frankfurter noted President Grant's effort in the 1870s to amend the Constitution to specifically prohibit the use of public funds for religious education consistent with the amendment of many state constitutions.[136] Frankfurter also quoted the lawyer and statesman Elihu Root for saying that "it is not a question of religion, or of creed, or of party; it is a question of declaring and maintaining the great American principle of eternal separation between Church and State,"[137] and quoted the following two chiasms from the American lawyer and judge Jeremiah Black:

> The manifest object of the men who framed the institutions of this country, was to have a *State without religion, and a Church without politics—* that is to say, they meant that one should never be used as an engine for any purpose of the other....Our fathers seem to have been perfectly sincere in their belief that the members of the Church would be more patriotic, and the citizens of the State more religious, by keeping their respective functions entirely separate.[138]

Frankfurter noted that the fact that Elihu Root and Jeremiah Black would agree on separationism despite their sharp political differences "affords striking proof of the respect to be accorded that principle."[139]

Justice Frankfurter then attributed the rise of released time programs to George Wenner's 1905 proposal to the Interfaith Conference on Federation that public schools "release" their monopoly on children's time by excusing them from school on Wednesday afternoons so that "churches could provide 'Sunday school on Wednesday,'" a proposal that Frankfurter noted "aroused considerable opposition."[140] Frankfurter nonetheless noted that released time programs had grown to two million participants in 2,200 communities by the time of *McCollum*, a scope which he wrote "indicates the importance of the problem" but also made the constitutional violations of the programs "ominous."[141] He amplified how much the programs differed, however, writing that "'released time' as a generalized conception, undefined by differentiating particularities, is not an issue for Constitutional adjudication," as programs "differ from each other in many and crucial respects," and therefore "we do not now attempt to weigh in the Constitutional scale every separate detail or various combination of factors which may establish a valid 'released time' program."[142] Because Illinois's released time program required religious teachers to obtain the permission of the school superintendent before they were allowed to teach in the program and required attendance reports to be submitted to school authorities, Frankfurter wrote, religious education was "patently woven into the working scheme of the school," actively furthering "inculcation in the religious tenets of some faiths," which "sharpens the consciousness of religious differences" in violation of the Establishment Clause.[143]

Justice Frankfurter returned to an epideictic register for the peroration of his opinion in the final two paragraphs, combining praise, exergasia, metaphor, antithesis, polyptoton, eloquence, the gnomic aspect, and affirmative modality to magnify the value of separationism:

> Separation means separation, not something less. Jefferson's metaphor in describing the relation between Church and State speaks of a "wall of separation," not of a fine line easily overstepped. The public school is at once the symbol of our democracy and the most pervasive means for promoting our common destiny. In no activity of the State is it more vital to keep out divisive forces than in its schools, to avoid confusing, not to say fusing,

what the Constitution sought to keep strictly apart. "The great American principle of eternal separation"—Elihu Root's phrase bears repetition—is one of the vital reliances of our Constitutional system for assuring unities among our people stronger than our diversities.[144]

After emphasizing that Jefferson's wall of separation is not a "fine line easily overstepped" in the penultimate paragraph of the opinion, Frankfurter ended by referencing Robert's Frost's poem "Mending Wall," as discussed above, writing that "if nowhere else, in the relation between Church and State, 'good fences make good neighbors.'"[145]

By ending on this poignant note, Justice Frankfurter substantially qualifies his enthusiasm for the wall metaphor, drawing as his conclusion does on the neighbor's rote repetition of the line in Frost's poem in response to the narrator's objections to the wall that separated them. It suggests a sublime perspective from which the wall is ultimately beyond the efficacy of law or our perceptual capacities, a perspective suggested earlier in the opinion when Frankfurter recognized that the common use of the metaphor did not preclude "a clash of views as to what the wall separates" and that the issue could not be resolved "by a mere phrase," as well as when he noted that the scale of potential breaches in the wall presented by the rapid growth of released time programs in the United States during the twentieth century had become "ominous."[146]

Justice Frankfurter's misgivings about the scope of the Court's decision reflected in his references to the wall metaphor, his characterization of the scale of released time programs as "ominous," and his effort to limit the holding to the unique facts of Illinois's program did not fully satisfy Justice Jackson, who joined Frankfurter's opinion but also wrote separately to express additional concerns about "the number of litigations likely to be started as a result of this decision" and the need to "place some bounds on the demands for interference with locals schools that we are empowered or willing to entertain."[147] Jackson's dissenting opinion was brief and began in a pragmatic register to note that the relief the Court granted was extraordinary in its breadth because it granted without qualification the plaintiff's request for a writ of mandamus directing the local board of education to "immediately adopt and enforce rules and regulations prohibiting all instruction in and teaching of religious education in all public schools," a writ that extended far beyond Illinois's released time program.[148] "The sweep and detail of these complaints is a danger signal," Jackson wrote, "which warns of the kind of local controversy we will be required to arbitrate if we do not place appropriate limitation on our decision."[149]

Justice Jackson then shifted into an epideictic register to amplify how intricately intertwined religion was with history and culture, raising difficult questions regarding how to implement separationism in public education that he admitted were "more than I know."[150] Beyond Illinois's released time program, Jackson wrote, the Court could "at all times prohibit teaching of creed and catechism and ceremonial and can forbid forthright proselytizing in the schools," but "it remains to be demonstrated whether it is possible, even if desirable, to comply with such demands as plaintiff's completely to isolate and cast out of secular education all that some people may reasonably regard as religious instruction."[151]

Expounding on the limits and desirability of completely eliminating religion from secular education, Justice Jackson used a dense convergence of praise, exergasia, enumeration, antithesis, mesodiplosis, eloquence, the gnomic aspect, and a relatively affirmative modality, although he used some epistemic qualifiers to emphasize the potentially insoluble nature of the relationship between religion and government:

> Perhaps subjects such as mathematics, physics or chemistry are, or can be, completely secularized. But it would not seem practical to teach either practice or appreciation of the arts if we are to forbid exposure of youth to any religious influences. Music without sacred music, architecture minus the cathedral, or painting without the scriptural themes would be eccentric and incomplete, even from a secular point of view. Yet the inspirational appeal of religion in these guises is often stronger than in forthright sermon. Even such a "science" as biology raises the issue between evolution and creation as an explanation of our presence on this planet. Certainly a course in English literature that omitted the Bible and other powerful uses of our mother tongue for religious ends would be pretty barren. And I should suppose it is a proper, if not an indispensable, part of preparation for a worldly life to know the roles that religion and religions have played in the tragic story of mankind.[152]

"The fact is," Jackson wrote, that "nearly everything in our culture worth transmitting, everything which gives meaning to life, is saturated with religious influences" derived from a variety of sources spanning world history, and "one can hardly respect a system of education that would leave the student wholly ignorant of the currents of religious thought that move the world society for a part in which he is being prepared."[153] Jackson concluded that it was unlikely people could teach such controversial subjects with perfect detachment and that "the task of separating the secular from the religious in education is one of magnitude, intricacy and delicacy."[154]

In the final paragraphs of his opinion, Justice Jackson objected to the Court's "uniform, rigid and, if we are consistent,...unchanging standard" effected by its decision in *McCollum* "for countless school boards representing and serving highly localized groups which not only differ from each other but which themselves from time to time change attitudes."[155] To apply such a standard, Jackson wrote, was to "allow zeal for our own ideas of what is good in public instruction to induce us to accept the role of a super board of education for every school in the nation."[156] Neither the Constitution nor any other legal authority, he wrote, provided one word to assist judges in determining "where the secular ends and the sectarian begins in education."[157] The Court had "no law but our prepossessions," Jackson wrote, and was likely to see many more cases like *McCollum* if it endeavored with no identifiable legal standard to decide "every variation of this controversy, raised by persons...who are dissatisfied with the way schools are dealing with the problem."[158] More importantly, Jackson wrote, the Court was likely to "make the legal 'wall of separation between church and state' as winding as the famous serpentine wall designed by Mr. Jefferson for the University he founded,"[159] a reference to the famous serpentine wall at the University of Virginia. Despite joining the decision of the case, Jackson's opinion betrays trepidation about the wall of separation metaphor, expressing both that it was too rigid and that it could become too serpentine.

A Blurred and Variable Barrier

In *Lemon v. Kurtzman* (1971), taxpayers and citizens challenged the constitutionality of statutory school programs in Pennsylvania and Rhode Island, which in Pennsylvania reimbursed the cost of teachers' salaries, textbooks, and instructional materials in secular subjects and in Rhode Island paid teachers in nonpublic elementary schools a supplement of 15 percent of their salary. In both cases, state aid was provided to church-related educational institutions.[160] The Court held that both programs were unconstitutional under the Religion Clauses of the First Amendment. Writing for a unanimous Court, Chief Justice Warren Burger began his discussion of the constitutional issue by writing that "candor compels acknowledgment…that we can only dimly perceive the lines of demarcation in this extraordinarily sensitive area of constitutional law."[161] The language of the Religion Clauses, he wrote, was "not precisely stated" but "at best opaque, particularly when compared with other portions of the Amendment," considering the use of the word *respecting* in the Establishment Clause's prohibition of any "law respecting an establishment of religion."[162]

In the absence of a more precisely stated provision, Justice Burger wrote, "we must draw lines with reference to the three main evils against which the Establishment Clause was designed to afford protection: sponsorship, financial support, and active involvement of the sovereign in religious activity."[163] He then announced a three-pronged test reflecting "cumulative criteria" developed by the Court over many years:

> First, the statute must have a secular legislative purpose; second, its principal or primary effect must be one that neither advances nor inhibits religion, finally, the statute must not foster "an excessive government entanglement with religion."[164]

Although the Pennsylvania and Rhode Island programs had a secular legislative purpose and did not advance religion, Burger concluded, the cumulative impact of the statutes "involves excessive entanglement between government and religion."[165] He acknowledged that "total separation is not possible in an absolute sense," because "some relationship between government and religious organizations is inevitable" insofar as "religious values pervade the fabric of our national life."[166]

The relationship between religion and government prescribed by the Religion Clauses was, Justice Burger wrote, "a blurred, indistinct, and variable barrier" rather than a wall.[167] In order to determine whether a statute fosters an "excessive entanglement" between religion and government, he wrote, the Court must examine "the character and purposes of the institutions that are benefited, the nature of the aid that the State provides, and the resulting relationship between the government and the religious authority." Both the Pennsylvania and Rhode Island education programs failed the test.[168]

Despite the fact that the wall of separation metaphor was all but discarded in *Lemon* and the epideictic registers of the opinion were muted relative to *Everson* and *McCollum*—perhaps because *Lemon* was not perceived to inaugurate change to the same extent as the Court's early Religion Clause cases—Justice Burger still drew substantially on chiasms to support the decision. Describing the divisive political potential of the education programs before the Court, for example, Burger wrote that it was inconsistent with history and tradition to let the Religion Clause issues preclude attending to the many legal questions involved in governance:

> The highways of church and state relationships are not likely to be one-way streets, and the Constitution's authors sought to protect religious worship from the pervasive power of government. The history of many countries attests to the hazards of religion's intruding into the political arena or of political power intruding into the legitimate and free exercise of religious belief.[169]

In the final paragraph of the opinion, Burger also used a chiasmus to support the boundary the decision marked. Although "some involvement and entanglement are inevitable, lines must be drawn" based on the choice made by our system of government that "government is to be entirely excluded from the area of religious instruction and churches excluded from the affairs of government."[170] Chiasms also appear in other opinions of the era, such as in Justice William Brennan's concurring opinion in *School District of Abington Township v. Schempp* (1963), in which Brennan quoted the same chiasma of Jeremiah Black quoted by Justice Frankfurter in his concurring opinion in *McCollum*: "The manifest object of the men who framed the institutions of this country, was to have a *State without religion*, and a *Church without politics*."[171]

A Variable Resolve

The epideictic registers in the Court's early Religion Clause jurisprudence, such as those in the Court's First Amendment free speech jurisprudence discussed in Chapter 2, illustrate the interdiscursive relationship between judicial discourse and the ritual and ceremonial discourse of epideictic. The Court's early Religion Clause cases also reveal the powerful intertextual influence of Madison's struggle for religious liberty and his *Remonstrance and Memorial for Religious Assessments*, particularly the figure of chiasmus that pervades the form and structure of the *Remonstrance* and of the Religion Clauses Madison authored. Similar to the role that paramologia played in the Court's First Amendment free speech cases, chiasmus formed a central gesture of the epideictic registers in the Court's early Religion Clause cases which equally magnified the value of both religious and secular life. The epideictic registers in the cases reflect less of a conflict between religion and government than conflicting approaches to the proper balance between them.

In the Court's early Religion Clause cases, the figure of chiasmus magnified the value of both religion and government without privileging either, a paean to both religious and secular life which proved more durable than the obstruction symbolized by the wall metaphor but one which in the end only resulted in the sort of "hermeneutical miasma" that Robert Hariman notes of chiasmus more generally.[172] The capacity of chiasmus to symbolize the Court's inability to find a more suitable metaphor for the relationship between religious and secular life may explain its durability. Although the judicial authors in the cases responded to the epideictic situation created by the inauguration of a new line of constitutional jurisprudence with broad social consequences by addressing the beliefs, desires, and ethical commitments that informed their decisions, they struggled to apprehend a national character or resolve regarding the issue.

When Justice Burger wrote in *Lemon* that "total separation" of religion and government was not possible "in an absolute sense" and that the language of the Religion Clauses was "not precisely stated" but "at best opaque," characterizing the separation of religion and government prescribed by the Religion Clauses as "a blurred, indistinct, and variable barrier" rather than a wall,[173] he expressed the culmination of a lengthy period in which the Court had become disillusioned with the wall metaphor and sought alternative metaphors through which to think about the Religion Clauses. At different times, the Court had alternatively construed the clauses to represent an imperfect "line," a "scale" on which to balance interests, a "boundary" designed to avoid excessive "entanglements," a "tight rope" to be "traversed,"[174] and had construed the wall metaphor itself with more concrete imagery as "serpentine,"[175] "warped and twisted,"[176] or through an allusion to the wall in Robert Frost's poem "Mending Wall."[177]

The figure of chiasmus captures the Court's failure to discover a stable principle of resolution in its Religion Clause jurisprudence, a conspicuous figure for magnifying the value of both religious and secular life without resolving their "proximity and distance."[178]

The central role of chiasmus in the Court's early Religion Clause cases also illustrates the philosophical significance of figures, which Jeanne Fahnestock notes "belong in the pragmatic or situational and functional dimension of language,"[179] revealing "a fundamental, generative cognitive process" no less than metaphor.[180] Far from representing a merely stylistic figure, as Rodolphe Gasché argues chiasmus is an "originary" form of thought that "allows the drawing apart and the bringing together of opposite functions or terms and entwines them within an identity of movements" while also infinitely deferring closure through the "substitutability implied by its asymmetry."[181] Rather than serving as mere ornamentation or artistic expression, chiasmus is "constitutive or iconic"[182] of the Court's thought regarding the relationship between religion and government, forming a "verbal summary that epitomizes a line of reasoning," a "condensed or even diagram-like rendering of the relationship among a set of terms, a relationship that constitutes the argument and that could be expressed at greater length."[183] The figure forms an essential part of the Court's thought.[184]

As discussed in Chapter 1, the Scientific Revolution and Enlightenment's insistence that invention be exclusively governed by deductive logic and the scientific method reduced rhetoric to a purely ornamental function by eliminating invention from its purview.[185] As Ernesto Grassi explains the thesis of modern rationalism, rhetoric and figurality were "to be appreciated primarily from the outside, for *pedagogical reasons*, that is, as aids to 'alleviate' the 'severity' and 'dryness' of rational language" or merely to make it "'easier' to absorb rational truth."[186] Metaphor and the "easy vanity of *fine speaking*" characterized by an elaborate use of tropes and figures was condemned as misleading because figures appeal to the senses rather than reason and because metaphor transfers and transforms meaning in a manner that frustrates logical precision.[187] Peter Ramus rejected the idea that rhetoric constituted a form of reasoning which had been widely recognized since the time of Aristotle, and Francis Bacon rejected the equally long-standing idea that rhetoric had an epistemic function of discovering new knowledge.[188] To modern reformers, rhetoric and the humanistic tradition of which it formed a central part—which "always concerned itself with the union of *res* and *verba*," of "*content*" and "*form*"—were considered only of literary and aesthetic, not philosophical, significance.[189]

As Fahnestock notes, however, "there has always been an undertow working against the separation of invention and style, and it is even possible to discover arguments stylistically."[190] Although in reference to the wall of separation metaphor Justice Reed wrote that "a rule of law should not be drawn from a figure of speech"[191] and Justice Frankfurter wrote that the Court's application of the Religion Clauses could not be achieved by "a mere phrase"[192]—comments which participated in the bias that figurality possesses only literary and aesthetic, not philosophical, significance—in the history of the Religion Clauses the figure of chiasmus first emerged as a fundamental habit of mind of Madison and symbolizes the Court's irresolution regarding the relationship between religious and secular life in its early Religion Clause cases. Ivo Strecker describes the potential of chiasmus to "shatter expectations and conventions," which forms its "rhetorical energy" and leads to both pleasure and pain as the figure first shatters expectations but ultimately fails to gain lasting adherence because it provides no principle of resolution between its terms.[193] While Madison's sententious chiasms may have shattered expectations in his struggle for religious liberty in the eighteenth century, in the Court's early Religion Clause jurisprudence they led only to the "small prison house of language" that Robert Hariman describes, a "perpetual oscillation" between chiastic terms.[194]

The following chapter examines the epideictic registers in the Court's privacy jurisprudence through an analysis of Justice Anthony Kennedy's majority opinion in *Obergefell v. Hodges* (2015) and a genealogy of the leading cases on which *Obergefell* relied, revealing both the accumulating force of epideictic across a century of cases as well as interpretive figures in the early development of the constitutional right of privacy that form important foundations of the Court's privacy jurisprudence, central figurations that amplify the basis of judicial authority to recognize rights such as privacy not explicitly enumerated in the Constitution.

CHAPTER 4

Storms, Shadows, and Privacy

In Daniel Boorstin's essay on Blackstone's *Commentaries on the Laws of England*, he writes that law's sublimity is created in part by its obscurity, not only the obscurity of its slow historical emergence and alterations but the obscurity of prophecy, "the indefiniteness of an institution which had to adapt itself to the indefinable necessities of the future."[1] When the Court first asserted its authority to review state court decisions in *Cohens v. Virginia* (1821), Chief Justice John Marshall included the following paean to the immortality of constitutions in his opinion for a unanimous Court:

> A constitution is framed for ages to come, and is designed to approach immortality as nearly as human institutions can approach it. Its course cannot always be tranquil. It is exposed to storms and tempests, and its framers must be unwise statesmen indeed if they have not provided it, so far as its nature will permit, with the means of self-preservation from the perils it may be destined to encounter. No government ought to be so defective in its organization as not to contain within itself the means of securing the execution of its own laws against other dangers than those which occur every day.[2]

In *McCulloch v. Maryland* (1819), Marshall had similarly written that the Constitution did not have the properties of a code but was "intended to endure for ages to come, and, consequently, to be adapted to the various crises of human affairs," not to provide, "by immutable rules, for exigencies which, if foreseen at all, must have been seen dimly."[3]

Justice Marshall's metaphor of an immortal constitution exposed to storms and tempests participated in a broader ship of state metaphor most often attributed to the Greek lyric poet Alcaeus of Mytilene of the late seventh and early sixth century BCE and developed by Plato, Horace, and many modern authors.[4] The epideictic register of the passage is reflected in its thematic metaphor of *storms and tempests* as a constitution navigates a "course" destined to encounter "perils" and "dangers," as well as in the figure of exergasia which develops the theme through similar statements in different forms, along with the specific repetition of the word *approach* in the opening sentence.

The passage magnified the value of the Constitution and the of Court's authority to review challenges to the constitutionality of state court decisions by using the gnomic aspect and addressing what it means for something to be called a constitution rather than a specific constitution such as that of the United States. Marshall did not use the simple present to discuss the meaning of a constitution to Americans in the early nineteenth century or even a hypothetical constitution, but used the unbounded present to address constitutionalism itself, infusing the United States Constitution with immortality. The unqualified opening phrase captures this quality: "A constitution is framed for ages to come." These features converge to amplify the subject beyond the reader's ability to perceptually encompass it, elevating it to the level of the sublime as a foundation of the Court's authority in response to a situation in which the Court inaugurated constitutional change with broad social consequences.

In the centuries since *Cohens*, Justice Marshall's paean to the Constitution's immortality has been cited and quoted in many judicial opinions, including *Weems v. United States* (1910), in which the Court held that a criminal sentence imposed in the Philippines that was disproportionate to the sentences imposed for more serious crimes was unconstitutionally cruel and unusual punishment, a conclusion which required the Court to consider its interpretation of cruel and unusual punishment under the Eighth Amendment to the United States Constitution.[5] In his opinion for the majority in *Weems*, Justice Joseph McKenna used an epideictic register to amplify the Court's interpretive authority by drawing on Marshall's immortal constitution metaphor, without citing *Cohens* specifically but attributing authorship to Marshall:

> Legislation, both statutory and constitutional, is enacted, it is true, from an experience of evils, but its general language should not, therefore, be necessarily confined to the form that evil had theretofore taken. Time works changes, brings into existence new conditions and purposes. Therefore a

principle to be vital must be capable of wider application than the mischief which gave it birth. This is peculiarly true of constitutions. They are not ephemeral enactments, designed to meet passing occasions. They are, to use the words of Chief Justice Marshall, "designed to approach immortality as nearly as human institutions can approach it." The future is their care and provision for events of good and bad tendencies of which no prophecy can be made. In the application of a constitution, therefore, our contemplation cannot be only of what has been but of what may be.[6]

Justice Louis Brandeis used this passage of *Weems* to thematically organize his dissenting opinion in *Olmstead v. United States* (1928), in which the Court held that the warrantless wiretapping of telephones used to convict defendants under the National Prohibition Act did not violate the Fourth or Fifth Amendments of the Constitution because the wiretaps had been made without physically trespassing on the defendants' property.[7] Brandeis's dissenting opinion in *Olmstead* is widely regarded as an early source of the Court's jurisprudence recognizing a constitutional right of privacy, although Brandeis and Samuel Warren had advocated a right of privacy as the basis of civil actions in an 1890 law review article which they coauthored.[8] In *Olmstead*, Brandeis argued that the authors of the Constitution sought to protect the spiritual and intellectual need to be left alone:

> The makers of our Constitution undertook to secure conditions favorable to the pursuit of happiness. They recognized the significance of man's spiritual nature, of his feelings and of his intellect. They knew that only a part of the pain, pleasure and satisfactions of life are to be found in material things. They sought to protect Americans in their beliefs, their thoughts, their emotions and their sensations. They conferred, as against the Government, the right to be let alone—the most comprehensive of rights and the right most valued by civilized men.[9]

The phrase "the right to be let alone" from Brandeis's opinion in *Olmstead* has been quoted at least 423 times in later judicial opinions in the United States.[10] Brandeis also wrote in *Olmstead* that "experience should teach us to be most on our guard to protect liberty when the Government's purposes are beneficent," because "the greatest dangers to liberty lurk in insidious encroachment by men of zeal, well-meaning but without understanding,"[11] a sentence quoted at least 105 times in later judicial opinions in the United States.[12]

At the beginning of Justice Brandeis's opinion in *Olmstead*, however, he also quoted Justice McKenna's opinion in *Weems* excerpted above and restated several sentences and phrases without attribution as he amplified the importance of the Constitution adapting to a changing world, beginning with the following passage in which Brandeis quoted McKenna's statement that constitutional language should not be "confined to the form that evil had theretofore taken":

> When the Fourth and Fifth Amendments were adopted, "the form that evil had theretofore taken," had been necessarily simple. Force and violence were then the only means known to man by which a Government could directly effect self-incrimination. It could compel the individual to testify—a compulsion effected, if need be, by torture. It could secure possession of his papers and other articles incident to his private life—a seizure effected, if need be, by breaking and entry. Protection against such invasion of "the sanctities of a man's home and the privacies of life" was provided in the Fourth and Fifth Amendments by specific language.[13]

Continuing his thematic development of Justice McKenna's opinion in *Weems*, Justice Brandeis quoted without attribution McKenna's gnomic saying "time works changes, brings into existence new conditions and purposes":

> But "time works changes, brings into existence new conditions and purposes." Subtler and more far-reaching means of invading privacy have become available to the Government. Discovery and invention have made it possible for the Government, by means far more effective than stretching upon the rack, to obtain disclosure in court of what is whispered in the closet.[14]

To conclude his development, Brandeis quoted without attribution McKenna's statement that "in the application of a constitution, our contemplation cannot be only of what has been but of what may be":

> Moreover, "in the application of a constitution, our contemplation cannot be only of what has been but of what may be." The progress of science

in furnishing the Government with means of espionage is not likely to stop with wiretapping. Ways may some day be developed by which the Government, without removing papers from secret drawers, can reproduce them in court, and by which it will be enabled to expose to a jury the most intimate occurrences of the home. Advances in the psychic and related sciences may bring means of exploring unexpressed beliefs, thoughts and emotions.[15]

Although Justice Brandeis did not explicitly reference Justice Marshall's metaphor of an immortal constitution from *Cohens*, he incorporated its influence in his dissenting opinion in *Olmstead* by relying heavily on Justice McKenna's elaboration of the metaphor in *Weems*. In both instances and in the influence that Brandeis's paean to privacy in *Olmstead* has had in the development of the Court's privacy jurisprudence, the intertextual power of Marshall's immortal constitution metaphor played a crucial role. It also served as a precursor to Justice William Douglas's metaphor of "emanations" of the Bill of Rights which form "penumbras" of those rights to support a constitutional right of privacy forty years after *Olmstead* in *Griswold v. Connecticut* (1965).[16] Both Marshall's and Douglas's metaphors are important figurations of living constitutionalism—the view that constitutional interpretation must adapt to the times rather than be limited to the conditions of the Constitution's original enactment—which is particularly important to the Court's authority to recognize a right such as privacy that is not explicitly enumerated in the Constitution.

This chapter examines the epideictic registers in the Court's privacy jurisprudence as the right of privacy was found to inhere in the penumbras of the Bill of Rights and in the liberty protected by the Due Process Clause of the Fourteenth Amendment, proceeding by means of an analysis of Justice Anthony Kennedy's majority opinion in *Obergefell* and a genealogy of the leading cases on which he relied, particularly *Lawrence v. Texas* (2003), *Griswold v. Connecticut* (1965), *Loving v. Virginia* (1967), and related cases. I argue that Chief Justice John Marshall's immortal constitution metaphor, which viewed the Constitution as a vessel designed to weather "storms and tempests," and Justice William Douglas's metaphor of "emanations" of the Bill of Rights which form "penumbras," serve as important foundations of the Court's privacy jurisprudence, functioning as central figurations in epideictic registers that amplify the basis of judicial authority to recognize rights such as privacy that are not explicitly enumerated in the Constitution. The often expansive intertextual power of epideictic registers is at its height in the Court's privacy cases, I argue, as the Court's affective commitments to the relationship between liberty and privacy accrue and take on new meanings across a wide range of subjects from searches and seizures to wiretapping, contraceptive use, sexual relations, and marriage. I argue that this jurisprudence and the metaphors on which it relied magnified the value of figurative reasoning itself to a sublime level as a premise of the Court's interpretive authority.

Obergefell's Wedding Speech

The third-century CE rhetorician Pseudo-Dionysius of Halicarnassus advises speakers to include the following topics in wedding speeches:

> Marriage is…helpful in facing the pains and hardships of life; it lightens these burdens, so to speak, when we share our troubles with our wives and are comforted by their companionship. Then, too, pleasures are bound to seem more gratifying when we do not enjoy them all by ourselves, but have children, wives, and relatives to celebrate and be joyful with us.[17]

One of the most expansive examples of an epideictic register in the Court's fundamental rights jurisprudence is Justice Anthony Kennedy's paean to marriage in his majority opinion in *Obergefell v. Hodges* (2015), in which the Court held that the right to marriage is guaranteed to same-sex couples by the Due Process and Equal Protection Clauses of the Fourteenth Amendment.[18] The opening sentence of Kennedy's opinion stated that "the Constitution promises liberty to all within its reach, a liberty that includes specific rights that allow persons, within a lawful realm, to define and express their identity,"[19] a sentence Justice Antonin Scalia described derisively in his dissenting opinion as a descent from the "disciplined legal reasoning of John Marshall and Joseph Story to the mystical aphorisms of the fortune cookie."[20]

Consistent with Pseudo-Dionysius of Halicarnassus's advice on wedding speeches, by the end of *Obergefell* Justice Kennedy had described marriage not only as a relationship that "allows two people to find a life that could not be found alone, for a marriage becomes greater than just the two persons,"[21] but as a response to the "universal" fear that "a lonely person might call out only to find no one there." He added the polysyndeton that marriage "offers the hope of companionship and understanding and assurance that while both still live there will be someone to care for the other."[22]

Following his opening paragraph and a brief three-paragraph procedural history, Justice Kennedy extolled marriage's role in history in order to "note the history of the subject now before the Court":

> From their beginning to their most recent page, the annals of human history reveal the transcendent importance of marriage. The lifelong union of a man and a woman always has promised nobility and dignity to all persons, without regard to their station in life. Marriage is sacred to those who live by their religions and offers unique fulfillment to those who find meaning in the secular realm....Rising from the most basic human needs, marriage is essential to our most profound hopes and aspirations.

> The centrality of marriage to the human condition makes it unsurprising that the institution has existed for millennia and across civilizations. Since the dawn of history, marriage has transformed strangers into relatives, binding families and societies together....There are untold references to the beauty of marriage in religious and philosophical texts spanning time, cultures, and faiths, as well as in art and literature in all their forms.[23]

In these passages, Kennedy not only used the superlatives *transcendent, most basic, essential, most profound, central,* and *untold,* but he used exergasia, parallelism, mesodiplosis, the gnomic aspect, and affirmative modality to magnify the value of marriage.

Following his introductory treatment of marriage's transcendent role in history, Justice Kennedy wrote that the history he outlined was "the beginning of these cases," but that the respondents said "it should be the end as well." He acknowledged that "to them, it would demean a timeless institution if the concept and lawful status of marriage were extended to two persons of the same sex," based on the long-held view that marriage is "by its nature a gender-differentiated union of man and woman." The petitioners, on the other hand, Kennedy wrote, "acknowledge this history but contend that these cases cannot end there." It is "the enduring importance of marriage that underlies the petitioners' contentions," wrote Kennedy, and "far from seeking to devalue marriage, petitioners seek it for themselves because of their respect—and need—for its privileges and responsibilities." Same-sex marriage, he noted, was their "only real path to this profound commitment" given the "immutable nature" of marriage.[24] After recounting the facts of the cases for the next few paragraphs, Kennedy concluded by stating that the petitioners' stories "reveal that they seek not to denigrate marriage but rather to live their lives, or honor their spouses' memory, joined in its bond."[25]

Justice Kennedy then recited historical developments in legal and societal perspectives on marriage and homosexuality before he addressed relevant legal precedent, beginning with what he called the Court's first "detailed consideration of the legal status of homosexuals" in *Bowers v. Hardwick* (1986), in which the Court upheld the constitutionality of laws criminalizing consensual sodomy between either heterosexual or gay couples but which were only enforced against gay couples,[26] and *Lawrence v. Texas* (2003), in which the Court overruled *Bowers* to hold that state laws criminalizing intimate sexual conduct between members of the same sex were unconstitutional.[27] With this precedent as background, Kennedy then summarized previous cases that had addressed same-sex marriage, noting that a substantial body of law existed which had almost unanimously held that it was unconstitutional to exclude same-sex couples from marriage.[28]

Intimate Choices

Justice Kennedy also wrote the majority opinion in *Lawrence*, and in *Obergefell* he cited his opinion in *Lawrence* extensively, quoting among other passages *Lawrence*'s acknowledgment that "when sexuality finds overt expression in intimate conduct with another person, the conduct can be but one element in a personal bond that is more enduring," and its conclusion that the state "cannot demean their existence or control their destiny by making their private sexual conduct a crime."[29] Compared to Kennedy's opinion in *Obergefell*, Kennedy only used brief epideictic registers in *Lawrence*, but much as he did in *Obergefell*, he began *Lawrence* with an epideictic register describing the liberty at stake as transcendent:

> Liberty protects the person from unwarranted government intrusions into a dwelling or other private places. In our tradition the State is not

omnipresent in the home. And there are other spheres of our lives and existence, outside the home, where the State should not be a dominant presence. Freedom extends beyond spatial bounds. Liberty presumes an autonomy of self that includes freedom of thought, belief, expression, and certain intimate conduct. The instant case involves liberty of the person both in its spatial and in its more transcendent dimensions.[30]

Robert Tsai notes that three of the four illustrations of liberty in the penultimate sentence of this passage of *Lawrence* are First Amendment freedoms. He argues that Kennedy hoped by citing rights at the beginning of his opinion which had already enjoyed broad support and then adding "the more contested right of sexual autonomy," the right of sexual autonomy "would gain something from its association with expressive rights."[31]

In *Lawrence*, Justice Kennedy framed the issue as one of determining "whether the petitioners were free as adults to engage in the private conduct in the exercise of their liberty under the Due Process Clause of the Fourteenth Amendment." He noted that there were "broad statements of the substantive reach of liberty under the Due Process Clause in earlier cases,"[32] the most pertinent of which was *Griswold v. Connecticut* (1965), in which the Court recognized a constitutional right of privacy to support its holding that a state law prohibiting the use of contraceptives or medical advice about their use was unconstitutional because it violated the privacy of marital relationships.[33] Kennedy wrote that both *Griswold* and *Eisenstadt v. Baird* (1972), in which the Court held that a state law prohibiting the distribution of contraceptives to unmarried people was no more constitutional than the contraceptive law invalidated in *Griswold*,[34] had formed the basis for *Roe v. Wade* (1973), in which the Court held that the Constitution limited the ability of states to restrict access to abortion,[35] and *Planned Parenthood v. Casey* (1992),[36] which reaffirmed *Roe*.[37] These cases, Kennedy wrote in *Lawrence*, "confirmed that the reasoning of *Griswold* could not be confined to the protection of rights of married adults."[38] In *Lawrence*, Justice Kennedy also noted that *Casey* and *Romer v. Evans* (1996), both decided after *Bowers*, had cast the decision in *Bowers* "into even more doubt."[39] In *Romer*, the Court invalidated as unconstitutional a state constitutional amendment which excepted gays, lesbians, and bisexuals from protection under antidiscrimination laws.[40]

Accordingly, Justice Kennedy concluded in *Lawrence* that the Court in *Bowers* failed to appreciate "the extent of liberty at stake." The penalties and purposes of the laws criminalizing intimate sexual relations between same-sex couples involved in *Bowers* and *Lawrence*, Kennedy wrote, impacted "the most private human conduct, sexual behavior, and in the most private of places, the home," and "when sexuality finds overt expression in intimate conduct with another person, the conduct can be but one element in a personal bond that is more enduring."[41]

In Justice Harry Blackmun's dissenting opinion in *Bowers*, joined by Justices William Brennan, Thurgood Marshall, and John Paul Stevens, Blackmun also used epideictic registers to magnify the value of privacy in intimate sexual relations, beginning his opinion by quoting Justice Brandeis's dissenting opinion in *Olmstead* to state that *Bowers* was about "'the most comprehensive of rights and the right most valued by civilized men,' namely, 'the right to be let alone.'"[42] According to Blackmun, the right of privacy was based on the value of individual autonomy rather than public welfare. "We protect those rights not because they contribute, in some direct and material way, to the general public welfare," wrote Blackmun, "but because they form so central a part of an individual's life." They embody "'the moral fact that a person belongs to himself and not others nor to society as a whole.'"[43]

Justice Blackmun then expounded on the importance of individual autonomy through a series of antitheses:

> We protect the decision whether to have a child because parenthood alters so dramatically an individual's self-definition, not because of demographic considerations or the Bible's command to be fruitful and multiply. And we protect the family because it contributes so powerfully to the happiness of individuals, not because of a preference for stereotypical households. The Court recognized in *Roberts* [v. *United States Jaycees* (1984)] that the "ability independently to define one's identity that is central to any concept of liberty" cannot truly be exercised in a vacuum; we all depend on the "emotional enrichment from close ties with others."[44]

Blackmun concluded that "only the most willful blindness could obscure the fact that sexual intimacy is 'a sensitive, key relationship of human existence, central to family life, community welfare, and the development of human personality.'"[45]

In *Lawrence*, Kennedy also quoted the following epideictic passage from the Court's plurality opinion in *Casey*, in which Kennedy joined

Justices Sandra Day O'Connor and David Souter to write the plurality opinion regarding constitutional limits on abortion restrictions:

> These matters, involving the most intimate and personal choices a person may make in a lifetime, choices central to personal dignity and autonomy, are central to the liberty protected by the Fourteenth Amendment. At the heart of liberty is the right to define one's own concept of existence, of meaning, of the universe, and of the mystery of human life. Beliefs about these matters could not define the attributes of personhood were they formed under compulsion of the State.[46]

The *Casey* opinion used substantial epideictic registers beyond this passage as well, beginning with the gnomic opening sentence: "Liberty finds no reference in a jurisprudence of doubt."[47] The plurality not only used epideictic registers to amplify the value of precedent to support its reaffirmation of the essential holding of *Roe* regarding a woman's right to abortion, but to magnify the value of privacy on which both *Roe* and *Casey* depended.

In its description of women's right to abortion, the *Casey* plurality magnified the value of liberty by dwelling on the sacrifices women make to give birth:

> The liberty of the woman is at stake in a sense unique to the human condition and so unique to the law. The mother who carries a child to full term is subject to anxieties, to physical constraints, to pain that only she must bear. That these sacrifices have from the beginning of the human race been endured by woman with a pride that ennobles her in the eyes of others and gives to the infant a bond of love cannot alone be grounds for the State to insist she make the sacrifice. Her suffering is too intimate and personal for the State to insist, without more, upon its own vision of the woman's role, however dominant that vision has been in the course of our history and our culture. The destiny of the woman must be shaped to a large extent on her own conception of her spiritual imperatives and her place in society.[48]

In this passage, the plurality used praise, exergasia, antithesis, asyndeton, the gnomic aspect, and a relatively affirmative modality to magnify the stakes of abortion rights for women, and in a particularly curious example of unbounded terminology the plurality even shifted from using the count nouns *the woman* and *the mother* to the uncountable noun *woman* in the third sentence of the passage, referring not to a specific or generic woman but to womankind.

Due Process in *Obergefell*

After addressing the legal precedent regarding the right of same-sex marriage and intimate relations, Justice Kennedy began his legal analysis in *Obergefell* by addressing the liberty protected by the Due Process Clause of the Fourteenth Amendment. The "fundamental liberties" protected by the clause, Kennedy wrote, include most of the rights enumerated in the Bill of Rights and "extend to certain personal choices central to individual dignity and autonomy, including intimate choices that define personal identity and beliefs," citing *Griswold, Eisenstadt,* and Justice John Harlan's dissenting opinion in *Poe v. Ullman* (1961), in which the Court held that plaintiffs who wanted to use contraceptives lacked standing to seek a declaratory judgment challenging the constitutionality of the same Connecticut statutes later held unconstitutional in *Griswold*.[49] Citing *Lawrence*, Kennedy wrote that "history and tradition guide and discipline this inquiry but do not set its outer boundaries," because "the nature of injustice is that we may not always see it in our own time."

Justice Kennedy also cited *Loving v. Virginia* (1967), in which the Court held miscegenation laws to be unconstitutional, for the proposition that the Court had "long held the right to marry...protected by the Constitution." Although Kennedy acknowledged that the right had previously presumed a relationship involving opposite-sex couples, he argued that four "principles and traditions" demonstrated that the reasons freedom in marriage was fundamental under the Constitution applied with equal force to same-sex couples: (1) it inheres in the concept of individual autonomy;[50] (2) it supports a two-person union "unlike any other in its importance to the committed individuals;"[51] (3) it "safeguards children and families," drawing from "related rights of childrearing, procreation, and education,"[52] and (4) it is a "keystone of our social order."[53]

To support his conclusion that the freedom to marry whoever one chooses inheres in the concept of individual autonomy, Justice Kennedy wrote that "the abiding connection between marriage and liberty is why

Loving invalidated interracial marriage bans under the Due Process Clause," and that decisions concerning marriage are "among the most intimate that an individual can make," similar to choices concerning contraception, family relationships, procreation, and childrearing, all of which were protected by the Constitution. "Choices about marriage shape an individual's destiny," Kennedy wrote, and he quoted the epideictic registers of the Massachusetts Supreme Court's opinion on same-sex marriage in *Goodridge v. Department of Public Health* (2003), in which Justice Margaret Marshall wrote that because marriage "fulfils yearnings for security, safe haven, and connection that express our common humanity," it is "an esteemed institution, and the decision whether and whom to marry is among life's momentous acts of self-definition." Through marriage's "enduring bond," Kennedy wrote, "all persons, whatever their sexual orientation," "can find other freedoms, such as expression, intimacy, and spirituality" together. "There is dignity in the bond between two men or two women," he affirmed, "who seek to marry and in their autonomy to make such profound choices."[54]

With regard to the principle that marriage supports a two-person union "unlike any other in its importance to the committed individuals,"[55] Justice Kennedy began by noting that this principle was central to *Griswold* and he quoted in its entirety the concluding mesodiplosis from Justice William Douglas's majority opinion for the Court in *Griswold*:

> We deal with a right of privacy older than the Bill of Rights—older than our political parties, older than our school system. Marriage is a coming together for better or for worse, hopefully enduring, and intimate to the degree of being sacred. It is an association that promotes a way of life, not causes; a harmony in living, not political faiths; a bilateral loyalty, not commercial or social projects. Yet it is an association for as noble a purpose as any involved in our prior decisions.[56]

The eloquence of this passage from Douglas's opinion in *Loving* began with its appeal to anteriority using the anaphora and asyndeton that repeat *older* at the beginning of successive clauses and concluded with the mesodiplosis surrounding the successive antitheses *a way of life, not causes; a harmony in living, not political faiths; a bilateral loyalty, not commercial or social projects*, which framed marriage as transcending commercial and political life. It is in this section of his opinion that Kennedy wrote that marriage responds to the "universal" fear that "a lonely person might call out only to find no one there," offering "the hope of companionship and understanding and assurance that while both still live there will be someone to care for the other," and he concluded that although *Lawrence* confirmed a measure of freedom, "outlaw to outcast may be a step forward, but it does not achieve the full promise of liberty."[57]

Justice Kennedy wrote that the Court had recognized the connection between marriage and childrearing, procreation, and education "by describing the varied rights as a unified whole," because the right to marry, establish a home, and raise children form a central part of the liberty protected by the Due Process Clause of the Fourteenth Amendment:

> Under the laws of the several States, some of marriage's protections for children and families are material. But marriage also confers more profound benefits. By giving recognition and legal structure to their parents' relationship, marriage allows children "to understand the integrity and closeness of their own family and its concord with other families in their community and in their daily lives." Marriage also affords the permanency and stability important to children's best interests.[58]

Finally, Kennedy supported the conclusion that both the Court and the nation's traditions had established marriage as a "keystone of our social order" by quoting the following passage of Alexis de Tocqueville's *Democracy in America*, in which Tocqueville exalts the "order and peace" of American family life as an important feature of politics:

> There is certainly no country in the world where the tie of marriage is so much respected as in America....[W]hen the American retires from the turmoil of public life to the bosom of his family, he finds in it the image of order and of peace....[H]e afterwards carries [that image] with him into public affairs.[59]

Kennedy wrote that the Court had echoed Tocqueville's remarks in *Maynard v. Hill* (1888) when it explained that marriage is "'the foundation of the family and of society, without which there would be neither civilization nor progress,'" an institution that gave "'character to our whole civil polity.'" This idea had been reiterated, Kennedy noted, even as the institution evolved, and "marriage remains a building block of our national community."[60]

Text and Penumbra

Because *Griswold* holds a central place in the development of the constitutional right of privacy which protects intimate relations and marriage, Justice Kennedy cited *Griswold* and its progeny many times in *Obergefell*. In *Griswold*, the Court considered a challenge to the constitutionality of Connecticut statutes that prohibited the use of contraceptives and medical advice relating to their use brought by the Executive Director of the Planned Parenthood League of Connecticut and a licensed physician and professor at Yale Medical School who served as Medical Director for Planned Parenthood in New Haven, both of whom were arrested by Connecticut authorities for providing medical advice to married persons relating to the use of contraceptives.[61] Before *Griswold*, the law had only protected the right of privacy between individuals as a private right of action rather than one guaranteed by the Constitution. As Bernard Schwartz notes, the constitutional right of privacy recognized in *Griswold* "proved as consequential as any constitutional right recognized by the Supreme Court," making it among the most important cases decided by the Warren Court.[62]

Writing for the majority in *Griswold*, Justice Douglas wrote that the case raised "a wide range of questions that implicate the Due Process Clause of the Fourteenth Amendment." He then addressed rights of association that the First Amendment had been construed to recognize but which were "not mentioned in the Constitution nor in the Bill of Rights," including the right to educate a child in a school of the parents' choice and the right to study a particular subject or foreign language.[63] As Robert Tsai notes, it is an "underappreciated fact" that Douglas "opened and closed his discussion [in *Griswold*] by casting the right to privacy—the 'intimate relation of husband and wife'—in First Amendment terms," and devoted most of his opinion to First Amendment freedoms.[64] Because the First Amendment rights Douglas identified were recognized despite not being mentioned in the First Amendment or the Bill of Rights, Douglas concluded that the First Amendment "has a penumbra where privacy is protected from governmental intrusion."[65] Such cases, he wrote, "suggest that specific guarantees in the Bill of Rights have penumbras, formed by emanations from those guarantees that help give them life and substance,"[66] a passage that has been quoted at least 196 times in later judicial opinions in the United States[67] and generated substantial controversy.[68]

Justice Douglas explained that "various guarantees create zones of privacy," and "the First Amendment is one."[69] Others, he wrote, included the Third Amendment's prohibition against the quartering of soldiers in time of peace, the Fourth Amendment's protection of the "right of the people to be secure in their persons, houses, papers, and effects, against unreasonable searches and seizures," the Fifth Amendment's protection against self-incrimination—which Douglas wrote "enables the citizen to create a zone of privacy which government may not force him to surrender to his detriment"—and the Ninth Amendment's provision that "the enumeration in the Constitution, of certain rights, shall not be construed to deny or disparage others retained by the people."[70] Douglas supported his conclusion by quoting Justice Joseph Bradley's statement in *Boyd v. United States* (1886) that the protection provided by the Fourth and Fifth Amendments "affect the very essence of constitutional liberty and security," reaching "farther than the concrete form of the case then before the court, with its adventitious circumstances," applying instead "to all invasions on the part of the government and its employés [sic] of the sanctity of a man's home and the privacies of life."[71]

Justice Douglas also quoted the following epideictic passage from *Boyd*, which has been quoted eighty-nine times in other judicial opinions in the United States,[72] exhibiting praise, a figurality which is particularly striking in the assonance and alliteration of the opening sentence, eloquence, the gnomic aspect, and a relatively affirmative modality:

> It is not the breaking of his doors, and the rummaging of his drawers, that constitutes the essence of the offence; but it is the invasion of his indefeasible right of personal security, personal liberty and private property, where that right has never been forfeited by his conviction of some public offence—it is the invasion of this sacred right which underlies and constitutes the essence of [the protection]. Breaking into a house and opening boxes and drawers are circumstances of aggravation; but any forcible and compulsory extortion of a man's own testimony or of his private papers to be used as evidence to convict him of crime or to forfeit his goods, is within

the condemnation....In this regard the Fourth and Fifth Amendments run almost into each other.⁷³

To conclude his opinion in *Griswold*, Justice Douglas recognized that the "penumbral rights of 'privacy and repose'" that the case recognized had given rise to many cases which "bear witness that the right of privacy which presses for recognition here is a legitimate one." He then ended the opinion with the mesodiplosis quoted by Justice Kennedy in *Obergefell* and eighty-four times in other judicial opinions in the United States as well as in judicial opinions of the supreme courts of Canada, India, and Ireland,⁷⁴ that marriage is "an association that promotes a way of life, not causes; a harmony in living, not political faiths; a bilateral loyalty, not commercial or social projects," but one with "as noble a purpose as any involved in our prior decisions."⁷⁵ As with the beginning of Douglas's discussion of privacy in *Griswold*, he concluded by casting the right of privacy in terms of associational rights typically protected by the First Amendment.

It is no surprise that Justice Douglas opened and closed his discussion of the constitutional right of privacy in *Griswold* by casting the right to privacy in First Amendment terms, as Robert Tsai notes,⁷⁶ because Douglas's first draft opinion in *Griswold* did not rely on the right of privacy at all but on the First Amendment right of association, comparing the marital relationship to other forms of association protected by the First Amendment.⁷⁷ In Douglas's draft opinion, his mesodiplosis on the marital "right of association" (or "right of privacy" in the published version) did not end the opinion. The draft opinion continued the epideictic register as follows:

> Yet it flourishes on the interchange of ideas. It is the main font of the population problem; and education of each spouse in the ramification of that problem, the health of the wife, and the well-being of the family, is central to family functioning. Those objects are the end products of free expression.

The draft opinion then concluded with what forms part of the penultimate paragraph of the published opinion, noting that the prospect of police searching the "sacred precincts of marital bedrooms for telltale signs of the use of contraceptives" was "repulsive to the idea of privacy and of association that make up a goodly part of the penumbra of the Constitution and Bill of Rights."[78] The references to privacy and a penumbra of rights in this final clause of the draft opinion are the only references to those terms in the draft, unlike the published version in which Douglas referenced privacy a dozen times and the penumbra metaphor four times.

We now know that Justice William Brennan persuaded Justice Douglas to edit his draft opinion in *Griswold* to abandon the First Amendment right of association approach in favor of a right of privacy after Douglas circulated his draft to the justices.[79] In a letter Brennan sent to Douglas regarding the draft opinion, Brennan noted that in the First Amendment context, in cases such as *NAACP* [National Association for the Advancement of Colored People] *v. Alabama* (1958)—a case Douglas cited in *Griswold* in which the Court held that a state's requirement that the NAACP disclose its membership list to conduct business in the state violated the Due Process Clause of the Fourteenth Amendment—privacy was necessary to "protect the capacity of an association for fruitful advocacy."[80] Brennan encouraged Douglas to consider what the Bill of Rights guaranteed as "but expressions of examples of those rights," without precluding "applications or extensions of those rights to situations unanticipated by the Framers." In other words, Brennan explained, the First, Third, Fourth, and Fifth Amendments, taken together, "indicate a fundamental concern with the sanctity of the home and the right of the individual to be alone,"[81] an allusion to Justice Brandeis's assertion of a "right to be let alone" in *Olmstead*.[82]

Despite Justice Brennan's influence on the published version of Justice Douglas's opinion in *Griswold*, Brennan ultimately joined Justice Arthur Goldberg's concurring opinion in which Goldberg wrote separately to emphasize the importance of the Ninth Amendment but agreed that "the concept of liberty protects those personal rights that are fundamental, and is not confined to the specific terms of the Bill of Rights." Although Goldberg's opinion was different in emphasis, it specifically endorsed Douglas's conclusion that "the right of marital privacy is protected, as being within the protected penumbra of specific guarantees of the Bill of Rights."[83]

David O'Brien writes that Justice Douglas's penumbra approach to privacy may have been "too imaginative to persuade many court watchers."[84] Although Justice John Harlan joined the decision in *Griswold*, he wrote a separate concurring opinion to express disagreement with the penumbra theory because he thought the case could be decided solely under the liberty protected by the Due Process Clause of the Fourteenth Amendment.[85]

In Justice Hugo Black's dissenting opinion, which Justice Potter Stewart joined, Black more broadly criticized living constitutionalism as an arrogation of authority to amend the Constitution, although he recognized the "rhapsodical" quality of epideictic registers often used to support the theory in relatively flattering terms: "I realize that many good and able men have eloquently spoken and written, sometimes in rhapsodical strains, about the duty of this Court to keep the Constitution in tune with the times."[86]

The penumbra metaphor did not originate in response to the privacy right recognized in *Griswold*. Instead, Justice Douglas had previously used the metaphor eight times and other federal judges and legal scholars had frequently used it.[87] The metaphor had a long history in legal reasoning beginning at least as early as the nineteenth century,[88] including its use by Justice Oliver Wendell Holmes in his dissenting opinion in *Olmstead*, in which Holmes wrote that he was "not prepared to say that the penumbra of the Fourth and Fifth Amendments covers the defendant" but that courts often erred by adhering too closely to the text of laws which "import a policy that goes beyond them."[89] In Douglas's dissenting opinion in *Poe v. Ullman* (1961), the predecessor to *Griswold* in which the Court held that the plaintiffs did not have standing to challenge the same contraceptive law at issue in *Griswold*, he also used the emanation metaphor closely linked with the penumbra metaphor. In *Poe*, Douglas wrote that "this notion of privacy is not drawn from the blue," but "emanates from the totality of the constitutional scheme under which we live."[90] Christopher Rideout writes that part of the criticism of Douglas's penumbra metaphor in *Griswold* derives from a general distrust of metaphor, although he recognizes that the penumbra metaphor provoked unique disdain among legal metaphors.[91] It faced the harshest critique from those like Justice Hugo Black, who simply objected to the recognition of any rights not explicitly enumerated in the Constitution.

In *Obergefell*, Justice Kennedy also relied on Justice John Harlan's dissenting opinion in *Poe*, which has been particularly influential in the Court's Due Process jurisprudence.[92] Both Justices Douglas and Harlan wrote dissenting opinions in *Poe* arguing that the plaintiffs had standing to sue and that the contraceptive law deprived the plaintiffs of liberty without due process of law under the Due Process Clause of the Fourteenth Amendment.[93] Although Douglas cited his own dissenting opinion in *Poe* in his majority opinion in *Griswold*, and both Douglas's and Harlan's opinions in *Poe* contain epideictic registers extolling the breadth and significance of liberty,[94] Harlan's opinion in *Poe* has been the more influential of the two.

In Justice Felix Frankfurter's plurality opinion in *Poe*, he argued that because the Connecticut contraceptive law had apparently only been enforced in a single case in 1940 since its original passage in 1879 despite contraceptives being "commonly and notoriously sold in Connecticut drug stores," Connecticut evinced a policy of nullification with no "real threat of enforcement."[95] The Court, he wrote, "cannot be umpire to debates concerning harmless, empty shadows."[96] By contrast, Harlan opened his discussion of the constitutional question in *Poe* by describing the law as "an intolerable and unjustifiable invasion of privacy in the conduct of the most intimate concerns of an individual's personal life."[97] Although he acknowledged that his conclusions were not based on any "explicit language of the Constitution, and have yet to find expression in any decision of this Court," he wrote that the Court must approach the text of the Constitution "not in a literalistic way, as if we had a tax statute before us, but as the basic charter of our society, setting out in spare but meaningful terms the principles of government."[98]

According to Justice Harlan, the scope of protection afforded to life, liberty, and property by the Due Process Clause of the Fourteenth Amendment was not determined by "the particular enumeration of rights in the first eight amendments" but embraced all of those rights considered fundamental.[99] In a gnomic saying that began a substantial paean to due process, he wrote that "due process has not been reduced to any formula; its content cannot be determined by reference to any code." Instead, he wrote, "the best that can be said is that through the course of this Court's decisions it has represented the balance which our Nation, built upon postulates of respect for the liberty of the individual, has struck between that liberty and the demands of organized society." This balance, Harlan concluded, is formed by tradition and determined with judgment and judicial restraint:

> The balance of which I speak is the balance struck by this country, having regard to what history teaches are the traditions from which it developed as well as the traditions from which it broke. That tradition is a living thing. A decision of this Court which radically departs from it could not

long survive, while a decision which builds on what has survived is likely to be sound. No formula could serve as a substitute, in this area, for judgment and restraint.[100]

After addressing the Connecticut law before the Court, Justice Harlan returned to an epideictic register in the final section of his opinion, first quoting at length from Justice Brandeis's dissenting opinion in *Olmstead* regarding the broad scope of the Bill of Rights to protect spiritual and intellectual needs through the "right to be let alone" and then expounding on the importance of the "privacy of the home" to liberty and security. The "sweep of the Court's decisions, under both the Fourth and Fourteenth Amendments," Harlan wrote, "amply shows that the Constitution protects the privacy of the home against all unreasonable intrusion of whatever character."[101] Quoting *Wolf v. Colorado* (1949), he added that "the security of one's privacy against arbitrary intrusion by the police—which is at the core of the Fourth Amendment—is basic to a free society."[102]

Loving and *Brown*

In *Obergefell*, Justice Kennedy also relied extensively on citations to *Loving v. Virginia* (1967), decided two years after *Griswold*, in which the Court held that Virginia's miscegenation law adopted to prevent marriages between persons based solely on their racial classification was unconstitutional under the Due Process and Equal Protection Clauses of the Fourteenth Amendment.[103] Writing for a unanimous Court in *Loving*, Justice Warren wrote that "the clear and central purpose of the Fourteenth Amendment was to eliminate all official state sources of invidious racial discrimination," and that there was "no question but that Virginia's miscegenation statutes rest solely upon distinctions drawn according to race" in violation of the Equal Protection Clause of the Fourteenth Amendment.[104]

In an otherwise brief and pragmatic opinion, Warren adopted an epideictic register in the final two paragraphs to announce the Court's conclusion that Virginia's miscegenation law also deprived the couple of liberty without due process of law in violation of the Due Process Clause of the Fourteenth Amendment. "The freedom to marry has long been recognized as one of the vital personal rights essential to the orderly pursuit of happiness by free men," Warren wrote, and in his final paragraph he elevated the freedom to marry to an existential necessity:

> Marriage is one of the "basic civil rights of man," fundamental to our very existence and survival. To deny this fundamental freedom on so unsupportable a basis as the racial classifications embodied in these statutes, classifications so directly subversive of the principle of equality at the heart of the Fourteenth Amendment, is surely to deprive all the State's citizens of liberty without due process of law. The Fourteenth Amendment requires that the freedom of choice to marry not be restricted by invidious racial discriminations. Under our Constitution, the freedom to marry, or not marry, a person of another race resides with the individual and cannot be infringed by the State.[105]

In *Obergefell*, Justice Kennedy quoted extensively from this final paragraph of *Loving* to support his conclusion that a prohibition on same-sex marriage violated the liberty protected by the Due Process Clause of the Fourteenth Amendment.[106]

Although in *Obergefell* Justice Kennedy does not cite *Brown v. Board of Education* (1954) and it is only cited in *Loving* for the purpose of rejecting the usefulness of consulting the legislative history surrounding the Fourteenth Amendment,[107] it is also useful to consider *Brown* part of a genealogy of *Obergefell*. As discussed briefly in the introduction to this book, Eugene Garver has argued that *Brown* constitutes an "epideictic declaration that equality and antidiscrimination are fundamental American constitutional values" which committed the Court and the nation to those values, a quality that created a new constitutional *ethos* connecting *Brown* to President Lincoln's Gettysburg Address and later to further desegregation orders which ultimately culminated in *Loving*.[108] An *ethos* such as that found in *Brown*, Garver writes, allowed practical reason to reach a conclusion "stronger than the premises that lead to it," creating an "ethical surplus" that made it "legitimately ampliative," an accomplishment unattainable by a strictly atemporal deductive logic but comparable to the ampliative possibilities of poetic work. According to Garver, *Brown*'s *ethos* "survives in the ethical surplus of the argument," the antidiscrimination principle that committed the Court to desegregation beyond the context of education.[109] Today the ethical surplus of *Brown* may also be observed in *Obergefell* through *Loving*.

Describing *Brown* as "an act of commitment," Garver argues that "had the *Brown* decision been more 'reasoned,' with more explicit ties of judgment to text and precedent, it would have been less persuasive."[110] He notes that Chief Justice Earl Warren stated that the opinions in *Brown* and its companion case *Bolling v. Sharpe* (1954) "should be short, readable to the lay public, nonrhetorical, unemotional and, above all, nonaccusatory,"[111] and according to Garver, "the brevity of the *Brown* opinion, which critics quickly characterized as 'containing almost no law,' is part of its persuasiveness because it is part of its legitimacy."[112] With regard to the need for the opinion's brevity, Garver's conclusion is premised on the observation that it needed to be readable by the lay public, "because it is they who decide whether the opinion is legitimate, and this particular opinion had to be legitimate in order to be successful."[113]

As discussed in Chapter 1, the brevity Garver describes may also refer to the gnomic aspect and affirmative modality characteristic of epideictic, or to the absence of "explicit ties of judgment to text and precedent" which Garver describes, rather than to the opinion's length alone. As Garver explains the necessity of a brief opinion:

> The Court could have written an opinion of nothing but footnotes, that is, constructed an opinion that deduced the violation of equal protection from constitutional text, history, and precedent, but for a case as monumental as *Brown* such a deduction would have been perceived as the Court hiding behind legal precedent and not taking responsibility for the decision.... The Court presents the opinion as ethically necessary precisely because it is not necessary and inevitable by narrow logical and legal criteria.[114]

This description refers to characteristic epideictic features, a discourse that is self-enclosed and unconstrained by evidence or attribution, expressing beliefs, desires, and ethical commitments knowable only through the practical imagination as common knowledge.[115]

Beyond the circumstances of its performance or its references to commitment, Justice Warren's opinion in *Brown* also contained discursive registers exemplifying all of the characteristic features of epideictic. At the heart of the opinion, for example, Warren extolled education as the foundation of good citizenship in a democratic society using an epideictic register that included praise, anaphora, eloquence, the gnomic aspect, and a relatively affirmative modality:

> Today, education is perhaps the most important function of state and local governments. Compulsory school attendance laws and the great expenditures for education both demonstrate our recognition of the importance of education to our democratic society. It is required in the performance of our most basic public responsibilities, even service in the armed forces. It is the very foundation of good citizenship. Today it is a principal instrument in awakening the child to cultural values, in preparing him for later professional training, and in helping him to adjust normally to his environment. In these days, it is doubtful that any child may reasonably be expected to succeed in life if he is denied the opportunity of an education.[116]

It is through such discursive practices that Warren constructed the *ethos* of the relationship between education and citizenship in a democratic society in *Brown*—an opinion not coincidentally issued during the Cold War when American ideology framed world affairs as a struggle between democracy and tyranny—discursive practices which allowed Warren to avoid, as Garver writes, "tackling the questions of whether the Fourteenth Amendment...changed meanings."[117]

An Epideictic Chorus

Following Justice Kennedy's discussion of due process in *Obergefell*, at the end of his opinion he turned to addressing the respondents, who had advanced among other things an equal protection argument. "The right of same-sex couples to marry that is part of the liberty promised by the Fourteenth Amendment is derived, too," he wrote, "from that Amendment's guarantee of the equal protection of the laws." The Due Process and Equal Protection Clauses are connected "in a profound way," he wrote, possessing a "synergy" or "interlocking nature" in which "each concept—liberty and equal protection—leads to a stronger understanding of the other."[118] In his peroration in the final paragraph of the opinion, Kennedy returned to an epideictic register to again extol the transcendent bond of marriage:

> No union is more profound than marriage, for it embodies the highest ideals of love, fidelity, devotion, sacrifice, and family. In forming a marital

union, two people become something greater than once they were. As some of the petitioners in these cases demonstrate, marriage embodies a love that may endure even past death.[119]

In these and similar passages throughout the opinion, Kennedy not only used praise, eloquence, and a variety of repetition devices to magnify the value of his subject, but he used the unbounded present tense to complement his often explicit depictions of marriage as a timeless institution.

The Court's decision in *Obergefell* was a particularly controversial one that followed decades of activism promoting the right to same-sex marriage and substantial resistance, including numerous actions by federal and state government authorities to stop such marriages. Such controversies regarding the inauguration of change with broad social consequences invite or even demand epideictic registers, making it unsurprising that Justice Kennedy's opinion in *Obergefell* represents one of the most elaborate examples of an epideictic register in the Court's history. Its impact is also exacerbated by the fact that the right of privacy on which it was based is not explicitly enumerated in the Constitution, which combined with the breadth of social consequences that privacy implicates may explain why epideictic registers appear prominently in so many of the Court's privacy cases.

Justice Kennedy's paean to marriage in *Obergefell* can of course be read to have addressed those expected to applaud the decision and benefit directly from it, but it appears to have also been specifically directed to the social conservatives who disapproved of the decision. In the concluding lines of the opinion, Kennedy addressed the conservative audience:

It would misunderstand these men and women to say they disrespect the idea of marriage. Their plea is that they do respect it, respect it so deeply that they seek to find its fulfillment for themselves. Their hope is not to be condemned to live in loneliness, excluded from one of civilization's oldest institutions. They ask for equal dignity in the eyes of the law. The Constitution grants them that right.[120]

By magnifying the value of marriage to a sublime level, Kennedy hoped to transfer the audience's commitment to marriage to the Court's decision so that if they could not agree with the decision, they might at least accept it. Because marriage is so timeless, transcendent, central, and profound, Kennedy argued, it cannot be denied to anyone.

As discussed in this chapter, Justice Kennedy's paean to marriage in *Obergefell* was not only elaborate in itself but it was preceded and fueled by over a century of other epideictic registers in judicial opinions addressing the constitutional right of privacy. Prominent examples include Justice Marshall's statement in *McCulloch* that the Constitution was "intended to endure for ages to come," not to provide rigid rules for exigencies which could only have been "seen dimly," if at all[121] and in *Cohens* that the Constitution is "designed to approach immortality" as nearly as possible despite facing "storms and tempests;"[122] Justice McKenna's statement in *Weems* that "a principle to be vital must be capable of wider application than the mischief which gave it birth;"[123] Justice Brandeis's statement in *Olmstead* that the "right to be let alone" was "the most comprehensive of rights and the right most valued by civilized men;"[124] Justice Douglas's statement in *Griswold* that "specific guarantees in the Bill of Rights have penumbras, formed by emanations from those guarantees that help give them life and substance;"[125] Justice Brennan's statement in *Roberts* that the "ability independently to define one's identity…is central to any concept of liberty,"[126] and the plurality's statement in *Casey* that "at the heart of liberty is the right to define one's own concept of existence, of meaning, of the universe, and of the mystery of human life."[127]

As Jeffrey Walker describes the "paradigms of eloquence" in ancient Greek epideictic from which pragmatic discourse derived its precedents, language, and power[128]—perhaps what Robert Tsai describes as "the precepts of eloquence" governing an era[129]—countless judicial opinions across more than a century contributed to a privacy jurisprudence "punctuated and pervaded by sententious flights of wisdom-invoking eloquence"[130] which shaped beliefs, desires, and ethical commitments. This intertextual power of the Court's epideictic registers may be at its height in its privacy jurisprudence because the right is not explicitly enumerated in the Constitution but can only be inferred. As the Court's commitment to a constitutional right of privacy has accumulated and taken on new meaning across a range of issues from searches and seizures to wiretapping, contraceptive use, sexual relations, and marriage, its privacy jurisprudence has specifically magnified the value of figurative reasoning as a premise of the Court's interpretive authority. As Don Le Duc argues, "the more vigorous or eloquent the judicial passage being quoted, the less likely it is to be an expression of existing law,"[131] and Jean-François Lyotard has claimed that "the retreat of regulation and rules is the cause of the feeling of the sublime" in response to Immanuel Kant's comment that the sublime emerges as a feeling of something formless.[132] Others have echoed this conception of the sublime as that which remains in some sense beyond representation, leading among other things to a call for a "sublime jurisprudence" that recognizes uncertainty, error, and incompleteness as inherent features of law.[133]

The figurative reasoning magnified by the Court's privacy jurisprudence is particularly apparent in Justice Marshall's immortal constitution metaphor and Justice Douglas's metaphor of "penumbras" of the Bill of Rights which include a constitutional right of privacy—a metaphor with a long legal history[134]—which formed central gestures in the epideictic registers of the Court's privacy jurisprudence, magnifying the Court's authority to recognize rights such as privacy which are not explicitly enumerated in the Constitution. While metaphors are ubiquitous in judicial discourse,[135] both Marshall's immortal constitution metaphor in *McCulloch* and *Cohens* and Douglas's penumbra metaphor in *Griswold* compare constitutional interpretation to situations involving a reduced visibility of light. Such imagery is suggested both by the storms through which constitutions must pass in *Cohens*[136] while facing exigencies "seen dimly," if at all, in *McCulloch*[137] and by the penumbras of the Bill of Rights in *Griswold*, referring to the partially shaded area "around the shadow of an opaque body, when the light source is larger than a point source and only part of its light is cut off."[138] The metaphors magnify the value of judicial authority at the outer limits of constitutional interpretation where meaning is difficult to discern.

According to David Zarefsky, the unit of analysis for argumentation can move beyond arguments advanced by individuals to social controversies that develop over time and involve many participants.[139] No less than the rhetorical acts of individuals or institutions, such collective discourse can create what Eugene Garver calls "ethical surplus," which is "legitimately ampliative,"[140] cumulating in a manner comparable to Kenneth Burke's description of a poetic process of development which arises from repeating something in various forms until it "increases in persuasiveness by the sheer accumulation"[141] or, in Longinus's words, when "the points of an argument allow of many pauses and many fresh starts from section to section, and the grand phrases come rolling out one after another with increasing effect."[142] The cumulative effect of epideictic is particularly apparent in the Court's privacy jurisprudence, which has produced numerous paeans to the constitutional right of privacy across more than a century. If, as Chaïm Perelman and Lucie Olbrechts-Tyteca write, epideictic is the only form of oratory that might be compared to the libretto of a cantata,[143] in the Court's privacy jurisprudence it can be compared to a chorus.

Conclusion: Truth Has No Bones

The epideictic registers of judicial opinions are not limited to fundamental rights cases, nor do they seem to be determined by the personal writing style of individual judges or their political ideology. Justices like Robert Jackson or Anthony Kennedy may betray more of a propensity for such writing than others, but judges appear to understand that its propriety is situational and epideictic registers appear in the writing both of liberal justices such as Earl Warren, Harry Blackmun, Louis Brandeis, William Brennan, William Douglas, Robert Jackson, Wiley Rutledge, and David Souter, and of conservative justices such as Felix Frankfurter, John Marshall, and William Rehnquist. Sometimes justices who vote on different outcomes in a case both use epideictic registers to voice their disagreement, as exemplified by the relationship between Justice Frankfurter's opinion in *Minersville School District v. Gobitis* (1940) and Justice Jackson's opinion in *West Virginia State Board of Education v. Barnette* (1943).[1] Epideictic also appears in the writing of swing justices such as Anthony Kennedy and Sandra Day O'Connor, and judges themselves have noted many panegyrics in the writing of William Blackstone.[2] Despite dissenting from the living constitutionalism that informed the majority opinion in *Griswold v. Connecticut* (1965), Justice Hugo Black even wrote sympathetically of the "rhapsodical strains" of those who were devoted to keeping the Constitution "in tune with the times," attributing the eloquence of such writing to "many good and able men."[3]

The pervasiveness of epideictic in judicial writing is also evident in the fact that it frequently appears in the writing of Justice Antonin Scalia, perhaps the Court's most outspoken critic of epideictic when it appeared in the writing of justices with whom he disagreed. Scalia's criticism of Justice Kennedy's paean to liberty in the opening sentence of *Obergefell v. Hodges*

(2015) as a descent from the "disciplined legal reasoning of John Marshall and Joseph Story to the mystical aphorisms of the fortune cookie"[4] is but one of many critiques Scalia advanced against epideictic writing in the Court's opinions. As noted in the Introduction to this book, Scalia derisively referred to Justice John Paul Stevens's concurring opinion in *Georgia v. Randolph* (2006) as a "panegyric to the *equal* rights of women,"[5] and in his dissenting opinion in *Lawrence v. Texas* (2003) Scalia criticized the plurality's opinion in *Planned Parenthood v. Casey* (1992) as a "paean to *stare decisis.*"[6] In *Lawrence*, Scalia specifically criticized the "sententious" opening sentence of *Casey*, "liberty finds no reference in a jurisprudence of doubt," because the same justices had voted to overrule *Bowers v. Hardwick* (1986). Scalia also referred to the *Casey* plurality's statement that "at the heart of liberty is the right to define one's own concept of existence, of meaning, of the universe, and of the mystery of human life" as the "famed sweet-mystery-of-life passage" and claimed that it was either dicta, or, if it purported to constrain the government's power to regulate actions based on one's self-defined "concept of existence, etc." it was "the passage that ate the rule of law."[7]

Despite Justice Scalia's critique of the epideictic registers of opinions with which he disagreed—a critique which sought to position his own writing as grounded in logical demonstration by contrast—he often used epideictic registers in his own writing. On the one hand he is known for a mode of debate steeped in negative modality and even sarcasm toward his opponents,[8] but Scalia is also notorious for using a wide variety of gnomic sayings in the form of maxims, aphorisms, idioms, metaphors or analogies, foreign phrases, and historical and cultural allusions, typically without attribution, which he at times called "truisms."[9] In his dissenting opinion in *Dickerson v. United States* (2000), for example, Scalia wrote that the majority overlooked "two truisms: that actions speak louder than silence, and that (in judge made law at least) logic will out."[10] The phrase *actions speak louder than silence* is an allusion to the idiom *actions speak louder than words*. In *Dickerson*, he used the phrase to mock what he perceived to be the majority's silent avoidance of the constitutionality of the Court's conclusion in *Miranda v. Arizona* (1966) that statements made in custodial interrogation were prohibited by the Fifth Amendment unless the defendant was first provided with a warning that the Court crafted, a conclusion Scalia perceived to be an unconstitutional arrogation of authority by the Court.¹¹ In a different case, Scalia wrote that "it is in fact comforting to witness the reality that he who lives by the *ipse dixit* dies by the *ipse dixit*."¹²

As Margaret Talbot writes, "occasionally, [Justice] Scalia [got] carried away with the notion of himself as the Court's littérateur,"¹³ perhaps unsurprising given that Scalia's father was a literary translator and professor of Romance languages and that Scalia himself received an intensive Jesuit education in the classics. Talbot notes that Scalia's originalism "echoes the scholarly sensibility of his father, which was in the spirit of the New Criticism," a philological method which disparaged consideration of an author's biography or a text's historical background rather than the language of the text itself. Scalia's classical education also appears to have had a powerful influence on his habits of thought. He described his education as a "very, very, classical" one beginning with "four years of Latin, Caesar to Cicero to Virgil and the poets," followed by "three years of Greek—Homer, more Homer, Aeschylus, and Euripides,"¹⁴ an education which is evident in his frequent use of Latin.

Beyond his many uses of gnomic sayings, the epideictic registers of Scalia's writing are exemplified in his dissenting opinion in *Morrison v. Olson* (1988), in which the Court upheld the constitutionality of the Independent Counsel Act. Scalia's dissenting opinion in *Morrison* formed an extended paean to separation of powers in a characteristically epideictic register. The opinion began with a dense convergence of praise, exergasia, antithesis, parallelism, epistrophe, eloquence, the gnomic aspect, and affirmative modality to extol the importance of separation of powers to the rule of law:

> It is the proud boast of our democracy that we have "a government of laws and not of men." Many Americans are familiar with that phrase; not many know its derivation. It comes from Part the First, Article XXX, of the Massachusetts Constitution of 1780, which reads in full as follows:
> In the government of this Commonwealth, the legislative department shall never exercise the executive and judicial powers, or either of them: The executive shall never exercise the legislative and judicial powers, or either of them: The judicial shall never exercise the legislative and executive powers, or either of them: to the end it may be a government of laws and not of men.¹⁵

The Framers of the Constitution, Scalia wrote, viewed separation of powers as "the absolutely central guarantee of a just Government." In *Federalist* No. 47, he added, James Madison wrote that "no political truth is certainly of greater intrinsic value, or is stamped with the authority of more enlightened patrons of liberty." Concluding his introductory paragraph of *Morrison*, Scalia wrote that "without a secure structure of separated powers, our Bill of Rights would be worthless, as are the bills of rights of many nations of the world that have adopted, or even improved upon, the mere words of ours."[16]

In one of Justice Scalia's more famous uses of gnomic sayings, he also drew on the idiom *a wolf in sheep's clothing* in *Morrison* to magnify the danger that the Court's decision posed to separation of powers. Alluding without attribution to Jesus's Sermon on the Mount in the Christian scriptures, in which the phrase *a wolf in sheep's clothing* serves as a metaphor for false prophets, Scalia wrote:

> That is what this suit is about. Power. The allocation of power among Congress, the President, and the courts in such fashion as to preserve the equilibrium the Constitution sought to establish—so that "a gradual concentration of the several powers in the same department," can effectively be resisted. Frequently an issue of this sort will come before the Court clad, so to speak, in sheep's clothing: the potential of the asserted principle to effect important change in the equilibrium of power is not immediately evident, and must be discerned by a careful and perceptive analysis. But this wolf comes as a wolf.[17]

"The mini-Executive that is the independent counsel," he wrote, operated "in an area where so little is law and so much is discretion," and in a similar antithesis he added, "how admirable the constitutional system that provides the means to avoid such a distortion," and "how unfortunate the judicial decision that has permitted it."[18]

Justice Scalia began his peroration in *Morrison* with the Latin legal maxim *fiat justicia, ruat coelum*, or "let justice be done, though the heavens may fall," noting that though the maxim was attractive, in reality "it is not an absolutely overriding value."[19] That reality, he wrote, was instead most suited to recognition by an unelected judiciary rather than the political branches of government who might have difficulty voting against a statute called the Ethics in Government Act. "If Congress is controlled by the party other than the one to which the President belongs, it has little incentive to repeal it," he argued, and "if it is controlled by the same party, it dare not."

Justice Scalia criticized not only the Court's decision in *Morrison* but accused the Court of arriving at the decision in an ad hoc manner that undermined the rule of law:

> A government of laws means a government of rules. Today's decision on the basic issue of fragmentation of executive power is ungoverned by rule, and hence ungoverned by law. It extends into the very heart of our most significant constitutional function the "totality of the circumstances" mode of analysis that this Court has in recent years become fond of. Taking all things into account, we conclude that the power taken away from the President here is not really *too* much. The next time executive power is assigned to someone other than the President we may conclude, taking all things into account, that it *is* too much. That opinion, like this one, will not be confined by any rule.[20]

Scalia then concluded his opinion by combining praise, anaphora, polysyndeton, eloquence, and affirmative modality to magnify the vision of separation of powers he attributed to the authors of the Constitution: "I prefer to rely upon the judgment of the wise men who constructed our system, and of the people who approved it, and of two centuries of history that have shown it to be sound." That judgment, "like it or not," he wrote, was "quite plainly, that '[t]he executive Power shall be vested in a President of the United States.'"[21]

Based on an approach to epideictic as "nontechnical" or "nonpropositional ceremonial speech" that intensifies adherence to values and affects "prejudgment and prejudice" in order to move discourse "in the long run," Colin Starger argues that Justice Scalia also used epideictic to "play the constitutional long game on abortion" in a series of First Amendment cases involving the free speech rights of abortion protesters.[22] Specifically, Starger argues that Scalia's dissenting opinions in the abortion speech cases of *Frisby v. Schultz* (1988),[23] *Madsen v. Women's Health Center* (1994),[24] *Schenck v. Pro-Choice Network of Western New York* (1997),[25] *Hill v. Colorado* (2000),[26] and *McCullen v. Coakley* (2014),[27] exemplify "what rhetoricians call epideictic" by intervening in "mainline abortion discourse" rather than the First Amendment issues that were before the

Court. Scalia's opinions in the abortion speech cases, according to Starger, did not "fundamentally concern free speech at all," but instead their "true subject" was abortion promoting an anti-abortion perspective that transcended the First Amendment by maintaining that "the only real explanation for the majority's doctrinal positions was its ideological commitment to abortion" and its bias against anti-abortion protest.[28] Scalia's "deeper and more essential rhetoric," Starger claims, promoted values undermining *Roe v. Wade* (1973) and other abortion decisions by associating abortion with the erosion of the rule of law.[29] "The crux of his argument," Starger concludes," was not First Amendment doctrine but opposition to the legitimacy of *Roe*.[30]

Not only did Justice Scalia use epideictic in his own writing, but his distinction between the epideictic registers of Justice Kennedy's opinion in *Obergefell* and the "disciplined legal reasoning"[31] of Justices John Marshall and Joseph Story neglected the extent to which Marshall and Story used such registers themselves. As discussed in Chapter 4, Marshall used epideictic to magnify the value of constitutionalism in *Cohens v. Virginia* (1922),[32] as he did in many of his opinions, and Story often used epideictic as well, both in some of his most important opinions such as *Martin v. Hunter's Lessee* (1816)[33] and in his 1833 treatise *Commentaries on the Constitution of the United States*. Story's *Commentaries* contains numerous epideictic registers, beginning with an effusive encomium dedicating the treatise to Marshall.[34] Following his dedication, Story immediately announces that he intends his *Commentaries* to instill an affection for the Constitution in his audience:

> [The reader's] judgment as well as his affections will be enlisted on the side of the Constitution, as the truest security of the Union, and the only solid basis, on which to rest the private rights, the public liberties, and the substantial prosperity of the people composing the American Republic.[35]

Story uses epideictic passages throughout his *Commentaries* to fulfill this purpose, culminating in a paean to American constitutionalism in the treatise's final paragraph:

> Let the American youth never forget, that they possess a noble inheritance, bought by the toils, and sufferings, and blood of their ancestors; and capable, if wisely improved, and faithfully guarded, of transmitting

to their latest posterity all the substantial blessings of life, the peaceful enjoyment of liberty, property, religion, and independence. The structure has been erected by architects of consummate skill and fidelity; its foundations are solid; its compartments are beautiful, as well as useful; its arrangements are full of wisdom and order; and its defences are impregnable from without. It has been reared for immortality, if the work of man may justly aspire to such a title.[36]

The final sentence of this passage powerfully echoes Marshall's immortal constitution metaphor in *Cohens*.

Beyond these examples from Justice Scalia's own writing and that of Justices Marshall and Story which undermine Scalia's distinction between disciplined legal reasoning and epideictic, Margaret Talbot notes that Scalia delivered a "rather purple" valedictorian speech at Georgetown which included among other passages the following paean to truth in a characteristically epideictic register:

> Truth has no bones, no flesh, no solid earthy form. You cannot hear her creeping through the forest glades by night; you cannot see her running through the forest paths by day; you cannot watch your arrow speeding straight to thud into her heart. For those who seek her, she is everywhere; for those who do not love her, she is nowhere.[37]

The appellation *purple prose* refers to an "ornate, brilliantly colored passage in a literary composition," deriving from the Latin phrase *purpureus pannus* which appears in Horace's first-century BCE poem *Ars Poetica* on the art of poetry and drama.[38] Horace's use may allude to the fact that ancient Greek rhapsodes wore purple robes to mark their function, and the Greek sophists Gorgias and Hippias were reputed to have worn purple robes as well.[39] Despite Scalia's comparison of Justice Kennedy's writing in *Obergefell* to a fortune cookie—a phrase which participates in the ethnic prejudices that caused classical authors to disparage epideictic as "Asianic"[40]—Scalia's classical education makes it likely he was trained in classical forms of epideictic and better versed in its practices than the average justice. Scalia was no stranger to the purple robe himself.

In addition to *Obergefell* and Justice Scalia's later opinions, epideictic registers appear in many other opinions of the Roberts Court. In Justice Samuel Alito's majority opinion in *Dobbs v. Jackson Women's Health*

Organization (2022), for example, in which the Court reversed its opinions in *Roe* and *Casey* regarding the constitutional standard for assessing abortion restrictions, Alito used epideictic registers to magnify the value of history, tradition, and legislative supremacy. In their jointly authored dissenting opinion in *Dobbs*, Justices Stephen Breyer, Sonia Sotomayor, and Elena Kagan opposed the decision using epideictic registers magnifying the value of liberty, equality, constitutionalism, and *stare decisis*. Although the epideictic registers of *Dobbs* are less elaborate than those of Justices Felix Frankfurter and Robert Jackson in *Gobitis* and *Barnette*, the conflict of belief, desire, and ethical commitment between originalism and living constitutionalism which supported the opposing positions on abortion in *Dobbs* is particularly evident in the epideictic registers of the opinions.

In *Dobbs*, Justice Alito's majority opinion largely consisted of an invective that framed the Court's opinions in *Roe* and *Casey* as an arrogation of judicial power which eroded legislative supremacy and the rule of law. He began by using epideictic registers to magnify the originalist position that historical sources regarding abortion restrictions prior to the Fourteenth Amendment did not support the assertion that abortion was sufficiently "rooted in the Nation's history and tradition"[41] to constitute a fundamental right. When assessing the status of *Roe* and *Casey* as *stare decisis*, he also emphasized the claim that the cases had distorted "many important but unrelated legal doctrines," using praise, enumeration, anaphora, and affirmative modality:

> The Court's abortion cases have diluted the strict standard for facial constitutional challenges. They have ignored the Court's third-party standing doctrine. They have disregarded standard *res judicata* principles. They have flouted the ordinary rules on the severability of unconstitutional provisions, as well as the rule that statutes should be read where possible to avoid unconstitutionality. And they have distorted First Amendment doctrines.[42]

Throughout the opinion, Alito magnifies the value of legislative supremacy and the rule of law, implying as Justice Scalia had that the ideological commitments of past justices had uniquely distorted the Court's doctrinal positions in abortion cases. "Respect for a legislature's judgment applies even when the laws at issue concern matters of great social significance and moral substance," he wrote, and any law regulating abortion, "like other health and welfare laws, is entitled to a 'strong presumption of validity.'"[43]

Justice Alito also used a convergence of praise, enumeration, anaphora, and affirmative modality to magnify the value of the "legitimate interests" the majority concluded legislatures could protect through abortion restrictions:

> These legitimate interests include respect for and preservation of prenatal life at all stages of development, the protection of maternal health and safety; the elimination of particularly gruesome or barbaric medical procedures; the preservation of the integrity of the medical profession; the mitigation of fetal pain; and the prevention of discrimination on the basis of race, sex, or disability.[44]

He framed the decision to overrule *Roe* and *Casey* as one of judicial restraint in contrast to the justices who beginning with *Roe* had found the right to abortion to be fundamental, writing that "we do not pretend to know how our political system or society will respond to today's decision," and "even if we could foresee what will happen, we would have no authority to let that knowledge influence our decision."[45] In the final passages of his opinion, Alito returned to the theme of legislative supremacy developed throughout the opinion, writing that "abortion presents a profound moral question," and "*Roe* and *Casey* arrogated [the] authority" conferred on the citizens of each State to regulate or prohibit it. "We now overrule those decisions," he wrote, and "return that authority to the people and their elected representatives."[46]

In their dissenting opinion in *Dobbs*, Justices Stephen Breyer, Sonia Sotomayor, and Elena Kagan used epideictic registers to accuse the majority of abandoning constitutionalism and the rule of law. They wrote that *Roe* and *Casey* had "deep connections to a broad swath of this Court's precedents," which from the start and even more so at the time of *Dobbs* were "embedded in core constitutional concepts of individual freedom, and of the equal rights of citizens to decide on the shape of their lives," which had "gone far toward defining what it means to be an American."[47] In contrast to the majority's paean to the legislative process, the dissenting justices wrote that "in this Nation, we do not believe that a government controlling all private choices is compatible with a free people" nor "place everything within 'the reach of majorities and [government] officials.'"[48] Instead, "we believe in a Constitution that puts some issues off limits to majority rule," particularly "the right of individuals—yes, including women—to make their own choices and chart their own futures," even "in the face of public opposition."[49]

Rejecting what they referred to as the majority's "pinched view" of the Constitution, the dissenting justices magnified the value of living constitutionalism through an epideictic register featuring praise, exergasia, antithesis, conduplicatio, eloquence, the gnomic aspect, and affirmative modality, specifically drawing on Justice Marshall's immortal constitution metaphor as expressed in *McCulloch v. Maryland* (1819):

> "The Founders," we recently wrote, "knew they were writing a document designed to apply to ever-changing circumstances over centuries." Or in the words of the great Chief Justice John Marshall, our Constitution is "intended to endure for ages to come," and must adapt itself to a future "seen dimly," if at all....The Framers (both in 1788 and 1868) understood that the world changes. So they did not define rights by reference to the specific practices existing at the time. Instead, the Framers defined rights in general terms, to permit future evolution in their scope and meaning.[50]

"Over the course of our history," the dissenting justices added, "this Court has taken up the Framers' invitation" and "it has kept true to the Framers' principles by applying them in new ways, responsive to new societal understandings and conditions."[51]

In their peroration of the opinion, the dissenting justices in *Dobbs* magnified the importance of the change that the decision inaugurated, beginning with a powerful antanaclasis of the word *stand* used to magnify the implications of the decision for *stare decisis*:

> "Power, not reason, is the new currency of this Court's decisionmaking." *Roe* has stood for fifty years. *Casey*, a precedent about precedent specifically confirming *Roe*, has stood for thirty. And the doctrine of *stare decisis*—a critical element of the rule of law—stands foursquare behind their continued existence.[52]

The right to abortion is "embedded in our constitutional law," the dissenting justices wrote, "both originating in and leading to other rights protecting bodily integrity, personal autonomy, and family relationships."

They then developed the theme of the right's embeddedness through an asyndeton combined with praise, enumeration, anaphora, eloquence, and affirmative modality, writing that it was "also embedded in the lives of women—shaping their expectations, influencing their choices about relationships and work, supporting (as all reproductive rights do) their social and economic equality." Immediately following this asyndeton, the dissenting justices magnified the deprivation of the right with the polysyndeton that "neither law nor facts nor attitudes have provided any new reasons to reach a different result," concluding instead that "all that has changed is this Court."[53] The epideictic registers in both the majority and dissenting opinions in *Dobbs* responded to the inauguration of change with broad social consequences that posed a threat to social unity, as did public discourse surrounding *Dobbs* which was framed in epideictic terms such as *eulogy* and *requiem*.[54]

In Gerald Wetlaufer's recognition that judicial opinion writing on "politically sensitive" topics such as racial discrimination, the American flag, the death penalty, privacy, abortion, and sexuality often reflects "a passion that sounds more like the rhetoric of politics" than the antirhetorical qualities he considers more typical of judicial opinions, he ultimately concludes that the more passionate writing in such cases is anomalous. "My understanding of these passages," he writes, "is that they *are* the rhetoric of politics and *not* the rhetoric of law."[55] In light of the many areas in which judges use epideictic registers, however, it is evident that such writing is not limited to a small sphere of "politically sensitive" topics.[56] As the interlocutor Crassus remarks in Cicero's dialogue *De Oratore* to those who are content with the formulaic rules of rhetorical handbooks, dismissing epideictic registers from the purview of legal rhetoric would make the orator "abandon a vast, immeasurable plain and confine himself to quite a narrow circle."[57] As this book demonstrates, the epideictic features of judicial opinions are necessary and endemic features of judicial discourse across a vast terrain of subject matter and of legal discourse more broadly, and they cannot simply be dismissed as the occasional rhetoric of United States Supreme Court justices acting as a political body.

As discussed in Chapter 1, there is no correct level on which to identify a register, and this book only identifies registral features of epideictic on the most general level. With further study, additional registral features or subregisters might be identified. The theory developed here goes further than previous studies of epideictic in understanding it as a register, however, first by identifying formal features of the register and how they function in specific situations and by illustrating how their formal features converge in honorific performances which fulfill epideictic's transcendent function. The features occur together, rather than in isolation, to a remarkable extent. Previous studies of epideictic have only observed that epideictic includes praise, figurality, eloquence, and nonverbal elements of the occasions on which it is delivered, most often in isolation from one another. None have applied linguistics to understand the grammatical aspect of epideictic, which tends to be imperfective and specifically gnomic, or to understand its linguistic modality, which tends to eliminate or subordinate negation and epistemic qualifiers, lending it a "resoundingly affirmative," "world-affirming" quality.[58] These discoveries help explain much of the commentary on epideictic and provide more precise criteria for identifying, predicting, critiquing, and producing it.

If epideictic situations are those in which social relationships begin, end, or in which an exigency arises to threaten social unity, we can predict a correlation between such situations and the features of the register. Recognizing that epideictic responds to specific types of situations substantially qualifies the view that it creates a disposition to act only at a future moment rather than immediately,[59] or is "less urgent" but "more lasting"[60] than more pragmatic registers. While it may not ask for immediate behavioral change, epideictic speaks to an immediate social need. Disagreements may arise about whether a situation inaugurates change, however, or whether change will have broad social consequences or threaten social unity. Judges may also differ in their perspectives on the value of opinion writing as an appropriate response or a means of legitimizing judicial decisions at all.

The possibility that judges may not equally value opinion writing of any sort—epideictic or not—is one concern of those who have criticized rulings made on what is called the "shadow docket" of the United States Supreme Court, which refers to various orders and summary decisions the Court routinely makes, typically without any written opinion or any of the other procedures that accompany its merits docket such as briefing and argument. As William Baude writes, the decisions on the shadow docket are made "without ceremony."[61] Although critiques of the shadow docket's lack of transparency have been advanced since the 1950s,[62] since 2017 it has become an increasingly prominent feature of the Roberts Court both in frequency and consequence, giving rise to increased criticism that this use harms the "public perception" of the Court.⁶³ Even the most consequential shadow docket rulings are difficult to classify as inaugurating change with broad social consequences that threaten social unity to the same degree as the landmark opinions issued from the merits docket, but the recent controversy surrounding the shadow docket is a useful reminder that the decision to write opinions is a rhetorical one about which judges may hold different views.

Not only can judges fail to recognize epideictic situations or writing as an appropriate response, but they can also misapprehend the beliefs, desires, and ethical commitments of the community despite heeding the call to produce epideictic. Their vision is rejected or they fail to formulate one. As discussed in Chapter 2, for example, Justice Frankfurter's epideictic registers in *Gobitis* and *Barnette* failed to recognize the nation's character or what it had resolved to become on the flag salute issue and were inconsistent with those of the Court's First Amendment free speech jurisprudence across the wider era. Similarly, as discussed in Chapter 3, the justices writing in the Court's early Religion Clause cases failed to develop a vision for the nation regarding the relationship between religious and secular life, as reflected in the irresolute figure of chiasmus on which they relied. Judges can also fail to write efficacious epideictic forms, such as in Justice Rehnquist's dissenting opinion in *Johnson*, discussed in Chapter 2, which relied on the perfective aspect and a highly qualified modality in a manner that privileged inexorable logic instead of addressing the beliefs, desires, and ethical commitments of the community in what otherwise appeared to be an epideictic effort. Not every speech produced in epideictic situations—even those occurring in traditionally recognized epideictic genres—will be either equally epideictic or efficacious.

The register theory developed in this book might also be used to successfully produce epideictic. It at least provides a set of features that admit of infinite combinations as well as criteria for determining when and why it might be appropriate to use them, but its utility as an aid to production is limited by how dependent epideictic is on social, cultural, and historical knowledge for its efficacy. A register approach offers a more precise understanding of the situations, forms, and functions of epideictic, but not everyone can magnify the value of "a measure or standard according to which the past and future can be evaluated," as Ernesto Grassi describes panegyrics and eulogies, or "what is exemplary and to which every judgment about men, actions, or situations must be referred,"⁶⁴ on behalf of a community at a moment when its social unity is threatened. Perhaps that explains Aristotle's conclusion that maxims are only appropriate for speakers with experience in their subjects,[65] and Cicero's conclusion that the ideal orator requires a broad education not only in philosophy but in "all the liberal arts."[66]

The contrast between the antirhetorical quality believed to characterize legal discourse today and the close relationship which is perceived to have existed between rhetoric and law in the classical rhetorical tradition of ancient Greece and Rome obscures the epideictic registers of legal discourse, which were disciplined, ignored, or both in the classical world as they are in ours. By attending closely to these registers, a more perennial and fraught relationship between law and rhetoric is discernible than historical developments since the classical period explain, evident in important sources of division in both the classical and contemporary worlds. In the classical world, Aristotle's effort to discipline the epideictic rhetorical practices of the ancient Greek sophists through his division of rhetoric into deliberative, judicial, and epideictic genres is an important source of this division, as it concomitantly sought to discipline judicial rhetoric.[67] The division between judicial and epideictic speech in the classical world is also evident in the belief that the province of rhetoric should be limited to case-specific questions, or *hypotheses*, while *theses*, or general questions, should be the domain of philosophy. Both the conclusion that contemporary legal discourse is antirhetorical, and that it was rhetorical in the classical world, require qualification.

The aspiration to reunite judicial and epideictic rhetoric is evident in Cicero's emphasis on the importance of *theses* to an orator in his *De Oratore* after opposing that view in his own *De Inventione*, and the epideictic registers in the United States Supreme Court's First Amendment free speech, Religion Clause, and privacy jurisprudence discussed in this book reflect similar practices of turning aside "from the particular matter in dispute to engage in an explanation of the meaning of the general issue, so as to enable the audience to base their verdict in regard to the particular parties and charges and actions in question on a knowledge of the nature and character of the matter as a whole."[68] As Justice Wiley Rutledge wrote in his dissenting opinion in *Everson v. Board of Education* (1947), for example, "this is not...just a little case over bus fares,"[69] or as Justice Frankfurter emphasized in *Barnette*, "this is no dry, technical matter," nor of "ephemeral significance," but an "august" one that "cuts deep into one's conception of the democratic process."[70] The power of eloquence to "subsume particulars within themes and frames of larger generality," as Thomas Farrell writes,[71] is closely connected to the epideictic practice of using *theses* which was widely rejected as inappropriate for legal speakers in the classical world and even by Cicero himself in his *De Inventione*.

In legal cases, epideictic registers interact with case-specific reasoning like the "flow-control mechanism" that Paul Hopper describes of the relationship between perfective and imperfective aspects:

> The aspects pick out the main route through the text and allow the listener (reader) to store the actual events of the discourse as a linear group while simultaneously processing accumulations of commentary and supportive information which add texture but not substance to the discourse itself.[72]

The commitments reflected in epideictic registers form crucial commentary on "the essential facts"[73] of legal cases. This closely intertwined relationship between judicial and epideictic discourse is paralleled in contemporary commentary such as James Boyd White's conclusion that legal discourse is inseparable from its cultural habitus, the rules of law less a command to be obeyed or disobeyed than one among many topics of argument available to participants in the legal process, other resources including "maxims, general understandings, conventional wisdom, and all the other resources, technical and nontechnical."[74] The perceived separation of these spheres which prompted White's course of study was equally evident in classical legal rhetoric, reflecting a perennial rather than a modern tension.

In contrast to White, however, Peter Goodrich writes that the antirhetorical foundation of English common law functions through a combination of positive and negative identification in which repression and rejection inheres in the "immemorial and monumental order of law" built on a rhetoric of affectivity and icons that produce a legal identity to which a subject can wish to belong. "In the marginalia of the doctrinal texts," he writes, "we thus learn of the excellence of the English, the longevity of their laws, the honesty of their people and the tranquility and obedience of their rustic and urban communities."[75] The common law develops around "clusters of legal affection by which the careful neighbor, the reasonable man, the incompetent child, the fiduciary relation, charitable purpose, legitimate expectation and the like" are protected by and define the common law and its value.[76] This positive identification also entails a negative one in which the English are depicted as a race "which is settled, united and defended by their opposition to French and Roman customs and laws."[77] Goodrich's account of identification in the English common law appears to refer to its epideictic content, viewing it not as rhetorical but as antirhetorical because praise implies exclusion,[78] a denunciation or "refusal to listen, a void or absence of speech."[79]

While it is always possible for the transcendent function of epideictic to promote a narrow social cohesion that results in or even leverages exclusions, since the time epideictic was first recognized as a rhetorical category in ancient Greece it has been understood to perform important social, cultural, and political functions, and both Isocrates and Plato concluded that it promoted social cohesion.[80] In contrast to this history, Goodrich participates in standard histories of rhetoric which have defined epideictic as a secondary, derivative, or inferior form of speech associated with propaganda which portends a "decline" of rhetoric compared with the practical civic oratory of legislative assemblies and courts as well as in modern language policies that harbor a general distrust of figurality in favor of a "plain style" of writing.[81]

For Eugene Garver, "democratic self-knowledge unfolds itself in successful epideictic rhetoric," as epideictic functions to convert knowledge "from something that each person knows to something that everybody knows and which therefore can figure in deliberations."[82] "The community as a whole must do the knowing," Garver writes, and when this emerges "so does friendship and a common *ethos*."[83] South Africa's Truth and Reconciliation Commission was a successful instance of epideictic, for example, because it proclaimed and reconstituted the community's values, "remaking the community in accordance with its declared values."[84] We get in trouble, Garver writes, when "pragmatic and symbolic politics are no longer genres of a single art of rhetoric," but "instead see themselves as all-consuming,"[85] and discursive forms such as philosophy, epideictic, and the "celebration of common symbols" are viewed as impractical.[86] Although Garver specifically refers to the separation of epideictic and deliberative speech, the same could be said of the relationship between epideictic and judicial speech. The effort to discipline epideictic in any sphere is an effort to limit democratic self-knowledge.

Because epideictic depends on situations, forms of repetition and insistence, and structured occasions for its delivery, it is also uniquely dependent on temporality. Time and mutability served as a central focus of the practical reasoning and diplomatic model of rhetoric that characterized the line of sophistic rhetoric from Protagoras and Isocrates to Cicero, sometimes referred to as Isocratean rhetoric. Following those who consider epideictic a quality of discourse or an entire approach to rhetoric characteristic of the ancient Greek sophists rather than belonging to a genre, attending to the epideictic registers of legal discourse might represent a sophistic rhetoric of law in the Isocratean tradition, a "humanist jurisprudence" or "rhetorical jurisprudence" that parallels the "humanist theology" or "rhetorical theology" John O'Malley attributes to the rise of epideictic sermons in the papal court of the Renaissance.[87] In such a jurisprudence, temporality is equally or perhaps even more important than a court's atemporal logic, revealing itself in the ways judges manage time in the discursive development of themes, at times in lyrical directions.

The amplifying and allusive dimension of epideictic inherently challenges views of legal discourse as "complete, autonomous, and hermetic,"[88] which due to its commitment to finality is inclined to a reduction and certainty that promotes "the one right (or best) answer to questions and the one true (or best) meaning of texts."[89] According to Chaïm Perelman and Lucie Olbrechts-Tyteca, the attempt to secure the univocal definitions, or terminological boundaries, that are necessary for logical demonstration is a means of "freezing time, emancipating [logical demonstration] from language."[90] This motivation prompted modern reformers to condemn figures because metaphor transfers and transforms meaning in a manner that frustrates logical precision.[91] In contrast to the frozen time of logical demonstration, a rhetorical approach to argumentation depends so essentially on time that, as Perelman and Olbrechts-Tyteca note, it may be "precisely the intervention of time that best allows us to distinguish argumentation from demonstration." In atemporal logic "nothing new is integrated on the way,"[92] but argumentation is directed at gaining adherence to claims presented for *assent* rather than dictated by necessity, an adherence always of "variable intensity," and therefore "never useless to reinforce." Perelman and Olbrechts-Tyteca write that the temporal dimension of argumentation "invites interest in repetition and insistence," while such forms are useless to logic.[93] Similarly, Ernesto Grassi writes that because logical demonstration "cannot be bound to times, places, or personalities," it is necessarily "*unrhetorical*."[94] It is incapable, for the same reason, of attestation or commitment.[95]

Contrary to the perspective that the "rhapsodical strains"[96] of judicial opinions reflect only an inferior, degenerate, or empty form of speech more closely aligned with propaganda than argument, I propose that such writing often reflects moments when judges acknowledge the limits of their power and seek to exercise their authority rhetorically by addressing the consequences of their decisions and seeking approval of them rather than relying on power alone. The epideictic registers of judicial opinions reveal a primary rhetorical dimension of judicial discourse that is necessary and endemic to legal reasoning, a "primal," "prophetic," or "evangelic" rhetoric that is both figurative and imaginative,[97] a "major source of the emergence of rhetorical knowledge,[98] and a "central part of the art of persuasion,"[99] not an anomaly or a corruption of legal reasoning. James Boyd White writes that "what matters most is who we are, who we are becoming, who we help each other become," which is "the deepest question of life, and not only for us as individuals, but for us as a nation, and for an institution like the Supreme Court too: Not what we do, what we have, but who we are."[100] Who we are is also a becoming, based in part on who we resolve to be through the beliefs and desires to which we commit ourselves. That is the vital activity of epideictic. It is not limited to a narrow set of genres but surrounds us, in law as in life, transforming our past experiences into common knowledge as we move into the future.

NOTES

Introduction: Rhapsodic Jurisprudence

1 Pierre Bourdieu, *Language and Symbolic Power*, new ed., trans. Gino Raymond and Matthew Adamson (Cambridge: Harvard Univ. Press, 1992), 42 (emphasis in original).

2 Chaïm Perelman and Lucie Olbrechts-Tyteca, *The New Rhetoric: A Treatise on Argumentation*, trans. John Wilkinson and Purcell Weaver (Notre Dame: Notre Dame Univ. Press, 1969), 51.

3 Benevolent and Protective Order of Elks No. 85 v. Tax Comm'n, 536 P.2d 1214 (Utah 1975) (Maughan, dissenting).

4 Chief Justice John Roberts, "2019 Year-End Report on the Federal Judiciary," Dec. 31, 2019, https://www.supremecourt.gov/publicinfo/year-end/2019year-endreport.pdf (accessed January 2, 2020), 2.

5 Ibid., 2–3.

6 Ibid., 4.

7 Planned Parenthood v. Casey, 505 U.S. 833, 865 (1992); see Roe v. Wade, 410 U.S. 113 (1973).

8 Lawrence Douglas, *The Memory of Judgment: Making Law and History in the Trials of the Holocaust* (New Haven: Yale Univ. Press, 2001), 114.

9 Chaïm Perelman, "Law and Rhetoric," in *Justice, Law, and Argument: Essays in Moral and Legal Reasoning*, trans. William Kluback (Dordrecht, Holland: D. Reidel Publishing, 1980), 120, 124; cf. Douglas, *Memory of Judgment*, 113–14 ("Any act of judging...implicitly involves a gesture of self-legitimation: at the same moment that judges sit in judgment on a person or a case, they, by the nature of their institutional role, will be called upon to engage in a performance that justifies their right to perform the judicial function."); cf. Frederic Gale, *Political Literacy: Rhetoric, Ideology, and the Possibility of Justice* (Albany: SUNY, 1994), 45 ("If cases are decided by a monarch or a local totalitarian leader whose word is accepted as law without the need for justice, no theories to explain his or her decisions are necessary.").

10 See Eugene Garver, *For the Sake of Argument: Practical Reasoning, Character, and the Ethics of Belief* (Chicago: Univ. of Chicago Press, 2004), 72.

11 See, e.g., Michael Dorf, "Dicta and Article III," *University of Pennsylvania Law Review* 142 (1994): 2037.

12 Frank Upham, "Japan: A Different Vision of Law and Justice," *Responsive Community* 1 (1991): 60; see also Josina Makau and David Lawrence, "Administrative Judicial Rhetoric: The Supreme Court's New Thesis of Political Morality," *Argumentation and Advocacy* 30, no. 4 (1994): 191–205.

13 See, e.g., James Gibson, Gregory Caldeira, and Vanessa Baird, "On the Legitimacy of National High Courts," *American Political Science Review* 92, no. 2 (1998): 345; Barbara Perry, *The Priestly Tribe: The Supreme Court's Image in the American Mind* (Westport: Praeger, 1999), 50–56.

14 See, e.g., Perry, *The Priestly Tribe*, 50–56. Robert Cover notes that the judicial opinions in antebellum slave cases typically justified the enforcement of slavery laws as a "'will-less' operation" constrained by precedent. Robert Cover, *Justice Accused: Antislavery and the Judicial Process* (New Haven: Yale Univ. Press, 1975), 25.

15 Robert Ferguson, "The Judicial Opinion as Literary Genre," *Yale Journal of Law and the Humanities* 2 (1990): 205.

16 See, e.g., Perry, *Priestly Tribe*, 50; cf. Walter Murphy, *Elements of Judicial Strategy* (1964; reprint, New Orleans: Quid Pro, 2016), 43–45 ("In situations where the Justice feels that the general political environment requires unanimity, he might play on the isolation of a would-be dissenter.").

17 See Perry, *The Priestly Tribe*, 50; cf. Maksymilian Del Mar, *Artefacts of Legal Inquiry: The Value of Imagination in Adjudication* (Oxford: Hart, 2020), 13–14 (arguing that the individuality of judgments is one of the most relevant features of common law legal reasoning, a practice both "central" and "valuable" to the common law tradition).

18 Perry, *The Priestly Tribe*, 50.

19 See Jeffrey Staton and Georg Vanberg, "The Value of Vagueness: Delegation, Defiance, and Judicial Opinions," *American Journal of Political Science* 52, no. 3 (2008): 504–19; cf. Jerome Frank, *Courts on Trial: Myth and Reality in American Justice* (Princeton: Princeton Univ. Press, 1949), 258 ("Judicial opinions usually omit many of the 'real reasons,' the factors which…'dare not be written down.'"). Prior research has also concluded that judges strategically use opinion language to obstruct appellate or congressional review of their decisions. See Ryan Owens, Justin Wedeking, and Patrick Wohlfarth, "How the Supreme Court Alters Opinion Language to Evade Congressional Review," *Journal of Law and Courts* 1, no. 1 (2013): 35–59; Max Schanzenbach and Emerson Tiller, "Strategic Judging Under the U.S. Sentencing Guidelines: Positive Theory and Evidence," *Journal of Law, Economics, and Organization* 23, no. 1 (2007): 24–56; Joseph Smith and Emerson Tiller, "The Strategy of Judging: Evidence from Administrative Law," *Journal of Legal Studies* 31, no. 1 (2002): 61–82.

20 Because it addresses boundless subjects situated neither in place nor time, the gnomic aspect not only magnifies the value of its subjects but evades challenge by presenting itself as generally known truth rather than new information. It is knowable only through the practical imagination, as common knowledge,

self-enclosed and unconstrained by evidence or attribution, a quality not unrelated to epideictic's tendency to feature an affirmative modality. See Ben Grant, *The Aphorism and Other Short Forms* (London: Routledge, 2016), 13–14, 38; Eugene Garver, "The Way We Live Now: Rhetorical Persuasion and Democratic Conversation," *Mercer Law Review* 63 (2012): 825–26. The gnomic aspect is found in the Bible and wisdom literature, sometimes in the form of gnomic poetry, giving it a unique authoritative *ethos*. See Barbara Czarniawska, "Styles of Organization Theory," in *Oxford Handbook of Organization Theory*, revised ed., eds. Haridimos Tsoukas and Christian Knudsen (Oxford: Oxford Univ. Press, 2005), 237–61; Grant, *The Aphorism*, 10; cf. Cynthia Sheard, "The Public Value of Epideictic Rhetoric," *College English* 58, no. 7 (1996): 768 (writing that the ceremonial functions of epideictic rhetoric "reflect a kind of discourse whose themes and exigencies might appear to its audience as timeless and transcendent or 'universal' rather than timely, kairotic, and culturally based."); see also Dierdre McCloskey, *The Rhetoric of Economics*, 2nd ed. (Madison: Univ. of Wisconsin Press, 1998), 11–12 (noting the rhetorical function of the gnomic present to construct an "*ethos* worthy of belief" in economic literature).

21 Perelman and Olbrechts-Tyteca, *New Rhetoric*, 51.

22 Palko v. Connecticut, 302 U.S. 319, 325 (1937). More recently, the Court has asserted that for a right to be fundamental it must also be "deeply rooted in the Nation's history and tradition." Dobbs v. Jackson Women's Health Org., No. 19-1392, slip op. at 5 (U.S. Supr. Ct. June 24, 2022).

23 See, e.g., Benton v. Maryland, 395 U.S. 784, 795 (1969).

24 *Palko*, 302 U.S. at 326.

25 Milton Konvitz, *Fundamental Rights: History of a Constitutional Doctrine* (New York: Routledge, 2001), ix.

26 Garver, *For the Sake of Argument*, 72.

27 Bourdieu, *Language and Symbolic Power*, 42.

28 See, e.g., *Benevolent and Protective Order*, 536 P.2d at 1214 (Maughan, dissenting).

29 See, e.g., Gerald Wetlaufer, "Rhetoric and Its Denial in Legal Discourse," *Virginia Law Review* 76 (1990): 1563.

30 Debora Shuger, *Sacred Rhetoric: The Christian Grand Style in the English Renaissance* (Princeton: Princeton Univ. Press, 1988), 173.

31 Cf. Ernesto Grassi, *Rhetoric as Philosophy: The Humanist Tradition*, trans. John Michael Krois and Azizeh Azodi (1980; reprint., Carbondale: Southern Illinois Press, 2001), 89 ("Because poetry is rooted in 'divine madness' there is an identity between the poet and the theologian.").

32 Griswold v. Connecticut, 381 U.S. 479, 486 (1965).

33 See generally Michael Abramowicz and Maxwell Stearns, "Defining Dicta," *Stanford Law Review* 57 (2005): 953–1094.

34 *Nexis Uni* database search (last visited Sept. 21, 2020); see McGee v Attorney General, [1974] I.R. 284 (Ireland); Miron v. Trudel, [1995] 2 S.C.R. 418 (Canada); Rajagopal v State of Tamil Nadu, [1995] 3 L.R.C. 566 (India).

35 Obergefell v. Hodges, 576 U.S. 644, 656–57 (2015).

36 Ibid., 666 (quoting Goodridge v. Dep't of Pub. Health, 440 Mass. 309, 322 (Mass. 2003)).

37 See Minersville Sch. Dist. v. Gobitis, 310 U.S. 586 (1940); West Virginia Board of Education v. Barnette, 319 U.S. 624 (1943).

38 Richard Posner, *The Problems of Jurisprudence* (Cambridge: Harvard Univ. Press, 1993), 147.

39 *Barnette*, 319 U.S. at 632–3.

40 Ibid., 640–1.

41 Ibid., 642.

42 *Nexis Uni* database search (last visited Nov. 8, 2020).

43 "Court Upholds Freedom of Conscience," *Christian Century*, June 23, 1943, 731.

44 "Blot Removed," *Time*, June 21, 1943, 16.

45 *Barnette*, 319 U.S. at 627.

46 Ibid., 627; see Ferguson, "Judicial Opinion as Literary Genre," 203 (noting that *Gobitis* and *Barnette* represent "one of those rare instances in which the Supreme Court has reversed itself on a crucial matter within a short period of time").

47 *Gobitis*, 310 U.S. at 600.

48 Ibid., 596.

49 Jeffrey Walker, *Rhetoric and Poetics in Antiquity* (Oxford: Oxford Univ. Press, 2000), 158 (writing that the Greek tradition of poetic *agôn* suggests that poets needed to competitively "distinguish themselves not only by the aesthetic or formal excellence of their verse but also by virtue of saying something both admirable and distinctive."); cf. Jonathan Pratt, "The Epideictic Agôn and Aristotle's Elusive Third Genre," *American Journal of Philology* 133, no. 2 (2012): 177–208.

50 Unsurprisingly, Justice Frankfurter wrote a lengthy and vitriolic dissenting opinion in *Barnette*. See *Barnette*, 319 U.S. at 646–71.

51 See, e.g., Justice Jackson's majority opinion in *Wickard v. Filburn*, 317 U.S. 111 (1942) (upholding congressional power to enact the Agricultural Adjustment Act of 1938, which regulated the number of acres of wheat a farmer could plant) or Justice Frankfurter's majority opinion in *Beauharnais v. Illinois*, 343 U.S. 250 (1952) (upholding an Illinois law making it illegal to exhibit in any public place any publication that portrayed "depravity, criminality, unchastity, or lack of virtue of a class of citizens of any race, color, creed or religion" which exposed them to "contempt, derision, or obloquy"); see also Richard Posner, *Cardozo: A Study in Reputation*, revised ed. (Chicago: Chicago Univ. Press, 1993), 140 (writing that Justice Jackson "cultivated a plain style with great success").

52 Urofsky v. Gilmore, 216 F.3d 401, 412 (4th Cir. 2000); see Sweezy v. New Hampshire, 354 U.S. 234, 250 (1957) ("No field of education is so thoroughly comprehended by man that new discoveries cannot yet be made. Particularly is that true in the social sciences, where few, if any, principles are accepted as absolutes. Scholarship cannot flourish in an atmosphere of suspicion and distrust. Teachers

and students must always remain free to inquire, to study and to evaluate, to gain new maturity and understanding; otherwise our civilization will stagnate and die.").

53 Miller v. Board of Public Works, 195 Cal. 477, 492–94 (Cal. 1925) ("It is axiomatic that the welfare, and indeed the very existence of a nation depends upon the character and caliber of its citizenry. The character and quality of manhood and womanhood are in a large measure the result of home environment. The home and its intrinsic influences are the very foundation of good citizenship, and any factor contributing to the establishment of homes and the fostering of home life doubtless tends to the enhancement not only of community life but of the life of the nation as a whole.").

54 Miller v. Clark County, 340 F.3d 959, 967 n.13 (9th Cir. 2003).

55 Maine v. Harriman, 75 Me. 562, 566–67 (Me. 1884) (Appleton, dissenting).

56 Pedersen v. United States, 115 Ct. Cl. 335, 338–39 (U.S. Ct. Cl. 1950) ("It was a dog that licked the wounds of Lazarus in his rags. Rin Tin Tin was a movie star. Neither poverty nor riches, success nor failure, affects his loyalty. It was the dog that served as a test for the army of Gideon. He also performed heroic services in the most modern and greatest of all wars."). The court in *Pedersen* concluded its paean to dogs by quoting without attribution Norah Holland's poem "The Little Dog-Angel": "The poet said that high in the courts of Heaven the one sure welcome that awaited was a little dog angel that 'sits alone at the gates,' and would not play with the others until his master arrived." See Norah Holland, *Spun-yarn and Spindrift* (London: J. M. Dent, 1918), 7.

In *Wiley v. Slater* (1856), Judge William Allen also quotes without attribution Isaac Watts's poem, "Let Dogs Delight to Bark and Bite," writing that

> I have been a firm believer with the poet in the instructive if not semi-divine right of dogs to fight; and with him would say,
> *Let dogs delight to bark and bite,*
> *For God hath made them so;*
> *Let bears and lions growl and fight, For 'tis their nature to.*

Wiley v. Slater, 22 Barb. 506, 509 (N.Y. Gen. Term 1856) (quoting Isaac Watts, "Let Dogs Delight to Bark and Bite," in *Watts' Divine Songs for the Use of Children* (New Haven: J. Babcock, 1824), 15). In *State v. Langford* (1899), the South Carolina Supreme Court also cited Shakespeare and Lord Byron, among others, to support its conclusion that dogs were sufficiently important to justify holding a person criminally responsible for stealing one. The dog's "intelligence, docility and devotion make it the servant, the companion and the faithful friend of man," the court wrote, and it enumerated a typology of dog breeds in a lengthy mesarchia which repeated the words *to the…dog* and *that* or *whose* at the beginning and middle of successive clauses with similar forms throughout the passage:

We should not let our contempt for sheep-killing dogs and our dread of hydrophobia do injustice to the noble Newfoundland, that braves the water to rescue the drowning child; to the Esquimaux dog, the burden bearer of the arctic regions; the sheep dog, that guards the shepherd's flocks and makes sheep raising possible in some countries; to the St. Bernard dog, trained to rescue travelers lost or buried in the snows of the Alps;...to the fleet fox hounds, whose music when opening on the fleeing fox is sweet to many ears; to the faithful watch dog, whose honest bark, as Byron says, bays "deep-mouthed welcome as we draw near home";...to even the pug, whose very ugliness inspires the adoration of the mistress;...and lastly, to the pet dog, the playmate of the American boy.

State v. Langford, 55 S.C. 322, 325 (S.C. 1899). See also Montgomery v. Maryland Cas. Co., 169 Ga. 746, 748 (Ga. 1930) ("In metal and in stone [the dog's] noble image has been perpetuated, but the dog's chief monument is in the heart of his friend, 'man.' As a house pet, a watchdog, a herder of sheep and cattle, in the field of sport, and as the motive power of transportation, especially in the ice fields of the far north as well as in the Antarctics, the dog has ever been a faithful companion and helper of man.").

57 See Miller v. Clark County, 340 F.3d at 967 n.13.

58 See, e.g., Sandra Berns, *To Speak as a Judge: Difference, Voice and Power* (Brookfield: Ashgate, 1999), 194 (noting that the legal trial "serves many of the same purposes as the ritual sacrifice," playing a major role in generating "public understandings of legality and legal process" and legitimizing legal change); Peter Winn, "Legal Ritual," *Law and Critique* 2, no. 2 (1991): 207 ("Ritual characterizes nearly all human institutions, especially legal institutions charged with resolving social conflict."); Robert Yelle, "Rhetorics of Law and Ritual: A Semiotic Comparison of the Law of Talion and Sympathetic Magic," *Journal of the American Academy of Religion* 69, no. 3 (2001): 628 (writing that "many punishments, including the well-known law of talion, which prescribes 'an eye for an eye,' are structured by the principles of similarity and contiguity, the same principles also found to structure religious rituals of the variety known as 'sympathetic magic'").

59 Cf. Wetlaufer, "Rhetoric and Its Denial," 1563.

60 See, e.g., Theodore Burgess, "Epideictic Literature," (PhD diss., Univ. of Chicago, 1902), 110–13; Celeste Condit, "The Functions of Epideictic: The Boston Massacre Orations as Exemplar," *Communication Quarterly* 33, no. 4 (1985): 287; Helen North, "The Use of Poetry in the Training of the Ancient Orator," *Traditio* 8 (1952): 2–3; Menander Rhetor, *An Analysis of Epideictic Speeches*, trans. William Race (Cambridge: Harvard Univ. Press, 2019) and Pseudo-Dionysius of Halicarnassus, *Ars Rhetorica*, trans. William Race (Cambridge: Harvard Univ. Press, 2019); Walker, *Rhetoric and Poetics*, 7–10; cf. Perelman and Olbrechts-Tyteca, *New Rhetoric*, 47–51; Davida Charney, "Performativity and Persuasion in the Hebrew Book of Psalms: A Rhetorical Analysis of Psalms 22 and 116," *Rhetoric Society Quarterly* 40, no. 3 (2010): 247–68. The second-century CE

rhetorician Hermogenes of Tarsus writes that "not only poetry and prose in general" exhibit the qualities of panegyric, but "history possesses them all in abundance," and he specifically discusses the panegyrical qualities of Herodotus's and Thucydides's histories. Hermogenes, *On Types of Style,* trans. Cecil Wooten (Chapel Hill: University of North Carolina Press, 1987), 2.12; cf. Burgess, "Epideictic Literature," 195–99 ("The epideictic tendency in history is conspicuous from the time of Isocrates.").

61 See Aristotle, *Rhetoric*, trans. W. Rhys Roberts, in *The Rhetoric and Poetics of Aristotle* (New York: Modern Library, 1984), 1358$^{a\text{-}b}$ ("The ceremonial orator is, properly speaking, concerned with the present, since all men praise or blame in view of the state of things existing at the time, though they often find it useful also to recall the past and to make guesses at the future."), 1366^a.

62 Ibid., 1368^a, 1392^a; cf. Quintilian, *The Institutio Oratoria of Quintilian*, trans. Harold Butler (Cambridge: Harvard Univ. Press, 1920), 3.7.6 ("The proper function...of panegyric is to amplify and embellish its themes."); Perelman and Olbrechts-Tyteca, *New Rhetoric*, 47–51 (noting that in epideictic discourse the speaker "uses the whole range of means available to the rhetorician for purposes of amplification and enhancement").

63 Kenneth Burke, *A Rhetoric of Motives* (New York: Prentice Hall, 1950), 69.

64 See, e.g., Shuger, *Sacred Rhetoric,* 174 ("In Christian rhetoric from Augustine on, epideictic oratory often receives the same condemnation meted out to all forms of ostentatious artistry.").

65 George Kennedy, *The Art of Persuasion in Greece* (Princeton: Princeton Univ. Press, 1963), 152; see also Edward Cope, *An Introduction to Aristotle's Rhetoric* (London: Macmillan, 1867), 121.

66 Tim Whitmarch, *The Second Sophistic* (Cambridge: Cambridge Univ. Press, 2005), 16–18.

67 Lawrence Rosenfield, "The Practical Celebration of Epideictic," in *Rhetoric in Transition: Studies in the Nature and Uses of Rhetoric,* ed. Eugene White (University Park: Penn State Univ. Press, 1980), 131.

68 Condit, "Functions of Epideictic," 284.

69 Laurent Pernot, *Epideictic Rhetoric: Questioning the Stakes of Ancient Praise* (Austin: Univ. of Texas Press, 2015), 69. But see Menander Rhetor, *An Analysis of Epideictic Speeches,* 2.14 (recommending that the speaker delivering a farewell speech should "display evenhandedness, avoiding both denigration and flattery").

70 Cope, *An Introduction to Aristotle's Rhetoric,* 122.

71 Perelman and Olbrechts-Tyteca, *New Rhetoric,* 51; see, e.g., Aristotle, *Rhetoric,* 1414^a ("It is ceremonial oratory that is most literary, for it is meant to be read."); Walter Beale, "Rhetorical Performative Discourse: A New Theory of Epideictic," *Philosophy and Rhetoric* 11, no. 4 (1978): 237–38; Condit, "Functions of Epideictic," 292; Grant, *The Aphorism,* 29 (noting the "peremptory and dictatorial" quality of aphorisms); Perelman and Olbrechts-Tyteca, *New Rhetoric,* 48–52 (describing the classical conception of epideictic as "a single orator, who often did not even appear in public, but merely circulated his written composition, made a speech, which no one opposed, on topics which were apparently uncontroversial

and without practical consequences."); Yun Lee Toon, "Epideictic Genre," in *Encyclopedia of Rhetoric*, ed. Thomas Sloane (Oxford: Oxford Univ. Press, 2001), 254–56.

72 See *Oxford English Dictionary*, 2nd ed., s.v. "Panegyric, *n.* and *adj.*"; Shadi Bartsch, "Panegyric," in *Encyclopedia of Rhetoric*, ed. Thomas Sloane (Oxford: Oxford Univ. Press, 2001), 549; Pernot, *Epideictic Rhetoric*, 52; David Timmerman, "Epideictic Oratory," in *Encyclopedia of Rhetoric and Composition: Communication from Ancient Times to the Information Age*, ed. Theresa Enos (New York: Routledge, 1996), 230; see also Richard Lanham, *A Handlist of Rhetorical Terms* (Berkeley: Univ. of California Press, 1991), 164.

73 Walker, *Rhetoric and Poetics*, vii.

74 "Extracts from Speeches," *Four Minute Men News*, October 1, 1918.

75 See John Oddo, *The Discourse of Propaganda: Case Studies from the Persian Gulf War and the War on Terror* (University Park: Penn State Univ. Press, 2018), 16, 37.

76 Antonio Gramsci, *Selections from Cultural Writings*, ed. David Forgacs and Geoffrey Nowell-Smith, trans. William Boelhower (Chicago: Haymarket, 1985), 377–80.

77 See, e.g., Elizabeth Wood, *Performing Justice: Agitation Trials in Early Soviet Russia* (Ithaca: Cornell Univ. Press, 2005).

78 See, e.g., Walter Ong, *Ramus, Method, and the Decay of Dialogue: From the Art of Discourse to the Art of Reason* (1958; reprint., Chicago: Univ. of Chicago Press, 2004), 4, 35; James Baumlin and Joseph Hughes, "Eloquence," in *Encyclopedia of Rhetoric and Composition: Communication from Ancient Times to the Information Age*, ed. Theresa Enos (New York: Routledge, 1996), 216–17.

79 Thomas Sprat, *The History of the Royal Society of London, for the Improving of Natural Knowledge*, 2nd ed. corrected (London, 1702), 112–13 ("Who can behold, without Indignation, how many mists and uncertainties, these specious *Tropes* and *Figures* have brought to our Knowledge? How many rewards, which are due to more profitable, and difficult *Arts*, have been still snatch'd away by the easy vanity of *fine speaking*."); cf. Grassi, *Rhetoric as Philosophy*, 96–97 ("The final consequence of rational speech is the demand for a mathematical symbolic language in which consequences can be drawn from the premises that we assume. Because its 'scientific' nature consists in its strictly deductive character, its essence is such that it can possess no 'inventive' character."); Joseph Story, *Commentaries on the Constitution of the United States*, abr. by the author (Boston: Hilliard, Gray, and Company, 1833), v ("The masterly reasoning of…Chief Justice [John Marshall] has followed [the powers and functions of the federal government] out to their ultimate results and boundaries, with a precision and clearness, approaching, as near as may be, to mathematical demonstration.").

80 Wilbur Samuel Howell, *Logic and Rhetoric in England, 1500–1700* (New York: Russell and Russell, 1961), 148.

81 John Locke, *An Essay Concerning Human Understanding*, ed. Alexander Campbell Fraser, 2 vols. (Oxford: Clarendon Press, 1894), 2.3.10.34.

82 Immanuel Kant, *The Critique of Judgement: Part I, Critique of Aesthetic Judgement*, trans. James Creed Meredith (Oxford: Clarendon Press, 1952), § 53 (emphasis in original).

83 John Genung, *The Working Principles of Rhetoric, Examined in Their Literary Relations and Illustrated with Examples* (Boston: Ginn and Co., 1900), 458–59 (noting that suspicion of amplification is only properly directed to its "abuse," however, which "rightly managed" is "simply the most vital and necessary process in all composition, it is in fact the summit of composition itself, approached from the inventive side").

84 Cf. Grassi, *Rhetoric as Philosophy*, 36 (describing René Descartes as concluding that "the best, if not the only, method to convince is the severity of logical proof, which leads to truth").

85 Ruggero Aldisert, *Opinion Writing*, 3rd ed. (Durham: Carolina Academic Press, 2012), 9 (noting among the most common criticisms of opinions that they are too long, burdened with too many citations, are over written and over footnoted, and "tend to ramble").

86 Irving Mehler, *Effective Legal Communication* (Denver: Philgor, 1975), 146–47. But cf. G. Edward White, "The Evolution of Reasoned Elaboration: Jurisprudential Criticism and Social Change," *Virginia Law Review* 59 (1973): 279–302 (discussing the tenets of the Reasoned Elaboration movement in Supreme Court criticism which critiqued the perfunctory reasoning and sweeping dogmatism in many of the Court's opinions, a movement that tended to desire longer rather than shorter opinions).

87 Nevin Laib, "Conciseness and Amplification," *College Composition and Communication* 41, no. 4 (1990): 447.

88 See Vijay Bhatia, *Analysing Genre: Language Use in Professional Settings* (London: Longman, 1993), 118–19; Ferguson, "Judicial Opinion as Literary Genre," 201–02.

89 Walker, *Rhetoric and Poetics*, viii; cf. Garver, "The Way We Live Now," 832 ("There is nothing inherently second-rate about epideictic rhetoric.").

90 Walker, *Rhetoric and Poetics*, 39; cf. Garver, "The Way We Live Now," 826–27 n.77 ("Deliberative and judicial rhetoric are Aristotelian species. Epideixis, on the other hand, looks like a bag for dumping all the instances of rhetoric that do not fit into the other two kinds.").

91 See, e.g., Thomas Cole, *The Origins of Rhetoric in Ancient Greece* (Baltimore: The Johns Hopkins Univ. Press, 1991), 89; Edward Schiappa with David Timmerman, "Aristotle's Disciplining of Epideictic," in Edward Schiappa, *The Beginnings of Rhetorical Theory in Classical Greece* (Hartford: Yale Univ. Press, 1999), 185, 198. Theodore Burgess notes that the voluminous amount of epideictic writing before Aristotle was connected with deliberative and judicial oratory until Aristotle took "a word used in a somewhat loose and general way by Plato, and with much greater definiteness by Isocrates, and makes it a full technical term, with distinct outlines and well-defined field." Burgess, "Epideictic Literature," 105. Similarly, Edward Schiappa and David Timmerman write that Aristotle's formulation of an epideictic genre was not representative

of fourth-century BCE rhetorical practices but an effort to discipline sophistic rhetorical theory and subordinate it to more exclusively pragmatic values. Schiappa with Timmerman, "Aristotle's Disciplining of Epideictic," 185; see also James Jasinski, *Sourcebook on Rhetoric: Key Concepts in Contemporary Rhetorical Studies* (Thousand Oaks: Sage, 2001), 209 ("For all practical purposes, the genre of epideictic discourse was invented by Aristotle."); Pernot, *Epideictic Rhetoric*, 5 ("Aristotle's *Rhetoric* is the first treatise that defines epideictic in a technical way."); Walker, *Rhetoric and Poetics*, 39.

92 See, e.g., Ilon Lauer, "Epideictic Rhetoric," *Communication Research Trends* 34, no. 2 (2015): 4–18; Burgess, "Epideictic Literature," 105.

93 Walker, *Rhetoric and Poetics*, 7–10, 14, 83, 115, 270–71 (noting that the ideal orator imagined in Cicero's *De Oratore* "looks remarkably like a sophist... whose major sources of emotive eloquence and power derive from epideictic registers" and that the second-century rhetorician Hermogenes of Tarsus "takes the epideictic/panegyric registers as the chief source and model for high eloquence in practical oratory"); cf. Perelman and Olbrechts-Tyteca, *New Rhetoric*, 47–51; Charney, "Performativity and Persuasion," 247–68.

94 See, e.g., Susanna Braund, "Praise and Protreptic in Early Imperial Panegyric: Cicero, Seneca, Pliny," in *Latin Panegyric*, ed. Roger Rees (Oxford: Oxford Univ. Press, 2012), 87; see also Roger Rees, "The Modern History of Latin Panegyric," in *Latin Panegyric*, 5–6.

95 John O'Malley, *Praise and Blame in Renaissance Rome: Rhetoric, Doctrine, and Reform in the Sacred Orators of the Papal Court, c. 1450–1521* (Durham: Duke Univ. Press, 1979), 59, 103.

96 Kathleen Jamieson and Jennifer Stromer-Galley, "Hybrid Genres," in *Encyclopedia of Rhetoric*, ed. Thomas Sloane (Oxford: Oxford Univ. Press, 2001), 362 (finding presidential inaugural addresses to be a relatively stable hybrid genre containing a fusion of epideictic and deliberative "elements").

97 Kathryn Olson, "An Epideictic Dimension of Symbolic Violence in Disney's *Beauty and the Beast*: Inter-Generational Lessons in Romanticizing and Tolerating Intimate Partner Violence," *Quarterly Journal of Speech* 99, no. 4 (2013): 448–80 (finding an "epideictic dimension" in texts that are not "generically epideictic").

98 O'Malley, *Praise and Blame in Renaissance Rome*, 59, 103; cf. Philodemus, *On Rhetoric Books 1 and 2*, trans. and exegetical essays by Clive Chandler (New York: Routledge, 2006), 101–02 (noting that for Philodemus "panegyric is synonymous with sophistic" rhetoric, the category he claimed constituted the entire art of rhetoric); cf. Lauer, "Epideictic Rhetoric," 4 (noting that epideictic is understood as an entire approach to rhetoric as well as a genre).

99 Sheard, "Public Value of Epideictic," 774.

100 See, e.g., Asif Agha, "Enregisterment and Communication in Social History," in *Registers of Communication*, ed. Asif Agha and Frog (Helsinki: Finnish Literature Society, 2015), 38 (noting that the term *genre* is used differently by different disciplines); Douglas Biber and Susan Conrad, *Register, Genre, and Style* (Cambridge: Cambridge Univ. Press, 2009), 2, 15 (finding the features of style, in

contrast to those of genre and register, to be functionally motivated by "aesthetic preferences, associated with particular authors or historical periods" rather than recurring situations).

101 See, e.g., Asif Agha and Frog, "An Introduction to Registers of Communication," introduction to *Registers of Communication*, ed. Asif Agha and Frog (Helsinki: Finnish Literature Society, 2015), 13–14; Biber and Conrad, *Register, Genre, and Style*, 2; James Wilce and Janina Fenigsen, "Mourning and Honor: Register in Karelian Lament," in *Registers of Communication*, 188–89.

102 Jamieson and Stromer-Galley, "Hybrid Genres," 361–63.

103 Mikhail Bakhtin, *Speech Genres and Other Late Essays*, trans. Vern McGee, eds. Caryl Emerson and Michael Holquist (Austin: Univ. of Texas Press, 1986): 60.

104 See Jamieson and Stromer-Galley, "Hybrid Genres," 362 ("Genres should not be viewed as static forms but as evolving phenomena.").

105 Norman Fairclough, *Critical Discourse Analysis: The Critical Study of Language*, 2nd ed. (Harlow: Pearson, 2010), 95; cf. Karlyn Campbell and Kathleen Jamieson, "Form and Genre in Rhetorical Criticism: An Introduction," in *Form and Genre: Shaping Rhetorical Action*, ed. Karlyn Campbell and Kathleen Jamieson (Falls Church: Speech Communication Association, 1978).

106 Cf. Halford Ryan, Introduction to *The Inaugural Addresses of Twentieth-Century American Presidents*, ed. Halford Ryan (Westport: Praeger, 1993), xvii ("At least in the case of inaugural addresses, genre theory hinders more than it helps."); see also, e.g., E. Johanna Hartelius, "Sentimentalism in Online Deliberation: Assessing the Generic Liability of Immigration Discourses," in *Emerging Genres in New Media Environments*, ed. Carolyn Miller and Ashley Kelly (Cham: Palgrave Macmillan, 2017), 239; Véronique Montagne, "Epideictic in the Renaissance," in *Encyclopedia of Renaissance Philosophy*, ed. Marco Scarbi (Cham: Springer, 2019).

107 O'Malley, *Praise and Blame in Renaissance Rome*, 39–41; see Burgess, "Epideictic Literature," 95.

108 *Rhetorica ad Alexandrum*, trans. Harris Rackham (1937; reprint. Cambridge: Loeb Classical Library, 1983), 1427^b. Anaximenes also recognizes elements common to all three types of oratory such as antithesis and irony, the anticipation of objections, and making demands on an audience. Ibid., 1427^b, 1441^a ("You must also magnify his deeds by conjecture, thus: 'Yet one who has become such a philosopher when young is likely to make a great advance when he gets older,' or 'One who had endured the toils of the gymnasium so sturdily will be an ardent devotee of the toilsome labor of philosophy.'").

109 Aristotle, *Rhetoric*, 1358^b.

110 Rees, "Modern History," 5.

111 *Rhetorica ad Herennium*, trans. Harry Caplan (1954; reprint. Cambridge: Loeb Classical Library, 2004), 3.15.

112 Rees, "Modern History," 3 (noting that epideictic rhetoric is a "versatile discourse with many applications across prose and verse"); see also Michael

Dewar, Introduction to *Panegyricus de Sexto Consulatu Honorii Augusti*, by Claudius, ed. and trans. Michael Dewar (Oxford: Oxford Univ. Press, 1996), xxii ("The history of panegyric is inseparable from the history of many other genres."). Rees cites the panegyrical mode in historiography from Late Antiquity through the Roman Republic, including Seneca the Younger's "On Clemency," in which Seneca addressed the young emperor Nero on the virtues of clemency in an effort to influence him in his new office. Rees, "Modern History," 6. Rees notes that the inventiveness of "On Clemency" contributed to its importance during the Middle Ages and the Renaissance. Ibid.

113 Quintilian, *Institutio Oratoria*, trans. Harold Butler (Cambridge: Harvard Univ. Press, 1920), 3.7.1–3. The Byzantine commentator John of Sardis notes in his commentary on Apthonius's *progymnasmata* that "in judicial speeches there is often need of encomium." John of Sardis, *Selections from the Commentary on the* Progymnasmata *of Apthonius*, in *Progymnasmata: Greek Textbooks of Prose Composition and Rhetoric*, translated with introductions and notes by George Kennedy (Atlanta: Society of Biblical Literature, 2003), 207.

114 Quintilian, *Institutio Oratoria*, 3.7.4–6; see Pernot, *Epideictic Rhetoric* 90.

115 See J. Richard Chase, "The Classical Conception of Epideictic," *Quarterly Journal of Speech* 37 (1961): 298.

116 Chaïm Perelman, *The Realm of Rhetoric*, trans. William Kluback (Notre Dame: Notre Dame Univ. Press, 1982), 20; cf. Perelman and Olbrechts-Tyteca, *New Rhetoric*, 54; cf. Nicole Loraux, *The Invention of Athens: The Funeral Oration in the Classical City*, trans. Alan Sheridan (New York: Zone Books, 2006), 142–43.

117 Perelman, *Realm of Rhetoric*, 20; Perelman and Olbrechts-Tyteca, *New Rhetoric*, 50–51.

118 Jeremy Engels, *Enemyship: Democracy and Counter-Revolution in the Early Republic* (East Lansing: Michigan State Univ. Press, 2010), 18; cf. Bradford Vivian, "Rhetorical Arts of Praise and Blame in Political Transformation," in *Conflict Transformation and Peacebuilding: Moving from Violence to Sustainable Peace*, ed. Bruce Dayton and Louis Kriesberg (New York: Routledge, 2009), 78 ("The appeal of epideictic rhetoric in its most publicly visible and consequential forms, despite roseate perceptions to the contrary, is often ardently nationalistic (if not xenophobic or militaristic).").

119 Perelman and Olbrechts-Tyteca, *New Rhetoric*, 50–51; see also Colin Starger, "A Separate, Abridged Edition of the First Amendment," in *Justice Scalia: Rhetoric and the Rule of Law*, eds. Brian Slocum and Francis Mootz, III (Chicago: Univ. of Chicago Press, 2019), 196 (suggesting that dissenting opinions in judicial cases might all have "an epideictic aspect" insofar as the author of a dissenting opinion has by definition "lost the instant judicial battle" but only aims to "win a long-term war"); cf. D. A. G. Hinks, "Tria Genera Causarum," *Classical Quarterly* 30, no. 3/4 (1936): 174 ("Epideictic is an essential part of oratory.").

120 Garver, "The Way We Live Now," 831–32.

121 Perelman and Olbrechts-Tyteca, *New Rhetoric*, 21.

122 Mark Osiel, *Mass Atrocity, Collective Memory, and the Law* (New Brunswick: Transaction, 1997), 99–101.

123 Rosenfield, "Practical Celebration," 133, 147–48.

124 Bradford Vivian, "Up from Memory: Epideictic Forgetting in Booker T. Washington's Cotton States Exposition Address," *Philosophy and Rhetoric* 45, no. 2 (2012), 191. Kenneth Burke writes that "martyrdom (bearing witness) is so essentially rhetorical, it even gets its name from the law courts." Burke, *Rhetoric of Motives*, 222.

125 Perelman and Olbrechts-Tyteca, *New Rhetoric*, 49.

126 Garver, "The Way We Live Now," 827.

127 See Garver, *For the Sake of Argument*, 71–73; Loving v. Virginia, 388 U.S. 1, 12 (1967).

128 Garver, *For the Sake of Argument*, 39, 71–73; cf. Susan Balter, "The Search for Grounds in Legal Argumentation: A Rhetorical Analysis of *Texas vs Johnson*," *Argumentation* 15, no. 4 (2001): 393 ("The Supreme Court primarily functions as an epideictic speaker. It establishes value hierarchies as a precursor to action.").

129 Robert Tsai, *Eloquence and Reason: Creating a First Amendment Culture* (New Haven: Yale Univ. Press, 2008), 28–29.

130 Starger, "A Separate, Abridged Edition," 185–86, 190, 192, 194.

131 Francis Mootz III, "Perelman's Theory of Argumentation and Natural Law," *Philosophy and Rhetoric* 43, no. 4 (2010): 399; cf. Chaïm Perelman, *The Idea of Justice and the Problem of Argument*, trans. John Petrie (New York: Routledge, 1963), 14 ("Justice is the eulogistic name we give to what we conceive to be good.").

132 Georgia v. Randolph, 547 U.S. 103, 124–125 (2006) (Stevens, concurring).

133 Ibid., 144 (Scalia, dissenting) (emphasis in original).

134 See Wash. ex. rel. Lumber & Sawmill Workers v. Sup. Ct., 164 P.2d 662, 678 (Wash. 1945) (Steinert, dissenting) (referring to judicial "encomium and panegyric addressed to the constitutional guaranty of free speech—with which we can all sincerely agree").

135 See *In re* Russo, 147 Misc. 2d 179, 187 (N.Y. Sup. Ct. 1990).

136 See Younger v. Smith, 106 Cal. Rptr. 225, 235 (Cal. Ct. App. 1973) ("The legal literature concerning freedom of the press needs no enrichment by yet another panegyric. Those who do not believe that a free press is one of the cornerstones of this republic, will not be swayed by us; those who do, need no refresher.").

137 See Wisconsin v. Hersh, 523 N.W.2d 210 (Wisc. Ct. App. 1994).

138 See McSwane v. Foreman, 167 Ind. 171, 176 (Ind. 1906) ("The tenderness of the common law for the right of privacy and personal security, which finds expression in the maxim 'every man's house is his castle,' does not call for a panegyric on our part.").

139 See Mackey v. Enzensperger, 11 Utah 154, 156 (Utah 1895).

140 See Boeing Co. v. Shipman, 411 F.2d 365, 378 (5th Cir. 1969) (Rives, concurring in part and dissenting in part) ("This is no occasion for an old common-law lawyer to indulge in a panegyric on the virtues of jury trial; how in our fallible system of human justice it is the best instrument yet devised for the determination of facts, how even its imperfections operate to rub the rough edges off of technical principles of law when they would result in unjust verdicts, how it is constantly improving."); *In re* Comm. for the Preservation of the Constitutional Right

to Trial by Jury, 1 Misc. 2d 548, 555 (N.Y. Sup. Ct. 1956) (referencing William Blackstone's "just panegyric" to the jury trial).

141 See Williams v. Bloomington, 108 Ill. App. 2d 307, 312 (Ill. Ct. App. 1969).

142 See Griset v. Fair Political Practices Comm'n, 82 Cal. Rptr. 2d 25, 34 (Cal. Ct. App. 1999).

143 See Barcon Assoc., Inc. v. Tri-County Asphalt Corp., 430 A.2d 214, 224 (N.J. 1981) (Clifford, dissenting).

144 See Snow v. Or. State Penitentiary, 780 P.2d 215, 220 (Or. 1989) (Fadeley, concurring) ("The panegyric to the polygraph which is sung in the lead opinion is not joined by me.").

145 See Pencovic v. Pencovic, 281 P.2d 261, 262 (Cal. Ct. App. 1955) ("This is not a case which calls for any religious panegyrics.").

146 Perry v. Edwards Mfg. Co., 26 Ohio Dec. 301, 302 (Ohio Cincinnati Super. Ct. 1915).

147 *Nexis Uni* database search (last accessed July 18, 2018).

148 See, e.g., Lawrence v. Texas, 539 U.S. 558, 567 (2003) (Scalia, dissenting) (describing the plurality opinion in *Planned Parenthood v. Casey* (1992) as a "paean to *stare decisis*"); Arizona State Legislature v. Arizona Indep. Redistricting Comm'n, 576 U.S. 787, 859 (2015) (Thomas, dissenting) ("The majority offers a paean to the ballot initiative."); Free Enterprise Fund v. Public Co. Accounting Oversight Bd., 561 U.S. 477, 499 (2010) (referring to the dissenting opinion as a "paean to the administrative state"); Keepseagle v. Vilsack, 118 F. Supp. 3d 98, 121 (D.C. Cir. 2015) (describing a judicial opinion written by another federal appeals court as "a paean to the sanctity of class-action settlement agreements"); Int'l Controls Corp. v. Vesco, 490 F.2d 1334, 1346 (2d Cir. 1974) (describing the dissenting opinion as a "paean to literalness"); Volmar Constr., Inc. v. United States, 32 Fed. Cl. 746, 761 (Fed. Cl. 1995) ("Litigation of related claims in one proceeding is a paean to judicial economy and conservation of the parties' resources."); United States v. Khan, 325 F. Supp. 2d 218, 225–26 (E.D.N.Y. 2004) ("The rationale of the majority in *Blakely* is summed up in its paean to the jury."); Conn. v. Guilbert, 49 A.3d 705, 740 n.49 (Conn. 2012) ("If the concurring justice means to do no more than sing a paean to § 4–3 of the Connecticut Code of Evidence, then we gladly lend our voices."); Kaya v. Partington, 681 A.2d 256, 264 (R.I. 1996) (Flanders, dissenting) ("Whatever may be the allure of the majority's paean to the interests of good order and discipline within paramilitary organizations, in my opinion it would resonate more from the well of the Senate floor than from the bench of the Supreme Court."). While the term *paean* may generally refer to any act of praise, admiration, or tribute, see *Oxford English Dictionary*, 2nd ed., s.v. "Paean, *n*," it more specifically refers to songs of praise originally deriving from the song sung to the Greek god of healing Paian, later confounded with Apollo, see Arthur Fairbanks, *A Study of the Greek Paean: With Appendixes Containing the Hymns Found at Delphi, and the Other Extant Fragments of Paeans* (Ithaca: Andrus and Church, 1900), 2.

149 See, e.g., United States v. Annigoni, 68 F.3d 279, 283 (9th Cir. 1995) ("Sustaining this conviction, the Supreme Court delivered an encomium

on peremptories, asserting that they eliminated 'extremes of partiality on both sides' and assured that justice satisfied the appearance of Justice."); Robertson v. Steele's Mills, 172 F.2d 817, 822 (4th Cir. 1949) ("The opinion of Circuit Judge Simons in the *Lincoln Electric* case,...contains an eloquent encomium of trusts created by employers for the benefit of employees. With that encomium we heartily agree."); Clark v. Container Corp. of Am., Inc., 589 So. 2d 184, 191 (Ala. 1991) ("When writing of the right to trial by jury there is, on one hand, a tendency to overwrite, to be too expansive of the right: to use 'encomiums' and 'panegyrics.'").

150 *Griswold*, 381 U.S. at 522 (Black, dissenting) ("I realize that many good and able men have eloquently spoken and written, sometimes in rhapsodical strains, about the duty of this Court to keep the Constitution in tune with the times."). Before it held any musical significance, the term *rhapsode* referred to those who recited epic poetry without musical accompaniment. In Europe, by the sixteenth century it was also used to refer to miscellaneous collections of writings and to any effusive expression of feeling before becoming associated with certain musical forms and eventually with the specific form of national epic. See John Rink, "Rhapsody," in *New Grove Dictionary of Music and Musicians*, eds. Stanley Sadie and John Tyrrell, 2nd ed. (London: Macmillan, 2001).

151 See, e.g., Bell Atlantic Corp. v. Twombly, 550 U.S. 544, 577 (2007) (Stevens, dissenting) ("If *Conley*'s 'no set of facts' language is to be interred, let it not be without a eulogy."); People v. McClellan, 71 Cal. 2d 793, 819 (Cal. 1969) (Mosk, concurring in part and dissenting in part) ("In the words of Francis Bacon: 'If it be that previous decisions must be rescinded, at least let them be interred with honour.' In lieu thereof, this eulogy in dissent must suffice."); MARTA v. Ledbetter, 361 S.E.2d 878, 880 (Ga. Ct. App. 1987) (Deen, dissenting) ("Because the majority opinion has mortally wounded the limitation period for filing a change in condition claim, I offer this dissent as a eulogy for O.C.G.A. § 34-9-104 (b)."); see also Linda Greenhouse, "Requiem for the Supreme Court," *New York Times*, June 26, 2022 (accessed July 4, 2022) (writing that the Court's decision in *Dobbs v. Jackson Women's Health Organization* (2022) is "a requiem for the right to abortion" and for the legitimacy of the Court); Radhika Rao, "A Eulogy to Roe," *SCOTUSblog*, June 28, 2022, https://www.scotusblog.com/2022/06/a-eulogy-to-roe/ (accessed June 29, 2022); cf. Gideon v. Wainwright, 372 U.S. 335, 349 (1963) (Harlan, dissenting) ("I agree that *Betts v. Brady* should be overruled, but consider it entitled to a more respectful burial than has been accorded, at least on the part of those of us who were not on the Court when that case was decided.").

152 *Elks*, 536 P.2d at 1214 (Maughan, dissenting).

153 *Hersh*, 523 N.W.2d at 210.

154 Evensen v. Dagostin, 183 A.3d 462, 465 n.3 (Pa. Super. Ct. 2018).

155 United States v. Alvarez, 567 U.S. 709, 750 (2012) (Alito, dissenting).

156 See Bhatia, *Analysing Genre*, 118–19; Ferguson, "Judicial Opinion as a Literary Genre," 201–2.

157 Perelman and Olbrechts-Tyteca, *New Rhetoric*, 471.

Judicial and Epideictic Rhetoric: A False Division

1 Gerald Wetlaufer, "Rhetoric and Its Denial in Legal Discourse," *Virginia Law Review* 76 (1990): 1552, 1555.

2 Sanford Levinson, "The Rhetoric of Judicial Opinions," in *Law's Stories: Narrative and Rhetoric in the Law*, eds. Peter Brooks and Paul Gewirtz (New Haven: Yale Univ. Press, 1996), 189.

3 Peter Goodrich, "The Continuance of the Antirrhetic," *Cardozo Studies in Law and Literature* 4, no. 2 (1992): 207.

4 Ibid., 207–8, 218.

5 Ibid., 207.

6 Robert Ferguson, "The Judicial Opinion as a Literary Genre," *Yale Journal of Law and the Humanities* 2 (1990): 204–7.

7 Ibid., 208.

8 Ibid., 210–13.

9 Ibid., 213–16; cf. Jerome Frank, *Courts on Trial: Myth and Reality in American Justice* (Princeton: Princeton Univ. Press, 1949), 258 ("The conventions of judicial opinion-writing—the uncolloquial vocabulary, the use of phrases carrying with them an air of finality, the parade of precedents, the display of seemingly rigorous logic, bedecked with 'therefores' and 'must-be-trues'—lend an air of thorough certainty, concealing the uncertainties inherent in the judging process."). But cf. Maksymilian Del Mar, *Artefacts of Legal Inquiry: The Value of Imagination in Adjudication* (Oxford: Hart, 2020), 15–16 (arguing that a "sheer variety of language uses, and thus also communication practices," are uniquely characteristic of common law judgments, including a dialogic quality, *obiter dicta*, and an absence of canonical formulations of rules or principles); John Leubsdorf, "The Structure of Judicial Opinions," *Minnesota Law Review* 86 (2001): 449–51 (acknowledging that "judicial opinions rarely rely much on suspense" and that judges "may hope to issue unanswerable opinions," but "the interweaving of different and sometimes conflicting stories and voices can make judicial opinions quite different from the model of impersonal, monologic, unquestioning declaration of which their authors, in the view of some, aspire," resulting instead in "an unexpectedly complicated and subtle genre.").

10 Eugene Garver, *For the Sake of Argument: Practical Reasoning, Character, and the Ethics of Belief* (Chicago: Univ. of Chicago Press, 2004), 119.

11 See, e.g., Malthon Anapol, "Rhetoric and Law: An Overview," *Today's Speech* 18, no. 4 (1970): 12–20; Peter Brooks, "Narrative Transactions—Does the Law Need a Narratology?," *Yale Journal of Law and the Humanities* 18 (2006): 20; Alessandro Giuliani, "The Influence of Rhetoric on the Law of Evidence and Pleading," *The Juridical Review*, new ser. 7 (1962): 216–51; Hans Hohmann, "The Dynamics of Stasis: Classical Rhetorical Theory and Modern Legal Argumentation," *The American Journal of Jurisprudence* 34 (1989): 171–97; Richard Schoeck, "Rhetoric and Law in Sixteenth-Century England," *Studies in Philology* 50, no. 2, (1953): 110–27; Barbara Shapiro, "Classical Rhetoric and the English Law of Evidence," in *Rhetoric and Law in Early Modern Europe*, eds. Victoria Kahn and Lorna Hutson (Hartford: Yale Univ. Press, 2001).

12 See, e.g., George Kennedy, *Classical Rhetoric and Its Christian and Secular Tradition from Ancient to Modern Times* (Chapel Hill: Univ. of North Carolina Press, 1980), 183.

13 See, e.g., Anapol, "Rhetoric and Law," (1970): 12-20; Giuliani, "Influence of Rhetoric," 216-51; Hohmann, "Dynamics of Stasis," 171-97; George Kennedy, *The Art of Rhetoric in the Roman World* (Princeton: Princeton Univ. Press, 1972), 88; Ronald Matlon, "Legal Communication: An Introduction," *Argumentation and Advocacy* 30, no. 4 (1994): 187-90; Terence Morrow, "Forensic Genre," in *Encyclopedia of Rhetoric*, ed. Thomas Sloane (Oxford: Oxford Univ. Press, 2001), 314-21; Schoeck, "Rhetoric and Law," 110-27; Shapiro, "Classical Rhetoric," cf. Stephen Toulmin, *The Uses of Argument* (Cambridge: Cambridge Univ. Press, 1958), 7-8 ("Law-suits are...a special kind of rational dispute, for which the procedures and rules of argument have hardened into institutions.").

14 See generally Michael Frost, *Introduction to Classical Legal Rhetoric: A Lost Heritage* (Burlington: Ashgate, 2005), vii; George Kennedy (trans.), *Progymnasmata: Greek Textbooks of Prose Composition and Rhetoric* (Atlanta: Society of Biblical Literature, 2003).

15 Chaïm Perelman, "Law and Rhetoric," in *Justice, Law, and Argument: Essays in Moral and Legal Reasoning*, trans. William Kluback (Dordrecht: D. Reidel Publishing, 1980), 121.

16 See Thomas Sloane, *On the Contrary: The Protocol of Traditional Rhetoric* (Washington: The Catholic Univ. of America Press, 1997), 106.

17 See David Cairns, *Advocacy and the Making of the Adversarial Criminal Trial 1800-1865* (Oxford: Clarendon Univ. Press, 1998), xi.

18 Frost, *Introduction to Classical Legal Rhetoric*, vii, 2.

19 Ibid., 36.

20 See Anapol, "Rhetoric and Law"; Hohmann, "Dynamics of Stasis"; Matlon, "Legal Communication;" Thomas McSweeney, *Priests of the Law: Roman Law and the Making of the Common Law's First Professionals* (Oxford: Oxford Univ. Press, 2020), 95 n.123 (noting that by the twelfth century some scholars began to skip the study of grammar and rhetoric to move directly to dialectic and law); Morrow, "Forensic Genre" ("With the decline of the Roman republic, forensic rhetoric was eviscerated in both practice and theory."); Richard Rieke, *Rhetorical Theory in American Legal Practice* (PhD diss., Ohio State Univ., 1964); Schoeck, "Rhetoric and Law"; Janice Schuetz and Kathryn Snedaker, *Communication and Litigation: Case Studies of Famous Trials* (Carbondale: Southern Illinois Univ. Press, 1988), ix ("As schools of law became more specialized ..., rhetoric gradually disappeared from the curriculum."); Shapiro, "Classical Rhetoric"; James Stratman, "Legal Rhetoric," in *Encyclopedia of Rhetoric and Composition: Communication from Ancient Times to the Information Age*, ed. Theresa Enos (New York: Routledge, 2010).

21 See, e.g., Thomas Conley, *Rhetoric in the European Tradition* (Chicago: Univ. of Chicago Press, 1990), 128-29; Wilbur Samuel Howell, *Logic and Rhetoric in England, 1500-1700* (New York: Russell and Russell, 1961), 148; James Jasinski, *Sourcebook on Rhetoric: Key Concepts in Contemporary Rhetorical Studies* (Thousand Oaks: Sage, 2001), xvii-xviii; Janice Lauer, *Invention in Rhetoric and*

Composition (West Lafayette: Parlor Press, 2004), 35, 38, 41; Walter Ong, *Ramus, Method, and the Decay of Dialogue: From the Art of Discourse to the Art of Reason* (1958; reprint, Chicago: Univ. of Chicago Press, 2004), 280–81, 288–89; Chaïm Perelman, *The Realm of Rhetoric*, trans. William Kluback (Notre Dame: Notre Dame Univ. Press, 1982), 3; Frances Yates, *The Art of Memory* (Chicago: Univ. of Chicago Press, 1966), 232–34.

22 Ong, *Ramus, Method, and the Decay of Dialogue*, 277.

23 See., e.g., Ernesto Grassi, *Rhetoric as Philosophy: The Humanist Tradition*, trans. John Michael Krois and Azizeh Azodi (1980; reprint, Carbondale: Southern Illinois Press, 2001), 35–37 (writing that by separating form and content, "from the very beginning [Descartes] strips the humanistic branches of their philosophical significance."); Lauer, *Invention in Rhetoric*, 38, 41; Thomas Sprat, *The History of the Royal Society of London, for the Improving of Natural Knowledge*, 2nd ed. corrected (London, 1702), 112–3.

24 Matlon, "Legal Communication," 187.

25 Frost, *Introduction to Classical Legal Rhetoric*.

26 See, e.g., Don Abbott, "The Jurisprudential Analogy: Argumentation and the New Rhetoric," *Central States Speech Journal* 25, no. 1 (1974): 50–55; Richard Gaskins, *Burdens of Proof in Modern Discourse* (New Haven: Yale Univ. Press, 1993), 15–20, 31; Robert Hariman, Introduction to *Popular Trials: Rhetoric, Mass Media, and the Law*, ed. Robert Hariman (Tuscaloosa: Alabama Univ. Press, 1993); Marouf Hasian Jr., *Legal Memories and Amnesias in America's Rhetorical Culture* (Boulder: Westview, 2000); John Lucaites, "Between Rhetoric and 'The Law': Power, Legitimacy, and Social Change," review of *A Guide to Critical Legal Studies*, by Mark Kelman, *Interpreting Law and Literature: A Hermeneutic Reader*, edited by Sanford Levinson and Steven Mailloux, and *The Critical Legal Studies Movement*, by Roberto Unger, *Quarterly Journal of Speech*, vol. 76, no. 4 (1990): 435–49; Francis Mootz, III, *Rhetorical Knowledge in Legal Practice and Critical Legal Theory* (Tuscaloosa: Alabama Univ. Press, 2006); Eileen Scallen, "Judgment, Justification and Junctions in the Rhetorical Criticism of Legal Texts," *Southern Communication Journal* vol. 60, no. 1 (1994): 68–74; James Boyd White, *Heracles' Bow: Essays on the Rhetoric and Poetics of the Law* (Madison: Wisconsin Univ. Press (1985).

27 See Stratman, "Legal Rhetoric," 383.

28 See Philodemus, *On Rhetoric Books 1 and 2*, trans. and exegetical essays by Clive Chandler (New York: Routledge, 2006), 101–2.

29 Walter Berns, "Judicial Rhetoric," in *Rhetoric and American Statesmanship*, eds. Glen Thurow and Jeffrey Wallin (Durham: Carolina Academic Press, 1984), 47–49.

30 See Edward Schiappa with David Timmerman, "Aristotle's Disciplining of Epideictic," in Edward Schiappa, *The Beginnings of Rhetorical Theory in Classical Greece* (Hartford: Yale Univ. Press, 1999), 185; Jasinski, *Sourcebook on Rhetoric*, 209; Jeffrey Walker, *Rhetoric and Poetics in Antiquity* (Oxford: Oxford Univ. Press, 2000), 39.

31 Aristotle, *Rhetoric*, trans. W. Rhys Roberts, in *The Rhetoric and Poetics of Aristotle* (New York: Modern Library, 1984), 1354^a; 1355^a; 1356^b; 1357^a ("The enthymeme must consist of few propositions, fewer often than those which make up the normal syllogism. For if any of these propositions is a familiar fact, there is no need to even mention it; the hearer adds it himself."). In *On Sophistical Refutations*, Aristotle advances a similar dismissal of the writers of rhetorical treatises. Comparing them to the sophist Gorgias of Leontini, Aristotle writes that "the teaching which they gave their pupils was rapid but unsystematic; for they conceived that they could train their pupils by imparting to them not an art but the results of an art." Aristotle, *On Sophistical Refutations*, trans. E. S. Forster and D. J. Furley (Cambridge: Loeb Classical Library, 1955), 34.

32 Aristotle, *Rhetoric*, 1354^a, 1355^a, 1357^a.

33 Ibid., 1368^a; cf. Chaïm Perelman and Lucie Olbrechts-Tyteca, *The New Rhetoric: A Treatise on Argumentation*, trans. John Wilkinson and Purcell Weaver (Notre Dame: Notre Dame Univ. Press, 1969), 230 (writing that "the attempts of the jurists to cast their reasoning into syllogistic form" should be understood as enthymematic reasoning in which quasi-logical argumentation is presented in syllogistic form, an "assimilation...with formal reasoning").

34 Aristotle, *Rhetoric*, 1354^{a-b}. The deep suspicion of judicial power that is expressed in the opening pages of Aristotle's *Rhetoric* persists in contemporary legal theory, with some theorists insisting that everything possible should be done to minimize the role of judges in the legal system. See Del Mar, *Artefacts of Legal Inquiry*, 18–19. Aristotle's view is not strictly limited to his suspicion of judicial power, however, but is more broadly suspicious of the role of rhetoric in judicial proceedings. At the beginning of his *Rhetoric*, Aristotle writes that a judge must refuse to consider the arguments of litigants regarding "whether a thing is important or unimportant, just or unjust," deciding such questions for himself where undefined by the legislature. Aristotle, *Rhetoric*, 1354^{a-b}. Yet near the end of the *Rhetoric*, Aristotle exhorts the reader to "magnify or minimize" the "importance" of the leading facts in the epilogue of a speech, which he describes as the "natural thing to do." Ibid., 1419^b. Aristotle at once recognizes the power of rhetoric in judicial situations and urges that it be strictly disciplined.

35 Aristotle, *Rhetoric*, 1354^b.

36 Eugene Garver, "Justice, Play, and Politics," *Mercer Law Review* 66 (2015): 353.

37 Eugene Garver, "The Contemporary Irrelevance of Aristotle's Practical Reason," in *Rereading Aristotle's Rhetoric*, eds. Alan Gross and Arthur Walzer (Carbondale: Southern Illinois Univ. Press, 2000), 70; cf. Walter Berns, "The Least Dangerous Branch. But Only If ...," in *The Judiciary in a Democratic Society*, ed. Leonard Theberge (Lexington: Lexington Books, 1979), 12 (writing that "judges have no constituents," but instead "represent the Constitution and derive all their authority from it").

38 Garver, "Justice, Play, and Politics," 353.

39 Aristotle, *Rhetoric*, 1354^b; cf. 1356^b ("Individual cases are so infinitely various that no systematic knowledge of them is possible.").

40 Ibid., 1374^{a-b}.

41 Ibid., 1354^{a-b}.

42 See, e.g., Christopher Blackwell, "The Council of the Areopagus," *Dēmos: Classical Athenian Democracy* (2003).

43 Jeffrey Walker, *The Genuine Teachers of This Art: Rhetorical Education in Antiquity* (Columbia: South Carolina Univ. Press, 2011), 17–19 ("In the *Rhetoric* the motives toward judgment and *theôria* are predominant.").

44 Cicero, *De Oratore*, trans. E. W. Sutton and H. Rackham (Cambridge: Loeb Classical Library, 1942), 2.160. Antonius argues that Aristotle surveyed the art of rhetoric "with that same keen insight, by which he had discerned the essential nature of all things," but rhetoricians "have dwelt upon the treatment of the single subject, without his sagacity, but, in this one instance, with larger practice and closer application." Ibid.

45 *Henry VI, Part 2, William Shakespeare: The Complete Works* (New York: Gramercy, 1975), 4.2.

46 Aristotle, *Rhetoric*, 1354^{a-b}.

47 Ibid., 1356^b.

48 Ibid., 1394^a.

49 Ibid., 1394^a.

50 Ibid., 1395^{a-b}.

51 Lawrence Rosenfield and Thomas Mader, "The Functions of Human Communication in Pleasing," in *Handbook of Rhetorical and Communication Theory*, ed. Carroll Arnold and John Bowers (Boston: Allyn and Bacon, 1984), 490.

52 Walker, *Rhetoric and Poetics*, 15–16.

53 Ibid.

54 Ibid.

55 Ibid., 6–7.

56 Ibid., 9. The author of the *Rhetorica ad Alexandrum* specifically notes the use of precedent among the means of amplification in epideictic discourse, introducing prior judgments that are either favorable or unfavorable depending on whether the purpose of the speech is praise or blame. *Rhetorica ad Alexandrum*, trans. Harris Rackham (1937; reprint, Cambridge: Loeb Classical Library, 1983), 1426^a. Citation practices in modern legal discourse, including the use of string citations and string parenthetical quotations, also form an important means of amplification and contribute to epideictic registers.

57 See Walker, *Rhetoric and Poetics*, 180, 183; see also Thomas Conley, "The Enthymeme in Perspective," *Quarterly Journal of Speech* 70 (1984): 171–72.

58 Walker, *Rhetoric and Poetics*, 172; Isocrates, *Panathenaicus*, in *Isocrates II*, ed. Jeffrey Henderson, trans. George Norlin (Cambridge: Loeb Classical Library, 1929), 2 ("I…devoted my own efforts to…writing in a style rich in many telling points.").

59 Walker, *Rhetoric and Poetics*, 171.

60 See Conley, "The Enthymeme in Perspective," 172.

61 See Walker, *Rhetoric and Poetics*, 175.

62 Ibid., 172, 174–75, 180; see also Conley, "The Enthymeme in Perspective," 171.

63 Walker, *Rhetoric and Poetics*, 180.

64 Aristotle, *Rhetoric*, 1354^a.

65 Ibid., 1354^{a-b}.

66 Cf. Garver, *For the Sake of Argument*, 34 (noting that "after establishing the primacy of reason, Aristotle explores in detail a series of emotions in Book II, with none of the hesitation one might expect from the polemics at the start of Book I").

67 Aristotle, *Rhetoric*, 1368^a.

68 Aristotle, *The Nicomachean Ethics*, trans. David Ross, revised by J. L. Ackrill and J. O. Urmson (1925; reprint, Oxford: Oxford Univ. Press, 1989), 1337^b.

69 Harold Berman, *Law and Revolution: The Formation of the Western Legal Tradition* (Cambridge: Harvard Univ. Press, 1983), 253; John Merryman, *The Civil Law Tradition: An Introduction to the Legal Systems of Western Europe and Latin America*, 2nd ed. (Stanford: Stanford Univ. Press, 1985), 49. Harold Berman notes that the legal concept of equity was also influenced by the Christian concept of mercy in the complex social and political society of eleventh- and twelfth-century Europe:

The belief in a God of justice who operates a lawful universe, punishing and rewarding according to principles of proportion, mercifully mitigated in exceptional cases, corresponded to the belief in a complex social unity, Christendom, in which the dialectic of interacting realms and polities was regulated by a similar kind of justice-based-on-law and law-based-on-justice, with mercy playing an exceptional role.

Berman, *Law and Revolution*, 168, 196–97.

70 Chaïm Perelman, *The Idea of Justice and the Problem of Argument*, trans. John Petrie (New York: Routledge, 1963), 32.

71 S. F. Bonner, *Roman Declamation in the Late Republic and Early Empire* (Liverpool: Univ. Press of Liverpool, 1949), 46.

72 Kennedy, *Art of Rhetoric in the Roman World*, 88.

73 Cf. Grassi, *Rhetoric as Philosophy*, 92 ("There is a parallel between the grammarian—the philologist as an interpreter of a text—and the rhetorician insofar as *both* began with the insight that particular cases *are bound up in a situation*.") (emphasis in original).

74 Albert Jonsen and Stephen Toulmin, *The Abuse of Casuistry: A History of Moral Reasoning* (Berkeley: Univ. of California Press, 1988), 258.

75 Stephen Toulmin, *Human Understanding: The Collective Use and Evolution of Concepts* (Princeton: Princeton Univ. Press, 1972), 95.

76 Jonsen and Toulmin, *Abuse of Casuistry*, 257, 293–94. Similarly, Ernesto Grassi writes that "the art of eloquence belongs to the realm of probability because it constantly directs its glance at the specific, variable psychic state of the audience,"

concerning itself with "the constantly variable individual case." Rationalism cannot determine rhetorical or poetic speech "because it cannot comprehend the particular, the individual, i.e., the concrete situation." Grassi, *Rhetoric as Philosophy*, 40, 44. For a broad-ranging discussion of the normative use of particularity in philosophy, literature, and law, see Michèle Lowrie and Susanne Lüdemann, eds., *Exemplarity and Singularity: Thinking through Particulars in Philosophy, Literature, and Law* (New York: Routledge, 2015).

77 See generally James Tallmon, "Casuistry," in *Encyclopedia of Rhetoric*, ed. Thomas Sloane (New York: Oxford Univ. press, 2001), 83–88.

78 Thomas De Quincey, "Casuistry," in *De Quincey's Writings: Theological Essays and Other Papers*, vol. 1. (1854; reprint, Madrid: HardPress, 2020).

79 Ibid. (emphasis in original).

80 Cicero, *De Inventione*, trans. H. M. Hubbell (Cambridge: Loeb Classical Library, 1949), 1.8.

81 Ibid.

82 Cicero, *De Or.* 3.120–21.

83 Ibid., 1.5.

84 See, e.g., Martin Clarke, *Rhetoric at Rome: A Historical Survey* (London: Cohen and West, 1953), 13–14; Donovan Ochs, "Cicero's Rhetorical Theory, with Synopses of Cicero's Seven Rhetorical Works," in *A Synoptic History of Classical Rhetoric*, edited by James Murphy and Richard Katula (Mahwah: Hermagoras Press, 2003), 151–99.

85 Cicero, *De Or.* 1.73; see Ochs, "Cicero's Rhetorical Theory," 151–52, 165.

86 Cicero, *De Or.* 1.158–59.

87 Conley, *Rhetoric in the European Tradition*, 37; see Michael Buckley, "Philosophic Method in Cicero," *Journal of the History of Philosophy* 8 (1970): 148.

88 Cf. Walker, *Rhetoric and Poetics*, 79.

89 Cicero, *De Or.*, 1.81.

90 Ibid., 2.84.

91 Ibid., 3.70.

92 Aristotle, *Rhetoric*, 1354[a–b].

93 Cicero, *De Or.*, 1.5.

94 Cicero also states in the prologue to the second book of *De Oratore* that "no man has ever succeeded in achieving splendor and excellence in oratory, I will not say merely without training in speaking, but without taking all knowledge for his province as well," and "all things whatsoever, that can fall under the discussion of human beings, must be aptly dealt with by him who professes to have this power, or he must abandon the name of eloquent." Cicero, *De Or.*, 2.5.

95 Ibid., 1.52–54.

96 Ibid., 1.56.

97 Ibid., 1.73.

98 Ibid., 1.173.

99 Ibid., 3.133–34.

100 Bonner, *Roman Declamation*, 29; see Kennedy, *Art of Rhetoric in the Roman World*, 95.

101 Cicero, *De Or.* 2.77–78, 2.134–36.
102 Cicero, *Orator*, in *Brutus and Orator*, trans. G. L. Hendrickson and H. M. Hubbell (Cambridge: Loeb Classical Library, 1939), 14–16.
103 Cicero, *Or.*, 45–46. In Crassus's discussion of amplification in *De Oratore*, he similarly advocates the use of commonplaces to argue both sides of a case:

> We orators are bound to possess the intelligence, capacity and skill to speak both *pro* and *contra* on the topics of virtue, duty, equity and good, moral growth and utility, honor and disgrace, reward and punishment, and like matters.

Cicero, *De Or.*, 3.107–8; cf. 3.104.
104 Sloane, *On the Contrary*, 97; Bonner, *Roman Declamation*, 30.
105 Richard Enos, *The Literate Mode of Cicero's Legal Rhetoric* (Carbondale: Southern Illinois Univ. Press, 1988), 1, 6.
106 Ibid., 29.
107 Walker, *Genuine Teachers*, 17, 25; cf. Clarke, *Rhetoric at Rome*, 55–56; Kennedy, *Art of Rhetoric in the Roman World*, 208
108 Walker, *Rhetoric and Poetics*, 7–10, 14, 83, 115, 270–71.
109 Theodore Burgess, "Epideictic Literature," (PhD diss., Univ. of Chicago, 1902), 216.
110 Perelman and Olbrechts-Tyteca, *New Rhetoric*, 471.
111 See Asif Agha and Frog, "An Introduction to Registers of Communication," Introduction to *Registers of Communication*, eds. Asif Agha and Frog (Helsinki: Finnish Literature Society, 2015), 14–15.
112 See, e.g., Asif Agha, *Language and Social Relations* (Cambridge: Cambridge Univ. Press, 2007), 80; Douglas Biber and Susan Conrad, *Register, Genre, and Style* (Cambridge: Cambridge Univ. Press, 2009), 36–47; Michael Halliday, *Halliday's Introduction to Functional Grammar*, revised by Christian Matthiessen (New York: Routledge, 2013), 33–34.
113 See Agha and Frog, "An Introduction to Registers of Communication," 14.
114 See Asif Agha, "Enregisterment and Communication in Social History," in *Registers of Communication*, ed. Asif Agha and Frog (Helsinki: Finnish Literature Society, 2015), 28; Margaret Bender, "Shifting Linguistic Registers and the Nature of the Sacred in Cherokee," in *Registers of Communication*, 247.
115 See Biber and Conrad, *Register, Genre, and Style*, 6, 8–9.
116 Ibid., 10, 32–33.
117 Perelman and Olbrechts-Tyteca, *New Rhetoric*, 160.
118 Celeste Condit, "The Functions of Epideictic: The Boston Massacre Orations as Exemplar," *Communication Quarterly* 33, no. 4 (1985): 288, 291.
119 Gray Matthews, "Epideictic Rhetoric and Baseball: Nurturing Community through Controversy," *Southern Journal of Communication* 60, no. 4 (1995): 277.
120 Lloyd Bitzer, "The Rhetorical Situation," *Philosophy and Rhetoric* 1, no. 1 (1968): 6; see also Lloyd Bitzer, "Functional Communication: A Situational

Perspective," in *Rhetoric in Transition: Studies in the Nature and Uses of Rhetoric*, ed. Eugene White (University Park: Pennsylvania Univ. Press, 1980), 28.

121 Bitzer, "Rhetorical Situation," 6–7.
122 Jasinski, *Sourcebook on Rhetoric*, 211–12.
123 Condit, "Functions of Epideictic, 288, 291.
124 See Menander Rhetor, *An Analysis of Epideictic Speeches*, trans. William Race (Cambridge: Harvard Univ. Press, 2019), 1.1.
125 Wetlaufer, "Rhetoric and Its Denial," 1562–63.
126 Ibid., 1563.
127 See West Virginia Board of Education v. Barnette, 319 U.S. 624 (1943).
128 Laurent Pernot, *Epideictic Rhetoric: Questioning the Stakes of Ancient Praise* (Austin: Univ. of Texas Press, 2015), 69.
129 J. Richard Chase, "The Classical Conception of Epideictic," *Quarterly Journal of Speech* 37, no. 3 (1961): 300.
130 See Aristotle, *Rhetoric*, 1358^b, 1366^a–1368^a.
131 Ibid., 1368^a.
132 *Rhetorica ad Alexandrum*, trans. Harris Rackham (1937; reprint, Cambridge: Loeb Classical Library, 1983), 1427^b.
133 See Cicero, *De Inv.*, 1.5; *Rhetorica ad Herennium*, trans. Harry Caplan (1954; reprint, Cambridge: Loeb Classical Library, 2004), 3.6.
134 See Menander Rhetor, *Analysis of Epideictic Speeches*, 1.1.
135 See Libanius, *Libanius's Progymnasmata: Model Exercises in Greek Prose Composition and Rhetoric*, trans. Craig Gibson (Atlanta: Society of Biblical Literature, 2008), 253; Kennedy, *Progymnasmata*, xii, 50, 81, 195–319.
136 Lawrence v. Texas, 539 U.S. 558, 567 (2003).
137 Minersville Sch. Dist. v. Gobitis, 310 U.S. 586, 596 (1940).
138 Burgess, "Epideictic Literature," 153.
139 Pernot, *Epideictic Rhetoric*, 89–90.
140 Obergefell v. Hodges, 576 U.S. 644, 681 (2015).
141 See generally Pernot, *Epideictic Rhetoric*, 88–90.
142 *Rhetorica ad Alexandrum*, 1421^b, 1422^a, 1426^a.
143 Aristotle, *Rhetoric*, 1366^{a-b}. Notably, Aristotelian virtues may not be modern virtues. Aristotle also writes that "it is noble to avenge oneself on one's enemies and not to come to terms with them; for requital is just, and the just is noble; and not to surrender is a sign of courage." Ibid., 1367^{a-b}; see Garver, "Contemporary Irrelevance," 57–73. As Aristotle himself notes, "it is not difficult to praise the Athenians to an Athenian audience." Aristotle, *Rhetoric*, 1367^{a-b}.
144 John O'Malley, *Praise and Blame in Renaissance Rome: Rhetoric, Doctrine, and Reform in the Sacred Orators of the Papal Court, c. 1450–1521* (Durham: Duke Univ. Press, 1979), 62.
145 Pernot, *Epideictic Rhetoric*, 88–90.
146 See Menander Rhetor, *Analysis of Epideictic Speeches*, 1.11, 1,15, 1.16.
147 Aristotle, *Rhetoric*, 1367^{a-b}.
148 Condit, "Functions of Epideictic," 285.

149 Pernot, *Epideictic Rhetoric*, 5; cf. Quintilian, *Institutio Oratoria*, 3.4.13–14 (noting that although the term *epideictic* "includes laudatory oratory, it does not confine itself thereto").
150 Chase, "Classical Conception," 294.
151 Lawrence Rosenfield, "The Practical Celebration of Epideictic," in *Rhetoric in Transition: Studies in the Nature and Uses of Rhetoric*, ed. Eugene White (University Park: Penn State Univ. Press, 1980), 133 (emphasis in original).
152 Ibid., 133–35, 142.
153 Ibid., 135.
154 Aristotle, *Rhetoric*, 1358^b; see Christine Oravec, "'Observation' in Aristotle's Theory of Epideictic," *Philosophy and Rhetoric* 9, no. 3 (1976): 162–74.
155 Chase, "Classical Conception," 298–300.
156 Quintilian, *Institutio Oratoria* 3.4.3–4.
157 J. L. Austin, *How to Do Things with Words*, edited by J. O. Urmson and Marina Sibsà, 2nd ed (Cambridge: Harvard Univ. Press, 1975), 1.
158 See Reed Dasenbrock, "Austin, J. L. (1911–1960)," in *Encyclopedia of Rhetoric and Composition: Communication from Ancient Times to the Information Age*, ed. Theresa Enos (New York: Routledge, 1996), 54 ("To say, as Austin does, that to speak is to act is to adopt a deeply rhetorical vision of language.").
159 Walter Beale, "Rhetorical Performative Discourse: A New Theory of Epideictic," *Philosophy and Rhetoric* 11, no. 4 (1978): 224–25.
160 Ibid., 232.
161 Aristotle, *Rhetoric*, 1368^a; 1392^a.
162 Longinus, *On the Sublime*, translated by T. S. Dorsch, in *Classical Literary Criticism* (New York: Penguin, 1965), 129.
163 Ibid., 128.
164 Kenneth Burke, *A Rhetoric of Motives* (New York: Prentice Hall, 1950), 69.
165 Burgess, "Epideictic Literature," 205, 208.
166 See Lawrence Kim, "Atticism and Asianism," in *The Oxford Handbook of the Second Sophistic*, eds. Daniel Richter and William Johnson (Oxford: Oxford Univ. Press, 2017), 41, 54–59; Pernot, *Epideictic Rhetoric*, 56.
167 Longinus, *On the Sublime*, 128.
168 Perelman and Olbrechts-Tyteca, *New Rhetoric*, 176–77.
169 See Desiderius Erasmus, *Copia: Foundations of the Abundant Style*, trans. Betty Knott, in *The Collected Works of Erasmus*, ed. Craig Thompson (Toronto: Univ. of Toronto Press, 1978).
170 Perelman and Olbrechts-Tyteca, *New Rhetoric*, 178.
171 Abraham Lincoln, *The Gettysburg Address and Other Speeches* (New York: Penguin, 1995).
172 United States v. Nixon, 418 U.S. 683, 708–9 (1974).
173 Perelman and Olbrechts-Tyteca, *New Rhetoric*, 145.
174 John Genung, *The Working Principles of Rhetoric, Examined in Their Literary Relations and Illustrated with Examples* (Boston: Ginn and Co., 1900), 458.
175 Perelman and Olbrechts-Tyteca, *New Rhetoric*, 169.

176 Ibid., 167.

177 Sprat, *History of the Royal-Society*, 112–13 ("Who can behold, without Indignation, how many mists and uncertainties, these specious *Tropes* and *Figures* have brought to our Knowledge? How many rewards, which are due to more profitable, and difficult *Arts*, have been still snatch'd away by the easy vanity of *fine speaking*.")

178 Perelman and Olbrechts-Tyteca, *New Rhetoric*, 171.

179 Jeanne Fahnestock, *Rhetorical Figures in Science* (Oxford: Oxford Univ. Press, 1999), 4.

180 See Ernesto Grassi, *The Primordial Metaphor*, trans. Laura Pietropaolo and Manuela Scarci (Binghamton: SUNY, 1994), 12; Sprat, *History of the Royal-Society*, 112–13.

181 Fahnestock, *Rhetorical Figures in Science*, 6.

182 Ibid., 10.

183 Ibid., 19–20.

184 See ibid., 168.

185 Ibid., 22.

186 Ibid., 24. Maksymilian Del Mar similarly argues that figural language makes substantial contributions to legal inquiry. See Del Mar, *Artefacts of Legal Inquiry*, 81.

187 Cf. Nevin Laib, "Conciseness and Amplification," *College Composition and Communication* 41, no. 4 (1990): 443–59.

188 Pseudo-Dionysius of Halicarnassus, *Ars Rhetorica*, trans. William Race (Cambridge: Harvard Univ. Press, 2019), 1.1.

189 Ibid., 1.8.

190 See Elaine Fantham, "Eloquence," in *Encyclopedia of Rhetoric*, ed. Thomas Sloane (Oxford: Oxford Univ. Press, 2001), 238.

191 See Pernot, *Epideictic Rhetoric*, 55–56.

192 Hermogenes, *On Types of Style*, trans. Cecil Wooten (Chapel Hill: University of North Carolina Press, 1987), 2.12.

193 Cf. James Wilce and Janina Fenigsen, "Mourning and Honor: Register in Karelian Lament," in *Registers of Communication*, 188–9 (noting the role of locally perceived "beautification" in honorific speech).

194 Perelman and Olbrechts-Tyteca, *New Rhetoric*, 51.

195 Ibid., 48–51.

196 Ibid., 450–55.

197 Fantham, "Eloquence," 238.

198 Perelman and Olbrechts-Tyteca, *New Rhetoric*, 52.

199 Pseudo-Dionysius of Halicarnassus, *Ars Rhetorica*, 1.1.

200 Condit, "Functions of Epideictic," 290–91.

201 Ralph Waldo Emerson, *The Complete Works of Ralph Waldo Emerson*, Concord ed. (Boston: Houghton Mifflin, 1904), 130.

202 Dale Sullivan, "The Ethos of Epideictic Encounter," *Philosophy and Rhetoric* 26, no. 2 (1993), 128.

203 Ralph Waldo Emerson, *Society and Solitude* (Boston: Houghton Mifflin, 1890), 76.
204 Thomas Farrell, *Norms of Rhetorical Culture* (New Haven: Yale Univ. Press, 1993), 266.
205 Cicero, *De Or.* 1.56; Cicero, *Or.* 45–46.
206 Giambattista Vico, *On the Study Methods of Our Time*, trans. Elio Gianturco (Ithaca: Cornell Univ. Press, 1990), 78.
207 Aristotle, *Rhetoric*, 1394[a]; 1395[a–b].
208 See *Bouvier's Law Dictionary*, revised 6th ed., s.v. "Maxims."
209 See, e.g., Cal. Civ. Code §§ 3509–3548 ("Maxims of Jurisprudence"). See generally Intisar Rabb, *Doubt in Islamic Law: A History of Legal Maxims, Interpretation, and Islamic Criminal Law* (Cambridge: Cambridge Univ. Press, 2015); Antonin Scalia and Bryan Garner, *Reading Law: The Interpretation of Legal Texts* (St. Paul: Thomson West, 2012); Peter Stein, *Regulae Iuris: From Juristic Rules to Legal Maxims* (Edinburgh: Edinburgh Univ. Press, 1966).
210 Donald Davis, Jr., "Maxims," in *The Oxford Handbook of Law and Humanities*, eds. Simon Stern, Maksymillian Del Mar, and Bernadette Mayler (Oxford: Oxford Univ. Press, 2020), 656, 658–59, 662 (noting both that interpretive maxims "function as shortcuts for argumentation" and that "ornamental or rhetorical uses of maxims in legal argument and decision are a prominent style of maxim usage").
211 Sweezy v. New Hampshire, 354 U.S. 234, 250 (1957).
212 Douglas v. Jeanette, 319 U.S. 157, 182 (1943) (Jackson, concurring).
213 Cabell v. Markham, 148 F.2d 737, 739 (2d Cir. 1945).
214 Dobbs v. Jackson Women's Health Org., No. 19-1392, slip op. at 50 (U.S. Supr. Ct. June 24, 2022) (Breyer, Sotomayor, and Kagan, dissenting); cf. ibid., 28 (Breyer, Sotomayor, and Kagan, dissenting) ("Logic and principle are not one-way ratchets.").
215 Richard Weaver, *The Ethics of Rhetoric* (1953; reprint, Davis: Hermagoras Press, 1985), 165–71. In Justice Felix Frankfurter's concurring opinion in *McCollum v. Board of Education* (1948), he referred to the separation of church and state as a "spacious conception." McCollum v. Bd. of Educ., 333 U.S. 203, 213 (1948) (Frankfurter, concurring).
216 Weaver, *Ethics of Rhetoric*, 178.
217 Sullivan, "Ethos of Epideictic Encounter," 123.
218 Condit, "Functions of Epideictic," 293–94.
219 Ibid., 294; cf. Oravec, "'Observation' in Aristotle's Theory of Epideictic," 163 (arguing that in epideictic "the audience receives new insights from the speaker's application of audience-supplied maxims and values to events and persons within their own experience").
220 Perelman and Olbrechts-Tyteca, *New Rhetoric*, 51.
221 Garver, *For the Sake of Argument*, 39–41; cf. Walker, *Rhetoric and Poetics*, 9 (writing that epideictic can "work to challenge or transform conventional beliefs" by shaping "the fundamental grounds, the 'deep' commitments

and presuppositions" of pragmatic arguments); cf. Giambattista Vico, *The New Science of Giambattista Vico*, trans. Thomas Goddard Bergin and Max Harold Fisch, unabr. ed. (Ithaca: Cornell Univ. Press, 1984), ¶ 142 ("Common sense [*il senso comune*] is judgment without reflection, shared by an entire class, an entire people, an entire nation, or the entire human race.").

222 Grassi, *Rhetoric as Philosophy*, 98–100.

223 Ibid., 93.

224 Aristotle, *Rhetoric*, 1358^b.

225 See Cynthia Sheard, "The Public Value of Epideictic Rhetoric," *College English* 58, no. 7 (1996): 768 (emphasis added).

226 Perelman and Olbrechts-Tyteca, *New Rhetoric*, 160.

227 Ibid., 165–66; cf. Robert Danisch, "Power and the Celebration of the Self: Michel Foucault's Epideictic Rhetoric," *Southern Communication Journal* 7, no. 3 (2006): 300 (comparing the association of epideictic and the present to Michel Foucault's critical project of writing a "history of the present").

228 Bernard Comrie, *Aspect: An Introduction to the Study of Verbal Aspect and Related Problems* (Cambridge: Cambridge Univ. Press, 1976), 3; William Frawley, *Linguistic Semantics* (New York: Routledge, 1992), 294; Andrew Sherrill, Anita Eerland, Rolf Zwaan, and Joseph Magliano, "Understanding How Grammatical Aspect Influences Legal Judgment," *PLoS ONE* 10, no. 10 (2015): 2.

229 Paul Hopper, "Aspect and Foregrounding in Discourse," in *Syntax and Semantics*, vol. 12, *Discourse and Syntax*, ed. Talmy Givón (New York: Academic Press, 1979), 239.

230 See Comrie, *Aspect*, 3–4, 12–13, 17–18, 24; Paul Hopper, "Some Observations on the Typology of Focus and Aspect in Narrative Language," *Studies in Language* 3, no. 1 (1979): 38–39, 60–61.

231 Ronald Langacker, *Foundations of Cognitive Grammar*, Vol. 1, *Theoretical Prerequisites* (Palo Alto: Stanford Univ. Press, 1999), 255; see also William Hart and Dolores Albarracín, "Learning About What Others Were Doing: Verb Aspect and Attributions of Mundane and Criminal Intent for Past Actions," *Psychological Science* 22, no. 2 (2011): 261–66; Carol Madden and Rolf Zwaan, "How Does Verb Aspect Constrain Event Representations?" *Memory and Cognition* 31, no. 5 (2003): 663–72.

232 See Åshlid Næss, *Prototypical Transitivity* (Amsterdam: John Benjamins, 2007), 78.

233 Olmstead v. United States, 277 U.S. 438, 479 (1928) (Brandeis, dissenting).

234 See, e.g., Comrie, *Aspect*, 2–3.

235 See, e.g., James Forsyth, *A Grammar of Aspect: Usage and Meaning in the Russian Verb* (Cambridge: Cambridge Univ. Press, 1970), 91; Hopper, "Aspect and Foregrounding in Discourse," 213; Hopper, "Some Observations," 38, 60–61; Paul Hopper, "Aspect between Discourse and Grammar," introduction to *Tense-Aspect: Between Semantics and Pragmatics*, edited by Paul Hopper (Amsterdam: John Benjamins, 1982), 9; Paul Hopper and Sandra Thompson, "Transitivity in Grammar and Discourse," *Language* 56, no. 2 (1980): 251–53.

236 Hopper, "Some Observations," 58, 60–61; cf. Aristotle, *Rhetoric*, 1414^a (writing that narration "surely is part of a forensic speech only: how in a political speech or a speech of display can there be 'narration' in the technical sense?").

237 Langacker, *Foundations of Cognitive Grammar*, 255; cf. Hopper, "Aspect and Foregrounding in Discourse," 215–16 ("Backgrounded clauses may be located at any point along the time axis or indeed may not be located on the time axis at all.").

238 See Hopper, "Some Observations," 60.

239 Hopper, "Aspect and Foregrounding in Discourse," 220.

240 Ibid.

241 Keith Tandy, "Verbal Aspect as Narrative Structure in Aelfric's *Lives of Saints*," in *The Old English Homily and Its Backgrounds*, ed. Paul Szarmach and Bernard Huppe (Albany: SUNY, 1978), 199.

242 See Bradford Vivian, "Rhetorical Arts of Praise and Blame in Political Transformation," in *Conflict Transformation and Peacebuilding: Moving from Violence to Sustainable Peace*, ed. Bruce Dayton and Louis Kriesberg (New York: Routledge, 2009), 78; Jeremy Engels, *Enemyship: Democracy and Counter-Revolution in the Early Republic* (East Lansing: Michigan State Univ. Press, 2010), 18.

243 Vivian, "Rhetorical Arts of Praise and Blame," 78.

244 Hugh Lee, "The 'Historical' Bundy and Encomiastic Relevance in Pindar," *The Classical World* 72, no. 2 (1978): 66.

245 Hopper, "Aspect and Foregrounding in Discourse," 215, 239.

246 Emerson, "Eloquence," 76.

247 Farrell, *Norms of Rhetorical Culture*, 266.

248 Barbara Czarniawska, "Styles of Organization Theory," in *Oxford Handbook of Organization Theory*, revised ed., eds. Haridimos Tsoukas and Christian Knudsen (Oxford: Oxford Univ. Press, 2005), 243; see also Dierdre McCloskey, *The Rhetoric of Economics*, 2nd ed. (Madison: Univ. of Wisconsin Press, 1998), 11–12 ("The advantage of the gnomic present is its claim to the authority of General Truth, which is another of its names in grammar.").

249 See, e.g., Günter Radden and René Dirven, *Cognitive English Grammar* (Amsterdam: John Benjamins Publishing, 2007), 64–65, 175–81.

250 Eugene Garver, "The Way We Live Now: Rhetorical Persuasion and Democratic Conversation," *Mercer Law Review* 63 (2012): 825–26.

251 Frawley, *Linguistic Semantics*, 384–85.

252 Frank Palmer, *Mood and Modality*, 2nd ed. (Cambridge: Cambridge Univ. Press, 2001), 1.

253 Frawley, *Linguistic Semantics*, 390.

254 O'Malley, *Praise and Blame in Renaissance Rome*, 75, 163.

255 Ibid., 240.

256 Perelman and Olbrechts-Tyteca, *New Rhetoric*, 51.

257 Condit, "Functions of Epideictic," 289–92.

258 Ibid., 289–90.

259 Ibid., 289.

260 O'Malley, *Praise and Blame in Renaissance Rome*, 61.

261 See, e.g., Jonathan Pratt, "The Epideictic Agōn and Aristotle's Elusive Third Genre," *American Journal of Philology* 133, no. 2 (2012): 177–208; Walker, *Rhetoric and Poetics*, 158.

262 Walker, *Rhetoric and Poetics*, 180, 183.

263 Thucydides, *History of the Peloponnesian War*, trans. Rex Warner (London: Penguin, 1972), 145.

264 Nicole Loraux, *The Invention of Athens: The Funeral Oration in the Classical City*, trans. Alan Sheridan (New York: Zone Books, 2006), 142–43.

265 Aristotle, *Rhetoric*, 1395^{a-b}.

266 Quintilian, *Institutio Oratoria*, 3.7.4–6; see Pernot, *Epideictic Rhetoric*, 90 ("All the subjects of epideictic speeches may present questionable aspects, which are no longer part of the 'acknowledged points' (*homologoumena*) and which as such require proofs and reasoning in addition to amplification.").

267 Nicolaus the Sophist, *Preliminary Exercises*, in Kennedy, *Progymnasmata*, 158.

268 Burgess, "Epideictic Literature," 216.

269 See Vivian, "Rhetorical Arts of Praise and Blame," 77–78.

270 Perelman, *Realm of Rhetoric*, 20; cf. Perelman and Olbrechts-Tyteca, *New Rhetoric*, 54; cf. Loraux, *The Invention of Athens*, 142–43.

271 Frederick Ahl, "The Art of Safe Criticism in Greece and Rome," *American Journal of Philology* 105, no. 2 (1984): 174–208.

272 See, e.g., Rees, "Modern History," 12–13; cf. Benjamin Gray, "A Civic Alternative to Stoicism: The Ethics of Hellenistic Honorary Decrees," *Classical Antiquity*, 37, no. 2 (2018): 198 (concluding that the inscriptions of Hellenistic *poleis*, especially decrees in honor of leading citizens, contributed to public argument)

273 O'Malley, *Praise and Blame in Renaissance Rome*, 74.

274 Ibid., 197.

275 Vivian, "Rhetorical Arts of Praise and Blame," 77.

276 See Ruth Smith and John Trimbur, "Rhetorics of Unity and Disunity: The Worcester Firefighters Memorial Service," *Rhetoric Society Quarterly* 33, no. 4 (2003): 7–24.

277 See Susan Zaeske, "Hearing the Silences in Lincoln's Temperance Address: Whig Masculinity as an Ethic of Rhetorical Civility," *Rhetoric and Public Affairs* 13, no. 3 (2010): 389–420; see also Michelle Yang, "President Nixon's Speeches and Toasts during His 1972 Trip to China: A Study in Diplomatic Rhetoric," *Rhetoric and Public Affairs* 14, no. 1 (2011): 1–44 (noting the intricate relationship between epideictic rhetoric and diplomacy in President Richard Nixon's speeches and toasts during his 1972 trip to China).

278 Condit, "Functions of Epideictic," 290–91.

279 Frawley, *Linguistic Semantics*, 388.

280 Palmer, *Mood and Modality*, 1.

281 Frawley, *Linguistic Semantics*, 407.
282 Grassi, *Rhetoric as Philosophy*, 103.
283 Frawley, *Linguistic Semantics*, 406–7 (emphasis in original).
284 Ibid., 408.
285 O'Malley, *Praise and Blame in Renaissance Rome*, 54.
286 Sullivan, "Ethos of Epideictic Encounter," 128.
287 Garver, *For the Sake of Argument*, 77.
288 Pierre Bourdieu, "The Force of Law: Toward a Sociology of the Juridical Field," *Hastings Law Journal* 38 (1987): 828.
289 See, e.g., Michael Carter, "The Ritual Functions of Epideictic Rhetoric: The Case of Socrates' Funeral Oration," *Rhetorica* 9, no. 3 (1991): 221; George Kennedy, *The Art of Persuasion in Greece* (Princeton: Princeton Univ. Press, 1963), 29, 154, 166–67.
290 Carter, "Ritual Functions of Epideictic," 211.
291 See Menander Rhetor, *Analysis of Epideictic Speeches*, 2.2, 2.4, 2.6, 2.10, 2.11, 2.12, 2.13, 2.14.
292 The extempore quality of epideictic speech exhibits the rhetorical concept of *kairos*, or the opportune, a concept attributed to the Greek sophists. See Debra Hawhee, "Kairotic Encounters," in *Perspectives on Rhetorical Invention*, eds. Janet Atwill and Janice Lauer (Knoxville: Univ. of Tennessee Press, 2002).
293 Bradford Vivian, "Neoliberal Epideictic: Rhetorical Form and Commemorative Politics on September 11, 2002," *Quarterly Journal of Speech* 92, no. 1 (2006): 2.
294 Edmund Thomas, "Performance Space," in *The Oxford Handbook of the Second Sophistic*, eds. Daniel Richter and William Johnson (Oxford: Oxford Univ. Press, 2017), 182–83.
295 See, e.g., Sandra Berns, *To Speak as a Judge: Difference, Voice and Power* (Brookfield: Ashgate, 1999), 194; Peter Winn, "Legal Ritual," *Law and Critique* 2, no. 2 (1991): 207; Robert Yelle, "Rhetorics of Law and Ritual: A Semiotic Comparison of the Law of Talion and Sympathetic Magic," *Journal of the American Academy of Religion* 69, no. 3 (2001): 628.
296 Judith Resnik and Dennis Curtis, *Representing Justice: Invention, Controversy, and Rights in City-States and Democratic Courtrooms* (New Haven: Yale Univ. Press, 2011), 25.
297 Ibid., 26.
298 Gerald Strauss, *Law, Resistance, and the State: The Opposition to Roman Law in Reformation Germany* (Princeton: Princeton Univ. Press, 1986), 111.
299 Martha McNamara, *From Tavern to Courthouse: Architecture and Ritual in American Law, 1658–1860* (Baltimore: Johns Hopkins Univ. Press, 2004), 3.
300 Resnik and Curtis, *Representing Justice*, 136; see also Lior Barshack, "The Constituent Power of Architecture," *Law, Culture, and the Humanities* 7, no. 2 (2010): 217–43; Judith Resnik, Dennis Curtis, and Allison Tait, "Constructing Courts: Architecture, the Ideology of Judging, and the Public Sphere," in *Law, Culture & Visual Studies*, eds. Richard Sherwin and Anne Wagner (New York: Springer, 2013) 547–72.

301 Quoted in Resnik and Curtis, *Representing Justice*, 172.

302 Barbara Perry, *The Priestly Tribe: The Supreme Court's Image in the American Mind* (Westport: Praeger, 1999), 8–11.

303 Aristotle, *Rhetoric*, 1395^a.

304 Beale, "Rhetorical Performative Discourse," 239.

305 Sullivan, "Ethos of Epideictic Encounter," 123.

306 See Condit, "Functions of Epideictic," 286.

307 Vivian, "Rhetorical Arts of Praise and Blame," 78.

308 W. N. Hargreaves-Mawdsley, *A History of Legal Dress in Europe until the End of the Eighteenth Century* (Oxford: Clarendon Press, 1963), 3.

309 See ibid., 56–102.

310 Ibid., 2–3, 53.

311 *In re* Amendments to the Florida Rules of Judicial Administration—New Rule 2.340, No. SC15-497 (Fl. Sup. Ct. Sept. 10, 2015), 3; Leslie Gordon, "Florida Supreme Court Orders Judges to Wear Black Robes," *ABA Journal*, Jan. 1, 2016, https://www.abajournal.com/magazine/article/florida_supreme_court_orders_judges_to_wear_black_robes (accessed October 10, 2020).

312 *In re* Amendments to the Florida Rules of Judicial Administration, 1–2, 7; cf. *Dobbs*, No. 19-1392, slip op. at 30 (Breyer, Sotomayor, and Kagan, dissenting) (noting that Chief Justice John Marshall is reputed to have donned a plain black robe when he swore his oath of office in order to "personif[y] an American tradition" of impartial justice).

313 Frank, *Courts on Trial*, 256–58.

314 Perelman, *Realm of Rhetoric*, 20; Perelman and Olbrechts-Tyteca, *New Rhetoric*, 50–51.

315 Cf. Biber and Conrad, *Register, Genre, and Style*, 10, 32–33.

316 Sheard, "Public Value of Epideictic," 773–74.

317 Ibid., 774.

318 See Kenneth Burke, *Attitudes Toward History* (Berkeley: Univ. of California Press, 1984), 86, 336.

319 Perelman and Olbrechts-Tyteca, *New Rhetoric*, 51.

320 Ibid., 471.

321 Ibid.

322 See ibid., 116.

323 Ibid., 117.

324 Translated in Michelle Bolduc and David Frank, "Chaïm Perelman and Lucie Olbrechts-Tyteca's 'On Temporality as a Characteristic of Argumentation,'" *Philosophy and Rhetoric* 43, no. 4 (2010), 319.

325 Carter, "Ritual Functions of Epideictic," 211–17, 226.

326 Debora Shuger, *Sacred Rhetoric: The Christian Grand Style in the English Renaissance* (Princeton: Princeton Univ. Press, 1988), 173–75.

327 Rosenfield, "Practical Celebration of Epideictic," 137.

328 See Carter, "Ritual Functions of Epideictic," 211–17, 226 ("Done well, such discourse connects a people to the cosmos and to a community that is a reflection of that cosmos.").

329 Shuger, *Sacred Rhetoric*, 173–75.

330 See Carter, "Ritual Functions of Epideictic," 211–12.

331 Oravec, "'Observation' in Aristotle's Theory of Epideictic," 163 (arguing that in epideictic "the audience receives new insights from the speaker's application of audience-supplied maxims and values to events and persons within their own experience").

332 Cristian Tileagă, "What Is a 'Revolution'? National Commemoration, Collective Memory and Managing Authenticity in the Representation of a Political Event," *Discourse and Society* 19, no. 3 (2008): 359–82 (emphasis in original).

333 Garver, *For the Sake of Argument*, 72 (emphasis in original); cf. *Dobbs*, No. 19-1392, slip op. at 30–31 (Breyer, Sotomayor, and Kagan, dissenting) (describing the American tradition of impartial justice as one in which "judges' personal preferences do not make law; rather, the law speaks through them").

334 E. Johanna Hartelius and Jennifer Asenas, "Citational Epideixis and a 'Thinking of Community': The Case of the Minuteman Project," *Rhetoric Society Quarterly* 40, no. 4 (2010): 378.

335 See Agha, "Enregisterment and Communication," 44; cf. Sullivan, "Ethos of Epideictic Encounter," 127 (concluding that epideictic creates an *ethos* that forms the "common dwelling place" of both speaker and audience).

336 Edmund Leach, *Culture and Communication: The Logic by Which Symbols Are Connected: An Introduction to the Use of Structuralist Analysis in Social Anthropology* (Cambridge: Cambridge Univ. Press, 1976), 45.

337 See Brooke Rollins, "The Ethics of Epideictic Rhetoric: Addressing the Problem of Presence through Derrida's Funeral Oration," *Rhetoric Society Quarterly* 35, no. 1 (2005): 8; Brian Vickers, *In Defence of Rhetoric* (Oxford: Clarendon Press, 1988), 55.

338 William Guthrie, *The Sophists* (1969; reprint, Cambridge: Cambridge Univ. Press, 1971), 44.

339 Vivian, "Rhetorical Arts of Praise and Blame," 78.

340 Waldo Braden and Harold Mixon, "Epideictic Speaking in the Post-Civil War South and the Southern Experience," *Southern Communication Journal* 54, no. 1 (1988): 47.

Freedom of Speech, Paramologia, and the Flag

1 See generally Michael Abramowicz and Maxwell Stearns, "Defining Dicta," *Stanford Law Review* 57 (2005): 953–1094.

2 Snow v. Oregon State Penitentiary, 308 Ore. 259, 270 (Or. 1989) (Fadeley, concurring).

3 Barbara Czarniawska, "Styles of Organization Theory," in *Oxford Handbook of Organization Theory*, revised ed., eds. Haridimos Tsoukas and Christian Knudsen (Oxford: Oxford Univ. Press, 2005), 243.

4 See, e.g., Eugene Garver, "The Way We Live Now: Rhetorical Persuasion and Democratic Conversation," *Mercer Law Review* 63 (2012): 825–26 ("As self-contained, the epideictic speech becomes a more organic body with its own internal standards for success.").

5 Donald Davis, Jr., "Maxims," in *The Oxford Handbook of Law and Humanities*, eds. Simon Stern, Maksymillian Del Mar, and Bernadette Mayler (Oxford: Oxford Univ. Press, 2020), 656, 658–59, 662 (noting both that interpretive maxims "function as shortcuts for argumentation" and that "ornamental or rhetorical uses of maxims in legal argument and decision are a prominent style of maxim usage").

6 Planned Parenthood v. Casey, 505 U.S. 833, 844 (1992).

7 Olmstead v. United States, 277 U.S. 438, 479 (1928) (Brandeis, dissenting).

8 Poe v. Ullman, 367 U.S. 497, 547 (1961) (Harlan, dissenting).

9 Cohen v. California, 403 U.S. 15, 25 (1971).

10 Whitney v. California, 274 U.S. 357, 375–376 (1927) (Brandeis, concurring).

11 Alexander Bickel and Harry Wellington, "Legislative Purpose and the Judicial Process: The Lincoln Mills Case," *Harvard Law Review* 71 (1957): 3, 5–6, 35; see G. Edward White, "The Evolution of Reasoned Elaboration: Jurisprudential Criticism and Social Change," *Virginia Law Review* 59 (1973): 287.

12 Robert Tsai, *Eloquence and Reason: Creating a First Amendment Culture* (New Haven: Yale Univ. Press, 2008), 2, 48.

13 Ibid., 48.

14 Paul Kahn, *Making the Case: The Art of the Judicial Opinion* (Hartford: Yale Univ. Press, 2016), xiv.

15 Don Le Duc, "'Free Speech' Decisions and the Legal Process: The Judicial Opinion in Context," *Quarterly Journal of Speech* 62, no. 3 (1976): 284.

16 Haig Bosmajian, *Metaphor and Reason in Judicial Opinions* (Carbondale: Southern Illinois Univ. Press, 1992), 205; see also Chad Oldfather, "The Hidden Ball: A Substantive Critique of Baseball Metaphors in Judicial Opinions," *Connecticut Law Review* 27 (1994): 17–51.

17 Maksymilian Del Mar, *Artefacts of Legal Inquiry: The Value of Imagination in Adjudication* (Oxford: Hart, 2020), 1, 47.

18 Jeanne Fahnestock, *Rhetorical Figures in Science* (Oxford: Oxford Univ. Press, 1999), 6.

19 Bosmajian, *Metaphor and Reason*, xii.

20 See Chaïm Perelman and Lucie Olbrechts-Tyteca, *The New Rhetoric: A Treatise on Argumentation*, trans. John Wilkinson and Purcell Weaver (Notre Dame: Notre Dame Univ. Press, 1969), 179 ("The objection may be made that by this approach we shall never deal with what some would deem essential aspects of the study of figures.").

21 Fahnestock, *Rhetorical Figures in Science*, 10; see Perelman and Olbrechts-Tyteca, *New Rhetoric*, 169.

22 Fahnestock, *Rhetorical Figures in Science*, 24.

23 Perelman and Olbrechts-Tyteca, *New Rhetoric*, 169.

24 See Del Mar, *Artefacts of Legal Inquiry*, 61, 122–23, 343.

25 Bosmajian, *Metaphor and Reason*, 201.

26 Del Mar, *Artefacts of Legal Inquiry*, 343.

27 Tsai, *Eloquence and Reason*, 48.

28 See James Jasinski, *Sourcebook on Rhetoric: Key Concepts in Contemporary Rhetorical Studies* (Thousand Oaks: Sage, 2001), 542, 557.

29 See Paul Baker and Sibonile Ellece, *Key Terms in Discourse Analysis* (New York: Continuum, 2011), 64.

30 See generally Milton Konvitz, *Fundamental Rights: History of a Constitutional Doctrine* (New York: Routledge, 2001), 2.

31 Palko v. Connecticut, 302 U.S. 319, 325 (1937). More recently, the Court has asserted that for a right to be fundamental it must also be "deeply rooted in the Nation's history and tradition." Dobbs v. Jackson Women's Health Org., No. 19-1392, slip op. at 5 (U.S. Supr. Ct. June 24, 2022).

32 See, e.g., Benton v. Maryland, 395 U.S. 784, 795 (1969).

33 *Palko*, 302 U.S. at 326.

34 Konvitz, *Fundamental Rights*, 2, 8.

35 Ibid., 8-10.

36 Tsai, *Eloquence and Reason*, 155.

37 Quoted in ibid., 155-57; cf. United States v. Darby, 312 U.S. 100, 124 (1941) (referring to the Tenth Amendment as merely "a truism").

38 See Konvitz, *Fundamental Rights*, 1.

39 Gitlow v. New York, 268 U.S. 652 (1925); see Konvitz, *Fundamental Rights*, 12.

40 *Palko*, 302 U.S. at 325; Konvitz, *Fundamental Rights*, 12-13.

41 *Palko*, 302 U.S. at 325, 327.

42 Konvitz, *Fundamental Rights*, 2-3.

43 Ibid., 4.

44 Ibid., 5-6.

45 See Francis Heller, "A Turning Point for Religious Liberty," *Virginia Law Review* 29 (1943): 444-46.

46 Minersville Sch. Dist. v. Gobitis, 310 U.S. 586, 591-92 (1940).

47 Gobitis v. Minersville Sch. Dist., 21 F. Supp. 581, 584 (E.D. Pa. 1937).

48 Ibid.

49 Gobitis v. Minersville Sch. Dist., 24 F. Supp. 271, 274 (E.D. Pa. 1938).

50 Minersville Sch. Dist. v. Gobitis, 108 F.2d 683, 683 (3d Cir. 1940).

51 Ibid., 688-89.

52 Ibid., 692.

53 Ibid., 692-93.

54 Ibid., 687.

55 Ibid., 683-92.

56 *Gobitis*, 310 U.S. at 591.

57 Ibid., 593.

58 Ibid., 593-94.

59 See ibid., 594-95.

60 Ibid., 595.

61 Ibid., 596.

62 Tsai, *Eloquence and Reason*, 48.

63 *Gobitis*, 310 U.S. at 596.
64 See Heller, "A Turning Point," 452–53.
65 *Gobitis*, 310 U.S. at 600.
66 See Chuck Smith, "The Persecution of West Virginia Jehovah's Witnesses and the Expansion of Legal Protection for Religious Liberty," *Journal of Church and State* 43, no. 3 (2001): 572.
67 West Virginia Board of Education v. Barnette, 319 U.S. 624, 626 (1943).
68 Ibid., 627.
69 Ibid., 630.
70 Ibid., 632–33.
71 Ibid., 636–37.
72 Ibid., 636–37.
73 Ibid., 640–41.
74 Ibid., 641.
75 Ibid.
76 Ibid.
77 Bosmajian, *Metaphor and Reason*, 201.
78 Sanford Levinson, *Constitutional Faith* (1988; reprint, Princeton: Princeton Univ. Press, 2011), 101.
79 *Barnette*, 319 U.S. at 643 (Black and Douglas, concurring).
80 Ibid., 644.
81 Ibid., 648–71 (Frankfurter, dissenting).
82 Ibid., 646–47.
83 *Gobitis*, 310 U.S. at 598.
84 *Barnette*, 319 U.S. at 661.
85 Ibid., 670.
86 Ibid., 661.
87 Ibid., 648–49.
88 Ibid., 650–52.
89 Ibid., 665.
90 Ibid., 667–70 (quoting James Thayer, *John Marshall* (Boston: Houghton Mifflin, 1901), 104–10).
91 *Gobitis*, 310 U.S. at 596.
92 *Barnette*, 319 U.S. at 669 (Frankfurter, dissenting).
93 Tsai, *Eloquence and Reason*, 125.
94 *Whitney*, 274 U.S. at 375–376 (Brandeis, concurring).
95 *Nexis Uni* database search (last visited June 5, 2022).
96 Bridges v. California, 314 US 252, 270 (1941).
97 United States v. Associated Press, 52 F. Supp. 362, 372 (S.D.N.Y. 1943).
98 New York Times v. Sullivan, 376 U.S. 254, 270 (1964).
99 United States v. White, 401 U.S. 745 (1971) (Douglas, dissenting).
100 Perelman and Olbrechts-Tyteca, *New Rhetoric*, 175.
101 Texas v. Johnson, 491 U.S. 397 (1989).
102 Ibid., 399.

103 John Leubsdorf, "The Structure of Judicial Opinions," *Minnesota Law Review* 86 (2001): 461 n. 56.
104 *Johnson*, 491 U.S. at 419–20.
105 Ibid., 419–20.
106 Ibid.
107 Jeffrey Walker, *Rhetoric and Poetics in Antiquity* (Oxford: Oxford Univ. Press, 2000), 158; cf. Jonathan Pratt, "The Epideictic Agōn and Aristotle's Elusive Third Genre," *American Journal of Philology* 133, no. 2 (2012): 177–208.
108 *Johnson*, 491 U.S. at 420–21 (Kennedy, concurring).
109 Ibid., 421.
110 Leubsdorf, "Structure of Judicial Opinions," 461 n. 56.
111 Celeste Condit, "The Functions of Epideictic: The Boston Massacre Orations as Exemplar," *Communication Quarterly* 33, no. 4 (1985): 294.
112 *Johnson*, 491 U.S. at 422 (Rehnquist, dissenting).
113 Ibid., 422–27 (Rehnquist, dissenting).
114 Ibid., 427 (Rehnquist, dissenting).
115 Ibid., 421–39 (Rehnquist, dissenting) (emphasis added).
116 John O'Malley, *Praise and Blame in Renaissance Rome: Rhetoric, Doctrine, and Reform in the Sacred Orators of the Papal Court, c. 1450–1521* (Durham: Duke Univ. Press, 1979), 75, 163.
117 Ibid., 240.
118 Perelman and Olbrechts-Tyteca, *New Rhetoric*, 51.
119 Michael Carter, "The Ritual Functions of Epideictic Rhetoric: The Case of Socrates' Funeral Oration," *Rhetorica* 9, no. 3 (1991): 211–17, 226.
120 Debora Shuger, *Sacred Rhetoric: The Christian Grand Style in the English Renaissance* (Princeton: Princeton Univ. Press, 1988), 173–75.
121 Lawrence Rosenfield, "The Practical Celebration of Epideictic," in *Rhetoric in Transition: Studies in the Nature and Uses of Rhetoric*, ed. Eugene White (University Park: Penn State Univ. Press, 1980), 137.
122 Del Mar, *Artefacts of Legal Inquiry*, 343–44.
123 See United States v. Eichman, 496 U.S. 310 (1990).
124 See Walker, *Rhetoric and Poetics*, 158; cf. Pratt, "The Epideictic Agōn," 177–208.
125 Ernesto Grassi, *Rhetoric as Philosophy: The Humanist Tradition*, trans. John Michael Krois and Azizeh Azodi (1980; reprint, Carbondale: Southern Illinois Press, 2001), 20, 33, 80.
126 Ibid., 20 (emphasis in original).
127 Ibid., 93.
128 Ibid., 20–21.
129 Ibid., 32.
130 Ibid.
131 Cicero, *De Oratore*, trans. E. W. Sutton and H. Rackham (Cambridge: Loeb Classical Library, 1942), 3.133–34.

132 Garver, *For the Sake of Argument*, 202; cf. Giambattista Vico, *On the Study Methods of Our Time*, trans. Elio Gianturco (Ithaca: Cornell Univ. Press, 1990), 13 ("Common sense, besides being the criterion of practical judgment, is also the guiding standard of eloquence."); Walker, *Rhetoric and Poetics*, 7–10, 14, 83, 115, 270–71 (writing that epideictic established and mnemonically sustained the "culturally authoritative codes of value and the paradigms of eloquence" from which deliberative and judicial rhetoric derived their "'precedents,'...language, and...power"); Perelman and Olbrechts-Tyteca, *New Rhetoric*, 47–51.

133 Garver, *For the Sake of Argument*, 10, 105.

134 Ibid., 4.

135 Ibid., 105.

136 Ibid., 119–20.

137 Ibid.

138 Walker, *Rhetoric and Poetics*, 7–10, 14, 83, 115, 270–71; see, e.g., Thomas Cole, *The Origins of Rhetoric in Ancient Greece* (Baltimore: The Johns Hopkins Univ. Press, 1991), 89; Edward Schiappa with David Timmerman, "Aristotle's Disciplining of Epideictic," in Edward Schiappa, *The Beginnings of Rhetorical Theory in Classical Greece* (Hartford: Yale Univ. Press, 1999), 185, 198.

Keeping Government Out of Religion and Vice Versa

1 See Goodson v. Northside Bible Church, 261 F. Supp. 99, 103 (S.D. Ala.1966).

2 Thomas Jefferson, Letter from President Thomas Jefferson to the Danbury Connecticut Baptist Association dated January 1, 1802, in Saul Padover, *The Complete Jefferson* (Freeport: Books for Library Press, 1943), 518–19; see Daniel Dreisbach, *Thomas Jefferson and the Wall of Separation Between Church and State* (New York: NYU Press, 2002), 205 n. 31 (noting that "the motif of a protective 'hedge' or 'wall' was ubiquitous in the rhetoric of colonial New England," providing "vital structures of demarcation between the degrading 'wilderness of the world' and the enclosed, fragrant 'garden of the church'"); Roger Williams, "Mr. Cotton's Letter Lately Printed, Examined, and Answered," in *The Complete Writings of Roger Williams*, ed. Reuben Aldridge Guild (New York: Russell and Russell, 1963: 1:392.

3 See *Goodson*, 261 F. Supp. at 103; see also Loren Beth, *The American Theory of Church and State* (Gainesville: Univ. of Florida Press, 1958), 65 (writing that both Madison and Jefferson were likely familiar with the ideas of Roger Williams, either directly or through Baptist views on religious liberty that were expressed in hundreds of petitions and memorials presented to state governments with which they were "exceedingly familiar").

4 Haig Bosmajian, *Metaphor and Reason in Judicial Opinions* (Carbondale: Southern Illinois Univ. Press, 1992), 73.

5 R. Freeman Butts, *The American Tradition in Religion and Education* (Boston: Beacon Press, 1950), 93.

6 Dreisbach, *Thomas Jefferson and the Wall of Separation*, 2–3.

7 Everson v. Bd. of Educ., 330 U.S. 1, 18 (1947).
8 Robert Tsai, *Eloquence and Reason: Creating a First Amendment Culture* (New Haven: Yale Univ. Press, 2008), 93.
9 McCollum v. Bd. of Educ., 333 U.S. 203, 247 (1948) (Reed, dissenting); see also Bosmajian, *Metaphor and Reason*, 82–83 (noting that Justice Reed relies on metaphor and personification elsewhere in *McCollum* and on metaphors and figures of speech in other opinions).
10 See generally Bosmajian, *Metaphor and Reason*, 73–90; Tsai, *Eloquence and Reason*, 93–97.
11 See Bosmajian, *Metaphor and Reason*, 83–88.
12 Lemon v. Kurtzman, 403 U.S. 602, 614 (1971).
13 *Everson*, 330 U.S. at 27 (Jackson, dissenting).
14 See Jeanne Fahnestock, *Rhetorical Figures in Science* (Oxford: Oxford Univ. Press, 1999), 122–26; Rodolphe Gasché, *Of Minimal Things: Studies on the Notion of Relation* (Stanford: Stanford Univ. Press, 1999), 272; Anthony Paul, "From Stasis to Ékstasis: Four Types of Chiasmus," in *Chiasmus and Culture*, eds. Boris Wiseman and Anthony Paul (New York: Berghahn Books, 2014), 21–23; Anthony Paul and Boris Wiseman, "Chiasmus in the Drama of Life," introduction to *Chiasmus and Culture*, 1–3.
15 *Everson*, 330 U.S. at 16.
16 See Fahnestock, *Rhetorical Figures in Science*, 126; see also Gasché, *Of Minimal Things*, 272; John Welch, ed., *Chiasmus in Antiquity: Structures, Analyses, Exegesis* (Eugene: Wipf and Stock, 1981); John Welch and Donald Parry, eds., *Chiasmus: The State of the Art* (Provo: BYU Studies, 2020).
17 See Robert Hariman, "What Is Chiasmus? Or, Why the Abyss Stares Back," in *Chiasmus and Culture*, eds. Boris Wiseman and Anthony Paul (New York: Berghahn Books, 2014), 57; Paul and Wiseman, "Chiasmus in the Drama of Life," 2–3.
18 Hariman, "What Is Chiasmus," 60.
19 Gasché, *Of Minimal Things*, 272–73.
20 Hariman, "What Is Chiasmus," 51, 57.
21 Aristotle, *Rhetoric*, trans. W. Rhys Roberts, in *The Rhetoric and Poetics of Aristotle* (New York: Modern Library, 1984), 1419^b (Aristotle adds "in which he was right").
22 Matthew 19:30 and 20:16 (King James).
23 See Gasché, *Of Minimal Things*, 272.
24 See Chuang Tzu, *The Book of Chuang Tzu*, trans. Martin Palmer with Elizabeth Breuilly, Chang Wai Ming, and Jay Ramsay (New York: Penguin, 2006), 20.
25 Maurice Merleau-Ponty, *The Visible and the Invisible*, ed. Claude Lefort, trans. Alphonso Lingis (Evanston: Northwestern Univ. Press, 1968), 215; cf. Alfred North Whitehead, *Process and Reality*, corrected ed., eds. David Griffin and Donald Sherburne (New York: Free Press, 1978), 339 ("The art of progress is to preserve order amid change, and to preserve change amid order.").

26 Ernesto Grassi, *Rhetoric as Philosophy: The Humanist Tradition*, trans. John Michael Krois and Azizeh Azodi (1980; reprint, Carbondale: Southern Illinois Press, 2001), 32 (also describing the true relationship between philosophy and rhetoric as "a philosophy which does not need an 'external' rhetoric to convince, and a rhetoric that does not need an 'external' content of verity"); see also ibid., 34 ("Every original philosophy is rhetoric and every true and not exterior rhetoric is philosophy.").

27 Cicero, *On the Laws*, trans. David Fott (Ithaca: Cornell Univ. Press. 2014), 3.2.

28 Brown v. Allen, 344 U.S. 443, 540 (1953) (Jackson, concurring); see also Marbury v. Madison, 5 U.S. 137, 178 (1803) (noting that where both a law and the Constitution apply to a particular case, the Court must either decide cases "conformably to the law, disregarding the constitution; or conformably to the constitution, disregarding the law").

29 See Dreisbach, *Thomas Jefferson and the Wall of Separation*, 86.

30 Cf. Eva Brann, "Madison's 'Memorial and Remonstrance,' Model of American Rhetoric," in *Rhetoric and American Statesmanship*, eds. Glen Thurow and Jeffrey Wallin (Durham: Carolina Academic Press, 1984), 10 (writing of Madison's "eloquence of measured passion and sober ardor, which knows what to say when and to whom without bending the truth").

31 Quoted in *Everson*, 330 U.S. at 68 (Rutledge, dissenting); see ibid., 63–72. Compare the symmetrical structure of the *Remonstrance and Memorial* observed by Eva Brann, recognizing the eighth paragraph as the central claim around which are "clustered...the other prudential and cautionary points to be addressed to the Christian communities which hoped to profit from the law." Brann, "Madison's 'Memorial and Remonstrance,'" 14–15. Madison also uses a sentence-level chiasmus in paragraph 5 when he writes that the bill "implies either that the Civil Magistrate is a competent Judge of Religious truth; or that he may employ Religion as an engine of Civil policy." Quoted in *Everson*, 330 U.S. at 67.

32 Quoted in *Everson*, 330 U.S. at 71 (Rutledge, dissenting); cf. Fahnestock, *Rhetorical Figures in Science*, 131 (noting that antimetabole is "less a static edifice than it is a movement," as "one enters the antimetabole at one conceptual location and comes out at another," having "the trajectory of a parabola").

33 James Madison, "Property," in James Madison, *James Madison: Writings*, ed. Jack Rakove (New York: Penguin, 1999), 515–17.

34 Paul and Wiseman, "Chiasmus in the Drama of Life," 5. Madison also used a chiasmus to describe the progress of the new nation in 1792: "In Europe, charters of liberty have been granted by power. America has set the example...of charters of power granted by liberty." Quoted in James Jasinski, *Sourcebook on Rhetoric: Key Concepts in Contemporary Rhetorical Studies* (Thousand Oaks: Sage, 2001), 209; Jeffrey Walker, *Rhetoric and Poetics in Antiquity* (Oxford: Oxford Univ. Press, 2000), 546.

35 Gasché, *Of Minimal Things*, 272–73.

36 Hariman, "What Is Chiasmus," 61.

37 Quoted in Gasché, 273.

38 Hariman, "What Is Chiasmus," 63.

39 Ibid., 62–63 ("We can recognize ourselves in the other and the other in oneself, but never to eliminate the empty space between us.").

40 John Ruffin, *The Rhetorlogue, Or, Study of the Rhetor or Orator* (New York: Edgar Werner, 1922), 140.

41 Fahnestock, *Rhetorical Figures in Science*, 141.

42 As defined in *Black's Law Dictionary*, in property law the term *abeyance* refers to a sequestration of title or expectant state of unfulfilled ownership:

Expectation; waiting; suspense; remembrance and contemplation in law. Where there is no person in existence in whom an inheritance can vest, it is said to be in abeyance, that is, in expectation; the law considering it as always potentially existing, and ready to vest whenever a proper owner appears. Or, in other words, it is said to be in the remembrance, consideration, and intendment of the law... . [I]n the case of maritime captures during war, it is said that, until the capture becomes invested with the character of prize by a sentence of condemnation, the right of property is in abeyance or in a state of legal sequestration. It has also been applied to the franchises of a corporation. "When a corporation is to be brought into existence by some future acts of the corporators, the franchises remain in abeyance, until such acts are done."

Black's Law Dictionary, 2nd ed. (St. Paul: West, 1910) s.v. "Abeyance" (citations omitted).

43 Hariman, "What Is Chiasmus," 51.

44 Ibid., 52.

45 Ibid., 50.

46 Ibid., 59. Jacques Derrida writes that the chiasm "folds itself with a supplementary flexion" rather than forming a unity of opposites. Jacques Derrida, *The Archaeology of the Frivolous*, trans. John Leavy (Pittsburgh: Duquesne Univ. Press, 1980), 134.

47 Hariman, "What Is Chiasmus," 59.

48 Elie Assis, "Chiasmus in Biblical Narrative: Rhetoric of Characterization," *Prooftexts: A Journal of Jewish Literary History* 22, no. 3 (2002): 287.

49 *Lemon*, 403 U.S. at 614.

50 *Everson*, 330 U.S. at 18.

51 Ibid., 1. The Court had previously applied the Free Exercise Clause of the First Amendment to the states under the Due Process Clause of the Fourteenth Amendment. See Murdock v. Pennsylvania, 319 U.S. 105 (1943).

52 *Everson*, 330 U.S. at 14–18.

53 Ibid., 16–18.

54 Ibid., 8.

55 Ibid., 9.

56 Ibid., 10.

57 Ibid., 11.

58 Ibid., 11 n.9.

59 Ibid., 12.
60 Ibid., 12–13.
61 Ibid., 5 (quoting Watson v. Jones, 13 Wall. 679, 730 (1871)).
62 *Nexis Uni* database search (last visited Dec. 27, 2021).
63 *Everson*, 330 U.S. at 15–16.
64 Ibid., 18.
65 Ibid., 19 (Jackson, dissenting). The quotation, unattributed except to the author, is from the first canto of Lord Byron's *Don Juan*. See Lord Byron, *Don Juan*, eds. T. G. Steffan, E. Steffan, and W. W. Pratt (1819–24; reprint, New York: Penguin, 1996).
66 *Everson*, 330 U.S. at 28 (Rutledge, dissenting).
67 Ibid., 12–13.
68 Ibid., 29 (Rutledge, dissenting).
69 Ibid., 31 (Rutledge, dissenting) (quoting Madison's description of Jefferson's *Virginia Bill for Religious Liberty*).
70 *Everson*, 330 U.S. at 31–32 (Rutledge, dissenting).
71 Ibid., 33 (Rutledge, dissenting).
72 Ibid., 34 (Rutledge, dissenting).
73 Ibid., 35 (Rutledge, dissenting).
74 Ibid., 37 (Rutledge, dissenting).
75 Ibid., 37–38 (Rutledge, dissenting).
76 Ibid., 39 (Rutledge, dissenting).
77 Ibid., 40 (Rutledge, dissenting).
78 Ibid., 40 n.29 (Rutledge, dissenting).
79 Ibid., 41 n.31 (Rutledge, dissenting).
80 Ibid., 47 (Rutledge, dissenting).
81 Ibid., 49–50 (Rutledge, dissenting).
82 Ibid., 56 (Rutledge, dissenting).
83 Ibid., 53–54 (Rutledge, dissenting) (citations to Madison's *Remonstrance and Memorial* omitted).
84 Ibid., 57 (Rutledge, dissenting).
85 Ibid., 57–58 (Rutledge, dissenting).
86 Ibid., 58 (Rutledge, dissenting).
87 Ibid., 58–59 (Rutledge, dissenting).
88 Ibid., 59 (Rutledge, dissenting) (citing with authorial attribution but without specific reference to either 1 Corinthians 6:20 (King James), "For ye are bought with a price: therefore glorify God in your body, and in your spirit, which are God's," or 7:23 (King James) "Ye are bought with a price; be not ye the servants of men.").
89 *Everson*, 330 U.S. at 60–63 (Rutledge, dissenting) (citations omitted).
90 Ibid., 18 (Jackson, dissenting).
91 Ibid., 20 (Jackson, dissenting).
92 See ibid., 21 (Jackson, dissenting).
93 Ibid., 24 (Jackson, dissenting).

94 Ibid., 24–25 (Jackson, dissenting).
95 Ibid., 25 (Jackson, dissenting).
96 Ibid., 26–27 (Jackson, dissenting).
97 Ibid., 28 (Jackson, dissenting).
98 Tsai, *Eloquence and Reason*, 94 (quoting *McCollum*, 333 U.S. at 211).
99 Tsai, *Eloquence and Reason*, 96–98 (quoting *McGowan v. Maryland*, 366 U.S. 420, 445–46, 450 (1961).
100 Tsai, *Eloquence and Reason*, 98.
101 *Lemon*, 403 U.S. at 612, 614.
102 *McCollum*, 333 U.S. at 247 (Reed, dissenting).
103 Bosmajian, *Metaphor and Reason*, 83; Zorach v. Clauson, 343 U.S. 306, 325 (1952) (Jackson, dissenting).
104 *Lemon*, 403 U.S. at 612, 614.
105 *Everson*, 330 U.S. at 18.
106 Hariman, "What Is Chiasmus," 50, 59.
107 Negation is notoriously difficult to process. As George Lakoff writes, "even when you negate a frame, you activate the frame." George Lakoff, *The All New Don't Think of an Elephant! Know Your Values and Frame the Debate* (White River Junction: Chelsea Green, 2014), xii.
108 Gasché, *Of Minimal Things*, 272–73.
109 Hariman, "What Is Chiasmus," 59.
110 Ibid., 51.
111 *Lemon*, 403 U.S. at 612, 614.
112 Brann, "Madison's 'Memorial and Remonstrance,'" 11.
113 Ibid., 29.
114 Quoted in *Everson*, 330 U.S. at 64 (Rutledge, dissenting). Eva Brann describes the first paragraph of Madison's *Remonstrance and Memorial*, from which these passages are drawn, as "an enchained sequence of sentences which has something of the quality of a liturgical response," with an "incantation-like" language, a "kind of rondel of reason." Brann, "Madison's 'Memorial and Remonstrance,'" 17.
115 See Matthew 22:21 (King James).
116 Chiasmus appears in scholarly commentary on the Religion Clauses as well. See, e.g., Dreisbach, *Thomas Jefferson and the Wall of Separation*, 2 (writing that the separation principle "inhibits religious intrusions on public life and politics as much as political intrusions on religion and the rights of conscience.").
117 See *McCollum*, 333 U.S. at 209–12.
118 Ibid., 209–10.
119 Ibid., 210–11 (quoting *Everson*, 330 U.S. at 15–16).
120 See ibid., 211–12.
121 Torcaso v. Watkins, 367 U.S. 488, 493 (1961).
122 *McCollum*, 333 U.S. at 216 (Frankfurter, concurring) (quoting Robert Frost, "Mending Wall," in *North of Boston* (1914; reprint, New York: Henry Holt, 1917), 11–13).

123 Frost, "Mending Wall."
124 *McCollum*, 333 U.S. at 212 (Frankfurter, concurring).
125 Ibid., 213 (Frankfurter, concurring).
126 Frost, "Mending Wall."
127 *McCollum*, 333 U.S. at 247 (Reed, dissenting).
128 Ibid., 213 (Frankfurter, concurring).
129 Ibid., 213–14 (Frankfurter, concurring).
130 Ibid., 214 (Frankfurter, concurring).
131 Ibid., 215 (Frankfurter, concurring).
132 Ibid., 216 (Frankfurter, concurring).
133 Ibid., 216–17 (Frankfurter, concurring).
134 Ibid., 227, 231 (Frankfurter, concurring).
135 *Gobitis*, 310 U.S. at 596, 600.
136 *McCollum*, 333 U.S. at 218–19 (Frankfurter, concurring).
137 Ibid., 219 (Frankfurter, concurring) (quoting Elihu Root, *Addresses on Government and Citizenship*, eds. Robert Bacon and James Brown Scott (Cambridge: Harvard Univ. Press, 1916), 137, 140).
138 Ibid., 219 n.8 (Frankfurter, concurring) (quoting Jeremiah Black, *Essays and Speeches of Jeremiah S. Black*, ed. Chauncey Black (New York: D. Appleton, 1885), 53).
139 *McCollum*, 333 U.S. at 219 n.8 (Frankfurter, concurring).
140 Ibid., 222–23 (Frankfurter, concurring).
141 Ibid., 222–25 (Frankfurter, concurring).
142 Ibid., 225, 231 (Frankfurter, concurring).
143 Ibid., 226–28 (Frankfurter, concurring).
144 Ibid., 231 (Frankfurter, concurring).
145 Ibid., 232 (Frankfurter, concurring).
146 Ibid., 213, 225 (Frankfurter, concurring).
147 Ibid., 232 (Jackson, concurring).
148 Ibid., 234–35 (Jackson, concurring).
149 Ibid., 235 (Jackson, concurring).
150 Ibid., 235–36 (Jackson, concurring).
151 Ibid., 235 (Jackson, concurring).
152 Ibid., 235–36 (Jackson, concurring).
153 Ibid., 235–36 (Jackson, concurring).
154 Ibid., 236–37 (Jackson, concurring).
155 Ibid., 237 (Jackson, concurring).
156 Ibid. (Jackson, concurring).
157 Ibid., 237–38 (Jackson, concurring).
158 Ibid., 238 (Jackson, concurring).
159 Ibid. (Jackson, concurring).
160 *Lemon*, 403 U.S. at 606–7.
161 Ibid., 612.
162 Ibid.

163 Ibid.
164 Ibid. 612–13 (citations omitted).
165 Ibid., 614.
166 Ibid., 614, 623.
167 Ibid., 614.
168 Ibid., 615.
169 Ibid., 623.
170 Ibid., 625.
171 Sch. Dist. of Abington Township v. Schempp, 374 U.S. 203, 304 (1963) (Brennan, concurring) (quoting Black, *Essays and Speeches*, 53); see *McCollum*, 333 U.S. 219 n.8 (Frankfurter, concurring).
172 Hariman, "What Is Chiasmus?," 52.
173 *Lemon*, 403 U.S. at 612, 614.
174 See Bosmajian, *Metaphor and Reason*, 83–88.
175 *McCollum*, 333 U.S. at 238 (Jackson, concurring).
176 *Zorach*, 343 U.S. at 325 (Jackson, dissenting)
177 *McCollum*, 333 U.S. at 216 (Frankfurter, concurring) (quoting Frost, "Mending Wall," 11–13).
178 Hariman, "What Is Chiasmus?, 62–63.
179 Fahnestock, *Rhetorical Figures in Science*, 10.
180 Ibid., 6.
181 Gasché, *Of Minimal Things*, 272–73.
182 Fahnestock, *Rhetorical Figures in Science*, 22.
183 Ibid., 24.
184 Cf. John Genung, *The Working Principles of Rhetoric, Examined in Their Literary Relations and Illustrated with Examples* (Boston: Ginn and Co., 1900), 458.
185 See, e.g., Thomas Conley, *Rhetoric in the European Tradition* (Chicago: Univ. of Chicago Press, 1990), 128–29; Wilbur Samuel Howell, *Logic and Rhetoric in England, 1500–1700* (New York: Russell and Russell, 1961), 148; James Jasinski, *Sourcebook on Rhetoric: Key Concepts in Contemporary Rhetorical Studies* (Thousand Oaks: Sage, 2001), xvii–xviii; Janice Lauer, *Invention in Rhetoric and Composition* (West Lafayette: Parlor Press, 2004), 35, 38, 41; Walter Ong, *Ramus, Method, and the Decay of Dialogue: From the Art of Discourse to the Art of Reason* (1958; reprint, Chicago: Univ. of Chicago Press, 2004), 280–81, 288–89; Chaïm Perelman, *The Realm of Rhetoric*, trans. William Kluback (Notre Dame: Notre Dame Univ. Press, 1982), 3; Frances Yates, *The Art of Memory* (Chicago: Univ. of Chicago Press, 1966), 232–34.
186 Grassi, *Rhetoric as Philosophy*, 26 (emphasis in original).
187 Thomas Sprat, *The History of the Royal Society of London, for the Improving of Natural Knowledge*, 2nd ed. corrected (London, 1702), 112–13 (emphasis in original); see Ernesto Grassi, *The Primordial Metaphor*, trans. Laura Pietropaolo and Manuela Scarci (Binghamton: SUNY, 1994), 12.

188 See., e.g., Lauer, *Invention in Rhetoric and Composition*, 38, 41 ("Bacon dealt a final blow to invention by proclaiming that rhetorical invention dealt only with retrieving the known, while science created new knowledge through an inductive investigation.").

189 Ibid., 35, 46.

190 Fahnestock, *Rhetorical Figures in Science*, 29.

191 *McCollum*, 333 U.S. at 247 (Reed, dissenting); cf. Berkey v. Third Ave. Ry. Co., 244 N.Y. 84, 94 (N.Y. 1926) ("The whole problem of the relation between parent and subsidiary corporations is still enveloped in the mists of metaphor.").

192 *McCollum*, 333 U.S. at 213 (Frankfurter, concurring).

193 Ivo Strecker, "Chiasmus and Metaphor," in *Chiasmus and Culture*, eds. Boris Wiseman and Anthony Paul (New York: Berghahn Books, 2014), 87.

194 Hariman, "What Is Chiasmus?," 59.

Storms, Shadows, and Privacy

1 Daniel Boorstin, *The Mysterious Science of the Law: An Essay on Blackstone's Commentaries Showing How Blackstone, Employing Eighteenth-Century Ideas of Science, Religion, History, Aesthetics, and Philosophy, Made of the Law at Once a Conservative and a Mysterious Science* (1941; reprint, Chicago: Univ. of Chicago Press, 1996), 104.

2 Cohens v. Virginia, 19 U.S. 264, 387 (1821).

3 McCulloch v. Maryland, 17 U.S. 316, 415 (1819).

4 See, e.g., Norma Thompson, *The Ship of State: Statecraft and Politics from Ancient Greece to Democratic America* (New Haven: Yale Univ. Press, 2001), 167; David Keyt, "Plato and the Ship of State," in *The Blackwell Guide to Plato's Republic*, ed. Gerasimos Santas (Malden: Blackwell, 2006), 189–213. Jeffrey Walker argues that Alcaeus's "ship of state" poems fused the audience's "seafaring knowledge with its code of manly, soldierly behavior," with the rhetorical purpose of maintaining the social cohesion of a political and fighting force "at a moment when it is threatened with defeat and disintegration." Jeffrey Walker, *Rhetoric and Poetics in Antiquity* (Oxford: Oxford Univ. Press, 2000), 212–14.

5 See Weems v. United States, 217 U.S. 349 (1910).

6 Ibid., 373.

7 See Olmstead v. United States, 277 U.S. 438 (1928).

8 See Bernard Schwartz, *The Unpublished Opinions of the Warren Court* (Oxford: Oxford Univ. Press, 1985), 227–28.

9 *Olmstead*, 277 U.S. at 478 (Brandeis, dissenting).

10 *Nexis Uni* database search (last visited Jan. 5, 2022).

11 *Olmstead*, 277 U.S. at 479 (Brandeis, dissenting).

12 *Nexis Uni* database search (last visited Jan. 5, 2022).

13 *Olmstead*, 277 U.S. at 473 (Brandeis, dissenting) (citations omitted).

14 Ibid., 412 (Brandeis, dissenting).

15 Ibid., 473–74 (Brandeis, dissenting).

16 Griswold v. Connecticut, 381 U.S. 479, 484 (1965).
17 Pseudo-Dionysius of Halicarnassus, *Ars Rhetorica*, trans. William Race (Cambridge: Harvard Univ. Press, 2019), 1.1.
18 Obergefell v. Hodges, 576 U.S. 644 (2015).
19 Ibid., 651–52.
20 Ibid., 719 n.22 (Scalia, dissenting).
21 Ibid., 657.
22 Ibid., 667.
23 Ibid., 656–57.
24 Ibid., 657–58.
25 Ibid., 658–59.
26 Bowers v. Hardwick, 476 U.S. 186, 199 (1986) (Blackmun, dissenting) (quoting *Olmstead*, 277 U.S. at 478 (Brandeis, dissenting)).
27 See Lawrence v. Texas, 539 U.S. 558 (2003).
28 See *Obergefell*, 576 U.S. at 661–63.
29 Ibid., 667, 675 (quoting *Lawrence*, 539 U.S. at 567, 578); see *Obergefell*, 576 U.S. at 647, 662, 664–67, 671, 674–75, 678. In *Obergefell*, Justice Kennedy also relied on his opinion for the majority in *United States v. Windsor* (2013), in which the Court held that the denial of federal recognition of same-sex marriages in the Defense of Marriage Act was unconstitutional. See ibid., 645–46, 662, 666–70; United States v. Windsor, 570 U.S. 744 (2013).
30 *Lawrence*, 539 U.S. at 562.
31 Robert Tsai, *Eloquence and Reason: Creating a First Amendment Culture* (New Haven: Yale Univ. Press, 2008), 137.
32 *Lawrence*, 539 U.S. at 537.
33 *Griswold*, 381 U.S. at 486.
34 Eisenstadt v. Baird, 405 U. S. 438 (1972).
35 Roe v. Wade, 410 U.S. 113 (1973).
36 Planned Parenthood v. Casey, 505 U.S. 833 (1992).
37 *Lawrence*, 539 U.S. at 565. Justice Kennedy also referenced *Carey v. Population Services International* (1977), in which the Court held that it was unconstitutional for a state to restrict the advertisement, sale, or distribution of contraceptives to individuals of any age. See ibid., 565–66; Carey v. Population Serv. Int'l, 431 U.S. 678 (1977).
38 *Lawrence*, 539 U.S. at 566.
39 Ibid., 573.
40 See Romer v. Evans, 517 U.S. 620 (1996).
41 *Lawrence*, 539 U.S. at 566–67.
42 *Bowers*, 476 U.S. at 199 (Blackmun, dissenting) (quoting *Olmstead*, 277 U.S. at 478 (Brandeis, dissenting)).
43 *Bowers*, 476 U.S. at 204 (Blackmun, dissenting) (quoting Thornburgh v. Am. Coll. of Obstetricians and Gynecologists, 476 U.S. 747, 777 n.5 (1986) (Stevens, concurring)).
44 *Bowers*, 476 U.S. at 204–5 (1986) (Blackmun, dissenting) (citations omitted) (quoting Roberts v. United States Jaycees, 468 U.S. 609, 619 (1984)).

45 *Bowers*, 476 U.S. at 204–5 (1986) (Blackmun, dissenting) (quoting Paris Adult Theatre I v. Slaton, 413 U.S. 49, 63 (1973)).

46 *Lawrence*, 539 U.S. at 574 (quoting *Casey*, 505 U.S. at 851). In his dissenting opinion in *Lawrence*, Justice Scalia referred to this passage of *Casey* as the "famed sweet-mystery-of-life passage." *Lawrence*, 539 U.S. at 588 (Scalia, dissenting).

47 *Casey*, 505 U.S. at 844.

48 Ibid., 852.

49 See *Obergefell*, 576 U.S. at 663.

50 Ibid., 665.

51 Ibid., 666.

52 Ibid., 667.

53 Ibid., 669.

54 Ibid., 666 (quoting Goodridge v. Dep't of Pub. Health, 440 Mass. 309, 322 (Mass. 2003)).

55 *Obergefell*, 576 U.S. at 666.

56 Ibid., 666–67 (quoting *Griswold*, 381 U.S. at 486).

57 *Obergefell*, 576 U.S. at 667.

58 Ibid., 668 (citations omitted).

59 Ibid., 669 (quoting Alexis de Tocqueville, *Democracy in America*, trans. Henry Reeve, revised ed., 2 vols. (New York: Vintage, 1990), 1:309).

60 *Obergefell*, 576 U.S. at 669 (quoting Maynard v. Hill, 125 U. S. 190, 211, 213 (1888)).

61 *Griswold*, 381 U.S. at 480.

62 Schwartz, *Unpublished Opinions*, 227–28.

63 *Griswold*, 381 U.S. at 481–82.

64 Tsai, *Eloquence and Reason*, 136.

65 *Griswold*, 381 U.S. at 483.

66 Ibid., 484.

67 *Nexis Uni* database search (last visited Jan. 3, 2022).

68 See, e.g., David O'Brien, *Storm Center: The Supreme Court in American Politics* (New York: Norton, 1986), 15; Christopher Rideout, "Penumbral Thinking Revisited: Metaphor in Legal Argumentation," *Journal of the Association of Legal Writing Directors* 7, no. 1 (2010): 157–58.

69 *Griswold*, 381 U.S. at 484.

70 Ibid.

71 *Griswold*, 381 U.S. at 484 (quoting Boyd v. United States, 116 U.S. 616, 630 (1886)).

72 *Nexus Uni* database search (last visited Jan. 4, 2022).

73 *Griswold*, 381 U.S. at 484–85 (quoting *Boyd*, 116 U.S. at 630).

74 *Nexus Uni* database search (last visited Sept. 21, 2020); see McGee v Attorney General, [1974] I.R. 284 (Ireland); Miron v. Trudel, [1995] 2 S.C.R. 418 (Canada); Rajagopal v State of Tamil Nadu, [1995] 3 L.R.C. 566 (India).

75 *Griswold*, 381 U.S. at 486.

76 See Tsai, *Eloquence and Reason*, 136.

77 See O'Brien, *Storm Center*, 275–76; Schwartz, *Unpublished Opinions*, 229.
78 Reproduced in Schwartz, *Unpublished Opinions*, 235–36.
79 Ibid., 237–38.
80 Quoted in O'Brien, *Storm Center*, 276; see NAACP v. Alabama, 357 U.S. 449 (1958).
81 Quoted in O'Brien, *Storm Center*, 276–77.
82 *Olmstead*, 277 U.S. at 478 (Brandeis, dissenting).
83 *Griswold*, 381 U.S. at 487 (Goldberg, concurring).
84 See O'Brien, *Storm Center*, 15.
85 *Griswold*, 381 U.S. at 499–500 (Harlan, concurring).
86 Ibid., 522 (Black, dissenting).
87 Rideout, "Penumbral Thinking Revisited," 181, 189.
88 See generally Burr Henly, "Penumbra: The Roots of a Legal Metaphor," *Hastings Constitutional Law Quarterly* 15, no. 1 (1987): 83–92; see also, e.g., Melville Bigelow, *Centralization and the Law: Scientific Legal Education* (Boston: Little, Brown, 1906), 144 ("Even in a stationary condition of society, the common law will seldom have sharply drawn lines. Even its most definite rules are almost certain to have a penumbra—a penumbra which may spread back towards the rule itself until the whole field becomes indistinct; to be lighted up again perhaps by a new rule, with a new penumbra, subject to the same process."); Henry Terry, *Some Leading Principles of Anglo-American Law: Expounded with a View to Its Arrangement and Codification* (Philadelphia: T. and J. W. Johnson and Co., 1884), 613 ("The situations of fact which call for the application of the various legal principles shade off into each other indistinguishably. Around each group of cases which fall clearly within any given principle lies a penumbra of equivocal ones where the principle overlaps with some other.").
89 *Olmstead*, 277 U.S. at 469 (Holmes, dissenting).
90 *Poe v. Ullman*, 367 U.S. 497, 521 (1961) (Douglas, dissenting).
91 Rideout, "Penumbral Thinking Revisited," 157–58.
92 *Obergefell*, 576 U.S. at 663–64.
93 *Poe*, 367 U.S. at 509–22 (Douglas, dissenting), 522–55 (Harlan, dissenting).
94 See *Griswold*, 367 U.S. at 484. Consider, for example, the following epideictic passage from Justice Douglas's dissenting opinion in *Poe*:
The regime of a free society needs room for vast experimentation. Crises, emergencies, experience at the individual and community levels produce new insights; problems emerge in new dimensions; needs, once never imagined, appear. To stop experimentation and the testing of new decrees and controls is to deprive society of a needed versatility. Yet to say that a legislature may do anything not within a specific guarantee of the Constitution may be as crippling to a free society as to allow it to override specific guarantees so long as what it does fails to shock the sensibilities of a majority of the Court.
Poe, 367 U.S. at 509–22 (Douglas, dissenting).
95 *Poe*, 367 U.S. at 501–02.
96 Ibid., 508.

97 *Poe*, 367 U.S. at 539 (Harlan, dissenting).
98 Ibid., 539–40 (Harlan, dissenting) (citing *McCulloch*, 17 U.S. at 316).
99 *Poe*, 367 U.S. at 541 (Harlan, dissenting).
100 Ibid., 542 (Harlan, dissenting).
101 Ibid., 550 (Harlan, dissenting).
102 Ibid. (Harlan, dissenting) (quoting Wolf v. Colorado, 338 U.S. 25, 27 (1949)).
103 See *Obergefell*, 576 U.S. at 645–47, 664–66, 671–74; Loving v. Virginia, 388 U.S. 1, 12 (1967).
104 *Loving*, 388 U.S. at 12.
105 Ibid., 12 (citations omitted).
106 See *Obergefell*, 576 U.S. at 673.
107 *Loving*, 388 U.S. at 9.
108 See Eugene Garver, *For the Sake of Argument: Practical Reasoning, Character, and the Ethics of Belief* (Chicago: Univ. of Chicago Press, 2004), 71–73; *Loving*, 388 U.S. at 12.
109 Garver, *For the Sake of Argument*, 39, 71–73.
110 Ibid., 77.
111 Ibid., (quoting O'Brien, *Storm Center*, 281); see Bolling v. Sharpe, 347 U.S. 497 (1954).
112 Garver, *For the Sake of Argument*, 77; cf. Ernesto Grassi, *Rhetoric as Philosophy: The Humanist Tradition*, trans. John Michael Krois and Azizeh Azodi (1980; reprint, Carbondale: Southern Illinois Press, 2001), 26 ("The emotive word affects us through its directness.").
113 Garver, *For the Sake of Argument*, 72.
114 Ibid., 77.
115 See, e.g., Ben Grant, *The Aphorism and Other Short Forms* (London: Routledge, 2016), 13–14, 38; cf. Eugene Garver, "The Way We Live Now: Rhetorical Persuasion and Democratic Conversation," *Mercer Law Review* 63 (2012): 825–26.
116 Brown v. Bd. of Educ., 347 U.S. 483, 493 (1954).
117 Garver, *For the Sake of Argument*, 79.
118 *Obergefell*, 576 U.S. at 672–74.
119 Ibid., 681.
120 Ibid.
121 *McCulloch*, 17 U.S. at 415.
122 *Cohens*, 19 U.S. at 387.
123 *Weems*, 217 U.S. at 373.
124 *Olmstead*, 277 U.S. at 478 (Brandeis, dissenting).
125 *Griswold*, 381 U.S. at 484.
126 *Roberts*, 468 U.S. at 619.
127 *Lawrence*, 539 U.S. at 574 (quoting *Casey*, 505 U.S. at 851).
128 Walker, *Rhetoric and Poetics*, 10.
129 Tsai, *Eloquence and Reason*, 94.

130 Walker, *Rhetoric and Poetics*, 7–10, 14, 83, 115, 270–71; cf. *Lawrence*, 539 U.S. at 586 (Scalia, dissenting) (describing the opening sentence of the plurality opinion in *Planned Parenthood v. Casey*—"liberty finds no refuge in a jurisprudence of doubt"—as the Court's "sententious response…to those seeking to overrule *Roe v. Wade*").

131 Don Le Duc, "'Free Speech' Decisions and the Legal Process: The Judicial Opinion in Context," *Quarterly Journal of Speech* 62, no. 3 (1976): 284.

132 Jean-François Lyotard, "Complexity and the Sublime," in *Postmodernism: ICA Documents 4 & 5*, ed. Lisa Appignanesi (London: Institute of Contemporary Arts Publications, 1986), 24.

133 See, e.g., Richard Sherwin, "Sublime Jurisprudence: On the Ethical Education of the Legal Imagination in Our Time," *Chicago-Kent Law Review* 83 (2008): 1174–96.

134 See generally Henly, "Penumbra: The Roots of a Legal Metaphor"; Rideout, "Penumbral Thinking Revisited." See also, e.g., Bigelow, *Centralization and the Law*, 144; Terry, *Some Leading Principles of Anglo-American Law*, 613.

135 See, e.g., Rideout, "Penumbral Thinking Revisited," 189. See generally Maksymilian Del Mar, *Artefacts of Legal Inquiry: The Value of Imagination in Adjudication* (Oxford: Hart, 2020); Tsai, *Eloquence and Reason*.

136 See *Cohens*, 19 U.S. at 387.

137 *McCulloch*, 17 U.S. at 415.

138 See *Oxford English Dictionary*, 2nd ed., s.v. "Penumbra, *n.*"

139 See David Zarefsky, "Argumentation," in *Encyclopedia of Rhetoric*, ed. Thomas Sloane (Oxford: Oxford Univ. Press, 2001), 33–37.

140 See Garver, *For the Sake of Argument*, 71–73.

141 Kenneth Burke, *A Rhetoric of Motives* (New York: Prentice Hall, 1950), 69.

142 Longinus, *On the Sublime*, translated by T.S. Dorsch, in *Classical Literary Criticism* (New York: Penguin, 1965), 128.

143 Chaïm Perelman and Lucie Olbrechts-Tyteca, *The New Rhetoric: A Treatise on Argumentation*, trans. John Wilkinson and Purcell Weaver (Notre Dame: Notre Dame Univ. Press, 1969), 51.

Conclusion: Truth Has No Bones

1 See Minersville Sch. Dist. v. Gobitis, 310 U.S. 586 (1940); West Virginia Board of Education v. Barnette, 319 U.S. 624 (1943).

2 See, e.g., *In re* Comm. for the Preservation of the Constitutional Right to Trial by Jury, 1 Misc. 2d 548, 555 (N.Y. Sup. Ct. 1956) (referencing Blackstone's "just panegyric" to the jury trial).

3 Griswold v. Connecticut, 381 U.S. 479, 522 (1965) (Black, dissenting).

4 Obergefell v. Hodges, 576 U.S. 644, 719 n.22 (2015) (Scalia, dissenting).

5 Georgia v. Randolph, 547 U.S. 103, 144 (2006) (Scalia, dissenting) (emphasis in original).

6 Lawrence v. Texas, 539 U.S. 558, 567 (2003) (Scalia, dissenting).

7 Ibid., 588 (2003) (Scalia, dissenting); cf. Yury Kapgan, "Of Golf and Ghouls: The Prose Style of Justice Scalia," *Legal Writing* 9 (2003): 81–82 (noting that the "adjectival catch phrase connected by hyphens," or "gaggle of hyphens," was a common feature of Justice Scalia's prose, and citing seventeen other examples from his opinions); Jeffrey Shaman, "Justice Scalia and the Art of Rhetoric," *Constitutional Commentary* 28 (2012): 288 (noting that Justice Scalia was "practiced at using abundant hyphenation in order to craft elongated compound phrases").

8 Cf. Mark Tushnet, "Style and the Supreme Court's Educational Role in Government," *Constitutional Commentary*, 11, no. 1 (1994) (writing that the "occasional acerbic tone" of Justice Scalia's opinions and "what might be called their 'mere' cleverness, may undermine the sense of seriousness necessary for a Justice to be an educator").

9 See, e.g., Kapgan, "Of Golf and Ghouls," 71; Shaman, "Justice Scalia and the Art of Rhetoric," 287, 290 (describing Justice Scalia as "a master of metaphor and other belletristic flourishes"); Margaret Talbot, "Supreme Confidence: The Jurisprudence of Justice Antonin Scalia," *New Yorker*, March 28, 2005.

10 Dickerson v. United States, 530 U.S. 428, 461 (2000) (Scalia, dissenting).

11 Ibid.

12 Morrison v. Olson, 487 U.S. 654, 726 (1988) (Scalia, dissenting).

13 Talbot, "Supreme Confidence."

14 Ibid.

15 *Morrison*, 487 U.S. at 697 (1988) (Scalia, dissenting) (citations omitted).

16 Ibid. (Scalia, dissenting) (citations omitted).

17 Ibid., 699 (Scalia, dissenting) (citations omitted); Matthew 7:15 (King James) ("Beware of false prophets, which come to you in sheep's clothing, but inwardly they are ravening wolves.").

18 *Morrison*, 487 U.S. at 732 (Scalia, dissenting).

19 Ibid.

20 Ibid., 733.

21 Ibid., 734.

22 Colin Starger, "A Separate, Abridged Edition of the First Amendment," in *Justice Scalia: Rhetoric and the Rule of* Law, eds. Brian Slocum and Francis Mootz, III (Chicago: Univ. of Chicago Press, 2019), 185, 194; cf. J. L. Austin, *How to Do Things with Words*, edited by J. O. Urmson and Marina Sibsà, 2nd ed (Cambridge: Harvard Univ. Press, 1975), 1; Walter Beale, "Rhetorical Performative Discourse: A New Theory of Epideictic," *Philosophy and Rhetoric* 11, no. 4 (1978): 224–25; Eugene Garver, "The Way We Live Now: Rhetorical Persuasion and Democratic Conversation," *Mercer Law Review* 63 (2012): 831–32; Chaïm Perelman, *The Realm of Rhetoric*, trans. William Kluback (Notre Dame: Notre Dame Univ. Press, 1982), 20; Chaïm Perelman and Lucie Olbrechts-Tyteca, *The New Rhetoric: A Treatise on Argumentation*, trans. John Wilkinson and Purcell Weaver (Notre Dame: Notre Dame Univ. Press, 1969), 50–51.

23 See Frisby v. Schultz, 487 U.S. 474 (1988).

24 See Madsen v. Women's Health Center, 512 U.S. 753 (1994).
25 See Schenck v. Pro-Choice Network of Western New York, 519 U.S. 537 (1997).
26 See Hill v. Colorado, 530 U.S. 703 (2000).
27 See McCullen v. Coakley, 573 U.S. 464 (2014).
28 Starger, "A Separate, Abridged Edition," 185–86, 190, 192.
29 Ibid., 185, 192.
30 Ibid., 190.
31 *Obergefell*, 576 U.S. at 719 n.22 (Scalia, dissenting).
32 See Cohens v. Virginia, 19 U.S. 264, 387 (1821).
33 See Martin v. Hunter's Lessee, 14 U.S. 304, 324 (1816) ("The questions involved in this judgment are of great importance and delicacy. Perhaps it is not too much to affirm, that, upon their right decision, rest some of the most solid principles which have hitherto been supposed to sustain and protect the constitution itself. The great respectability, too, of the court whose decisions we are called upon to review, and the entire deference which we entertain for the learning and ability of that court, add much to the difficulty of the task which has so unwelcomely fallen upon us.").
34 Joseph Story, *Commentaries on the Constitution of the United States*, abr. by the author (Boston: Hilliard, Gray, and Company, 1833), iii–iv ("Your expositions of constitutional law enjoy a rare and extraordinary authority. They constitute a monument of fame far beyond the ordinary memorials of political and military glory. They are destined to enlighten, instruct, and convince future generations; and can scarcely perish but with the memory of the constitution itself.").
35 Ibid., 2.
36 Ibid., 388–90.
37 Talbot, "Supreme Confidence."
38 Bryan Garner, *Garner's Modern American Usage*, 3rd ed. (Oxford: Oxford Univ. Press, 2009), 915.
39 See Jeffrey Walker, *Rhetoric and Poetics in Antiquity* (Oxford: Oxford Univ. Press, 2000), 25 (citing the Roman orator Aelian's third-century CE *Miscellaneous History*, 12.32).
40 See Lawrence Kim, "Atticism and Asianism," in *The Oxford Handbook of the Second Sophistic*, eds. Daniel Richter and William Johnson (Oxford: Oxford Univ. Press, 2017), 41, 54–59 ("The term 'Asian' was primarily a derogatory label cast upon one's opponents and never used by individual orators to characterize their *own* style."); Laurent Pernot, *Epideictic Rhetoric: Questioning the Stakes of Ancient Praise* (Austin: Univ. of Texas Press, 2015), 56.
41 Dobbs v. Jackson Women's Health Org., No. 19-1392, slip op. at 5 (U.S. Supr. Ct. June 24, 2022).
42 Ibid., 63.
43 Ibid., 77.
44 Ibid., 78 (citations omitted).
45 Ibid., 68–69 (citations omitted).

46 Ibid., 78–79.

47 Ibid., 6–7 (Breyer, Sotomayor, and Kagan, dissenting).

48 Ibid., 7 (Breyer, Sotomayor, and Kagan, dissenting) (citation omitted).

49 Ibid. (Breyer, Sotomayor, and Kagan, dissenting).

50 Ibid., 16 (Breyer, Sotomayor, and Kagan, dissenting) (quoting McCulloch v. Maryland, 17 U.S. 316, 415 (1819)).

51 Ibid. (Breyer, Sotomayor, and Kagan, dissenting).

52 Ibid., 57 (Breyer, Sotomayor, and Kagan, dissenting) (citations omitted); cf. ibid., 19 (Breyer, Sotomayor, and Kagan, dissenting) ("It was settled at the time of *Roe*, settled at the time of *Casey*, and settled yesterday that the Constitution places limits on a State's power to assert control over an individual's body and most personal decisionmaking.").

53 Ibid., 57 (Breyer, Sotomayor, and Kagan, dissenting).

54 See, e.g., Linda Greenhouse, "Requiem for the Supreme Court," *New York Times*, June 26, 2022 (accessed July 4, 2022); Radhika Rao, "A Eulogy to Roe," *SCOTUSblog*, June 28, 2022, https://www.scotusblog.com/2022/06/a-eulogy-to-roe/ (accessed June 29, 2022).

55 Gerald Wetlaufer, "Rhetoric and Its Denial in Legal Discourse," *Virginia Law Review* 76 (1990): 1563 (emphasis in original).

56 Ibid., 1562–63.

57 Cicero, *De Oratore*, trans. E. W. Sutton and H. Rackham (Cambridge: Loeb Classical Library, 1942), 3.70.

58 John O'Malley, *Praise and Blame in Renaissance Rome: Rhetoric, Doctrine, and Reform in the Sacred Orators of the Papal Court, c. 1450–1521* (Durham: Duke Univ. Press, 1979), 75, 163.

59 Perelman and Olbrechts-Tyteca, *New Rhetoric*, 50–51; see also Starger, "A Separate, Abridged Edition," 196 (suggesting that dissenting opinions in judicial cases might all have "an epideictic aspect" insofar as the author of a dissenting opinion has by definition "lost the instant judicial battle" but only aims to "win a long-term war").

60 Garver, "The Way We Live Now," 831–32.

61 William Baude, "Foreword: The Supreme Court's Shadow Docket," *New York University Journal of Law and Liberty* 9, no. 1 (2015): 1–6.

62 See generally G. Edward White, "The Evolution of Reasoned Elaboration: Jurisprudential Criticism and Social Change," *Virginia Law Review* 59 (1973): 279–302.

63 Testimony of Stephen Vladeck, Hearing on "The Supreme Court's Shadow Docket" before the Subcommittee on Courts, Intellectual Property, and the Internet of the House Committee on the Judiciary, 117th Cong., 1st Sess., Feb. 18, 2021, at 4, 17; see also Baude, "Foreword," 12 ("Procedural regularity begets substantive legitimacy.").

64 Ernesto Grassi, *Rhetoric as Philosophy: The Humanist Tradition*, trans. John Michael Krois and Azizeh Azodi (1980; reprint, Carbondale: Southern Illinois Press, 2001), 93.

65 Aristotle, *Rhetoric*, trans. W. Rhys Roberts, in *The Rhetoric and Poetics of Aristotle* (New York: Modern Library, 1984), 1395[a-b].

66 Cicero, *De Or.* 1.73.

67 See Edward Schiappa with David Timmerman, "Aristotle's Disciplining of Epideictic," in Edward Schiappa, *The Beginnings of Rhetorical Theory in Classical Greece* (Hartford: Yale Univ. Press, 1999), 185; James Jasinski, *Sourcebook on Rhetoric: Key Concepts in Contemporary Rhetorical Studies* (Thousand Oaks: Sage, 2001), 209; Walker, *Rhetoric and Poetics*, 39.

68 Cicero, *De Or.*, 3.120–21.

69 Everson v. Bd. of Educ., 300 U.S. 1, 52–54 (1947).

70 Ibid., 650–52.

71 Thomas Farrell, *Norms of Rhetorical Culture* (New Haven: Yale Univ. Press, 1993), 266.

72 Paul Hopper, "Aspect and Foregrounding in Discourse," in *Syntax and Semantics*, vol. 12, *Discourse and Syntax*, ed. Talmy Givón (New York: Academic Press, 1979), 220.

73 Aristotle, *Rhetoric*, 1354[a-b].

74 James Boyd White, *Heracles' Bow: Essays on the Rhetoric and Poetics of the Law* (Madison: Wisconsin Univ. Press (1985), 33 n.2; cf. Jessica Findley and Bruce Sales, *The Science of Attorney Advocacy: How Courtroom Behavior Affects Jury Decision Making* (Washington, DC: American Psychological Association, 2012), 166 (noting that trial discourse draws on many sources, including symbols, song titles, bible phrases, slogans, lyrics, proverbs, parables, children's rhymes, and literary sources such as stories, religious writings, and parental lessons).

75 Peter Goodrich, "The Continuance of the Antirrhetic," *Cardozo Studies in Law and Literature* 4, no. 2 (1992): 212.

76 Ibid., 213.

77 Ibid., 212.

78 See Bradford Vivian, "Rhetorical Arts of Praise and Blame in Political Transformation," in *Conflict Transformation and Peacebuilding: Moving from Violence to Sustainable Peace*, ed. Bruce Dayton and Louis Kriesberg (New York: Routledge, 2009), 77–78.

79 Goodrich, "The Continuance of the Antirrhetic," 207–8, 218.

80 See Thomas Cole, *The Origins of Rhetoric in Ancient Greece* (Baltimore: The Johns Hopkins Univ. Press, 1991), 89; Brooke Rollins, "The Ethics of Epideictic Rhetoric: Addressing the Problem of Presence through Derrida's Funeral Oration," *Rhetoric Society Quarterly* 35, no. 1 (2005): 8; Edward Schiappa with David Timmerman, "Aristotle's Disciplining of Epideictic," 185, 198; Brian Vickers, *In Defence of Rhetoric* (Oxford: Clarendon Press, 1988), 55.

81 See James Baumlin and Joseph Hughes, "Eloquence," in *Encyclopedia of Rhetoric and Composition: Communication from Ancient Times to the Information Age*, ed. Theresa Enos (New York: Routledge, 1996), 216–17; Garver, "The Way We Live Now," 832 ("There is nothing inherently second-rate about epideictic rhetoric."); Jeffrey Walker, *Rhetoric and Poetics in Antiquity* (New York: Oxford Univ. Press, 2000), viii.

82 Eugene Garver, *For the Sake of Argument: Practical Reasoning, Character, and the Ethics of Belief* (Chicago: Univ. of Chicago Press, 2004), 32, 39–41.

83 Ibid., 42.

84 Ibid., 32.

85 Garver, "The Way We Live Now," 824.

86 Garver, *For the Sake of Argument*, 202.

87 O'Malley, *Praise and Blame in Renaissance Rome*, 59, 103.

88 Peter Brooks, "Narrative Transactions—Does the Law Need a Narratology?," *Yale Journal of Law and the Humanities* 18 (2006): 20.

89 Wetlaufer, "Rhetoric and Its Denial," 1552, 1555.

90 Translated in Michelle Bolduc and David Frank, "Chaïm Perelman and Lucie Olbrechts-Tyteca's 'On Temporality as a Characteristic of Argumentation,'" *Philosophy and Rhetoric* 43, no. 4 (2010): 323.

91 See Ernesto Grassi, *The Primordial Metaphor*, trans. Laura Pietropaolo and Manuela Scarci (Binghamton: SUNY, 1994), 12; Thomas Sprat, *The History of the Royal Society of London, for the Improving of Natural Knowledge*, 2nd ed. corrected (London, 1702), 112–13.

92 Translated in Bolduc and Frank, "On Temporality," 316.

93 Ibid., 318; see Perelman and Olbrechts-Tyteca, *New Rhetoric*, 4, 175–75.

94 Grassi, *Rhetoric as Philosophy*, 96.

95 See ibid., 27 (noting that for modern rationalism, among other things, "attestation loses its significance altogether; the only valid testimony is the logical process").

96 *Griswold*, 381 U.S. at 522 (Black, dissenting).

97 Grassi, *Rhetoric as Philosophy*, 20.

98 Walker, *Rhetoric and Poetics*, viii.

99 See Perelman, *Realm of Rhetoric*, 20; Perelman and Olbrechts-Tyteca, *New Rhetoric*, 50–51.

100 James Boyd White, *Living Speech: Resisting the Empire of Force* (Princeton: Princeton Univ. Press, 2006), 28.

GLOSSARY OF FIGURES

Anadiplosis	Repetition of a word or phrase from the end of a passage at the beginning of the next.
Anaphora	Repetition of a word or phrase at the beginning of successive passages.
Antanaclasis	Repetition of a word in different senses.
Antimetabole	A specific form of chiasmus in which a pair of words is repeated in reverse order, often as an inverted bicolon.
Antirrhesis	Denunciation of an authority or opinion as improper.
Antithesis	Juxtaposition of contrasting words or ideas.
Asyndeton	Omission of expected conjunctions.
Chiasmus	Repetition of a pair of words, phrases, structures, or ideas in reverse order.
Conduplicatio	Repetition of a word in adjacent passages.
Consonance	Repetition of similar consonant sounds.
Dirimens Copulatio	The qualification of a statement with countervailing considerations for balance.
Epexegesis	Interpretation or explanation of what has just been said.
Epistrophe	Repetition of a word or phrase at the end of successive passages.
Exergasia	Repetition of the same or essentially the same idea in different forms.
Mesarchia	Repetition of a word or phrase at the beginning and in the middle of successive passages.
Mesodiplosis	Repetition of a word or phrase in the middle of successive passages.

Parataxis	A succession of speech elements without conjunctions, especially without subordinating conjunctions.
Personification	Giving human attributes to the nonhuman.
Polyptoton	Repetition of words derived from the same root but with different cases, inflections, or voice.
Polysyndeton	Addition of unexpected conjunctions, often in close succession.
Paramologia	A partial concession made to magnify what is unconceded by contrast.
Ploce	Repetition of a word in various parts of a passage.

BIBLIOGRAPHY

Abbott, Don. "The Jurisprudential Analogy: Argumentation and the New Rhetoric." *Central States Speech Journal* 25, no. 1 (1974): 50–55.
Abramowicz, Michael, and Maxwell Stearns. "Defining Dicta." *Stanford Law Review* 57 (2005): 953–1094.
Aldisert, Ruggero. *Opinion Writing*. 3rd ed. Durham: Carolina Academic Press, 2012.
Agha, Asif. *Language and Social Relations*. Cambridge: Cambridge Univ. Press, 2007.
Agha, Asif. "Enregisterment and Communication in Social History." In *Registers of Communication*, edited by Asif Agha and Frog, 27–53. Helsinki: Finnish Literature Society, 2015.
Agha, Asif, and Frog. "An Introduction to Registers of Communication." In *Registers of Communication*, edited by Asif Agha and Frog, 13–23. Helsinki: Finnish Literature Society, 2015.
Ahl, Frederick. "The Art of Safe Criticism in Greece and Rome." *American Journal of Philology* 105, no. 2 (1984): 174–208.
Anapol, Malthon. "Rhetoric and Law: An Overview." *Today's Speech* 18, no. 4 (1970): 12–20.
Aristotle. *The Nicomachean Ethics*. Translated by David Ross. Revised by J. L. Ackrill and J. O. Urmson. 1925. Reprint, Oxford: Oxford Univ. Press, 1989).
Aristotle. *On Sophistical Refutations*. Translated by E. S. Forster and D. J. Furley. Cambridge: Loeb Classical Library, 1955.
Aristotle. *Rhetoric*. In *The Rhetoric and Poetics of Aristotle*, translated by W. Rhys Roberts. New York: Modern Library, 1984.
Assis, Elie. "Chiasmus in Biblical Narrative: Rhetoric of Characterization." *Prooftexts: A Journal of Jewish Literary History* 22, no. 3 (2002): 273–304.
Austin, J. L. *How to Do Things with Words*. Edited by J. O. Urmson and Marina Sibsà. 2nd edition. Cambridge: Harvard Univ. Press, 1975.
Baker, Paul, and Sibonile Ellece. *Key Terms in Discourse Analysis*. New York: Continuum, 2011.

Bakhtin, Mikhail. *Speech Genres and Other Late Essays*. Edited by Caryl Emerson and Michael Holquist. Translated by Vern McGee. Austin: Univ. of Texas Press, 1986.

Balter, Susan. "The Search for Grounds in Legal Argumentation: A Rhetorical Analysis of *Texas vs Johnson*." *Argumentation* 15, no. 4 (2001): 381–95.

Barshack, Lior. "The Constituent Power of Architecture." *Law, Culture, and the Humanities* 7, no. 2 (2010): 217–43.

Bartsch, Shadi. "Panegyric." In *Encyclopedia of Rhetoric*, edited by Thomas Sloane, 549–51. Oxford: Oxford Univ. Press, 2001.

Baude, William. "Foreword: The Supreme Court's Shadow Docket." *New York University Journal of Law and Liberty* 9, no. 1 (2015): 1–63.

Baumlin, James and Joseph Hughes. "Eloquence." In *Encyclopedia of Rhetoric and Composition: Communication from Ancient Times to the Information Age*, edited by Theresa Enos, 216–17. New York: Routledge, 1996.

Beale, Walter. "Rhetorical Performative Discourse: A New Theory of Epideictic." *Philosophy and Rhetoric* 11, no. 4 (1978): 221–46.

Bender, Margaret. "Shifting Linguistic Registers and the Nature of the Sacred in Cherokee." In *Registers of Communication*, edited by Asif Agha and Frog, 247–57. Helsinki: Finnish Literature Society, 2015.

Berman, Harold. *Law and Revolution: The Formation of the Western Legal Tradition*. Cambridge: Harvard Univ. Press, 1983.

Berns, Sandra. *To Speak as a Judge: Difference, Voice and Power*. Brookfield: Ashgate, 1999.

Berns, Walter. "The Least Dangerous Branch. But Only If …" In *The Judiciary in a Democratic Society*, edited by Leonard Theberge, 1–17. Lexington: Lexington Books, 1979.

Berns, Walter. "Judicial Rhetoric." In *Rhetoric and American Statesmanship*, edited by Glen Thurow and Jeffrey Wallin, 47–56. Durham: Carolina Academic Press, 1984.

Beth, Loren. *The American Theory of Church and State*. Gainesville: Univ. of Florida Press, 1958.

Bhatia, Vijay. *Analysing Genre: Language Use in Professional Settings*. London: Longman, 1993.

Bickel, Alexander, and Harry Wellington. "Legislative Purpose and the Judicial Process: The Lincoln Mills Case." *Harvard Law Review* 71 (1957): 1–39.

Biber, Douglas, and Susan Conrad. *Register, Genre, and Style*. Cambridge: Cambridge Univ. Press, 2009.

Bigelow, Melville. *Centralization and the Law: Scientific Legal Education*. Boston: Little, Brown, 1906.

Bitzer, Lloyd. "The Rhetorical Situation," *Philosophy and Rhetoric* 1, no. 1 (1968): 1–14.

Bitzer, Lloyd. "Functional Communication: A Situational Perspective." In *Rhetoric in Transition: Studies in the Nature and Uses of Rhetoric*, edited by Eugene White, 21–38. University Park: Pennsylvania Univ. Press, 1980.

Black, Jeremiah. *Essays and Speeches of Jeremiah S. Black*. Edited by Chauncey Black. New York: D. Appleton, 1885.

Blackwell, Christopher. "The Council of the Areopagus." *Dēmos: Classical Athenian Democracy* (2003): 1–38.

Black's Law Dictionary. 2nd ed. St. Paul: West, 1910.

Bolduc, Michelle, and David Frank, "Chaïm Perelman and Lucie Olbrechts-Tyteca's 'On Temporality as a Characteristic of Argumentation,'" *Philosophy and Rhetoric* 43, no. 4 (2010): 308–36.

Bonner, S. F. *Roman Declamation in the Late Republic and Early Empire*. Liverpool: Univ. Press of Liverpool, 1949.

Boorstin, Daniel. *The Mysterious Science of the Law: An Essay on Blackstone's Commentaries Showing How Blackstone, Employing Eighteenth-Century Ideas of Science, Religion, History, Aesthetics, and Philosophy, Made of the Law at Once a Conservative and a Mysterious Science*. 1941. Reprint, Chicago: Univ. of Chicago Press, 1996.

Bosmajian, Haig. *Metaphor and Reason in Judicial Opinions*. Carbondale: Southern Illinois Univ. Press, 1992.

Bourdieu, Pierre. *Language and Symbolic Power*. New ed. Translated by Gino Raymond and Matthew Adamson. Cambridge: Harvard Univ. Press, 1992.

Bourdieu, Pierre. "The Force of Law: Toward a Sociology of the Juridical Field." *Hastings Law Journal* 38 (1987): 805–53.

Braden, Waldo, and Harold Mixon. "Epideictic Speaking in the Post-Civil War South and the Southern Experience." *Southern Communication Journal* 54, no. 1 (1988): 40–57.

Brann, Eva. "Madison's 'Memorial and Remonstrance,' Model of American Rhetoric." In *Rhetoric and American Statesmanship*, edited by Glen Thurow and Jeffrey Wallin, 9–46. Durham: Carolina Academic Press, 1984.

Braund, Susanna. "Praise and Protreptic in Early Imperial Panegyric: Cicero, Seneca, Pliny." In *Latin Panegyric*, edited by Roger Rees, 85–108. Oxford: Oxford Univ. Press, 2012.

Brooks, Peter. "Narrative Transactions—Does the Law Need a Narratology?" *Yale Journal of Law and the Humanities* 18 (2006): 1–28.

Buckley, Michael. "Philosophic Method in Cicero." *Journal of the History of Philosophy* 8 (1970): 143–54.

Burgess, Theodore. "Epideictic Literature." PhD diss., Univ. of Chicago, 1902.

Burke, Kenneth. *A Rhetoric of Motives*. Calif. ed. Berkeley: California Univ. Press, 1969.

Burke, Kenneth. *Attitudes Toward History*. Berkeley: Univ. of California Press, 1984.

Butts, R. Freeman. *The American Tradition in Religion and Education*. Boston: Beacon Press, 1950.

Byron, Lord. *Don Juan*. Edited by T. G. Steffan, E. Steffan, and W. W. Pratt. 1819–24. Reprint, New York: Penguin, 1996.

Cairns, David. *Advocacy and the Making of the Adversarial Criminal Trial 1800-1865*. Oxford: Clarendon, 1998.
Campbell, Karlyn, and Kathleen Jamieson. "Form and Genre in Rhetorical Criticism: An Introduction." In *Form and Genre: Shaping Rhetorical Action*, edited by Karlyn Campbell and Kathleen Jamieson, 9–32. Falls Church: Speech Communication Association, 1978.
Carter, Michael. "The Ritual Functions of Epideictic Rhetoric: The Case of Socrates' Funeral Oration." *Rhetorica* 9, no. 3 (1991): 209–32.
Charney, Davida. "Performativity and Persuasion in the Hebrew Book of Psalms: A Rhetorical Analysis of Psalms 22 and 116." *Rhetoric Society Quarterly* 40, no. 3 (2010): 247–68.
Chase, J. Richard. "The Classical Conception of Epideictic." *Quarterly Journal of Speech* 37 (1961): 293–300.
Chuang Tzu. *The Book of Chuang Tzu*. Translated by Martin Palmer with Elizabeth Breuilly, Chang Wai Ming, and Jay Ramsay. New York: Penguin, 2006.
Cicero. *Brutus and Orator*. Translated by G. L. Hendrickson and H. M. Hubbell. Cambridge: Loeb Classical Library, 1939.
Cicero. *De Inventione*. Translated by H. M. Hubbell. Cambridge, Mass.: Loeb Classical Library, 1949.
Cicero. *On the Laws*. Translated by David Fott. Ithaca: Cornell Univ. Press. 2014.
Cicero. *De Oratore*. Translated by E. W. Sutton and H. Rackham. 2 vols. Cambridge: Loeb Classical Library, 1942.
Clarke, Martin. *Rhetoric at Rome: A Historical Survey*. London: Cohen and West, 1953.
Cole, Thomas. *The Origins of Rhetoric in Ancient Greece*. Baltimore: The Johns Hopkins Univ. Press, 1991.
Comrie, Bernard. *Aspect: An Introduction to the Study of Verbal Aspect and Related Problems*. Cambridge: Cambridge Univ. Press, 1976.
Condit, Celeste. "The Functions of Epideictic: The Boston Massacre Orations as Exemplar." *Communication Quarterly* 33, no. 4 (1985): 284–99.
Conley, Thomas. "The Enthymeme in Perspective." *Quarterly Journal of Speech* 70 (1984): 168–87.
Conley, Thomas. *Rhetoric in the European Tradition*. Chicago: Univ. of Chicago Press, 1990.
Cope, Edward. *An Introduction to Aristotle's Rhetoric*. London: Macmillan, 1867.
Coulson, Doug. "The Devil's Advocate and Legal Oratory in the *Processus Sathanae*." *Rhetorica: A Journal of the History of Rhetoric* 33, no. 4 (2015): 409–30.
Coulson, Doug. "Law as Epideictic: The Complex Publics of Legal Discourse." In *Rhetoric's Change*, edited by Jenny Rice, Chelsea Graham, and Eric Detweiler. Anderson: Parlor Press, 2018.
Coulson, Doug. "More Than Verbs: An Introduction to Transitivity in Legal Argument." *The Scribes Journal of Legal Writing* 19 (2020): 81–125.

Cover, Robert. *Justice Accused: Antislavery and the Judicial Process.* New Haven: Yale Univ. Press, 1975.

Czarniawska, Barbara. "Styles of Organization Theory." In *Oxford Handbook of Organization Theory*, revised ed., edited by Haridimos Tsoukas and Christian Knudsen, 237–61. Oxford: Oxford Univ. Press, 2005.

Danisch, Robert. "Power and the Celebration of the Self: Michel Foucault's Epideictic Rhetoric." *Southern Communication Journal* 7, no. 3 (2006): 291–307.

Dasenbrock, Reed. "Austin, J. L. (1911–1960)." In *Encyclopedia of Rhetoric and Composition: Communication from Ancient Times to the Information Age*, edited by Theresa Enos. New York: Routledge, 1996.

Davis, Donald Jr. "Maxims." In *The Oxford Handbook of Law and Humanities*, edited by Simon Stern, Maksymillian Del Mar, and Bernadette Mayler, 655–69. Oxford: Oxford Univ. Press, 2020.

Del Mar, Maksymilian. *Artefacts of Legal Inquiry: The Value of Imagination in Adjudication.* Oxford: Hart, 2020.

Derrida, Jacques. *The Archaeology of the Frivolous.* Translated by John Leavy. Pittsburgh: Duquesne Univ. Press, 1980.

Derrida, Jacques. "The Law of Genre." Translated by Avital Ronell. In *Glyph 7*, edited by Samuel Weber, 202–32. Baltimore: Johns Hopkins Univ. Press, 1980.

De Quincey, Thomas. "Casuistry." In *De Quincey's Writings: Theological Essays and Other Papers*, vol. 1. 1854. Reprint, Madrid: HardPress, 2020.

Dewar, Michael, ed. and trans. "Introduction." In *Panegyricus de Sexto Consulatu Honorii Augusti*, by Claudius. Oxford: Oxford Univ. Press, 1996.

Dionysius of Halicarnassus. *Ars Rhetorica.* Translated by William Race. Cambridge: Harvard Univ. Press, 2019.

Dorf, Michael. "Dicta and Article III." *University of Pennsylvania Law Review* 142 (1994): 2009–40.

Douglas, Lawrence. *The Memory of Judgment: Making Law and History in the Trials of the Holocaust.* New Haven: Yale Univ. Press, 2001.

Dreisbach, Daniel. *Thomas Jefferson and the Wall of Separation Between Church and State.* New York: New York Univ. Press, 2002.

Engels, Jeremy. *Enemyship: Democracy and Counter-Revolution in the Early Republic.* East Lansing: Michigan State Univ. Press, 2010.

Emerson, Ralph Waldo. *Society and Solitude.* Boston: Houghton Mifflin, 1890.

Emerson, Ralph Waldo. *The Complete Works of Ralph Waldo Emerson.* Concord ed. Boston: Houghton Mifflin, 1904.

Enos, Richard. *The Literate Mode of Cicero's Legal Rhetoric.* Carbondale: Southern Illinois Univ. Press, 1988.

Enos, Theresa, ed. *Encyclopedia of Rhetoric and Composition: Communication from Ancient Times to the Information Age.* New York: Routledge, 1996.

Erasmus, Desiderius. *Copia: Foundations of the Abundant Style.* Translated by Betty Knott. In *The Collected Works of Erasmus*, edited by Craig Thompson. Toronto: Univ. of Toronto Press, 1978.

Fahnestock, Jeanne. *Rhetorical Figures in Science.* Oxford: Oxford Univ. Press, 1999.
Fantham, Elaine. "Eloquence." In *Encyclopedia of Rhetoric*, edited by Thomas Sloane, 237–47. Oxford: Oxford Univ. Press, 2001.
Farrell, Thomas. *Norms of Rhetorical Culture.* New Haven: Yale Univ. Press, 1993.
Fairbanks, Arthur. *A Study of the Greek Paean: With Appendixes Containing the Hymns Found at Delphi, and the Other Extant Fragments of Paeans.* Ithaca: Andrus and Church, 1900.
Fairclough, Norman. *Critical Discourse Analysis: The Critical Study of Language.* 2nd ed. Harlow: Pearson, 2010.
Ferguson, Robert. "The Judicial Opinion as a Literary Genre." *Yale Journal of Law and the Humanities* 2 (1990): 201–19.
Findley, Jessica, and Bruce Sales. *The Science of Attorney Advocacy: How Courtroom Behavior Affects Jury Decision Making.* Washington, DC: American Psychological Association, 2012.
Forsyth, James. *A Grammar of Aspect: Usage and Meaning in the Russian Verb.* Cambridge: Cambridge Univ. Press, 1970.
Frank, Jerome. *Courts on Trial: Myth and Reality in American Justice.* Princeton: Princeton Univ. Press, 1949.
Frawley, William. *Linguistic Semantics.* London: Routledge, 2013.
Frost, Michael. *Introduction to Classical Legal Rhetoric: A Lost Heritage.* Burlington: Ashgate, 2005.
Frost, Robert. *North of Boston.* 1914. Reprint, New York: Henry Holt, 1917.
Gale, Frederic. *Political Literacy: Rhetoric, Ideology, and the Possibility of Justice.* Albany: SUNY, 1994.
Garner, Bryan. *Garner's Modern American Usage.* 3rd ed. Oxford: Oxford Univ. Press, 2009.
Garver, Eugene. "The Contemporary Irrelevance of Aristotle's Practical Reason." In *Rereading Aristotle's* Rhetoric, edited by Alan Gross and Arthur Walzer, 57–73. Carbondale: Southern Illinois Univ. Press, 2000.
Garver, Eugene. *For the Sake of Argument: Practical Reasoning, Character, and the Ethics of Belief.* Chicago: Univ. of Chicago Press, 2004.
Garver, Eugene. "The Way We Live Now: Rhetorical Persuasion and Democratic Conversation." *Mercer Law Review* 63 (2012): 807–33.
Garver, Eugene. "Justice, Play, and Politics." *Mercer Law Review* 66 (2015): 345–64.
Gasché, Rodolphe. *Of Minimal Things: Studies on the Notion of Relation.* Stanford: Stanford Univ. Press, 1999.
Gaskins, Richard. *Burdens of Proof in Modern Discourse.* New Haven: Yale Univ. Press, 1993.
Genung, John. *The Working Principles of Rhetoric, Examined in Their Literary Relations and Illustrated with Examples.* Boston: Ginn and Co., 1900.
Gibson, James, Gregory Caldeira, and Vanessa Baird. "On the Legitimacy of National High Courts." *American Political Science Review* 92, no. 2 (1998): 343–58.

Giuliani, Alessandro. "The Influence of Rhetoric on the Law of Evidence and Pleading." *Juridical Review*, new series, vol. 7 (1962): 216–51.
Goodrich, Peter. "The Continuance of the Antirrhetic." *Cardozo Studies in Law and Literature* 4, no. 2 (1992): 207–22.
Gordon, Leslie. "Florida Supreme Court Orders Judges to Wear Black Robes," *ABA Journal*, Jan. 1, 2016, https://www.abajournal.com/magazine/article/florida_supreme_court_orders_judges_to_wear_black_robes (accessed October 10, 2020).
Gramsci, Antonio. *Selections from Cultural Writings*. Edited by David Forgacs and Geoffrey Nowell-Smith. Translated by William Boelhower. Chicago: Haymarket, 1985.
Grant, Ben. *The Aphorism and Other Short Forms*. London: Routledge, 2016.
Grassi, Ernesto. *The Primordial Metaphor*. Translated by Laura Pietropaolo and Manuela Scarci. Binghamton: SUNY, 1994.
Grassi, Ernesto. *Rhetoric as Philosophy: The Humanist Tradition*. Translated by John Michael Krois and Azizeh Azodi. 1980. Reprint, Carbondale: Southern Illinois Press, 2001.
Gray, Benjamin. "A Civic Alternative to Stoicism: The Ethics of Hellenistic Honorary Decrees." *Classical Antiquity* 37, no. 2 (2018): 187–235.
Greenhouse, Linda. "Requiem for the Supreme Court," *New York Times*, June 26, 2022.
Guthrie, William. *The Sophists*. 1969. Reprint, Cambridge: Cambridge Univ. Press, 1971.
Halliday, Michael. *Halliday's Introduction to Functional Grammar*. Revised by Christian Matthiessen. New York: Routledge, 2014.
Hamilton, Alexander. "Federalist no. 78." In *The Federalist Papers*, edited by Clinton Rossiter. New York: Penguin Books, 1961.
Hargreaves-Mawdsley, W. N. *A History of Legal Dress in Europe until the End of the Eighteenth Century*. Oxford: Clarendon Press, 1963.
Hariman, Robert. "Introduction." In *Popular Trials: Rhetoric, Mass Media, and the Law*, edited by Robert Hariman. Tuscaloosa: Alabama Univ. Press, 1993.
Hariman, Robert. "What Is Chiasmus? Or, Why the Abyss Stares Back." In *Chiasmus and Culture*, edited by Boris Wiseman and Anthony Paul, 45–68. New York: Berghahn Books, 2014.
Hart, William, and Dolores Albarracín. "Learning About What Others Were Doing: Verb Aspect and Attributions of Mundane and Criminal Intent for Past Actions." *Psychological Science* 22, no. 2 (2011): 261–66.
Hartelius, E. Johanna. "Sentimentalism in Online Deliberation: Assessing the Generic Liability of Immigration Discourses." In *Emerging Genres in New Media Environments*, edited by Carolyn Miller and Ashley Kelly, 225–41. Cham: Palgrave Macmillan, 2017.
Hartelius, E. Johanna, and Jennifer Asenas. "Citational Epideixis and a 'Thinking of Community': The Case of the Minuteman Project." *Rhetoric Society Quarterly* 40, no. 4 (2010): 360–84.

Hasian, Marouf, Jr. *Legal Memories and Amnesias in America's Rhetorical Culture.* Boulder: Westview, 2000.

Hasian, Marouf, Jr., Celeste Condit, and John Lucaites. "The Rhetorical Boundaries of 'the Law': A Consideration of the Rhetorical Culture of Legal Practice and the Case of the 'Separate but Equal' Doctrine." *Quarterly Journal of Speech* 82, no. 4 (1996): 323-42.

Hawhee, Debra. "Kairotic Encounters." In *Perspectives on Rhetorical Invention*, edited by Janet Atwill and Janice Lauer, 16-35. Knoxville: Univ. of Tennessee Press, 2002.

Heller, Francis. "A Turning Point for Religious Liberty." *Virginia Law Review* 29 (1943): 440-59.

Henly, Burr. "Penumbra: The Roots of a Legal Metaphor." *Hastings Constitutional Law Quarterly* 15, no. 1 (1987): 81-100.

Herman, Susan. *The Right to a Speedy and Public Trial: A Reference Guide to the United States Constitution.* Westport: Praeger, 2006.

Hermogenes. *On Types of Style.* Translated by Cecil Wooten. Chapel Hill: University of North Carolina Press, 1987.

Hinks, D. A. G. "Tria Genera Causarum." *Classical Quarterly* 30, no. 3/4 (1936): 170-76.

Hohmann, Hans. "The Dynamics of Stasis: Classical Rhetorical Theory and Modern Legal Argumentation." *American Journal of Jurisprudence* 34 (1989): 171-97.

Hopper, Paul. "Aspect and Foregrounding in Discourse." In *Syntax and Semantics*, vol. 12, *Discourse and Syntax*, edited by Talmy Givón, 213-41. New York: Academic Press, 1979.

Hopper, Paul. "Some Observations on the Typology of Focus and Aspect in Narrative Language." *Studies in Language* 3, no. 1 (1979): 37-64.

Hopper, Paul. "Introduction: Aspect between Discourse and Grammar." In *Tense-Aspect: Between Semantics and Pragmatics*, edited by Paul Hopper. Amsterdam: John Benjamins, 1982.

Hopper, Paul, and Sandra Thompson. "Transitivity in Grammar and Discourse." *Language* 56, no. 2 (1980): 251-53.

Howell, Wilbur Samuel. *Logic and Rhetoric in England, 1500-1700.* New York: Russell and Russell, 1961.

Isocrates. *Panathenaicus.* In *Isocrates II*, edited by Jeffrey Henderson and translated by George Norlin. Cambridge: Loeb Classical Library, 1929.

Jamieson, Kathleen, and Jennifer Stromer-Galley. "Hybrid Genres." In *Encyclopedia of Rhetoric*, edited by Thomas Sloane, 361-63. Oxford: Oxford Univ. Press, 2001.

Jasinski, James. *Sourcebook on Rhetoric: Key Concepts in Contemporary Rhetorical Studies.* Thousand Oaks: Sage, 2001.

Jefferson, Thomas. Letter to the Danbury Connecticut Baptist Association dated January 1, 1802. In Saul Padover, *The Complete Jefferson*, 518-19. Freeport: Books for Library Press, 1943.

John of Sardis. *Selections from the Commentary on the Progymnasmata of Apthonius*. In *Progymnasmata: Greek Textbooks of Prose Composition and Rhetoric*, translated with introductions and notes by George Kennedy, 173–228. Atlanta: Society of Biblical Literature, 2003.

Jonsen, Albert, and Stephen Toulmin. *The Abuse of Casuistry: A History of Moral Reasoning*. Berkeley: Univ. of California Press, 1988.

Just, Peter. "Law, Ritual, and Order." In *Order and Disorder: Anthropological Perspectives*, edited by Keebet von Benda-Beckmann and Fernanda Pirie, 112–31. New York: Berghahn, 2007.

Kahn, Paul. *Making the Case: The Art of the Judicial Opinion*. Hartford: Yale Univ. Press, 2016.

Kant, Immanuel. *The Critique of Judgement: Part I, Critique of Aesthetic Judgement*. Translated by James Creed Meredith. Oxford: Clarendon Press, 1952.

Kapgan, Yury. "Of Golf and Ghouls: The Prose Style of Justice Scalia." *Legal Writing* 9 (2003): 71–108.

Kennedy, George. *The Art of Persuasion in Greece*. Princeton: Princeton Univ. Press, 1963.

Kennedy, George. *The Art of Rhetoric in the Roman World*. Princeton: Princeton Univ. Press, 1972.

Kennedy, George (trans.). *Progymnasmata: Greek Textbooks of Prose Composition and Rhetoric*. Atlanta: Society of Biblical Literature, 2003.

Kennedy, George. *Classical Rhetoric and Its Christian and Secular Tradition from Ancient to Modern Times*. Chapel Hill: Univ. of North Carolina Press, 1980.

Keyt, David. "Plato and the Ship of State." In *The Blackwell Guide to Plato's Republic*, edited by Gerasimos Santas, 189–213. Malden: Blackwell, 2006.

Kim, Lawrence. "Atticism and Asianism." In *The Oxford Handbook of the Second Sophistic*, edited by Daniel Richter and William Johnson, 41–66. Oxford: Oxford Univ. Press, 2017.

Konvitz, Milton. *Fundamental Rights: History of a Constitutional Doctrine*. New York: Routledge, 2001.

Laib, Nevin. "Conciseness and Amplification," *College Composition and Communication* 41, no. 4 (1990): 443–59.

Lakoff, George. *The All New Don't Think of an Elephant! Know Your Values and Frame the Debate*. White River Junction: Chelsea Green, 2014.

Langacker, Ronald. *Foundations of Cognitive Grammar*. Vol. 1. *Theoretical Prerequisites*. Palo Alto: Stanford Univ. Press, 1999.

Lanham, Richard. *A Handlist of Rhetorical Terms*. Berkeley: Univ. of California Press, 1991.

LaRue, Lewis. *Constitutional Law as Fiction: Narrative in the Rhetoric of Authority*. University Park: Penn State Univ. Press, 1995.

Lauer, Ilon. "Epideictic Rhetoric." *Communication Research Trends* 34, no. 2 (2015): 4–18.

Lauer, Janice. *Invention in Rhetoric and Composition*. West Lafayette: Parlor Press, 2004.

Leach, Edmund. *Culture and Communication: The Logic by Which Symbols Are Connected: An Introduction to the Use of Structuralist Analysis in Social Anthropology.* Cambridge: Cambridge Univ. Press, 1976.

Le Duc, Don. "'Free Speech' Decisions and the Legal Process: The Judicial Opinion in Context." *Quarterly Journal of Speech* 62, no. 3 (1976): 279–87

Lee, Hugh. "The 'Historical' Bundy and Encomiastic Relevance in Pindar." *The Classical World* 72, no. 2 (1978): 65–70.

Leubsdorf, John. "The Structure of Judicial Opinions." *Minnesota Law Review* 86 (2001): 447–96.

Levinson, Sanford. *Constitutional Faith.* 1988. Reprint, Princeton: Princeton Univ. Press, 2011.

Levinson, Sanford. "The Rhetoric of Judicial Opinions." In *Law's Stories: Narrative and Rhetoric in the Law,* edited by Peter Brooks and Paul Gewirtz, 187–205. New Haven: Yale Univ. Press, 1996.

Libanius, *Libanius's Progymnasmata: Model Exercises in Greek Prose Composition and Rhetoric,* translated by Craig Gibson. Atlanta: Society of Biblical Literature, 2008, 253

Lincoln, Abraham. *The Gettysburg Address and Other Speeches.* New York: Penguin, 1995.

Locke, John. *An Essay Concerning Human Understanding.* Edited by Alexander Campbell Fraser. 2 vols. Oxford: Clarendon Press, 1894.

Longinus. *On the Sublime.* Translated by T. S. Dorsch. In *Classical Literary Criticism,* 113–66. New York: Penguin, 1965.

Loraux, Nicole. *The Invention of Athens: The Funeral Oration in the Classical City.* Translated by Alan Sheridan. New York: Zone Books, 2006.

Lowrie, Michèle, and Susanne Lüdemann, eds. *Exemplarity and Singularity: Thinking through Particulars in Philosophy, Literature, and Law.* New York: Routledge, 2015.

Lucaites, John. "Between Rhetoric and 'The Law': Power, Legitimacy, and Social Change." Review of *A Guide to Critical Legal Studies,* by Mark Kelman, *Interpreting Law and Literature: A Hermeneutic Reader,* edited by Sanford Levinson and Steven Mailloux, and *The Critical Legal Studies Movement,* by Roberto Unger. *Quarterly Journal of Speech,* 76, no. 4 (1990): 435–49.

Lyotard, Jean-François. "Complexity and the Sublime." In *Postmodernism: ICA Documents 4 & 5,* edited by Lisa Appignanesi. London: Institute of Contemporary Arts Publications, 1986.

Madden, Carol, and Rolf Zwaan. "How Does Verb Aspect Constrain Event Representations?" *Memory and Cognition* 31, no. 5 (2003): 663–72.

Madison, James. "Property." In *James Madison: Writings,* edited by Jack Rakove, 515–17. New York: Penguin, 1999.

Makau, Josina, and David Lawrence. "Administrative Judicial Rhetoric: The Supreme Court's New Thesis of Political Morality." *Argumentation and Advocacy* 30, no. 4 (1994): 191–205.

Matlon, Ronald. "Legal Communication: An Introduction." *Argumentation and Advocacy* 30, no. 4 (1994): 187–90.
Matthews, Gray. "Epideictic Rhetoric and Baseball: Nurturing Community through Controversy." *Southern Journal of Communication* 60, no. 4 (1995): 275–91.
McCloskey, Dierdre. *The Rhetoric of Economics*. 2nd ed. Madison: Univ. of Wisconsin Press, 1998.
McNamara, Martha. *From Tavern to Courthouse: Architecture and Ritual in American Law, 1658–1860*. Baltimore: Johns Hopkins Univ. Press, 2004.
McSweeney, Thomas. *Priests of the Law: Roman Law and the Making of the Common Law's First Professionals*. Oxford: Oxford Univ. Press, 2020.
Mehler, Irving. *Effective Legal Communication*. Denver: Philgor, 1975.
Menander Rhetor. *An Analysis of Epideictic Speeches*. Translated by William Race. Cambridge: Harvard Univ. Press, 2019.
Merleau-Ponty, Maurice. *The Visible and the Invisible*. Edited by Claude Lefort. Translated by Alphonso Lingis. Evanston: Northwestern Univ. Press, 1968.
Merryman, John. *The Civil Law Tradition: An Introduction to the Legal Systems of Western Europe and Latin America*. 2nd ed. Stanford: Stanford Univ. Press, 1985.
Montagne, Véronique. "Epideictic in the Renaissance." In *Encyclopedia of Renaissance Philosophy*, edited by Marco Scarbi. Cham: Springer, 2019.
Mootz, Francis III. *Rhetorical Knowledge in Legal Practice and Critical Legal Theory*. Tuscaloosa: Alabama Univ. Press, 2006.
Mootz, Francis III. "Perelman's Theory of Argumentation and Natural Law." *Philosophy and Rhetoric* 43, no. 4 (2010): 383–402.
Mootz, Francis III, and Leticia Saucedo. "The 'Ethical' Surplus of the War on Illegal Immigration." *Journal of Gender, Race and Justice* 15 (2012): 257–79.
Morrow, Terence. "Forensic Genre." In *Encyclopedia of Rhetoric*, edited by Thomas Sloane, 314–21. Oxford: Oxford Univ. Press, 2001.
Murphy, Walter. *Elements of Judicial Strategy*. 1964. Reprint, New Orleans: Quid Pro, 2016.
Næss, Åshlid. *Prototypical Transitivity*. Amsterdam: John Benjamins, 2007.
North, Helen. "The Use of Poetry in the Training of the Ancient Orator." *Traditio* 8 (1952): 1–33.
O'Brien, David. *Storm Center: The Supreme Court in American Politics*. New York: Norton, 1986.
Ochs, Donovan. "Cicero's Rhetorical Theory, with Synopses of Cicero's Seven Rhetorical Works." In *A Synoptic History of Classical Rhetoric*, edited by James Murphy and Richard Katula, 151–99. Mahwah: Hermagoras Press, 2003. 151–99.
Oddo, John. *The Discourse of Propaganda: Case Studies from the Persian Gulf War and the War on Terror*. University Park: Penn State Univ. Press, 2018.

Olson, Kathryn. "An Epideictic Dimension of Symbolic Violence in Disney's *Beauty and the Beast*: Inter-Generational Lessons in Romanticizing and Tolerating Intimate Partner Violence." *Quarterly Journal of Speech* 99, no. 4 (2013): 448–80.

Oldfather, Chad. "The Hidden Ball: A Substantive Critique of Baseball Metaphors in Judicial Opinions." *Connecticut Law Review* 27 (1994): 17–51.

O'Malley, John. *Praise and Blame in Renaissance Rome: Rhetoric, Doctrine, and Reform in the Sacred Orators of the Papal Court, c. 1450–1521*. Durham: Duke Univ. Press, 1979.

Ong, Walter. *Ramus, Method, and the Decay of Dialogue: From the Art of Discourse to the Art of Reason*. 1958. Reprint, Chicago: Univ. of Chicago Press, 2004.

Oravec, Christine. "'Observation' in Aristotle's Theory of Epideictic." *Philosophy and Rhetoric* 9, no. 3 (1976): 162–74.

Osiel, Mark. *Mass Atrocity, Collective Memory, and the Law*. New Brunswick: Transaction, 1997.

Owens, Ryan, Justin Wedeking, and Patrick Wohlfarth. "How the Supreme Court Alters Opinion Language to Evade Congressional Review." *Journal of Law and Courts* 1, no. 1 (2013): 35–59.

Palmer, Frank. *Mood and Modality*. 2nd ed. Cambridge: Cambridge Univ. Press, 2001.

Paul, Anthony. "From Stasis to Ékstasis: Four Types of Chiasmus." In *Chiasmus and Culture*, edited by Boris Wiseman and Anthony Paul, 19–44. New York: Berghahn Books, 2014.

Paul, Anthony, and Boris Wiseman. "Chiasmus in the Drama of Life." Introduction to *Chiasmus and Culture*, edited by Boris Wiseman and Anthony Paul, 1–16. New York: Berghahn Books, 2014.

Perelman, Chaïm. *The Idea of Justice and the Problem of Argument*. Translated by John Petrie. New York: Routledge, 1963.

Perelman, Chaïm. *The Realm of Rhetoric*. Translated by William Kluback. Notre Dame: Notre Dame Univ. Press, 1982.

Perelman, Chaïm. "Law and Rhetoric." In *Justice, Law, and Argument: Essays in Moral and Legal Reasoning*, 120–24. Translated by William Kluback. Dordrecht: D. Reidel Publishing, 1980.

Perelman, Chaïm, and Lucie Olbrechts-Tyteca. *The New Rhetoric: A Treatise on Argumentation*. Translated by John Wilkinson and Purcell Weaver. Notre Dame: Notre Dame Univ. Press, 1969.

Pernot, Laurent. *Epideictic Rhetoric: Questioning the Stakes of Ancient Praise*. Austin: Univ. of Texas Press, 2015.

Perry, Barbara. *The Priestly Tribe: The Supreme Court's Image in the American Mind*. Westport: Praeger, 1999.

Philodemus. *On Rhetoric Books 1 and 2*. Translation and exegetical essays by Clive Chandler. New York: Routledge, 2006.

Posner, Richard. *Cardozo: A Study in Reputation*. Revised ed. Chicago: Chicago Univ. Press, 1993.

Posner, Richard. *The Problems of Jurisprudence*. Cambridge: Harvard Univ. Press, 1993.

Pratt, Jonathan. "The Epideictic Agōn and Aristotle's Elusive Third Genre." *American Journal of Philology* 133, no. 2 (2012): 177–208.

Pseudo-Dionysius of Halicarnassus. *Ars Rhetorica*. Translated by William Race. Cambridge: Harvard Univ. Press, 2019.

Quintilian. *The Institutio Oratoria of Quintilian*. Translated by Harold Butler. Cambridge: Harvard Univ. Press, 1920.

Rabb, Intisar. *Doubt in Islamic Law: A History of Legal Maxims, Interpretation, and Islamic Criminal Law*. Cambridge: Cambridge Univ. Press, 2015.

Radden, Günter, and René Dirven. *Cognitive English Grammar*. Amsterdam: John Benjamins Publishing, 2007.

Rao, Radhika. "A Eulogy to Roe," *SCOTUSblog*, June 28, 2022, https://www.scotusblog.com/2022/06/a-eulogy-to-roe/ (accessed June 29, 2022).

Rees, Roger. "The Modern History of Latin Panegyric." In *Latin Panegyric*, edited by Roger Rees, 85–108. Oxford: Oxford Univ. Press, 2012.

Resnik, Judith, and Dennis Curtis. *Representing Justice: Invention, Controversy, and Rights in City-States and Democratic Courtrooms*. New Haven: Yale Univ. Press, 2011.

Resnik, Judith, Dennis Curtis, and Allison Tait. "Constructing Courts: Architecture, the Ideology of Judging, and the Public Sphere." In *Law, Culture & Visual Studies*, edited by Richard Sherwin and Anne Wagner, 547–72. New York: Springer, 2013.

Rhetorica ad Alexandrum. Translated by Harris Rackham. 1937. Reprint, Cambridge: Loeb Classical Library, 1983.

Rhetorica ad Herennium. Translated by Harry Caplan. 1954. Reprint, Cambridge: Loeb Classical Library, 2004.

Rideout, Christopher. "Penumbral Thinking Revisited: Metaphor in Legal Argumentation." *Journal of the Association of Legal Writing Directors* 7, no. 1 (2010): 155–92.

Rieke, Richard. *Rhetorical Theory in American Legal Practice*. PhD diss., Ohio State Univ., 1964.

Rink, John. "Rhapsody." In *New Grove Dictionary of Music and Musicians*, edited by Stanley Sadie and John Tyrrell. 2nd ed. London: Macmillan, 2001.

Roberts, John G., Jr. "2019 Year-End Report on the Federal Judiciary," Dec. 31, 2019, https://www.supremecourt.gov/publicinfo/year-end/2019year-endreport.pdf (accessed January 2, 2020).

Rollins, Brooke. "The Ethics of Epideictic Rhetoric: Addressing the Problem of Presence through Derrida's Funeral Oration." *Rhetoric Society Quarterly* 35, no. 1 (2005), 5–23.

Root, Elihu. *Addresses on Government and Citizenship*. Edited by Robert Bacon and James Brown Scott. Cambridge: Harvard Univ. Press, 1916.

Rosenfield, Lawrence. "The Practical Celebration of Epideictic." In *Rhetoric in Transition: Studies in the Nature and Uses of Rhetoric*, edited by Eugene White, 131–55. University Park: Penn State Univ. Press, 1980.

Rosenfield, Lawrence and Thomas Mader. "The Functions of Human Communication in Pleasing." In *Handbook of Rhetorical and Communication Theory*, edited by Carroll Arnold and John Bowers, 475–543. Boston: Allyn and Bacon, 1984.

Ruffin, John. *The Rhetorlogue, Or, Study of the Rhetor or Orator*. New York: Edgar Werner, 1922.

Ryan, Halford, ed. *The Inaugural Addresses of Twentieth-Century American Presidents*. Westport: Praeger, 1993.

Scalia, Antonin, and Bryan Garner. *Reading Law: The Interpretation of Legal Texts*. St. Paul: Thomson West, 2012.

Scallen, Eileen. "Judgment, Justification and Junctions in the Rhetorical Criticism of Legal Texts." *Southern Communication Journal* 60, no. 1 (1994): 68–74.

Schanzenbach, Max, and Emerson Tiller. "Strategic Judging Under the U.S. Sentencing Guidelines: Positive Theory and Evidence." *Journal of Law, Economics, and Organization* 23, no. 1 (2007): 24–56.

Shaman, Jeffrey. "Justice Scalia and the Art of Rhetoric." *Constitutional Commentary* 28 (2012): 287–92.

Sheard, Cynthia. "The Public Value of Epideictic Rhetoric." *College English* 58, no. 7 (1996): 765–94.

Sherwin, Richard. "Sublime Jurisprudence: On the Ethical Education of the Legal Imagination in Our Time." *Chicago-Kent Law Review* 83 (2008): 1174–96.

Schiappa, Edward, with David Timmerman. "Aristotle's Disciplining of Epideictic." In Edward Schiappa, *The Beginnings of Rhetorical Theory in Classical Greece*, 185–206. Hartford: Yale Univ. Press, 1999.

Schoeck, Richard. "Rhetoric and Law in Sixteenth-Century England." *Studies in Philology* 50, no. 2 (1953): 110–27.

Schuetz, Janice, and Kathryn Snedaker. *Communication and Litigation: Case Studies of Famous Trials*. Carbondale: Southern Illinois Univ. Press, 1988.

Schwartz, Bernard. *The Unpublished Opinions of the Warren Court*. Oxford: Oxford Univ. Press, 1985.

Shakespeare, William. *Henry VI, Part 2*. In *William Shakespeare: The Complete Works*. New York: Gramercy, 1975.

Shapiro, Barbara. "Classical Rhetoric and the English Law of Evidence." In *Rhetoric and Law in Early Modern Europe*, edited by Victoria Kahn and Lorna Hutson, 54–72. Hartford: Yale Univ. Press, 2001.

Sherrill, Andrew, Anita Eerland, Rolf Zwaan, and Joseph Magliano. "Understanding How Grammatical Aspect Influences Legal Judgment." *PLoS ONE* 10, no. 10 (2015): 1–19.

Shuger, Debora. *Sacred Rhetoric: The Christian Grand Style in the English Renaissance*. Princeton: Princeton Univ. Press, 1988.

Sloane, Thomas. *On the Contrary: The Protocol of Traditional Rhetoric.* Washington, DC: Catholic Univ. of America Press, 1997.

Smith, Chuck. "The Persecution of West Virginia Jehovah's Witnesses and the Expansion of Legal Protection for Religious Liberty." *Journal of Church and State* 43, no. 3 (2001): 539–77.

Smith, Joseph, and Emerson Tiller. "The Strategy of Judging: Evidence from Administrative Law." *Journal of Legal Studies* 31, no. 1 (2002): 61–82.

Smith, Ruth, and John Trimbur. "Rhetorics of Unity and Disunity: The Worcester Firefighters Memorial Service." *Rhetoric Society Quarterly* 33, no. 4 (2003): 7–24.

Sprat, Thomas. *The History of the Royal-Society of London, for the Improving of Natural Knowledge.* 2nd ed. corrected. London, 1702.

Starger, Colin. "A Separate, Abridged Edition of the First Amendment." In *Justice Scalia: Rhetoric and the Rule of Law,* edited by Brian Slocum and Francis Mootz, III, 185–96. Chicago: Univ. of Chicago Press, 2019.

Staton, Jeffrey, and Georg Vanberg. "The Value of Vagueness: Delegation, Defiance, and Judicial Opinions." *American Journal of Political Science* 52, no. 3 (2008): 504–19.

Stein, Peter. *Regulae Iuris: From Juristic Rules to Legal Maxims.* Edinburgh: Edinburgh Univ. Press, 1966.

Stone, Julius. *Legal System and Lawyers' Reasonings.* Stanford: Stanford Univ. Press, 1968.

Story, Joseph. *Commentaries on the Constitution of the United States.* Abridged by the author. Boston: Hilliard, Gray, and Company, 1833.

Stratman, James. "Legal Rhetoric." In *Encyclopedia of Rhetoric and Composition: Communication from Ancient Times to the Information Age,* edited by Theresa Enos, 383–85. New York: Routledge, 2010.

Strauss, Gerald. *Law, Resistance, and the State: The Opposition to Roman Law in Reformation Germany.* Princeton: Princeton Univ. Press, 1986.

Strecker, Ivo. "Chiasmus and Metaphor." In *Chiasmus and Culture,* edited by Boris Wiseman and Anthony Paul, 69–88. New York: Berghahn Books, 2014.

Sullivan, Dale. "The Epideictic Character of Rhetorical Criticism." *Rhetoric Review* 11, no. 2 (1993): 339–49.

Sullivan, Dale. "The Ethos of Epideictic Encounter." *Philosophy and Rhetoric* 26, no. 2 (1993): 113–33.

Talbot, Margaret. "Supreme Confidence: The Jurisprudence of Justice Antonin Scalia." *New Yorker.* March 28, 2005.

Tallmon, James. "Casuistry." In *Encyclopedia of Rhetoric,* edited by Thomas Sloane, 83–88. New York: Oxford Univ. press, 2001.

Tandy, Keith. "Verbal Aspect as Narrative Structure in Aelfric's *Lives of Saints.*" In *The Old English Homily and Its Backgrounds,* edited by Paul Szarmach and Bernard Huppe, 181–202. Albany: SUNY, 1978.

Terry, Henry. *Some Leading Principles of Anglo-American Law: Expounded with a View to Its Arrangement and Codification.* Philadelphia: T. & J. W. Johnson & Co., 1884.

Thomas, Edmund. "Performance Space." In *The Oxford Handbook of the Second Sophistic*, edited by Daniel Richter and William Johnson, 181–201. Oxford: Oxford Univ. Press, 2017.

Thompson, Norma. *The Ship of State: Statecraft and Politics from Ancient Greece to Democratic America.* New Haven: Yale Univ. Press, 2001.

Thucydides. *History of the Peloponnesian War.* Translated by Rex Warner. London: Penguin, 1972.

Tileagă, Cristian. "What Is a 'Revolution'? National Commemoration, Collective Memory and Managing Authenticity in the Representation of a Political Event." *Discourse and Society* 19, no. 3 (2008): 359–82.

Timmerman, David. "Epideictic Oratory." In *Encyclopedia of Rhetoric and Composition: Communication from Ancient Times to the Information Age*, edited by Theresa Enos, 228–32. New York: Routledge, 1996.

Tocqueville, Alexis de. *Democracy in America.* Translated by Henry Reeve. Revised ed. 2 vols. New York: Vintage, 1990.

Toon, Yun Lee. "Epideictic Genre." In *Encyclopedia of Rhetoric*, edited by Thomas Sloane, 251–57. Oxford: Oxford Univ. Press, 2001.

Topf, Mel. "Communicating Legitimacy in U.S. Supreme Court Opinions." *Language and Communication* 12, no. 1 (1992): 17–29.

Toulmin, Stephen. *The Uses of Argument.* Cambridge: Cambridge Univ. Press, 1958.

Toulmin, Stephen. *Human Understanding: The Collective Use and Evolution of Concepts.* Princeton: Princeton Univ. Press, 1972.

Tsai, Robert. *Eloquence and Reason: Creating a First Amendment Culture.* New Haven: Yale Univ. Press, 2008.

Tushnet, Mark. "Style and the Supreme Court's Educational Role in Government." *Constitutional Commentary* 11, no. 1 (1994).

Upham, Frank. "Japan: A Different Vision of Law and Justice." *Responsive Community* 1 (1991): 52–63.

Vickers, Brian. *In Defence of Rhetoric.* Oxford: Clarendon Press, 1988.

Vico, Giambattista. *The New Science of Giambattista Vico.* Translated by Thomas Goddard Bergin and Max Harold Fisch. Unabridged ed. Ithaca: Cornell Univ. Press, 1984.

Vico, Giambattista. *On the Study Methods of Our Time.* Translated by Elio Gianturco. Ithaca: Cornell Univ. Press, 1990.

Vivian, Bradford. "Neoliberal Epideictic: Rhetorical Form and Commemorative Politics on September 11, 2002." *Quarterly Journal of Speech* 92, no. 1 (2006): 1–26.

Vivian, Bradford. "Rhetorical Arts of Praise and Blame in Political Transformation." In *Conflict Transformation and Peacebuilding: Moving from Violence to Sustainable Peace*, edited by Bruce Dayton and Louis Kriesberg, 74–90. New York: Routledge, 2009.

Vivian, Bradford. "Up from Memory: Epideictic Forgetting in Booker T. Washington's Cotton States Exposition Address." *Philosophy and Rhetoric* 45, no. 2 (2012), 189–212.

Vladeck, Stephen. Testimony during Hearing on "The Supreme Court's Shadow Docket" before the Subcommittee on Courts, Intellectual Property, and the Internet of the House Committee on the Judiciary, 117th Cong., 1st Sess., Feb. 18, 2021.

Voth, Ben. "A Case Study in Metaphor as Argument: A Longitudinal Analysis of the Wall Separating Church and State." *Argumentation and Advocacy* 34, no. 3 (1998): 127–39.

Walker, Jeffrey. *Rhetoric and Poetics in Antiquity*. Oxford: Oxford Univ. Press, 2000.

Walker, Jeffrey. *The Genuine Teachers of This Art: Rhetorical Education in Antiquity*. Columbia: South Carolina Univ. Press, 2011.

Weaver, Richard. *The Ethics of Rhetoric*. 1953. Reprint, Davis: Hermagoras Press, 1985.

Welch, John, ed. *Chiasmus in Antiquity: Structures, Analyses, Exegesis*. Eugene: Wipf and Stock, 1981.

Welch, John, and Donald Parry, eds. *Chiasmus: The State of the Art*. Provo: BYU Studies, 2020.

Wetlaufer, Gerald. "Rhetoric and Its Denial in Legal Discourse," *Virginia Law Review* 76 (1990): 1545–97.

White, G. Edward. "The Evolution of Reasoned Elaboration: Jurisprudential Criticism and Social Change." *Virginia Law Review* 59 (1973): 279–302.

White, James Boyd. *Heracles' Bow: Essays on the Rhetoric and Poetics of the Law*. Madison: Wisconsin Univ. Press, 1985.

White, James Boyd. *Living Speech: Resisting the Empire of Force*. Princeton: Princeton Univ. Press, 2006.

Whitehead, Alfred North. *Process and Reality*. Corrected ed. Edited by David Griffin and Donald Sherburne. New York: Free Press, 1978.

Whitmarch, Tim. *The Second Sophistic*. Cambridge: Cambridge Univ. Press, 2005.

Wilce, James, and Janina Fenigsen. "Mourning and Honor: Register in Karelian Lament." In *Registers of Communication*, edited by Asif Agha and Frog, 187–209. Helsinki: Finnish Literature Society, 2015.

Williams, Roger. *The Complete Writings of Roger Williams*. Edited by Reuben Aldridge Guild. New York: Russell and Russell, 1963.

Winn, Peter. "Legal Ritual." *Law and Critique* 2, no. 2 (1991): 207–32.

Wood, Elizabeth. *Performing Justice: Agitation Trials in Early Soviet Russia*. Ithaca: Cornell Univ. Press, 2005.

Yang, Michelle. "President Nixon's Speeches and Toasts during His 1972 Trip to China: A Study in Diplomatic Rhetoric." *Rhetoric and Public Affairs* 14, no. 1 (2011): 1–44.

Yates, Frances. *The Art of Memory*. Chicago: Univ. of Chicago Press, 1966.

Yelle, Robert. "Rhetorics of Law and Ritual: A Semiotic Comparison of the Law of Talion and Sympathetic Magic." *Journal of the American Academy of Religion* 69, no. 3 (2001): 627–47.

Zaeske, Susan. "Hearing the Silences in Lincoln's Temperance Address: Whig Masculinity as an Ethic of Rhetorical Civility," *Rhetoric and Public Affairs* 13, no. 3 (2010).

Zarefsky, David. "Argumentation." In *Encyclopedia of Rhetoric*, edited by Thomas Sloane, 33–37. Oxford: Oxford Univ. Press, 2001.

TABLE OF CASES

Arizona State Legislature v. Arizona Indep. Redistricting Comm'n, 576 U.S. 787 (2015)
Barcon Assoc., Inc. v. Tri-County Asphalt Corp., 430 A.2d 214 (N.J. 1981)
Beauharnais v. Illinois, 343 U.S. 250 (1952)
Bell Atlantic Corp. v. Twombly, 550 U.S. 544 (2007)
Benevolent and Protective Order of Elks No. 85 v. Tax Comm'n, 536 P.2d 1214 (Utah 1975)
Benton v. Maryland, 395 U.S. 784 (1969)
Boeing v. Shipman, 411 F.2d 365 (5th Cir. 1969)
Berkey v. Third Ave. Ry. Co., 244 N.Y. 84 (N.Y. 1926)
Bolling v. Sharpe, 347 U.S. 497 (1954)
Bowers v. Hardwick, 476 U.S. 186 (1986)
Boyd v. United States, 116 U.S. 616 (1886)
Brandenburg v. Ohio, 395 U.S. 444 (1969)
Bridges v. California, 314 U.S. 252 (1941)
Brown v. Allen, 344 U.S. 443 (1953)
Brown v. Bd. of Educ., 347 U.S. 483 (1954)
Cabell v. Markham, 148 F.2d 737 (2d Cir. 1945)
Carey v. Population Serv. Int'l, 431 U.S. 678 (1977)
Clark v. Container Corp. of Am., Inc., 589 So. 2d 184 (Ala. 1991)
Cohen v. California, 403 U.S. 15 (1971)
Cohens v. Virginia, 19 U.S. 264 (1821)
In re *Comm. for the Preservation of the Constitutional Right to Trial by Jury*, 1 Misc. 2d 548 (N.Y. Sup. Ct. 1956)
Connecticut v. Guilbert, 49 A.3d 705 (Conn. 2012)
Dickerson v. United States, 530 U.S. 428 (2000)
Dobbs v. Jackson Women's Health Org., No. 19-1392, slip op. (U.S. Supr. Ct. June 24, 2022).
Douglas v. Jeanette, 319 U.S. 157 (1943)
Eisenstadt v. Baird, 405 U. S. 438 (1972)
Engel v. Vitale, 370 U.S. 421 (1962)
Epperson v. Arkansas, 393 U.S. 97 (1968)

Evensen v. Dagostin, 183 A.3d 462 (Pa. Super. Ct. 2018)
Everson v. Bd. of Educ., 330 U.S. 1 (1947)
Free Enterprise Fund v. Public Co. Accounting Oversight Bd., 561 U.S. 477, 499 (2010)
Frisby v. Schultz, 487 U.S. 474 (1988)
Georgia v. Randolph, 547 U.S. 103 (2006)
Gideon v. Wainwright, 372 U.S. 335 (1963)
Gitlow v. New York, 268 U. S. 652 (1925)
Gobitis v. Minersville Sch. Dist., 21 F. Supp. 581 (E.D. Pa. 1937)
Gobitis v. Minersville Sch. Dist., 24 F. Supp. 271 (E.D. Pa. 1938)
Goodridge v. Dep't of Pub. Health, 440 Mass. 309 (Mass. 2003)
Goodson v. Northside Bible Church, 261 F. Supp. 99 (S.D. Ala.1966)
Griset v. Fair Political Practices Comm'n, 82 Cal. Rptr. 2d 25 (Cal. Ct. App. 1999)
Griswold v. Connecticut, 381 U.S. 479 (1965)
Halter v. Nebraska, 205 U. S. 34 (1907)
Hill v. Colorado, 530 U.S. 703 (2000)
Hustler Magazine, Inc. v. Falwell, 485 U.S. 46 (1988)
Int'l Controls Corp. v. Vesco, 490 F.2d 1334 (2d Cir. 1974)
Kaya v. Partington, 681 A.2d 256 (R.I. 1996)
Keepseagle v. Vilsack, 118 F. Supp. 3d 98 (D.C. Cir. 2015)
Kennedy v. Bremerton Sch. Dist., No. 21–418, slip op. (U.S. Supr. Ct. June 27, 2022)
Lawrence v. Texas, 539 U.S. 558 (2003)
Lemon v. Kurtzman, 403 U.S. 602 (1971)
Mackey v. Enzensperger, 11 Utah 154 (Utah 1895)
Madsen v. Women's Health Center, 512 U.S. 753 (1994)
Maine v. Harriman, 75 Me. 562 (Me. 1884)
Marbury v. Madison, 5 U.S. 137 (1803)
MARTA v. Ledbetter, 361 S.E.2d 878 (Ga. Ct. App. 1987)
Martin v. Hunter's Lessee, 14 U.S. 304 (1816)
Maynard v. Hill, 125 U. S. 190 (1888)
McCulloch v. Maryland, 17 U.S. 316 (1819)
McCollum v. Bd. of Educ., 333 U.S. 203 (1948)
McCullen v. Coakley, 573 U.S. 464 (2014)
McGee v Attorney General, [1974] I.R. 284 (Ireland)
McGowan v. Maryland, 366 U.S. 420 (1961)
McSwane v. Foreman, 167 Ind. 171 (Ind. 1906)
Miller v. Bd. of Pub. Works, 195 Cal. 477 (Cal. 1925)
Miller v. Clark County, 340 F.3d 959 (9th Cir. 2003)
Minersville Sch. Dist. v. Gobitis, 108 F.2d 683 (3d Cir. 1940)
Minersville Sch. District v. Gobitis, 310 U.S. 586 (1940)
Miranda v. Arizona, 384 U.S. 436 (1966)
Miron v. Trudel, [1995] 2 S.C.R. 418 (Canada)

Missouri v. Holland, 252 U.S. 416 (1920)
Montgomery v. Maryland Cas. Co., 169 Ga. 746 (Ga. 1930)
Morrison v. Olson, 487 U.S. 654 (1988)
Murdock v. Pennsylvania, 319 U.S. 105 (1943)
NAACP v. Alabama, 357 U.S. 449 (1958)
New York Times v. Sullivan, 376 U.S. 254 (1964)
Obergefell v. Hodges, 576 U.S. 644 (2015)
Olmstead v. United States, 277 U.S. 438 (1928)
Palko v. Connecticut, 302 U.S. 319 (1937)
Paris Adult Theatre I v. Slaton, 413 U.S. 49 (1973)
Pedersen v. United States, 115 Ct. Cl. 335 (U.S. Ct. Cl. 1950)
Pencovic v. Pencovic, 281 P.2d 261 (Cal. Ct. App. 1955)
People v. McClellan, 71 Cal. 2d 793 (Cal. 1969)
Perry v. Edwards Mfg. Co., 26 Ohio Dec. 301 (Ohio Cincinnati Super. Ct. 1915)
Planned Parenthood v. Casey, 505 U.S. 833 (1992)
Poe v. Ullman, 367 U.S. 497 (1961)
Rajagopal v State of Tamil Nadu, [1995] 3 L.R.C. 566 (India)
Roberts v. United States Jaycees, 468 U.S. 609 (1984)
Robertson v. Steele's Mills, 172 F.2d 817 (4th Cir. 1949)
Roe v. Wade, 410 U.S. 113 (1973)
Romer v. Evans, 517 U.S. 620 (1996)
In re *Russo*, 147 Misc. 2d 179 (N.Y. Sup. Ct. 1990)
Schenck v. Pro-Choice Network of Western New York, 519 U.S. 537 (1997)
Sch. Dist. of Abington Township v. Schempp, 374 U.S. 203 (1963)
Snow v. Oregon State Penitentiary, 780 P.2d 215 (Or. 1989)
State v. Langford, 55 S.C. 322 (S.C. 1899)
Sweezy v. New Hampshire, 354 U.S. 234 (1957)
Texas v. Johnson, 491 U.S. 397 (1989)
Thornburgh v. Am. Coll. of Obstetricians and Gynecologists, 476 U.S. 747 (1986)
Torcaso v. Watkins 367 U.S. 488 (1961)
United States v. Alvarez, 567 U.S. 709 (2012)
United States v. Annigoni, 68 F.3d 279 (9th Cir. 1995)
United States v. Associated Press, 52 F. Supp. 362 (S.D.N.Y. 1943)
United States v. Darby, 312 U.S. 100 (1941)
United States v. Eichman, 496 U.S. 310 (1990)
United States v. Khan, 325 F. Supp. 2d 218 (E.D.N.Y. 2004)
United States v. Nixon, 418 U.S. 683 (1974)
United States v. White, 401 U.S. 745 (1971)
United States v. Windsor, 570 U.S. 744 (2013)
Urofsky v. Gilmore, 216 F.3d 401 (4th Cir. 2000)
Volmar Constr., Inc. v. United States, 32 Fed. Cl. 746 (Fed. Cl. 1995)
Washington ex. rel. *Lumber and Sawmill Workers v. Superior Court*, 164 P.2d 662 (Wash. 1945)

Watson v. Jones, 13 Wall. 679 (1871)
Weems v. United States, 217 U.S. 349 (1910)
West Virginia Bd. of Educ. v. Barnette, 319 U.S. 624 (1943)
Whitney v. California, 274 U.S. 357 (1927)
Wickard v. Filburn, 317 U.S. 111 (1942)
Wiley v. Slater, 22 Barb. 506 (N.Y. Gen. Term 1856)
Williams v. Bloomington, 108 Ill. App. 2d 307 (Ill. Ct. App. 1969)
Wisconsin v. Hersh, 523 N.W.2d 210 (Wisc. Ct. App. 1994)
Wolf v. Colorado, 338 U.S. 25 (1949)
Younger v. Smith, 106 Cal. Rptr. 225 (Cal. Ct. App. 1973)
Zorach v. Clauson, 343 U.S. 306 (1952)

INDEX

abeyance, 106, 221n42
abortion and birth control, 2, 7, 19, 143, 144–46, 149–55, 167–71, 227/n37. *See also* privacy jurisprudence and *Obergefell v. Hodges*; *specific cases*
The Abuse of Casuistry (Jonsen and Toulmin), 34–35
accumulation, 4, 48
Ælfric of Eynsham, 57–58
Aeschylus, 165
affirmative modality: in *Dobbs* opinions, 170, 171, 172, 173; in flag jurisprudence, 78–81, 83, 85, 87, 90, 93; gnomic aspect and, 182–83n20; in privacy jurisprudence, 141, 145, 150, 157; register theory of epideictic and, 59–63, 174; in Religion Clause jurisprudence, 108, 114, 117, 124, 126, 128; Scalia's use of, 165, 167
Agricultural Adjustment Act (1938), 184n51
Alcaeus of Mytilene, 135–36, 226n4
Aldisert, Ruggero, 189n85
Alito, Samuel, 21, 169–71
Allen, William, 185–86n56
amplification devices: as dicta, 71; figural devices and patterns of, 4; multiple rhetorical uses of, 12, 17; negative associations of, 14; register theory of epideictic and, 46–50, 200n56
anadiplosis, 47, 90, 117, 237
anaphora, 4, 47, 48, 73, 110, 147, 157, 167, 170, 171, 173, 237
Anaximenes, 43
Angelou, Maya, 12
antanaclasis, 172, 237
Antidosis (Isocrates), 17
antimetabole, 32, 47, 73, 102–3, 220n32, 237
antirhetorical tendency, 25–27, 41, 173, 176–78
antirrhesis, 25, 237
antithesis: defined, 237; in *Dobbs* dissent, 172; in flag jurisprudence, 73, 78, 80, 81, 83, 85, 86, 90, 93; in privacy jurisprudence, 144, 145, 147; register theory of epideictic and, 8, 33, 46, 47, 50, 60, 61, 191n108; in Religion Clause jurisprudence, 105, 117, 126, 128; Scalia's use of, 165, 166
Appleton, John, 10–11
Areopagus, Council of, 30
Aristotle: on amplification, 46; on antitheses, 60; characterization of epideictic by, 18, 187n61, 187n71, 189–90n91; distinguishing epideictic and deliberative rhetoric, 11–12,

15, 18, 26, 28–34, 176, 200n39;
on emotions, 200n66; on
enthymemes, 31–34, 199n31;
on gnomic aspect, 52, 55, 60,
66, 176; judicial power, suspicion of, 199n34; motives toward
judgment and *theôria*, 200n43;
on narration, 209n236; on
praise, 42–43, 44, 45; *Rhetoric*,
11, 15, 28–33, 42, 45, 60, 187n61,
187n71, 199n31, 199n34, 200n39,
200n43, 204n143, 209n236; *On
Sophistical Refutations*, 199n31;
theses and *hypotheses*, proper
domain of, 36, 39; on virtues,
204n143
*Arizona State Legislature v. Arizona
Indep. Redistricting Comm'n*
(2015), 194n148
Arspoetica (Horace), 169
Asenas, Jennifer, 69
"Asianic," as term for epideictic, 47,
169, 233n40
Assis, Elie, 106
association, right of, 149, 151, 152
asyndeton: defined, 237; in *Dobbs* dissent, 173; in flag jurisprudence,
73, 81, 85, 93; in privacy jurisprudence, 145, 147; in register
theory of epideictic, 8, 47; in
Religion Clause jurisprudence,
108, 110, 124
Austin, John, 45–46, 205n158

Bacon, Francis, 27, 133, 195n151,
226n188
Baker, Paul, 74
Bakhtin, Mikhail, 16
Balter, Susan, 193n128
"Barbara Fritchie" (Whittier), 95
*Barnette. See West Virginia State
Board of Education v. Barnette*
Baude, William, 174
Beale, Walter, 46, 66

Beauharnais v. Illinois (1952), 184n51
Bell Atlantic Corp. v. Twombly (2007),
195n151
Bellamy salute, 9, 77, 84
*Benevolent and Protective Order of
Elks No. 85 v. Tax Commission*
(1975), 1, 7
Berkey v. Third Ave. Ry. Co. (1926),
226n191
Berman, Harold, 201n69
Berns, Sandra, 186n58
Berns, Walter, 28, 199n37
Beth, Loren, 218n3
Biber, Douglas, 40, 190n100
Bill of Rights: flag jurisprudence and,
75–77, 80, 85; fundamental
rights doctrine and, 5, 9, 75–77;
privacy jurisprudence and, 23,
139, 146, 147, 149, 150, 152, 155,
160, 161; Religion Clause jurisprudence and, 108, 117, 139, 146,
147, 149, 150, 152, 155, 160, 161;
separation of powers and, 166
birth control. *See* abortion and birth
control
Bitzer, Lloyd, 41
Black, Hugo, 87, 91, 101–2, 103, 107–11,
121–22, 153, 163
Black, Jeremiah, 125–26
Blackmun, Harry, 144, 163
Blackstone, William, 135, 163, 193n140
blame. *See* praise and blame
Boeing Co. v. Shipman (1969), 194n140
Bolling v. Sharpe (1954), 157
Boorstin, Daniel, 135
Bosmajian, Haig, 73–74, 86, 101,
119, 219n9
Boston Massacre orations, 54
Bourdieu, Pierre, 1, 6, 63
Bowers v. Hardwick (1986), 142, 143–
44, 164
Boyd v. United States (1886), 150–51
Braden, Waldo, 70
Bradley, Joseph, 150–51

Brandeis, Louis, 56, 72, 90, 137–39, 144, 152, 155, 160, 163
Brandenburg v. Ohio (1969), 90
Brann, Eva, 220nn30–31, 223n114
Brennan, William, 74, 91, 92–93, 131, 144, 152, 160, 163
Breyer, Stephen, 53, 170, 171–73
Bridges v. California (1941), 90–91
Brown v. Allen (1953), 220n28
Brown v. Board of Education (1954), 4, 19, 63, 156–58
Burger, Warren, 48, 102, 106, 119, 130–31, 132
Burgess, Theodor, 39, 47, 60, 189n91
Burke, Kenneth, 12, 47, 68, 161, 193n124
burning the flag, 92–97
Burton, Harold, 119, 121
bus voucher program for schools. See *Everson v. Board of Education*
Butts, R. Freeman, 101
Byron, George Gordon, Lord, 111, 222n65

Cabell v. Markham (1945), 53
Cairns, David, 26
California: Criminal Syndicalism Act, 90; Red Flag Law, 76
Cardozo, Benjamin, 76
Carey v. Population Services International (1977), 227n37
Carter, Michael, 64, 69, 212n328
Casey. See *Planned Parenthood v. Casey*
castle doctrine, 20
casuistry, 34–35
ceremonial/ritual occasions, association of epideictic with, 63–67, 69–70
Chase, J. Richard, 42, 45
chiasmus: defined, 102–3, 237; Derrida on, 221n46; in flag jurisprudence, 85, 86; Madison's use of, 103–7, 113–14, 116, 120–21, 132, 220n31, 220n34; in register theory of epideictic, 4, 22–23, 32, 47; in Religion Clause jurisprudence, 100, 102–8, 110, 113–14, 116–17, 119–22, 125, 131–34; in scholarly commentary on the Religion Clauses, 223n116; "vice versa," as expression of, 103, 110, 122
church-related educational institutions, state aid for. See *Lemon v. Kurtzman*
Cicero: chiasmus, use of, 104; *De Inventione*, 35, 36, 43, 176, 177; *De Oratore*, 30, 35–39, 173, 176, 190n93, 200n44, 202n94, 203n103; register theory of epideictic and, 30, 35–39, 43, 52, 176, 179, 190n93, 200n44, 202n94, 203n103; Scalia's education in, 165
Civil War, U.S., 5, 70, 75, 82
Clark, William, 79–80
Clark v. Container Corp. of Am., Inc. (1991), 195n149
classical world, relationship between rhetoric and law in, 26
Cohens v. Virginia (1821), 135–36, 139, 160, 161, 168, 169
Commentaries on the Constitution of the United States (Story), 168–69, 233n34
Commentary on the Laws of England (Blackstone), 135
common law, 3, 4, 6, 10, 20, 25, 34, 47, 53, 177–78, 182n17, 193n138, 196n9, 229n88
The Common Law (Holmes), 34
compulsory flag salutes, 8–10, 22, 74, 77–89
concession, strategic. See paramologia
"Concord Hymn" (Emerson), 95
Condit, Celeste, 40, 41, 44–45, 51, 54, 59–60, 61

conduplicatio, 86, 172, 237
confrontation and epideictic, 59–61, 98–99
Conn. v. Guilbert (2012), 194n148
Conrad, Susan, 40, 190n100
consonance, 117, 237
contingent reasoning, 29, 30
contraception. *See* abortion and birth control
Copia (Erasmus), 47
correctio, 48
Cotton, John, 101
Cover, Robert, 182n14
cruel and unusual punishment, 136–37
Curtis, Dennis, 65
Cuvier, George, 10
Czarniawska, Barbara, 58, 71

Danbury Baptists, Jefferson's letter to, 101
Danisch, Robert, 208n227
Dasenbrock, Reed, 205n158
Davis, Donald, Jr., 207n210, 214n5
De Inventione (Cicero), 35, 36, 43, 176, 177
De Oratore (Cicero), 30, 35–39, 173, 176, 190n93, 200n44, 202n94, 203n103
De Quincey, Thomas, 35
Defense of Marriage Act, 227n29
Del Mar, Maksymilian, 73, 74, 97, 196n9, 206n186
deliberative rhetoric falsely distinguished from epideictic, 11–15, 24, 25–34, 176
Democracy in America (Tocqueville), 148
Demosthenes, 17, 19
Derrida, Jacques, 221n46
Descartes, René, 27, 49, 189n84, 198n23
desecration of the flag, 22, 74, 92–97
Dewar, Michael, 191n112

Dickerson v. United States (2000), 164–65
dicta, judicial metaphors and figures regarded as, 71–73, 97
dirimenscopulatio, 78, 237
Dobbs v. Jackson Women's Health Organization (2022), 24, 53, 169–73, 183n22, 195n151, 207n214, 212n312, 213n333, 215n31, 234n52
dogmatism, epideictic's reputation for, 60–61
dogs, judicial paeans to, 10–11, 185–86n56
Don Juan (Byron), 111, 222n65
Douglas, Lawrence, 3, 181n9
Douglas, William, 6–7, 23, 87, 91, 139, 147, 149–53, 161, 163, 229n94
Douglas v. Jeanette (1943), 53
Dreisbach, Daniel, 101, 218n2, 223n116
Due Process Clause, Fourteenth Amendment, 2, 5, 23, 75–76, 107, 118, 139, 143, 146–49, 152–56, 221n51

Eighth Amendment, 136
Eisenstadt v. Baird (1972), 143, 146
Ellece, Sibonile, 74
eloquence: in *Dobbs* opinions, 172, 173; Farrell on, 177; in flag jurisprudence, 78–81, 83, 85, 87, 90, 93, 94; in previous studies of epideictic, 174; in privacy jurisprudence, 147, 150, 157, 159, 160; in register theory of epideictic, 8, 14–16, 21, 22, 32, 37, 39, 50–52, 53, 58, 67, 69; in Religion Clause jurisprudence, 108, 114, 117, 118, 126, 128; Scalia's use of, 165, 167
emanation metaphor, 23, 139, 150, 153, 160
Emancipation Proclamation, 19
Emerson, Ralph Waldo, 51–52, 95

encomium: John of Sardis on, 192n113; judicial reference to, 6, 19, 20, 21, 193n134, 194–95n149; Pernot on, 43; Quintilian on, 60; Story's encomium to Marshall, 168
Encomium to Helen (Gorgias of Leontini), 17
Engels, Jeremy, 18, 58
Enlightenment/Scientific Revolution, 13–14, 27, 133
Enos, Richard, 38
enthymemes, 29, 31–34, 52, 66, 199n31
enumeration: in *Dobbs* opinions, 170, 171, 173; in flag jurisprudence, 75, 78, 83, 85, 94; in privacy jurisprudence, 150, 154; register theory of epideictic and, 4, 5, 8, 48, 68; in Religion Clause jurisprudence, 108, 128
epanalepsis, 85
epea, 32–33
epexegesis, 48, 237
Epicurean philosophy, 28
epideictic register, judicial use of: affective dimension of, 6; antirhetorical tendency and, 25–27, 41, 173, 176–78; examples of, 6–11; false distinction of deliberative and epideictic rhetoric, 11–15, 24, 25–34, 176; fundamental rights jurisprudence, focus on, 2, 5, 21–22; as genre versus register, 15–17, 32–34; interdiscursivity of epideictic and practical argument, recognition of, 17–19; judges' appreciation of, 174–75; judges' references to, 6, 19–21; judicial opinions as legitimation strategy, 1–6, 11, 182n19; methodological approach, 21–22; negative, inferior, or degenerate associations of, 12–15, 24, 177–80; political ideology and, 6, 11, 163, 173; religious speech, parallels to, 6; by Roberts Court, 169–73; Scalia's criticism/use of, 163–69; successful production of, 175–80; temporality in judicial discourse, role of, 24; ubiquity of, 163. *See also* flag jurisprudence; privacy jurisprudence; register theory of epideictic; Religion Clause jurisprudence
Epideictic Rhetoric: Questioning the Stakes of Ancient Praise (Pernot), 42
epistemic modality, 29, 61–62
epistrophe, 47, 165, 237
Equal Protection Clause, Fourteenth Amendment, 140, 155, 157, 158
equity, 30, 34–35, 201n69
Erasmus, Desiderius, 47
ethical dimensions of epideictic, 100
ethical surplus, 19, 156, 161
eulogy, 11, 16, 20–21, 41, 54, 55, 61, 99, 103, 173, 175, 193n131, 195n151
Euripides, 31, 165
Everson v. Board of Education (1947), 23, 106–8; Black's majority opinion, 107–11; Jackson's dissenting opinion, 116–18; *Lemon* compared, 131; *McCollum* and, 121, 122, 123; Rutledge's dissenting opinion, 107, 111–16, 176; wall metaphor used in, 101–2, 106–8, 110–11
exergasia: defined, 237; in *Dobbs* dissent, 172; flag jurisprudence and, 78, 82, 85, 88; privacy jurisprudence and, 136, 141, 145; register theory of epideictic and, 4, 47–48; Religion Clause jurisprudence and, 114, 124, 126, 128; Scalia's use of, 165

Fadeley, Edward, 71
Fahnestock, Jeanne, 49–50, 73, 105, 133–34, 220n32
Fantham, Elaine, 50, 51
Farrell, Thomas, 52, 177
Faulkner, William, 12
The Federalist Papers, 2, 166
Fenigsen, Janina, 206n193
Ferguson, Robert, 25
Fifth Amendment, 75, 137, 138, 150–53, 164
figurality, 47–50, 52, 53, 73, 80, 101, 104, 133, 134, 150, 174, 178
Findley, Jessica, 236n74
First Amendment: abortion cases, 19, 167–68; association, right of, 149, 151, 152; free speech cases, 19, 22 (See also flag jurisprudence); paramologia in risks of free speech, 88, 89–92; in privacy jurisprudence, 143, 149–52; religious freedom cases, 23 (See also Religion Clause jurisprudence); rhetorical strategies shaping development of culture of, 72
flag jurisprudence, 22–23, 71–100; Bellamy salute, 9, 77, 84; compelled speech argument, 84–87; compulsory flag salutes, 8–10, 22, 74, 77–89; desecration cases, 22, 74, 92–97; function of judicial metaphors and figures in, 71–74; fundamental rights doctrine and, 75–77; interdiscursive relationship between judicial and epideictic discourse, revealing, 97–100; paramologia in, 22, 74, 82, 86, 88–90, 92, 97–100; religious liberty arguments, 77–82, 84, 88, 98; risks of free speech, judicial concessions to, 89–92
Foucault, Michel, 208n227

Four Minute Man Speech, 13
Fourteenth Amendment: Due Process Clause, 2, 5, 23, 75–76, 107, 118, 139, 143, 146–49, 152–56, 221n51; Equal Protection Clause, 140, 155, 157, 158
Fourth Amendment, 91, 137, 138, 150–53, 155
Frank, Jerome, 67, 182n19, 196n9
Frankfurter, Felix: *Barnette*, dissenting opinion in, 87–89, 98, 170, 175, 176–77; flag desecration opinions compared to flag salute opinions of, 93; *Gobitis*, opinion in, 22–23, 78, 81–83, 98, 125, 170, 175; Robert Jackson commenting on *Gobitis* opinion of, in *Barnette*, 85–86; *Poe*, plurality opinion in, 154; register theory of epideictic and, 8–10, 43, 184n51; Religion Clause jurisprudence of, 107, 119, 121, 122–27, 134; use of epideictic register by, 163
Frawley, William, 59, 61–62
Free Enterprise Fund v. Public Co. Accounting Oversight Bd. (2010), 194n148
free speech, 19, 22. See also flag jurisprudence
freedom of religion, 23. See also Religion Clause jurisprudence
freedom to marry, 146–49, 155–56. See also privacy jurisprudence and *Obergefell v. Hodges*
Frisby v. Schultz (1988), 167
Frost, Michael, 26, 27
Frost, Robert, 122–23, 127, 132
fundamental rights doctrine and jurisprudence, 5, 21–22, 75–77, 146, 215n31
funerals and funeral orations, 12, 13, 16, 17, 20, 43, 60–61, 64, 69

Gale, Frederick, 181n9
Garver, Eugene: on ethical surplus, 19, 156, 161; on *ethos* of *Brown v. Board of Education* (1954), 156–58; flag jurisprudence and, 99–100, 213n4; on judicial use of epideictic thought, 6, 18, 19; on practical reasoning, 99–100; register theory of epideictic and, 25–26, 30, 54, 59, 63, 69, 201n66, 207–8n221; on successful epideictic rhetoric, 178, 235n81
Gasché, Rodolphe, 103, 133
genre versus register, epideictic viewed as, 15–17, 32–34
Genung, John, 14, 48, 188–89n83
Georgia v. Randolph (2006), 19–20, 164
Gettysburg Address, 19, 48, 53–54, 74, 156
Gideon v. Wainwright (1963), 195n151
Gilbert, Cass, 65
Gitlow v. New York (1925), 76
gnomic aspect: Aristotle of, 52, 55, 60, 66, 176; as dicta, 71–72; in *Dobbs* dissent, 172; enthymemes and, 31–32, 52; in flag jurisprudence, 78–85, 87, 90, 93, 94; grammar of epideictic and, 174; judicial use of epideictic and, 4, 8, 182–83n20; living constitutionalism, in judicial oratory on, 136, 138; in privacy jurisprudence, 141, 145, 150, 154, 157; in register theory of epideictic, 52–59, 62, 210n207; in Religion Clause jurisprudence, 102, 108, 114, 117, 123, 124, 126, 128; Scalia's use of, 164–66
Gobitis. See Minersville School District v. Gobitis
Goldberg, Arthur J., 152
Goodrich, Peter, 25, 177–78
Goodridge v. Department of Public Health (2003), 8, 147

Goodson v. Northside Bible Church (1966), 101
Gorgias of Leontini, 17, 70, 103, 169, 199n31
Gorman, Amanda, 12
Gramsci, Antonio, 13
Grant, Ulysses S., 125
Grassi, Ernesto: on chiasmus, 104; judicial use of epideictic and, 183n31, 187n79, 189n84; on logical demonstration, 179; on modern rationalism thesis, 133, 236n95; original assertions, on figurative and metaphorical nature of, 99–100; on panegyrics and eulogies, 175; register theory of epideictic and, 54–55, 61, 198n23, 201–2n76, 201n73; on relationship between philosophy and rhetoric, 220n26
Gray, Benjamin, 210n272
Greenhouse, Linda, 195n151
Griswold v. Connecticut (1965), 7, 23, 139, 143, 146, 147, 149–53, 155, 160, 161, 163, 195n150
Gulag Archipelago (Solzhenitsyn), 18

Hand, Learned, 53, 91
Hargreaves-Mawdsley, W. N., 65
Hariman, Robert, 103, 105, 106, 132, 134, 221n39
Harlan, John, 76, 146, 152, 153–55
Hartelius, Johannes, 69
Hayne, Robert, 74
Henly, Burr, 339n88
Henry, Patrick, 120
Hermogenes of Tarsus, 50, 186n60, 190n93
Hesiod, 32
Hill v. Colorado (2000), 167
"The Hill We Climb" (Gorman), 12
Hippias of Elis, 70, 169
Holmes, Oliver Wendell, 34, 94–95, 153

Homer, 32, 165
homosexual acts, 142–44. *See also* *Lawrence v. Texas*; same-sex marriage
Hopper, Paul, 56, 57, 58, 177
Horace, 136, 169
hyperbole, 47
hypotheses versus *theses*, 34–39, 176
hysteron proteron, 103

"I Have a Dream" speech (King), 74
immortal constitution, 23, 135–36, 139, 161, 169, 172. *See also* living constitutionalism
imperfective aspect, 52, 55–57, 174, 177
In re *Comm. for the Preservation of the Constitutional Right to Trial by Jury* (2956), 193n140
Independent Counsel Act, 165–66
Institutio Oratoria (Quintilian), 17, 45, 187n62
Interfaith Conference on Federation, 126
interracial marriage, 7–8, 19, 146–47, 155–56
Int'l Controls Corp. v. Vesco (1974), 194n148
An Introduction to Legal Reasoning (Levi), 34
irrealis mode, 61
Isocrates, 17, 33, 70, 178, 179, 189n91, 200n58

Jackson, Robert: flag jurisprudence of, 74, 78, 84–86, 93, 170; propensity for epideictic, 163; register theory of epideictic and, 8–10, 42, 53, 184n51; Religion Clause jurisprudence of, 102, 104, 107, 116–18, 121, 123, 127–29
Jamieson, Kathleen, 16, 190n96
Jasinski, James, 74, 189–90n91
Jefferson, Thomas, 101, 107, 109, 111, 112, 126–27, 218n3

Jehovah's Witnesses, 77, 83, 84
John of Sardis, 192n113
Johnson. See Texas v. Johnson
Johnson, Gregory, 92, 94
Johnson, Samuel, 10
Jonsen, Albert, 34–35
judicial opinions: brevity in, 157; judges' appreciation of, 174–75; lack of legal requirement for, 3; as legitimation strategy, 1–6, 11, 182n19; use of epideictic register in (*See* epideictic register, judicial use of)
judicial restraint, 3–4, 81, 87–88, 154–55, 171
judicial robes, 65–66, 212n312

Kagan, Elena, 53, 170, 171–73
Kahn, Paul, 7
kairos, 211n292
Kant, Immanuel, 14, 161
Kapgan, Yury, 232n7
Kaya v. Partington (1996), 194n148
Keepseagle v. Vilsack (2015), 194n148
Kennedy, Anthony: on abortion and birth control, 2, 144–45; analysis of majority opinion in *Obergefell*, 23, 134, 139 (*See also* privacy jurisprudence and *Obergefell v. Hodges*); on Defense of Marriage Act, in *United States v. Windsor* (2013), 227n29; flag jurisprudence of, 22, 74, 92, 94; intimate conduct, protective statements about, in *Lawrence v. Texas* (2003), 142–44; marriage, paean to, 7–8, 43, 140–42; propensity for epideictic, 163; Scalia's critique of, 163–64, 168, 169
Kennedy, George, 34
Kim, Lawrence, 233n40
King, Martin Luther, Jr., 12, 74
Konvitz, Milton, 5, 75, 76

Laib, Nevin, 14
Lakoff, George, 223n107
Langacker, Ronald, 57
Language and Symbolic Power (Bourdieu), 1
Lauer, Ilon, 190n98
Lauer, Janice, 226n188
Lawrence v. Texas (2003), 43, 139, 142–44, 146, 148, 164, 194n148
Le Duc, Don, 7, 160
Leach, Edmund, 69–70
Lee, Hugh, 58
Lemon v. Kurtzman (1971), 23, 102, 106, 119, 120, 121, 129–31, 132
Leubsdorf, John, 196n9
Levi, Edward, 34
Levinas, Emmanuel, 105
Levinson, Sanford, 25, 86
lex talionis, 186n58
Lincoln, Abraham, 19, 48, 53–54, 61, 74, 82, 85, 156
Lives of Saints (Ælfric of Eynsham), 57–58
living constitutionalism, 24, 135–39, 153, 160, 161, 163, 172
Locke, John, 14
Longinus, 46, 47, 48
Loraux, Nicole, 60
Loving v. Virginia (1967), 19, 23, 139, 146–47, 155–56
Lyotard, Jean-François, 160–61

Mader, Thomas, 32
Madison, James: on Bill of Rights, 75; Hugo Black citing, in *Everson*, 107, 108–9; chiasmus used by, 103–7, 113–14, 116, 120–21, 132, 134, 220n31, 220n34; "Property" essay, 105, 120; *Remonstrance and Memorial against Religious Assessments*, 23, 101, 103–7, 109, 111–14, 116, 120–21, 124, 132, 220n31, 223n114; Rutledge citing, in *Everson*

dissent, 111–15; on separation of powers, 166; Roger Williams, familiarity with ideas of, 218n3
Madsen v. Women's Health Center (1994), 167
Magna Carta, 10, 20
Maine v. Harriman (1884), 10
Marbury v. Madison (1803), 220n28
Maris, Albert, 78–79
marriage and sexual relations, 6–8, 10, 19, 23–24, 140–42, 146–49, 155–56, 158–59. *See also* privacy jurisprudence and *Obergefell v. Hodges*
Marshall, John, 23, 88, 135–37, 139, 140, 160, 161, 163, 164, 168, 169, 187n79, 212n312
Marshall, Margaret, 8, 147
Marshall, Thurgood, 144
MARTA v. Ledbetter (1987), 195n151
Martin v. Hunter's Lessee (1816), 168–69, 233n33
Matlon, Ronald, 27
Matthews, Gray, 40–41
Maughan, Richard, 1, 6
maxims. *See* gnomic aspect
Maynard v. Hill (1888), 148
McCloskey, Dierdre, 183n21, 209n248
McCollum v. Board of Education (1948), 23, 102, 106, 119–29, 131
McCullen v. Coakley (2014), 167
McCulloch v. Maryland (1819), 135, 160, 161, 172
McGowan v. Maryland (1961), 119
McKenna, Joseph, 136–37, 138–39, 160
McSwane v. Foreman (1906), 193n138
McSweeney, Thomas, 197n20
Medea (Euripides), 31
Menander of Laodicea, 41, 43, 44, 64
"Mending Wall" (Frost), 122–23, 127, 132
mercy and equity, 201n69
Merleau-Ponty, Maurice, 104, 219n25
mesarchia, 47, 93, 185n56, 237

mesodiplosis, 6–7, 47, 114, 117, 128, 141, 147, 151, 237
metaphor: in flag jurisprudence, 71, 72–74, 80, 81, 86, 93, 99; in privacy jurisprudence, 135–36, 139–40, 152–53, 161; register theory of epideictic and, 8–9, 23–24, 44, 49, 54; in Religion Clause jurisprudence, 101–2, 106, 108, 110, 118, 119, 123–24, 126–27, 129, 131–34, 219n9; wall metaphor for separation of church and state, 101–2, 106–8, 110–11, 118–21, 123–24, 126–27, 129, 131, 132, 134
Miller v. Board of Public Works (1925), 10, 185n53
Miller v. Clark County (2003), 10, 11
Minersville School District v. Gobitis (1940), 8–10, 22, 43, 74, 77–90, 93, 97, 98, 125, 163, 170, 175, 184n46
Miranda v. Arizona (1966), 164
miscegenation laws, 7–8, 19, 146–47, 155–56
Mixon, Harold, 70
modality, concept of, 59
Montgomery v. Maryland Cas. Co. (1930), 186n56
Mootz, Francis, III, 19, 193n131
Morrison v. Olson (1988), 165–67
Morrow, Terence, 197n20

NAACP v. Alabama (1958), 152
National Prohibition Act, 137
negation, 4, 59, 61, 63, 174, 223n107
Nero (emperor), 192n112
New Criticism, 165
The New Rhetoric (Perelman and Olbrechts-Tyteca): cantata, epideictic compared to libretto of, 1, 5, 50, 162; on figures in argumentation, 47–50, 73; judicial use of epideictic and, 1, 5, 12, 18–19, 22, 187n71; on paramologia or concession, 92; register theory of epideictic and, 39, 40, 47–51, 54, 55, 59, 68–69, 199n33; on temporal dimension of argumentation, 179
New Testament, 80, 103, 115, 121, 166, 222n88
New York Times v. Sullivan (1964), 91
Nicolaus the Sophist, 60
Ninth Amendment, 150, 152
Nixon, Richard, 48, 210n277
nonverbal features of epideictic, 39, 63–67, 69, 177

Obergefell v. Hodges (2015). *See* privacy jurisprudence and *Obergefell v. Hodges*
O'Brien, David, 152
O'Connor, Sandra Day, 2, 92, 145, 163
Olbrechts-Tyteca, Lucie. *See New Rhetoric*
Olmstead v. United States (1928), 56, 137–38, 144, 152, 153, 155, 160
Olson, Kathryn, 190n97
O'Malley, John, 17, 44, 59, 60, 61, 62, 97, 179, 190n98
"On Clemency" (Seneca the Younger), 192n112
On Sophistical Refutations (Aristotle), 199n31
On the Crown (Demosthenes), 17
"On the Pulse of the Morning" (Angelou), 12
On the Sublime (Longinus), 46
Ong, Walter, 27
Oravec, Christine, 207n219, 213n331
originalism, 20, 24, 165
Osiel, Mark, 18

paean: defined, 194n148; judicial reference to, 6, 10, 19, 20, 21 194n148
Palko v. Connecticut (1937), 76

panegyric: Cicero's *De Oratore* and, 39; defined, 12; epideictic, connection to, 19–20, 64, 190n93, 191–92n112; Grassi on, 55, 99, 175; Hermogenes on, 50, 186n60, 190n93; [in]sincerity of, 60–61; judicial reference to, 6, 16, 19–20, 71, 163, 164, 193n134, 193n136, 193n138, 193n140, 194nn144–45, 195n149, 231n2; Philodemus on, 190n98; Pseudo-Dionysius of Halicarnassus on, 50; Quintilian on, 187n62
parallelism, 13, 50, 80, 81, 83, 85, 87, 102–3, 108, 124, 141, 165
paramologia: defined, 238; in flag jurisprudence, 22, 74, 82, 86, 88–90, 97–100; in free speech jurisprudence, 22, 88, 91–92
parataxis, 73, 238
Pedersen v. United States (1950), 185n56
Pencovic v. Pencovic (1955), 194n145
Pennsylvania Right to Farm Act, 21
penumbral rights, 23, 139, 149–53, 160–61, 229n88
People v. McClellan (1969), 195n151
Perelman, Chaïm, 3, 17, 26, 27, 34. *See also* New Rhetoric
perfective aspect, 55–57, 95, 98, 175, 177
Pericles, 12, 60
Pernot, Laurent, 42, 43, 45, 190n91, 205n149, 210n266
Perry, Barbara, 3, 4, 66, 182n16
personification, 73, 219n9, 238
Philodemus, 28, 190n98
Pindar, 58
Planned Parenthood, in *Griswold*, 149
Planned Parenthood v. Casey (1992), 2, 3, 143, 144–46, 160, 164, 170–72, 194n148, 228n46, 231n130, 234n52
Plato, 70, 136, 178, 189n91

Pledge of Allegiance, 9, 77, 96. *See also* flag jurisprudence
ploce, 124, 238
Poe v. Ullman (1961), 146, 153–55, 229n94
polarity, 59, 61
political ideology and use of epideictic register, 6, 11, 163, 173
polyptoton, 114, 126, 238
polysyndeton, 47, 141, 167, 173, 238
Posner, Richard, 8
practical reasoning, 35, 97, 100, 156, 179
praise and blame: in *Dobbs* opinions, 170, 171, 172, 173; in flag jurisprudence, 71, 78, 79, 80, 81, 82, 85, 87, 90, 93, 94, 96; implications of, 178; in judicial use of epideictic, 4, 8, 11–12, 16–17, 21, 22; in previous studies of epideictic, 174; in privacy jurisprudence, 145, 150, 157, 159; register theory of epideictic and, 32, 39, 42–46, 48, 52, 53, 55, 58, 60–61, 67, 69; in Religion Clause jurisprudence, 108, 109, 114, 117, 124, 126, 128; Scalia's use of, 165, 167
precedent: in antebellum slavery cases, 182n14; in *Dobbs* opinions, 171, 172; flag jurisprudence and, 71, 73, 85; Frank on, 196n9; privacy jurisprudence and, 142, 145, 146, 157, 160; register theory of epideictic and, 3, 4, 9, 14, 15, 20, 32, 34, 53, 63, 218n132; Religion Clause jurisprudence and, 105, 111, 113, 115, 116, 120; *Rhetorica ad Alexandrum* on, 200n56
present tense, association of epideictic with, 55, 136

privacy jurisprudence and *Obergefell v. Hodges* (2015), 23–24, 135–62; abortion and birth control, 2, 7, 19, 143, 144–46, 149–55, 167–71, 227/n37; *Bowers v. Hardwick* (1986), 142, 143–44; centrality of *Obergefell* to privacy jurisprudence, 23, 134, 139; due process considerations, 139, 143, 146–49, 152–56; emanation metaphor, 23, 139, 150, 153, 160; equal protection, 140, 155, 157, 158; First Amendment in, 143, 149–52; freedom to marry, 146–48, 155–56; *Griswold v. Connecticut* (1965), 139, 143, 146, 147, 149–53, 155, 160, 161; homosexual acts, 142–44; intimate conduct, protective statements about, 142–46; *Lawrence v. Texas* (2003), 139, 142–44, 146, 148; living constitutionalism and, 24, 135–39, 153, 160, 161; *Loving v. Virginia* (1967), 23, 139, 146–47, 155–56; marriage and sexual relations, 6–8, 10, 19, 23–24, 140–42, 146–49, 155–56, 158–59; paean to marriage in *Obergefells*, 7–8, 43, 140–42, 158–60; penumbral rights, 23, 139, 149–53, 160–61, 229n88; *Planned Parenthood v. Casey* (1992), 143, 144–46; *Poe v. Ullman* (1961), 146, 153–55, 229n94; proliferation of epideictic rhetoric in, 158–62; "right to be let alone," 137–38, 152, 155, 160; *Roe v. Wade* (1973), 143, 145; same-sex marriage, 7–8, 140, 141–42, 146, 147, 158, 159, 227n29; Scalia's critique of Kennedy's *Obergefell* opinion, 163–64, 168, 169

progymnasmata, 43, 60

propaganda, association of epideictic with, 13

"Property" (Madison), 105, 120

Protagoras, 179

Pseudo-Dionysius of Halicarnassus, 50, 51, 140

public schools and religion. *See* Religion Clause jurisprudence

purple prose, 169

Quakers, Washington's letter to, 79–80

qualifiers, 4, 29, 59, 61–63, 81, 128, 174

quartering of soldiers, 150

Quintilian, 17, 26, 28, 45, 60, 187n62

race discrimination/segregation: *Bolling v. Sharpe* (1954), 157; *Brown v. Board of Education* (1954), 4, 19, 63, 156–58; *Loving v. Virginia* (1967), 19, 23, 139, 146–47, 155–56; slavery cases, antebellum, 182n14

Ramus, Peter, 27, 48–49, 133

realis mode, 61

Reed, Stanley, 102, 119, 121, 122, 124, 134, 219n9

Rees, Roger, 17, 191–92n112

register theory of epideictic, 22, 25–70; affirmative modality, 59–63; amplification devices and figures of thought, 46–50, 200n56; ceremonial/ritual occasions, association of epideictic with, 63–67, 69–70; confrontation and, 59–61, 98–99; convergence of features, transcendent effect of, 67–70; definition of register, 39–40; eloquence, 50–52; false distinction between judicial and epideictic rhetoric, 11–15, 24, 25–34, 176; genre versus register approaches to epideictic, 15–17, 32–34;

Index 273

gnomic aspect, 52–59, 62, 210n207; nonverbal features, 39, 63–67, 69; praise and blame, 42–46, 58, 60–61; previous studies of, 173–74; social exigencies, epideictic situations arising from, 39–42, 174; successful production of epideictic through, 175–80; *theses* and *hypotheses,* proper domain of, 34–39
Rehnquist, William, 23, 74, 94–97, 98–99, 163, 175
released time programs. *See McCollum v. Board of Education*
Religion Clause jurisprudence, 23, 101–34; chiasmus in, 100, 102–8, 110, 113–14, 116–17, 119–22, 125, 131–34, 175; Establishment Clause and Free Exercise Clause, chaiastic relationship between, 121; flag cases and, 77–82, 84, 88, 98; Frost's "Mending Wall" and, 122–23, 127, 132; interdiscursive relationship between judicial and epideictic discourse, revealing, 131–34; Jefferson's *Virginia Bill for Religious Liberty* and, 107, 109, 111–12; *Lemon v. Kurtzman* (1971), 23, 102, 106, 119, 120, 121, 129–31, 132; Madison's *Remonstrance* and, 23, 75, 101, 103, 104–9, 111–16, 120–21, 124, 132, 134; *McCollum v. Board of Education* (1948), 23, 102, 106, 119–29; wall metaphor for separation of church and state, 101–2, 106–8, 110–11, 118–21, 123–24, 126–27, 129, 131, 132, 134. *See also Everson v. Board of Education*
Remonstrance and Memorial against Religious Assessments (Madison),
23, 101, 103–7, 109, 111–14, 116, 120–21, 124, 132, 220n31, 223n114
repetition: in chiasmus, 102; in flag jurisprudence, 46–48, 71, 81, 87, 9313; in privacy jurisprudence, 136, 159; in register theory of epideictic, 13, 46–48; in Religion Clause jurisprudence, 108, 110, 117, 124, 127
Resnik, Judith, 65
Revolutionary War, 95
rhapsode/rhapsody: defined, 195n150; judicial reference to, 6, 10, 19, 20, 21, 195n150
Rhetoric (Aristotle), 11, 15, 28–33, 42, 45, 60, 187n61, 187n71, 199n31, 199n34, 200n39, 200n43, 204n143, 209n236. *See also* Aristotle
Rhetorica ad Alexandrum, 17, 43, 44, 191n108, 200n56
Rhetorica ad Herennium, 17, 43
ritual/ceremonial occasions, association of epideictic with, 63–67, 69–70
Roberts, John, and Roberts Court, 2, 169–73, 174–75
Roberts v. United States Jaycees (1984), 144, 160
Robertson v. Steele's Mills (1949), 195n149
Roe v. Wade (1973), 2, 19, 143, 145, 168, 170–72, 234n52
Romer v. Evans (1996), 143
Root, Elihu, 125–26, 127
Rosenfield, Lawrence, 32, 45
Royal Society of London, 13–14, 27, 49, 188n79, 206n177
Ruffin, John, 105
Rutledge, Wiley, 107, 111–16, 119, 121, 163, 176
Ryan, Halford, 191n106

Sales, Bruce, 236n74
same-sex marriage, 7–8, 140, 141–42, 146, 147, 158, 159, 227n29. *See also* privacy jurisprudence and *Obergefell v. Hodges*
Scalia, Antonin, 19, 20, 24, 140, 163–69, 170, 228n46, 231n130, 232nn7–8
Schenck v. Pro-Choice Network of Western New York (1997), 167
Schiappa, Edward, 189n91
School District of Abington Township v. Schempp (1963), 131
schools and religion. *See* Religion Clause jurisprudence
Schuetz, Janice, 197n20
Schwartz, Bernard, 149
Scientific Revolution/Enlightenment, 13–14, 27, 133
search and seizure, 91, 137, 140, 150–51, 155
Second Sophistic, 64
self-incrimination, 76, 138, 150–51
Seneca the Younger, 192n112
sensus communis, 54–55
separation of powers, 165–66
sex/sexuality: abortion and birth control, 2, 7, 19, 143, 144–46, 149–55, 167–71, 227/n37; homosexual acts, 142–44; marriage and sexual relations, 6–8, 10, 19, 23–24, 140–42, 146–49, 155–56, 158–59. *See also* privacy jurisprudence and *Obergefell v. Hodges*; same-sex marriage; women's rights
shadow docket, 174–75
Shakespeare, William, 31
Shaman, Jeffrey, 232n7
Sheard, Cynthia, 55, 68, 183n21
Sherman Antitrust Act, 91
Shuger, Debora, 187n64
slavery cases, antebellum, 182n14
Sloane, Thomas, 38

Snedaker, Kathryn, 197n20
Snow v. Or. State Penitentiary (1989), 194n144
Snow v. Oregon State Penitentiary (1989), 71
social exigencies, epideictic situations arising from, 39–42, 174
soldiers, quartering of, 150
Solzhenitsyn, Aleksandr, 18
sophistic rhetoric, 28, 32, 33–34, 179, 189n91, 190n98
sophists, 15, 28, 33, 39, 64, 70, 169, 176, 179, 190n93, 199n31, 211n292. *See also specific sophists*
Sotomayor, Sonia, 53, 170–73
Souter, David, 2, 145, 163
South Africa, Truth and Reconciliation Commission, 178
speech, freedom of, 19, 22. *See also* flag jurisprudence
speech act theory, 22, 39, 45–46
stare decisis, 3, 4, 7, 10, 20, 164, 170, 172, 194n148
Starger, Colin, 19, 167–68, 192n118, 234n59
"Star-Spangled Banner," 95, 96
state governments, applicability of Bill of Rights to, 5, 75
State v. Langford (1899), 186n56
Stevens, John Paul, 19–20, 144, 164
Stewart, Potter, 153
Stolen Valor Act, 21
Story, Joseph, 140, 164, 168–69, 197n79, 233n34
Strassburger, Eugene, 21
strategic concession. *See* paramologia
Strecker, Ivo, 134
Stromberg v. California (1931), 76
Stromer-Galley, Jennifer, 16, 190n96
the sublime, 6, 24, 35, 46, 87, 108, 127, 136, 160–61
Sullivan, Dale, 52, 54, 62–63, 66, 213n335
Sunday closing laws, 119

Supreme Court's use of epideictic register. *See* epideictic register, judicial use of
Sweezy v. New Hampshire (1957), 10, 53, 184–85n52

Talbot, Margaret, 165, 169
talionic law, 186n58
Tandy, Keith, 57–58
Temperance Address (Lincoln), 61
Terry, Henry, 339n88
Texas v. Johnson (1989), 8–10, 22, 74, 92–97, 98, 175
Thayer, James, 88–89
theses versus *hypotheses*, 34–39, 176
Third Amendment, 150, 152
Thomas, Daniel, 101
Thomas, Edmund, 64
Tileagă, Cristian, 69
Time magazine, 9
Timmerman, David, 189n91
Tocqueville, Alexis de, 148
Torcaso v. Watkins (1961), 122
Toulmin, Stephen, 27, 29, 34–35, 197n13
truth, Scalia on, 169
Truth and Reconciliation Commission, South Africa, 178
Tsai, Robert, 19, 72, 89, 102, 118–19, 143, 149, 151, 160
Tusnet, Mark, 232n7

United States v. Annigoni (1995), 194–95n149
United States v. Associated Press (1943), 91
United States v. Eichman (1990), 98
United States v. Khan (2004), 194n148
United States v. Nixon (1974), 48
United States v. White (1971), 91
United States v. Windsor (2013), 227n29
Upham, Frank, 3
U.S. Courts Design Guide, 65

U.S. Supreme Court building, 65–66
U.S. Supreme Court's use of epideictic register. *See* epideictic register, judicial use of

"vice versa," as expression of chiasmus, 103, 110, 122
Vico, Giambatista, 52, 208n221, 218n132
Vignon, Pierre, 65
Virgil, 10, 165
Virginia Bill for Religious Liberty (Jefferson), 107, 109, 111–12
Vivian, Bradford, 18, 58, 61, 64, 66, 70, 192n118
Volmar Constr., Inc. v. United States (1995), 194n148

Walker, Jeffrey: on Alcaeus of Mytilene, 226n4; on ethical dimensions of epideictic, 100; on judicial use of epideictic, 15–16, 184n49, 189n90, 190n93, 218n132; on privacy jurisprudence, 160; register theory of epideictic and, 32–33, 38–39, 60, 200n43
wall metaphor for separation of church and state, 101–2, 106–8, 110–11, 118–21, 123–24, 126–27, 129, 131, 132, 134
Warren, Earl, and Warren Court, 10, 118–19, 149, 155–58, 163
Warren, Samuel, 137
Wash. ex. rel. Lumber & Sawmill Workers v. Sup. Ct. (1945), 193n134
Washington, George, 79–80
Watson v. Jones (1871), 110
Weaver, Richard, 53, 54
Webster, Daniel, 74, 80
Weems v. United States (1910), 136–37, 138–39, 160
Wenner, George, 126

West Virginia State Board of Education v. Barnette (1943), 8–10, 22, 42, 74, 77, 78, 82, 83–89, 90, 93, 97, 98, 163, 170, 175, 176–77, 184n46
Wetlaufer, Gerald, 41–42, 173
White, Byron, 92
White, Edward, 189n86
White, James Boyd, 177
Whitney v. California (1927), 90
Whittier, John Greenleaf, 95
Wickard v. Filburn (1942), 184n51
Wilce, James, 206n193
Wiley v. Slater (1856), 185–86n56
Williams, Roger, 79, 101, 218n3
Winn, Peter, 186n58

wiretapping, warrantless, 137, 140
Wolf v. Colorado (1949), 155
women's rights, 20, 164, 172
World War I, 13
World War II, 9, 18, 77, 89

Yang, Michelle, 210n277
Yelle, Robert, 186n58
Younger v. Smith (1973), 193n136
Yousafzai, Malala, 12

Zarefsky, David, 161
Zhuangzi, 103–4
Zorach v. Clauson (1952), 119

www.ingramcontent.com/pod-product-compliance
Lightning Source LLC
Chambersburg PA
CBHW070838160426
43192CB00012B/2226